Ahead of her Time

a Biography of Nikki Archer
former head of
The King Alfred School
Hampstead

By John Stafford Archer

First published 1998
by Clayton-Wright
Edgecombe, Brook Street Mews
Alcombe, Minehead
Somerset TA24 6BT

ISBN 0 9528957 0 6

Printed in Great Britain by

Redwood Books
Kennet Way, Trowbridge
Wiltshire, BA14 8RN

Dedication

For Nikki, with love

Contents

Illustrations are located between Parts 1 and 2

Acknowledgements

I have first to thank Nikki herself for her patience, understanding and indispensable collaboration throughout the whole course of this venture.

Next I would like to express my gratitude to Frances Moran and King Alfred School for permission to use the resources of the KAS archives and to Brian Rance, the school's archivist, for his guidance and practical support.

My thanks are also due to the following for providing variously, general, textual and technical advice, oral history and related documentation:

Sir William Wood, Jack Pole, Margaret Maxwell, Katie Munden; Denise Gibbs; Roy Greenfield; Bernard Igra; Alan Gershon; John Izbicki; Diane Chanteau; Bob Parvin; Virginia Edwards; Marian Elichaoff; Margot Holbrook; Alan Humphries; Maurice Ash; Mana and Michael Brearley; Marie-Elene Vafiadis; Peter Graff, Marjorie Chanteau, Pam Oliver.

A sentence is reserved for Richard Paul-Jones who, not for the first time in relation to my literary endeavours, has contributed to the labours of production his technical expertise as well as untold hours of sheer hard work.

Finally, for their permission to use copyright material, my acknowledgements are due to the following:

Times Newspapers Ltd., for permission to use 'A Quiz for Parents' devised by Nikki Archer and featured in 'Look!', Sunday Times, 22nd January 1978; The Ham & High for innumerable accounts of the activities of KAS over the years; International Music Publications Ltd., for permission to quote from Dorothy Field's lyrics of Jerome Kern's 'Pick Yourself Up'; International Thomson Publishing Services, for permission to quote material from M.Ash (ed) 'Who are the Progressives Now?' Routledge and Kegan Paul (1968); The British Broadcasting Corporation Written Archives Centre, for permission to reproduce selected material from broadcast recordings of 'Petticoat Line', 'You and Yours', 'Parents and Children', 'Good Afternoon'; The New Era in Education (International), Journal of the World Education Fellowship, for permission to quote from a conference report 'Notions of Authority' (1968).

Preface

Professor J.R.Pole, F.B.A.,F.R.Hist S; Hon
Fellow of King Alfred School Society,
Old Alfredian and former member of KAS Council

A first impression of Nikki Archer was - and I imagine, still is - a lasting impression: remarkable for its consistency. You - the person to whom she was talking - were at the centre of her interest and concentration. You could count on her to be candid, forthright, clear - sometimes clearer than you might have wished. And these qualities, blended with compassion, considerable human understanding and a commanding sense of her own obligations and responsibilities combined to earn the respect of her staff and the confidence, as far as one can judge these things, of the children at King Alfred School. Certainly they won the confidence of the mass of the parents who concerned themselves with the welfare of the School as a whole.

These qualities - and Nikki's ebullient and abounding energy - contributed powerfully to the remarkable success of the School under her leadership. No-one with any knowledge of KAS would claim that it measured success exclusively by examination results or subsequent careers; it has always remained loyal to the principle that it owed some openings to children with difficulties of one sort of another. This makes its distinguished academic record all the more creditable. KAS has always been distinctive in its encouragement of individuality, and Nikki had to bring her own human qualities to bear not only on a strikingly individualistic collection of children, but on equally individualistic parents, who sent their children to the School because they wanted to be consulted about and to some extent to contribute to their schooling. She retained, through difficult times, the support of a staff who were dedicated to the School's ideals. Like any head of KAS she could expect a certain amount of contention and a large amount of co-operation. She emerged over the years as one of the most respected head teachers in London.

The School had to be steered through periods when its financial survival was uncertain. Over the years Nikki worked with two former treasurers, Gerd Weiss (a contemporary of mine), and Teddy Epstein, both of whom made important contributions towards keeping the finances on a safe footing; but it is the considered opinion of those who were close to events at the time that the School's recovery in the late seventies was due largely to the heroic dedication and expertise of its honorary treasurer Bernard Igra. But this, in an important sense, was characteristic. The ideals which brought the School into existence, and which continued to attract parents to it, ensured that professional experts among the governing body, such as architects, accountants and lawyers, were willing to offer their services gratis when the School needed them. With her own gifts and qualifications, and with these advantages, not to mention the School's satisfactory record of achievement, it must seem extraordinary that Nikki's last three years were enveloped in increasingly bitter controversy, ending in her premature retirement on the alleged grounds of her having reached the age of sixty.

The file in my possession of much correspondence that took place in the final period of the winter of 1982-83, (though a necessarily incomplete one - it contains nothing that passed among the Head Teacher's critics) reveals one striking negative feature: the opposition were either unable or unwilling to define the issues. There was no specific criticism relating to issues of educational policy, nor any complaint of specific errors or failures in the School's performance. The Head's opponents comprised an always small group - their numbers could never be accurately ascertained - who proposed each other for election without disclosing to the Society at large their ulterior aim of unseating the Head of the School. Their failure to reveal the grounds of their hostility was due, no doubt, to the fact that the problems were of personality. And here Nikki's difficulties may well have been compounded by her own forceful candour. She knew infinitely more than her critics about the School from every point of view, from the abilities and personalities of the Staff to the individual needs of the children. She had well-thought-out reasons for everything she did, but in responding to critical questions she did not always leave as much room as a trained diplomat might have done for the recovery of her critics' *amour propre*. The School's governance, which involved parents by election to the council, required for its successful operation not only co-operation but a certain degree of self-restraint as to the Head's conduct both of policy and of day-to-day affairs. It was right, and indeed integral to the School's *modus operandi,* that the council should appoint committees on such matters as buildings; but it was disruptive to the School's operation when the council intervened in staff appointments and even in the conduct of teachers in their class rooms. Before the whole business was over, members of the opposition were undermining their Head Teacher's authority by sending directives to individual teachers without notifying the Head herself.

Nations, private clubs, schools, have constitutions. But those bodies, whatever their scale, also operate according to conventions of procedure and conduct. As I write, the government of the United States of America has recently been brought to a standstill by the controversy between the Republican majority in Congress and the President. There is nothing in the United States constitution either to prevent this from happening or to indicate a resolution. Such occasions of impasse have been brief in the past because everybody concerned understood that there were higher values than the satisfaction of their personal opinions or even the gratification of their self-esteem. The principles at issue do not vary very greatly between large and small institutions. The successful operation of a school like King Alfred, which requires the involvement of parents loyal to its principles, also calls for an appropriate measure on the council's part of trust in the staff and the head - trust implying discretion and self- restraint.

It would be regrettable, however, if the history of this important period in the School's life were made to turn on the way Nikki Archer's headship came to an end. It would be much more appropriate to reflect on the ways in which she maintained the twin KAS values of personal compassion and intellectual excellence throughout a period which was inherently difficult for private schools - especially for such a small one as KAS, which had minimal resources beyond its fees. One thing Nikki proved was that reasonable expectations are compatible with - indeed are best served by - an atmosphere of confidence and happiness.

It is probably not known to most Old Alfrdians that during her service as Head, Nikki spent a term as a schoolmistress fellow commoner at Churchill College, Cambridge - of which I happened to be a fellow. The College had instituted this system for bringing to Cambridge exceptional schoolteachers who needed time to do some thinking. I had no idea that she was coming and, as years had elapsed since my daughter had been at King Alfred, Nikki had to reintroduce herself to me, if I remember correctly. Her qualities of warmth, humour and intellect were much appreciated in our senior combination room, and I strongly suspect that she would have been fully equal to running a college.

Jack Pole

Introduction

'Ahead of her Time' is the authorised biography of Nikki Archer, who, after twenty-four years at the King Alfred School in Hampstead, North London, became, on her retirement in 1983, its longest-serving head. An independent co-educational day school, King Alfred was founded in 1898 by a small group of eminent Hampstead residents who sought to provide, as an alternative to the existing state and private systems, an education based on liberal and scientific principles now widely recognised but at that time rarely adopted. At first it was designated as a 'rational' school but this gained little currency and it was under the ambiguous label 'progressive' that the school, together with others dedicated to similar objectives, subsequently became known to the general public.

The educational philosophy of the founders was largely derived from ideas which long antedated the English progressive school movement. In essence, this placed the child - and not the needs of society - at the centre of the educational process, and allowed the individual child the fullest possible freedom within a framework of social responsibility.

The creation of a learning environment incorporating these principles had been relatively uncomplicated in the early years when numbers were small and most of the pupils were under twelve years of age.. But, with subsequent growth and transformation into an all-age school, the need for modification and compromise became imperative, and reconciliation of change with conservation of the educational ideals of the founders became a recurrent problem at King Alfred thereafter.

The story of Nikki Archer is unlike traditional biographies of school heads, where the subject is invested with supreme authority, credited with an almost mystical charisma, and acclaimed as the sole agent of outstanding educational reforms. While charisma and achievement may remain constant attributes in the lives of heads today, the definition and function of authority have undergone radical change. This has so altered the concept of leadership that biographies like that of Arnold of Rugby are today hardly conceivable; and it is questionable whether a 'deconstructed' Arnold might not be exposed as less the sole architect of reform than historians have led us to believe.

Nikki saw her role as enabling and sustaining conditions which ensured the efficient conduct of the school and the achievement of its educational aims and objectives, in which the children's interests were paramount.

Her time at King Alfred School coincided with a period of accelerating social, economic, and cultural change, and an effective transformation of the major institutions of society.

The actual as distinct from the ideological state of the democratic process in Britain underwent critical scrutiny, and related concepts of freedom, authority, and accountability became the foci of political debate and public discussion. A heightened consciousness of social inequalities led to growing concern over questions of social justice and equal opportunity, while an obsessional preoccupation with rights threatened to obscure the equally important issue of responsibilities.

The consequent weakening of established values and social consensus, typified by the 'permissive society' and the 'swinging sixties', and reinforced by the growing influence of the communications media, created a pervasive uncertainty over moral principles and sanctions.

Finally, rapid advances in science and technology were effecting a reconstruction of both the economic system of production and the occupational structure.

All these changes had wide-ranging implications for education in general and King Alfred School in particular, confronting the council, heads and staff with problems of adaptation neither they not their predecessors had encountered before. 'The sixties were more of a shock than the seventies,' Nikki Archer observed, 'probably because, by the seventies, adaptation had become second nature.'

It was a particularly challenging time for heads, and more especially so for a woman in a school which had always accepted in principle the idea of women in authority but, like society at large, was ambivalent about it in practice. At every stage of her career at the school (first as co-head and later as sole head) this ambivalence had to be faced and dealt with on countless occasions. She was philosophical about this: 'All social reform tends to be slow: the reform of social attitudes the slowest of all.'

A powerful advocate of women's rights, she nevertheless had little patience with the fashionable delusion which mistook strident expressions of female petulance for a genuine concern with women's needs and interests. In particular, she deplored the anti-male, anti-family and ultimately anti-female tendencies currently appearing in feminist literature. The question, in her view, was no longer merely one of discrimination against women. It was far more to do with finding a rationale for the development of mature reciprocal relationships between the sexes.

To a school like King Alfred the moral and educational implications of accelerating social change were of paramount importance. Nikki considered that, in the prevailing social conditions, an essential function of the school was the provision of a stable environment. To achieve this end she strove tirelessly for unity and cohesion in a community prone by its nature to periodic dissension and factionalism. Success in this endeavour was largely attributable to the openness of her approach, avoidance of confrontation, and quiet insistence on the more positive solution of heuristic discussion. She encouraged a free exchange of ideas, regarding it as a fertile source of innovation and change. And, because she had seen so much potential achievement go to waste through fear and inhibition, her idea of freedom included being allowed to make mistakes as a legitimate component of learning. In token of which, over her desk was to be seen a

10

small notice saying, 'I have given myself permission to be wrong.' It was less a statement about herself than a philosophical observation about the folly of unreflective certitude.

As to the dysfunctional effects of social change and their implications for education, she felt that the school's inherited culture of secular morality was cause for optimism, because it stressed the development of individual responsibility, a sense of values, and independent judgment.

'My own feeling at that time' she recalled, 'was that we had to assess what these new freedoms would do to and for education, and to and for our children.. We were not there to reform society, nor were we the agents of revolutionary change. Our traditional role was to stand out against extremism at both ends of the political spectrum, not in the sense of compromise, but as an expression of independence of judgment. Children had to live in the world as it was going to be, and be prepared for it; but not sent into it either with blind acceptance or with an attitude of total rejection of what was happening. It was all to do with respect for children as individuals and enabling them to develop faith in their own judgment - and this was what we tried to do.'

Another change, which had proved harmful to King Alfred School, was the increasing semantic confusion surrounding the term 'progressive' in the context of education. Following the Plowden Report (1967) many state schools had come to apply this label to themselves. Conversely, there was a reaction by a body of opinion on the political Right against progressive education because of the excesses of a few schools and because it was thought to be associated with the spread of permissiveness. In fact, there was research evidence to show that the degree of liberalisation in the maintained system was far less extensive than was generally supposed.

Nikki was prompted to write on this subject: 'When some of the state schools claimed to have assumed leadership of the progressive movement, it was based on a misconception. They failed to appreciate the fundamental difference between our understanding of the educational principles involved and their own. For them, because of their large numbers, child-centredness meant in practice treating children as units, whereas we were able to treat them as persons.

'Pioneering ideas require two things for their implementation: first, they must be genuinely understood; second, they must be supported by proper financial and other provision. If either of these is lacking, no more than lip service can be paid to them in practice. At the time when money appeared most plentiful in state-funded education, priority was given to prestigious buildings and lavish technical resources, but not to any significant reduction of class numbers - the real key to authentic child-centredness.'

King Alfred School moved with the times, modernising itself in a way consistent with the educational ideals of its founders - ideals the essentials of which have still not been implemented in more than a minority of schools in the maintained system. It is in this respect that the school remains at the forefront of educational thought and practice - the same 'demonstration' school that was envisaged at its inception.

During the course of a long and eventful career at King Alfred, Nikki Archer made a distinctive contribution to this collective achievement.

In the text which follows I have adopted a linear approach, presenting in chronological order as true and objective an account of her life as possible. Any ventures into the field of psychobiography have been restricted to the empirically verifiable and have avoided the more ontological areas of depth psychology.

Nikki's collaboration at every stage in the production of the book has been invaluable both as a source of oral history and as a corrective to my errors of fact and judgment.   For any that remain I must be held solely accountable.

Minehead 1998   *John Stafford Archer*

Part One

1　Family Origins

Nikki was not her baptismal name but a sobriquet she acquired as an undergraduate at Bristol University. Born on November 13th, 1921 in the market town of Skipton, West Yorkshire, she was christened Audrey Barbara, two names she later came to dislike on grounds of cacophony and negative historical association. 'Too many 'R's, for one thing; and the shoddy goods of St. Audrey's Fair were the origin of 'tawdry'.

Although blessed with a strong constitution, she contracted pneumonia in her first year, but made a complete recovery without complications or subsequent ill effects. In spite of which, her mother treated her from this time onwards with an over-protective solicitude far more suited to a delicate child than to the evidently robust daughter she actually had.

Her parents, Frank and Margaret (Meg) Greenall, both came from a Yorkshire background, grew up in Leeds, and settled after their marriage in Skipton, where he was employed in the Midland Bank.

In 1923, her father was required to transfer to the main Bristol branch, and in consequence Nikki was left for three months in the care of her aunt and her grandmother in Middlesbrough, while her parents searched for suitable accommodation in Bristol and made all the necessary arrangements for the removal. This kind of separation was not thought of as unusual at the time, the conventional wisdom being that infants provided with substitute care suffered no harm from the occasional absence of their parents. Frank noted in his diary that 'Audrey did not fret, and seemed to understand that Mummy was in Bristol making a new home for us all'. And, when she finally joined them at Goldney Road in Clifton, her repeated assertions that she had 'waited and waited and waited!'. were perceived as amusing chatter and evidence of precocious linguistic development rather than as signals of distress or a remembered sense of having been abandoned.

In the years that followed, her sleep was frequently disturbed by nightmares from which she awoke screaming with terror. These almost invariably expressed in one form or another the fear that everyone had left her and that she was entirely alone. It is probable she repressed the painful emotions aroused by this early separation, as she had no recall whatsoever of the Middlesbrough 'exile'.

Of her infancy in Yorkshire she retained only one memory which she could be sure was not hearsay - that of being wheeled along in a large black perambulator, struggling to see round the canopy and glimpsing a brilliant yellow cornfield scattered with red poppies.

Her early childhood in Bristol could not, as a whole, be described as happy, and she felt an extraordinary sense of elation and relief when it was over and she was eventually able to gain some degree of independence.

Not that she suffered in any way from material deprivation or that she lacked parental care and affection.

The underlying causes of this troubled stage of her development were not uncommon. As an only child, she was the focus of parents who, because of difficulties in their own relationship, lived in a state of intermittent personal conflict. They projected much of the ensuing frustration onto Nikki, and tried persistently to involve her in taking sides in their quarrels. With hindsight, she attributed her own early difficulty in making friends to this experience of having the undivided attention of her parents, forming in her mind unrealistic expectations of what relationships might ,or ought to be about.

Frank Greenall came from a middle class Leeds family. His father, John Greenall, a refrigerator manufacturer, was responsible for the introduction of refrigeration in ships carrying perishable cargoes. However, like many inventors, he never received the financial rewards that his achievement deserved.

John Greenall's father-in-law was Henry Brambles, a distinguished Yorkshire journalist, whose long career included appointments on the Huddersfield Chronicle, the Leeds Intelligencer, and, finally, the Leeds Mercury, of which he ultimately became leader writer and sub-editor.

Frank was one of seven children, the only one to survive infancy, and, whilst the impact of this on his emotional development can only be conjectured, it certainly influenced the nature of his relationship with his mother. Her reaction to the only surviving child was to become excessively protective, jealous, and possessive. By making him the centre of her life, she contributed to the formation of the egocentricity that was to become such a marked personality trait in his later life. He was a gifted child and, after a successful career at Leeds Grammar School, instead of continuing his education at university, he spent two years studying French and music in France and Belgium, a period which included a course in harmony and composition at the Paris Conservatoire.

It was soon after his return to England that, against his own inclination and largely at the insistence of his mother, he joined the Midland Bank, in whose employment he remained, but for the interruption of the first world war, until ill-health compelled him to retire in 1946.

Such was his exceptional ability that by the age of twenty-five he had passed all the examinations of the Institute of Bankers, being placed, in the final examination, among the top five candidates in England.

On the outbreak of war in 1914 he joined the Army and, owing to his fluency in French, was posted as an interpreter to the staff of General Weygand, one of the Allied commanders in Europe. He was present at the battle of the Somme, became a casualty as a result of shell-shock, and was invalided out in 1917, afterwards spending many months in hospital in England before his ultimate demobilisation.

His wartime experiences served to confirm him in the socialist beliefs he had developed some years before. He was widely read in radical literature and deeply interested in social and political reform, more from the dialectical than the activist point of view.

After resuming his career in the bank, he experienced periods of ill-health, twice suffering physical and nervous breakdown, first when Nikki was five, and again when she was thirteen. These attacks were complicated by a form of colitis, which he endured intermittently for the rest of his life.

Nikki's maternal grandmother, Elizabeth Ann Holiday, was the eldest daughter of William Clayton, who, in tragic circumstances, deserted his family and ran away to Australia, where he died shortly afterwards in a paupers' workhouse. He was an expert in cloth dyeing, a qualified chemist and partner in a firm later to become world famous as the Bradford Dyers' Association. An inquiry into the case established that his partner had absconded with most of the firm's liquid assets and that William, although entirely innocent, yet fearing incrimination, had left the country, hoping that blame would not fall on his family, and consequently retribution would not be exacted by the directors. Had he not been driven to take such precipitate action, the story would have undoubtedly had a less pitiable ending, because the directors, having discovered the real culprit, decided to invest more capital and set the business on its feet again. His widow was left in impoverished circumstances and, existing on a very small pension, moved into the country, rented an isolated cottage on the moors, and set herself to the task of bringing up her children on her own. Elizabeth Ann, without any trace of resentment or self-pity, used to describe the hardships they had to endure. Most of her sympathy was reserved for those she considered worse off than herself, and she had little patience with anyone who was self-indulgent or lazy. 'If he had to be down the mine before five in the morning', she would say, 'he'd have something to grumble about'.

Every morning, as the eldest child, she walked three miles to a local farm for milk, returned to the cottage in time to give the younger children their breakfast, and then walked two more miles to the village school. In cold weather, they each carried a hot potato in a sock to warm their hands and to eat at the morning break. Soon after her sixteenth birthday she met the young man she was later to marry, Samuel Greenwood Holiday, then barely eighteen. Both their families forbade even an engagement at that time because of their lack of prospects. Sam asked her to wait for him, and emigrated to South Africa, where he spent nine years in the Cape Mounted Police. He saw active service at the time of the Basuto Revolt and in the Zulu War in the 1870s.

While he was away, Elizabeth Ann went into domestic service as a personal maid to Mrs Urquhart, a wealthy Scottish widow, who had no children of her own and had obviously taken a great liking to her. When she discovered the girl's exceptional qualities and strength of character, Mrs

Ahead of her Time

Urquhart offered to send her to college, pay for her education, and adopt her as her own child. Elizabeth Ann, who had left the village school at the age of twelve, refused the offer on the grounds that education was not what women needed, and, if 'her Sam' wanted her to be any different when he returned, he would tell her so.

This was how she had been brought up to think of women's place in society but it was an attitude which became in later years a contentious issue with her two daughters and, less directly, with her granddaughter. For her daughters it represented a challenge which determined them to acquire all the education they could. For Nikki, growing up in a period when educational opportunity for girls was an accomplished fact, it was a cause for reflection on the gender inequalities that remained and the related struggles yet to come.

In the meantime Elizabeth Ann waited, worked, and would hear nothing more of her employer's desire to change her pattern of life, and, in due course, nine years after he had left the country, Sam Holiday returned. Everyone, including Mrs Urquhart, knew the story of their past disappointment and long separation, and those who had never met Sam questioned her constantly about him. She would answer all these questions with a shrug and say offhandedly, 'Oh, he's a Leeds loiner', (a colloquial term rather similar to 'Geordie' today), 'and he's nought but a lile bow-legged man' (lile = little or short). Sam was, in fact, six feet two inches tall, and broad in proportion, as befitted a Cape mounted policeman. She was exactly five feet tall, and would maintain her equality when any dispute took place by looking up at him and saying, 'If you're as big as a church, Sam Holiday, I'm not afraid of you!' And nor was she.

He adored her and was happy to live on her terms in all except two particulars. Butter, a great luxury in her childhood days, remained to the end of her life a symbol of self-indulgence and she doled it out with miserly economy. Some weeks after their marriage he picked her up one day and put her on top of the dresser in the dining room, fetched himself a pound of butter which he put on a plate, and refused to lift her down until she promised to let him have as much as he wanted. She, unwilling to allow anyone to see her in this undignified position, was forced to agree, and it was never referred to again.

The other bone of contention was smoking which she, in common with most women of her generation, thought of as a dirty habit which men should be permitted to indulge only in a smoking room. As their small house had no such amenity she sent him into the greenhouse or, in fine weather, the garden. Give it up he would not, and she accepted the compromise with becoming dignity. Sam Holiday's time in South Africa had changed him in many ways, and Nikki used to listen fascinated as a child to the stories her grandmother told of his life in the Cape Mounted Police. One of these was of a time when her grandfather had been riding on patrol with a colleague and they had been discussing the alleged powers of fortune-telling in some of the tribal groups. Both men dismissed the supposed powers as superstitious nonsense and shortly afterwards passed an elderly woman who held up her hand to stop them. Thinking she was begging, Sam's companion pushed her roughly off the path. Sam asked her what she wanted and she said that she could foretell the future. At this he laughed and asked her to tell his future and she said that in 'three years more and three years again' he would cross the sea and find his woman. They would have four children: two sons and two daughters, and would have a good life. The other man then asked her to tell his fortune but she shook her head and he rode onward, angered by her refusal. Sam asked the woman why she had refused and she said, 'Baas. him die this one day'. Two hours later, as they dismounted to make camp, the man was bitten by a poisonous snake and died. Sam buried him on the veldt and returned to barracks to report the fate of his companion to the commanding officer. The whole experience had left him in a state of shock, the result not only of the sudden death of his comrade but also of the apparent clairvoyance of the old woman they had encountered. As he told Elizabeth Ann years later, there were many things in Africa that were not susceptible to rational or scientific explanation.

He brought back many mementoes of his years in Africa, including three huge amethyst rocks which were kept for years in the front garden but eventually stolen. By the time Nikki first visited her grandmother in Horsforth in the 1920s, few of these souvenirs remained but Elizabeth Ann still had his spurs and a bead purse which she kept by her bedside to the end of her life.

There also remained several sets of magnificent horns, rather badly mounted, which hung in various parts of the house and included wildebeest, kudu and gazelle. The largest of these was suspended in a great curling spread at the top of the stairs and was the centre of some of the fears and fantasies Nikki associated with the house at Horsforth. Every night she had to go up the staircase and pass underneath it, always in a state of apprehension that it was about to fall and crush her. At times, she would pause, heart in mouth, at the foot of the stairs, summoning up the courage to risk the headlong dash up the first flight. The noise she made as she pounded fearfully upstairs often brought her grandmother to the door exclaiming 'for goodness sake, child! I tell you every night to come up quietly. Whatever is the matter with you?' Nikki was six years old and it never occurred to her to mention the horns. Perhaps she intuited that the animistic beliefs and apprehensions of childhood, let alone those of Africa, would receive little sympathy from the redoubtable Grandma Holiday.

The prophecy made in South Africa came true. Sam and Elizabeth Ann had four children but only three survived. Their first child, a boy, died at birth. Nikki's mother, Margaret Ellen (Meg) came next, and then Constance Mary, five years her junior. Finally there was Richard Alan, born at the turn of the century, who lied about his age to join the Royal Flying Corps during the first world war. Shortly after qualifying as a pilot he was lost over France in 1916, a few days before his seventeenth birthday. Not long after his return to England, Sam, who had accumulated a modest amount of capital during his service overseas, formed a partnership with Elizabeth Ann and started a laundry business. This prospered to such an extent that the other part of the prophecy, forecasting 'a good life', must have appeared amply fulfilled, but nothing had been predicted about the length of his own life. Sadly, soon after Meg's sixteenth birthday, her father died prematurely at the age of forty-six.

Obliged in the circumstances to forego the further education for which she had been destined, Meg withdrew from college and joined her mother in the management of the business. She learned book-keeping and enough commercial law and practice to deal with contract matters and tax returns. She made herself wholly responsible for the horse-drawn transport and when, later, the laundry converted to mechanized vehicles, she taught herself to drive and became one of the first women in Leeds to qualify for a licence. During the war she made all the deliveries, crossing the Yorkshire moors in all weathers, taking and collecting the laundry for hospitals.

Her sister Constance (Con), who joined them later, took over all the book-keeping, and the three women kept the business going until Elizabeth Ann retired. After this, it was taken over by Harold Mason, a young man whom she had adopted unofficially and supported through college and university after the death of her son Alan. There was an element of sibling jealousy between the sisters. Con was clever but of a more passive nature than Meg. With her curling golden-blonde hair, pink and white complexion and large blue eyes, she was clearly the prettier of the two, and tended to be admired by friends and relatives alike. Meg was fully aware of this and accepted it with equanimity, but, together with their brother Alan, felt a sense of injustice when Con escaped the punishments to which misbehaviour exposed all three at one time or another.

Meg, with her brilliant red hair and extraordinary vitality, was herself a very attractive woman and, as a result of her premature managerial experience, unusually emancipated for a woman at that time. In addition to driving a motor vehicle, she was a fearless horsewoman and possessed of a beautiful soprano voice for which she was much in demand in local choirs and the Leeds Choral Society. During the war she had married Gordon Powell, a young teacher, and one of six brothers, but sadly she was to lose him after only six months, when he was killed in action serving with the British Expeditionary Force in France. Later, his five brothers successively followed him to Europe and met with the same fate. Meg's grief outlasted the war, and only very gradually was she able to come to terms with Gordon's death and resume her life with some sense of normality. She had known Frank Greenall from childhood and they met again after the war when he was still convalescent and suffering from the effects of shell-shock. She felt a deep compassion for him and a strong impulse to do all in her power to help him towards complete recovery. They married in 1920.

It was not an easy relationship and quarrels were prolonged and frequent. Egotistical and obsessed with a sense of his own intellectual superiority, Frank was a difficult man to live with. He was subject to recurrent spells of physical and mental illness and these together with medication served to aggravate the impatience, intolerance, and fractiousness which periodically characterised his behaviour. He had very considerable charm when he was prepared to exercise it, which was not often; was acutely sensitive about his own feelings but less so about the feelings of others.

His general attitude towards people and things was sceptical and cynical. His wit and verbal facility, which were to influence Nikki's own delight in the use of language, were often used negatively to ridicule or belittle. Years later Nikki came to understand the causes underlying her father's personality and behaviour, and was able to say in retrospect:

'Frank had such a strong sense of justice and compassion. He defended himself against the horror of war and the bitterness of being cheated of his career in music by taking refuge in cynicism and suspicion. Poor dear, he wanted so much to love and be loved, but didn't know how'.

Meg, for her part, was a warm, impulsive Yorkshirewoman, with a great sense of fun and a love of company, an impish mischief always ready to pop out when Frank was not lecturing her.

Quarrels in the early years of their married life were mainly about money. Meg wanted to invite guests and entertain, while Frank, who was as mean as his wife was generous, was constantly seeking ways of economising. Waste of any kind infuriated him and there were times when he went to absurd lengths to prevent it. He would, for example, exasperate Meg by hovering around in the kitchen and suddenly turning off the taps of the gas cooker while she was in the process of cooking. This anxiety neurosis extended also to the choice of a family dentist. Frank employed the least expensive practitioner he could find, a man unfortunately afflicted with Parkinson's Disease. This had disastrous consequences for Nikki, in particular, for, apart from exposing her to excruciating pain, it imbued her with a fear of dentists which lasted for many years.

In her early childhood she found her parents' quarrels both bewildering and frightening because she could not understand what they were about. Later on, when she could comprehend the nature of their mutual frustrations, she took steps to avoid their conflicts, seeking some private space where she would not be emotionally overwhelmed by them.

2   Early Stages

In common with many middle class parents during this period, Meg and Frank were well acquainted with the latest research in child psychology and its implications for the upbringing of children. Recognising the important connection between infant care and subsequent mental and physical development, they wanted to bring up their daughter with due regard for scientific principles. Well-intentioned as this was, the practical results, as far as she was concerned, were less than satisfactory, and the pressures exerted upon her were premature and excessive. At the age of three she was able to read the Times as well as showing other indications of remarkable precocity. Swept along by their own enthusiasm, her parents became so obsessed with theories of child-rearing that they began to lose sight of the child, and Nikki found herself being treated more like a laboratory specimen than an individual person. While material needs were amply satisfied, her emotional needs were often neglected, and she would, in effect, have gained more had common sense rather than impersonal theory prevailed. Frank sought to encourage learning by the negative reinforcement of constant fault-finding and correction. Conversely, by giving little positive recognition to Nikki's achievement and progress, he fostered the growth of a negative self-image from which, because it was buried in the unconscious, she could never entirely free herself. Well into adult life she would sometimes respond with genuine surprise and disbelief when people expressed admiration for the extraordinary range of her talents and the high standard of her achievements. Against all the evidence to the contrary, she regarded her abilities as no more than ordinary, and believed that anything she could do, anyone else was capable of doing as well if not better.

However, the positive side of her father's relentless criticism was the transmission of a capacity for rational thought and reasoned argument which greatly enhanced her intellectual growth and development. It was not that Frank wanted a son instead of a daughter. He loved Nikki in his own way and wanted to be proud of her, but he expressed his approval only if she did absolutely what he wanted, and did not like the independence of a lively child who wanted to go off in her own direction all the time.

Meg, in spite of all her loving care, was equally demanding in her own fashion, being anxious, fussy, and over-protective, investing the child with irrational fears and free-floating anxieties.

For all that Nikki was gregarious by nature, several factors conspired to draw her into a relatively solitary existence in her early years. The social disadvantages of being an only child were compounded by the fact that her parents failed to encourage any form of social interaction with other children of the same age. That they were comparative newcomers from the north may have accounted for this reluctance. Meg often unwittingly alienated potential friends in the neighbourhood by showing Nikki off as the 'clever little girl'. Added to this, Nikki herself chose solitude from time to time in order to escape from the constant and almost suffocating attention of one if not both of her parents.

She thus lived for the most part in a world of adults, had no difficulty in relating to them, conversed with them confidently and fluently, and was used to being the focus of their admiring attention. This influenced her language, thought and behaviour. She seldom had to be told, as were most children of her age, to walk and not to run.

With this background it is not surprising that Nikki had problems of social adjustment when, at the age of six, she began her formal education. She was intellectually advanced for her years and quickly singled out by her peers as different from themselves in her attitudes, behaviour, and speech which bore traces of Yorkshire dialect. Nikki recalls that she spoke four dialects during her Bristol childhood: broad Yorkshire for visits to relatives in the north; slight Yorkshire at home (Meg still retained traces of the accent, though Frank spoke standard English); local Bristolian; and conventional middle-class English.

Her first school, Duncan House, was for girls only, and privately run by two elderly ladies with advanced ideas on education. They had adopted the American Dalton Plan, a system intended to foster the cognitive development of children through individual learning projects or assignments. There was no routine class teaching and each pupil had a degree of free choice, being able to set her own goals and work at her own pace. Individual tasks involved problem-solving activities and could be spread over varying periods of time up to a month in duration. The method had been chosen in preference to formal teaching because it was said to have greater motivational value as well as more beneficial effects on character and self-discipline. The aim was to provide liberty in a controlled environment. Nikki profited from these arrangements since they enabled her to spend hours reading by herself under a grand piano which, with a fringed shawl draped over it, concealed her from view and left her undisturbed by her peers.

This did nothing to resolve her problems of social integration, and she soon had to come to terms with the complex relationships of the peer group of which she was now inescapably a member. Three archetypal bullies fixed upon her as a victim and made her life miserable by various acts of petty malice like pushing, hiding her books, and snatching her hat or satchel. Unprovoked aggression of this kind was a new and frightening experience and, not knowing how to deal with it, she neither offered resistance nor reported to anyone in authority. Her tormentors were encouraged by this and the bullying continued intermittently during the three years she spent at the school. Nikki told her mother something of what was happening during the first year, but Meg had not seen fit to take any action at that time. It was only in the third year when the persecution became worse that she was persuaded that something had to be done. She went with Frank to see the Head and together they complained about the behaviour of the three girls, adding an ultimatum that, unless they were punished either by expulsion or some other means of stopping their activities, Nikki would be immediately withdrawn.

This was not the way things were done at Duncan House, and left very little room for compromise, since the Head clearly thought expulsion disproportionate and unwarranted by the circumstances. She promised, however, to enquire into the allegations and take whatever action she deemed appropriate in the light of her findings. Meg and Frank found this totally unacceptable and, true to their earlier resolution, gave notice that Nikki would leave the school at the end of the term.

Reflecting on these early years, she acknowledged with characteristic fairness that she must have been an awkward child to deal with. Far from being a passive victim, she was at times sharp-tongued and had her father's propensity for cutting remarks. Her outspokenness expressed exactly what she thought and felt, with little concession to conventional ideas of politeness. She had not learned that arguing with adults, permitted and encouraged at home, could meet with disapproval elsewhere.

The atmosphere of high drama which prevailed at home was to some extent alleviated by the calming influence of music. Her parents made a conscious attempt to imbue her with a love of good music, and any sign of an appreciative response met with their approval. The desire to obtain this left her wondering how far her enjoyment was real and to what extent merely simulated. That she loved Mozart there could be no doubt, but she was less sure about some of the works of Chopin and Tchaikovsky, which her father played with a theatrical bravura that invariably reduced her to a state of acute embarrassment.

Occasionally her parents performed duets but these were seldom harmonious and frequently ended in one of their familiar rows. Meg complained he had failed to accompany her properly, to which he retorted her singing was at fault, adding furthermore that she was never likely to amount to anything as a singer.

When Nikki was eight they decided she should learn to play a musical instrument. The choice of instrument, on which Nikki was not consulted, was a small cello, and apparently determined more by the fact that Frank had been able to buy it cheaply than that it was particularly suited to a small girl of eight. A teacher was employed and lessons began, but after a few weeks Nikki gave up in despair, no longer able to bear the absurdity of it all: 'A small fat girl sitting with a cello between my legs, and I didn't even like the sound it made.'

Piano lessons followed. Meg arranged these without telling Frank, intending to surprise him at the end of several weeks' tuition. The piano teacher, to whom Nikki took an instant dislike, was a disagreeable and impatient woman with an unpleasant body odour. She complained that

Ahead of her Time

Nikki would not practise between lessons and, to her pupil's secret delight, pronounced her quite hopeless and unlikely to ever succeed in playing the piano, however hard she tried. And with that the piano lessons came to an end.

To refute the teacher's prognosis and to prove that she was not hopeless, Nikki taught herself to play 'I saw three ships come sailing in' using both hands and, having succeeded in doing this to her own satisfaction, gave up the piano for ever.

Soon after her ninth birthday Frank and Meg became agitated because she had been peering at her father through the smoked-glass upper half of the lavatory door in an attempt to see what he was doing. A simple act of curiosity was magnified into a case of abnormal behaviour requiring specialist investigation, and she was taken to London to see the psychologist Cyril (later Sir Cyril) Burt. After an hour in the waiting-room, reading old copies of Punch, she was ushered into his study and introduced to him. He gazed down at her as she sat on the other side of his desk and said rather pompously, 'Well, little girl, what do you think of me? Do you like me?' 'No' she replied in her usual direct manner, 'not very much'. Cyril Burt showed no signs of being surprised or perturbed by this and, after a few more attempts to win her confidence, finally succeeded in establishing a more friendly and co-operative relationship. He gave her a series of mental tests ranging from conventional verbal reasoning to non-verbal abstract problem-solving; carried out an analysis of the results, and sent for her parents. She was, he said, an exceptionally intelligent child and quite the most uninhibited he had ever encountered. She appeared to be entirely without guile, thought seriously before speaking, and then came out directly with what she thought and felt. In conclusion, said Mr Burt, the behaviour which had aroused so much concern should not be a cause for anxiety, being no more than normal sexual curiosity in a child of her age. Considering the time and expense involved in the whole operation, it is reasonable to ask whether Frank and Meg were relieved or disappointed by this disclosure - at the conscious level it was presumably the former. If, on the other hand, they had been anticipating a complex Freudian diagnosis, it is more likely that they experienced a sense of deflation and anti-climax. Nikki, knowing nothing of the ulterior motive for the excursion, understood that it was all to do with the tests, but, as these had revealed nothing they did not already know, she was left wondering what it had all been about.

It was at about this time that Nikki met Percy Leonard, an elderly man who was to become a significant and formative influence in her early life. He was a naturalist who, after graduating many years before at Bristol University, had emigrated to the United States. He remained there for most of his working life and achieved distinction as an entomologist, specialising in the study of ants. He was a lifelong Theosophist and during the last years of his life he returned to Bristol in order to be near his brother, a professor at the University, and settled in a house near the Greenalls. He soon came to know the family and became a close friend and regular visitor at the house. Out of this there grew a special relationship with Nikki, whose quick intelligence he recognized, and in whom he found a willing and eager listener, fascinated by the vast range of his knowledge and experience of plant and animal life. While her father had greatly influenced her intellectual development, it was Percy Leonard who opened her eyes to the wonders of the natural world. In the walks they took together and on the excursions they made into the countryside he was able to train her powers of observation, enabling her to experience the joys of discovery and to understand the elementary principles of scientific investigation.

In 1932, in hospital with a terminal illness, he sent her a letter, enclosed with which were some verses he had written out for her: : presumably an echo of his theosophic convictions.

> God and the Child
> God and I in space alone
> and nobody else in view.
> 'And where are the people, oh Lord', I said,
> 'the earth below and the sky o'erhead,
> and the dead whom once I knew?'
> 'That was a dream', the good God said,
> 'a dream that seemed to be true.
> There are no people living or dead,
> there is no earth, and no sky o'erhead,
> there is only Myself - and you.
> 'Why do I feel no fear?', I asked,
> 'meeting you here this way;
> for I have sinned, I know full well
> and is there a heaven and is there is a hell,
> and is this the judgement day?'
> 'Nay, all are but dreams', the great God said,
> 'dreams that have ceased to be.
> There is no such thing as fear or sin;
> there is no you - and never has been -
> there is nothing at all but Me.'

He had been a valued friend of the family and was greatly missed after his death, most poignantly by Nikki herself. She attributed to him in large measure her openness to knowledge and experience of all kinds, and the joy of learning and discovery, particularly when these were the outcome of intrinsic rather than extrinsic motivation.

Reflecting, years later, on her friendship with Percy Leonard, she came to appreciate how much more she owed to his influence than she had formerly realised. He had been like another member of the family, providing an alternative role model to that of her father. He was kindly, encouraging, approving, and reflected back to her a more positive self-image than she had ever known before. Some of the sources of her negative feelings about herself have already been suggested in the foregoing account of her relationship with her parents. They had constituted the major part of her social environment and, having no other children, their influence on her was direct and unmediated. At an impressionable age, she internalised some of their least, as well as some of their most admirable characteristics. For example, she assimilated some of her father's insensitivity to the feelings of others, but, whereas his grew out of generalised prejudice, hers was ephemeral, no more than imitative behaviour calculated to give him pleasure. However, what was tolerated in the family circle did not necessarily transfer to other social situations, as she was to discover to her cost. On one occasion the adults were discussing Darwinian theory and she joined in with more enthusiasm than tact, informing one of their friends, a Cambridge don, that he indeed did resemble an anthropoid ape. When her father angrily reprimanded her for this she felt badly let down, having fully expected approval for her intelligence and observation.

The anxieties she inherited from her mother were compounded by the sense of insecurity she had known since the time when her parents had left her for three months during the move from Yorkshire to Bristol. But to her mother also she owed a wealth - almost an excess - of protective and loving care, something of her bubbling curiosity about the nature of things, and her lively anticipation of the course of future events.

Being the sole focus of parental attention was a stifling experience and led Nikki insensibly to adopt whatever self-protective strategies were open to her. She lied to her parents to prevent their controlling every aspect of her life and to create the private space essential to a sense of separate identity. Sulking, she recalls, became a way of life which she learned to adopt as a shield against the constant criticism to which she was exposed. Neither of these kinds of behaviour outlasted the situations which generated them, for mendacity and ill-humour were quite alien to her moral sensibility and natural disposition. Looking back with detachment at this stage of her development provided her with a valuable insight into the ways in which teachers, parents and other figures of authority can unwittingly, and paradoxically, induce in children the very behaviour they so earnestly seek to prevent.

Her argumentativeness was in due course modified by the academic discipline of high school and university; and, with greater experience of the social world beyond the family, she rapidly outgrew any residual insensitivity to the feelings of others.

3   Adolescence

A regular feature of the Sunday Review in 1934 was a column by Victor Neuberg entitled Poet's Corner. The issue of November 25th announced the award of a prize to Audrey B. Greenall (aged 13) for 'a beautiful poem'. 'The prizes', Neuberg explained, 'go to those who manage to express their poems in their own way rather than to those who copy, sometimes with great care, what they hear and read. Accuracy and memory are useful, as those who flourish in examinations know well; but the world's real workers are those who have imagination in abundance - and allow themselves to use it.   Life's failures are those whose imaginations have shrunk and withered.... The wise poet knows something of history and also watches what is happening around him/her; that is, sees history in the making. We are all ourselves living history, and writing about this, if the poet is gifted, sometimes makes good poetry'.   Nikki's entry in the competition well exemplified these principles and showed a remarkable maturity for her age as well as an early manifestation of adolescent idealism.

Armistice Day
The trumpets blew in praise of knights who won,
The dead celebrities of yesterday -
The talk of one day till the set of sun,
And at the rise of dawn but useless clay.
But as the pageantry of Time goes on,
And with it goes the pomp and all the praise
That wastes men's lives to give an Empire fame;
And as they feed the famous, people gaze.
Do they but stop to think, 'What is it worth?'
While honouring the dead, men starve on earth.

For Nikki, puberty and rebellion - the critical phases of adolescence in Western society - were not sources of 'sturm und drang' as they are for so many young people during this stage of development.

She took puberty in her stride and this was facilitated by her mother's instinctive empathy and intelligent anticipation of her need for relevant information and practical advice. Her emotional life was so closely bound up with that of her parents that she was spared the complications of premature emotional involvement with adolescent males, a circumstance reinforced by attendance during her teenage years at a single-sex school. She had, furthermore, become so accustomed to being treated like a boy by her father that she went through a period of tomboyishness, probably out of a subconscious desire to please him. She was interested in men, but in a frightened and immature way; whilst she in turn found boys of her own age comparatively immature and intolerably gauche.

At fifteen she fell hopelessly in love with a young communist Adonis, seven years her senior, a friend of her parents and a frequent visitor at the house. He was at first totally unaware of this, being himself in love with one of two sisters who were also regular visitors at the Greenalls. Nikki did her best to disguise her feelings but was not entirely successful, thereby causing him some embarrassment but no lasting injury to his *'amour propre'*.

He was later to take part in the civil war in Spain, where in 1938 he lost his life fighting for the International Brigade. Nikki was disillusioned to learn some time afterwards that, before leaving for Spain, he had deserted his mistress in Bristol, leaving her pregnant and suffering from a sexually-transmitted disease. If his political idealism and personal courage in the field of battle were not in doubt, his moral character as a whole was patently not without blemish. The romantic hero of her imagination had proved to be human and fallible after all.

Nikki's ultimate achievement of independence from her parents without recourse to the confrontation so commonly experienced in later adolescence is attributable to hers having been a silent rather than an overt rebellion. This had started many years before in reaction to her parents' well-intentioned attempts to control every aspect of her life. As an only child, she was outnumbered by two parents, both with strong personalities and both excessively concerned with every detail of her upbringing. Unfortunately they were not content to be what Bruno Bettelheim calls 'the good enough parent' but had to be perfect parents and were intent on the production of a perfect child. 'They wanted to know', she recalls, 'what I thought and felt; where I had been and what I had been doing, and always these interrogations involved giving reasons for my thoughts, feelings, and actions.'

Overt rebellion and direct confrontation were out of the question. Detachment from Frank and Meg, and the development of an independent personality had to be achieved by other means, and these had been employed since early childhood.

By the time adolescence began she had transferred from her Dalton school to La Retraite High School in Clifton, which she attended from the age of nine until she was nineteen. This was a Roman Catholic foundation which, in return for increasing financial support from Bristol Education Authority, had been obliged to develop as an integrated school, offering 50% of its places to pupils from Christian denominations other than Catholic.

It was a fee-paying grammar school for girls, had a distinguished academic record, and a dedicated staff of highly qualified graduate nuns. It was predominantly a day school but had a small number of boarders. The choice of a convent school clearly involved Frank and Meg in some degree of ambivalence. As a doctrinaire socialist and self-confessed atheist, Frank had to compromise his Marxist principles by allowing his daughter to be exposed to the possibility of religious indoctrination. The advantages of the school were compelling: it was conveniently situated half a mile away from home, it was academically sound, and the fees were affordable. Ideology yielded to pragmatism and the decision went in favour of the school. Meg was happy in the thought that the nuns would be kind to Nikki, while Frank appeased his radical conscience by insisting that the Head should provide them with a written undertaking that she would not be exposed to any kind of religious indoctrination or proselytization. This the Head agreed to without demur, reassuring him that this was already an article of the school's policy.

It is doubtful whether Frank and Meg made any deliberate resolution to test the credibility of this undertaking but they exercised a constant vigilance and showed a critical interest in everything Nikki was taught during the time she spent at the school.

In Frank's case there was rather more to it than this. Having broken away from the Anglican Church, in which he had had a strict upbringing, he was a classic example of the apostate still deeply bound up with the faith he has repudiated. In Nikki's judgment he was not so much an atheist as a high-minded agnostic, perpetually searching for God and never finding him. He was a collector of religions and, whenever he heard of any new belief system, would send off for detailed information about it. On receiving this, he would subject it to a relentless critical analysis, and invariably conclude by rejecting it entirely.

Thus, apart from supervising her studies, Frank was also conducting a proxy theological debate with her teachers, and, on a larger scale, a continuous disputation with the Roman hierarchy as a whole. With Nikki as his channel of communication he was able to represent to her teachers his own scepticism about Christianity and his critical responses to what he regarded as their unexamined philosophical assumptions. In this he sought to justify to himself the rightness of his own convictions.

Whilst he had no conscious intention of setting her up as an *agent provocateur*, this was in effect what she in all innocence became. It was not that he fed her specific questions to put to the teachers but that he suggested areas of inquiry in such a way that she became personally concerned about them not merely as his ideas but as questions in which they were both interested. The Immaculate Conception, for example, was of consuming interest to them both, as it remains to many people today, and she posed the question in class: 'How did they know Mary was a virgin?'. So she was far from playing a passive role in this process of intercommunication, being often as deeply involved as Frank in what they saw as the anomalies of Catholic rules and dogmas, especially where these impinged on matters of social concern. It was the mental agony of a Catholic friend whose infant sister had died unbaptized that prompted Nikki one day to protest in class against the Catholic belief that the unbaptized are consigned to limbo - a belief held with less conviction today than it was at the time. On another occasion she expressed indignation about the ascribed authority of priests in the private sphere of family life. This derived from the case of a local maidservant whose life had been made miserable during her first year of marriage by what amounted to persecution by a priest who repeatedly demanded to know why she was showing no visible signs of pregnancy and whether she had committed the sin of practising birth control.

The opportunity for raising these subjects occurred in history and scripture, when liberal discussion, if not positively encouraged, was at least not expressly prohibited, and she took a leading role on these occasions. When she could report to Frank some success in her polemical encounters he was delighted, and she observed 'Daddy liked me on those days!' Unfortunately the approval of her father was offset by the unfavourable impression she was creating on some members of the staff, who were unsure of their ability to deal with her precocity, articulacy, and independence of mind. Realizing she had at times clearly gone too far, Nikki commented 'Of course I was the one who opened my silly mouth'. No blame attached to Frank for encouraging her to ask questions or suggesting to her the questions to ask. What, in her interests, he failed to suggest was that she would do better to listen and learn rather than attack, challenge and provoke, which is what she thought he wanted.

On one occasion in 1937 the nuns invited pupils to put up on a notice board written petitions or prayers of their own choice. Several of the prayers that were subsequently displayed referred to the Spanish Civil War, and all of these reflected the official views of the nuns in seeking God's intercession on the side of the rebel forces led by General Franco. Nikki related this to Frank the same evening, whereupon he suggested she should put up a prayer on behalf of the legitimate Left-wing Government forces. This Nikki did the following day and recalls that it was met by 'a deafening silence' and, two days later, was quietly removed without a word being spoken. When Frank heard of this he urged her to put up a copy of the petition that had been removed. This time all the petitions to do with the Spanish War disappeared and Nikki was apprehensive when she was summoned by the head. Mother St. Paul, however, received her with her usual kindliness and merely observed 'You should always be careful, child, whose opinions you accept'.

If this was an injunction to distinguish fact from opinion it was a precept in which Nikki was already well grounded and one which she usually attempted to apply. It was a fact that the Left-wing Republicans were at the time the legitimate government of Spain. However, authority had to prevail, and she discreetly remained silent. Mother St. Paul stood up, took her face in her hands, kissed her on the forehead, and dismissed her with a blessing.

Nikki had been brought up to say her prayers at bedtime in her early years, but, as Frank and Meg had not insisted upon it, the practice had declined gradually until it came to a stop when she was about eight.

The importance of prayer in the life of the convent school revived her interest in it, but at a different level of understanding, so that she was concerned with it from both a theoretical as well as a practical point of view. She observed the way in which people spoke about prayer, endowed it with a sacred quality, and believed in its efficacy, and decided to learn more about it by empirical means. In a cupboard beside her bed at home she erected a kind of altar, with a crucifix, holy pictures and two candlesticks. Then, in an existential venture into the unknown, she gave herself up to the subjective experience of prayer. It was an attempt to see if she could communicate with God, not with the intention of asking for any material benefit, but in an indefinable way to see whether anything would happen. She knelt by her icons on several occasions during the ensuing weeks, experimenting with prayer and eventually came to the conclusion that, as far as she was concerned, God was inaccessible.

One day, Frank came into her bedroom, discovered the sacred emblems, and expressed his disapproval in the strongest terms, somewhat illogically invoking God to witness such sentimental nonsense. He made her feel that she had let him down by committing what was for him the cardinal sin of acting unintelligently. Meg showed more restraint in the matter and urged him to leave her alone, for she would grow out of it in due course. Nikki did indeed grow out of it, but kept the icons on display measurably longer than she would have done had Frank not made such a drama of the whole affair.

She made few lasting friendships in her peer group at school. Lacking siblings and influenced by an almost exclusively adult social circle at home, she continued to experience difficulty in relating to young people of her own age. For some years she played intermittently with the daughter of neighbours in the same road, but, as each of them went to a different school, this came to an end and their paths separated during their early teens. Of three friends made at La Retraite, one, not destined for an academic career either by ability or aspiration, became pregnant at sixteen and left to get married. Another went on to the university with Nikki but they lost touch with each other soon afterwards, parted by different faculties and academic courses. The third, who became one of her closest friends, and remains so to the present day, was a classmate called Peggy Scully, the daughter of a Bristol manufacturer who had settled with his family in the small residential area of Severn Beach.

One summer, in order to escape the atmospheric pollution they anticipated would follow from repairs taking place on the local drainage system, Frank and Meg bought a caravan and had it moved to Severn Beach, and here they stayed for the next six months. Nikki slept in a tent and greatly enjoyed the sense of independence it gave her, but joined her mother in the caravan on the occasions when Frank stayed in Bristol.

They had not been there long before they discovered that the Scullys lived only a short distance from the camp site and, as a result, the two girls spent a great deal of time together, and the friendship which had begun at school matured rapidly during the months which followed. Peggy's family was, in Nikki's estimation, everything that a family ought to be: affectionate, tolerant, good-humoured, and united. In their company she felt at ease and was able to enjoy herself and have fun in a way she had never experienced before. 'Peggy and her family', she recalls, 'were friendly without being intense. Hospitable in an easy-going way, they managed somehow to combine good sense with a total absence of fuss. In their company I felt almost free from the pervading sense of inadequacy and guilt which characterised my relationship with my father and coloured my social outlook. Peggy's elder brother Raymond, a handsome boy with a passion for motorbikes, was the only person I knew of my own age and of the opposite sex with whom I felt completely at ease. I gather everyone thought that something was going between us, but we were unaware of it at the time. I admired particularly Peggy's ability to maintain undemanding relationships with at least six boys at once, and hoped that perhaps the magic of her good looks and attractiveness would rub off on me. It never did. The first dance I ever went to was spoiled by my mother's insistence on my wearing a frock which she considered suitable but which made me look dumpy and inelegant. Peggy was, of course, as beautiful as ever, and dressed in a modern style which she carried off to perfection. I remember thinking that, if my mother had been less sentimental about pink tulle and more like Peggy's mother, I might not have hated the evening so much'.

Peggy, however, was the exception to the pattern of Nikki's adolescent relationships. It remains a fact that, for the most part, Nikki related better to her teachers at this stage of her life than she did to her peers.

She had little to do with Mother Superior, or Reverend Mother as she was called, the spiritual head of the whole establishment. An Irishwoman largely concerned with religious affairs and administration, she tended to be a remote and shadowy figure.

The teacher she most esteemed and with whom she formed a lasting relationship of enduring value was Mother St. Paul, the academic head. An American psychology graduate, Nikki admired and respected her and came to recognise years later that she had been a major influence on her own personal development. They corresponded for several years after Nikki had left La Retraite, and she occasionally visited her when she was at Bristol University, but they lost touch with each other in the 1950s when Mother St. Paul left the convent after a long illness and removed to the Mother Church in France.

In common with other convent schools, La Retraite was furnished with devotional pictures and figure sculptures, the former being of an excessively sanguine design and the latter being conspicuous examples of uninspiring mass production. She once asked the head why the school had to have such terrible paintings and statuary. Mother St Paul's response was characteristic. She made no attempt to excuse the cruelly explicit portrayal of Christ's passion - the subject of most of the paintings - or the poor quality of the statues. On the contrary, she tacitly accepted the validity of the implied criticism, and quietly explained that they had no money to buy anything better, and were thus obliged to exhibit the gifts donated to the school by the Catholic parents.

At a later stage in her life at the school she asked Mother St Paul if she never had any doubts about her vocation, a question to which the latter replied, 'Why should you think I never have any doubts? We all have doubts as long as we live. It is never easy. Faith lies in overcoming our doubts'. She did not fully understand the significance of this at the time, being too much under the influence of Frank's sceptical attitude to Catholic absolutism, which appeared to preclude the likelihood of doubt. Years later, with more knowledge and understanding of Catholic doctrine, she came to reflect upon and acknowledge the profound wisdom of Mother St Paul's remarks.

Nikki was one of the many children who, throughout the history of education, have, for no obvious reason, experienced difficulty in learning mathematics. For her, the trouble started in the lower school at the convent, where her teacher appeared to be more concerned with disciplined behaviour than with the academic discipline she was responsible for teaching. She was inordinately concerned with the cleanliness of her pupils' fingernails and made a routine inspection of these at the beginning of every lesson. Whenever she found any that fell below her exacting standards she struck the fingers of the offending pupil with a 12-inch ruler, causing acute pain, and sometimes tears. This created a negative learning environment in the classroom, and concentration was distracted by fears that mistakes in calculation would be punished with equal severity.

In the constant state of apprehension to which they were reduced it is not surprising that many of her pupils were under-achievers in mathematics at this stage of their academic careers.

Corporal punishment was not officially allowed in the school, but a few individual teachers still believed in the spiritual value of mortifying the flesh, whether they practised it or not.

Nikki's difficulties were compounded by intermittent absences from school as a result of ill-health, when she missed parts of the mathematics syllabus which were essential to the understanding of the whole. As the teacher kept no record of sequences missed by individual pupils, and made no attempt to make up for these, she found herself falling behind, and, as almost invariably happens in childhood, believed it was all her own fault.

Fortunately, her experience of this subject did not end in dismal failure, as it has done for so many before and since. As she moved up the school, so her teachers changed, and she entered the class of Miss Prior, a gifted teacher, and one who was capable of demystifying the arcane subject matter that mathematics - beyond simple calculations - had become for her up to this time.

An interval of remedial tuition was followed by a period of accelerated learning as she quickly made up for lost ground and discovered for the first time something of the scope and the excitement of mathematics. Miss Prior was the first person to explain to her the meaning of 'light years' and she elucidated trigonometry for her as no-one had been able to do before.

It was at about this time, in the 1930s, that Nikki's mother, through her connections at the university, happened to meet Maria Montessori, the Italian educationist. Dr Montessori had started her long career of missionary work, teaching abroad at first to disseminate her innovatory teaching methods, and later because there was no freedom to teach at home under the fascist government of Benito Mussolini. She was accompanied everywhere by her nephew, a man in his early thirties who spoke English fluently and acted as her interpreter. Always interested in reform and reformers, Meg invited them both to dinner. Perhaps by prearrangement with Meg, perhaps for other reasons, the distinguished guest brought with her a suitcase full of practical teaching apparatus. When the methodological principles of individual problem-solving and self-tuition had been outlined, Nikki was asked if there was any mathematical problem she had never fully understood. 'Yes', she replied, without hesitation, 'the Pythagoras theorem', and went on to give a faultless account of the well-known formula relating to the properties of right -angled triangles. 'But I still didn't know what it meant', she concluded, 'or why'. Signora Montessori produced a cut-out triangle and laid it flat on the table. She than aligned each of three geometric squares against the corresponding sides of the triangle and left her, without further intervention, to draw her own conclusions. 'Oh, it means 'square'!' Nikki exclaimed delightedly, 'but why didn't anyone ever show me?' The experience was of lasting value: far more than explaining the theorem, it had demystified Euclidian geometry.

Another member of staff who facilitated her academic progress was Mother St Christopher, a brilliant and inspired teacher of English. On one occasion Nikki lent her a copy of Olaf Stapleton's 'Odd John', one of the first science fiction books she had read, and one she had much enjoyed. Mother St Christopher returned the book the following day, much sooner than expected, looking visibly shaken and holding the book as if it were a live thing possessed of diabolical power. She had obviously undergone some profound psychic disturbance, and disclosed that, the night before, she had thrust the book outside the door, unable to endure its presence in the room with her. As she made no further comment, and did not mention the affair subsequently, the precise reasons for her actions never transpired. It seemed improbable that the book itself or the category to which it belonged came under the Papal Index Expurgatorius, but it was possible Mother St Christopher's instinctive reaction was to regard it as taboo. If any of these conjectures was the case, she did not say so.

Physical education at the school included the conventional individual and team games, the virtues of which were almost entirely lost upon Nikki. Her relatively isolated upbringing had not accustomed her to gregarious pursuits; she felt she was over-weight, and had been alienated from outdoor exercise by her father's insistence on joining him in a programme of diet and exercise prescribed by his doctor. As far as she was concerned, team games were an abomination, typified by winter afternoons playing hockey. She recalls standing about shivering in freezing temperatures, waiting for a ball which seldom came in her direction, and wondering what to do with the hockey stick when it did. Her ankles were kicked and struck with sticks, and she could not understand how it could ever have come to be called a game, as for her it represented nothing but unrelieved torture.

If there was no relief, there was at least the occasional distraction, provided by the spectacle of Mother Theresa, in full sail, charging down the field brandishing her hockey stick and shouting 'Holy Mary, Mother of God!' and 'Take that!' as she propelled the ball in front of her. Presumably she was calling on the saintly company of Heaven to witness if not to further her endeavours.

It would be possible to exaggerate the elements of cultural conflict that marked the relations between home and school. That she confronted her teachers from time to time, challenging their system of beliefs, has already been established, just as, by the same token, it has been shown that she was sensitised to and thus armed against the possibilities of religious indoctrination. It does not follow from this - and it would be absurd to suggest that, outside the formal and secular contents of the curriculum, she did not learn anything of permanent value from the school.

Where her father had been conspicuously incapable of respecting those with whom he was in dissent, Nikki learned that she could like, respect and work with people with whose beliefs she fundamentally disagreed. She came to recognise and to dissociate herself from her father's prejudice against the Roman Catholic Church. She both admired and respected the selfless and dedicated way of life of the nuns and the religious faith which sustained it. The drama and symbolism inherent in the rituals and ceremonies of the Church made a deep impression on her, while the myths and parables stimulated her imagination and opened her mind to a higher order of philosophical thought. For all this, she remained detached, objective and quite incapable of experiencing any sense of identity with the Catholic world view. Her growing awareness of sexual inequality in the wider society was increased by observing the unequal distribution of power in the Catholic hierarchy. Her experience at the convent left her with the impression that the priests, a considerable number of whom regularly visited the school, were on the whole conspicuously inferior to the nuns, in character, intelligence, and education, and yet were everywhere in authority. She recalls a graphic example of what she then perceived as the nuns' subordination, when a ceremony held at the school was attended in his official capacity by a grossly fat and worldly-looking bishop. At one stage of the proceedings, in accordance with the normal ritual, Mother St Paul genuflected and kissed the bishop's ring. Nikki was shocked and revolted by what she saw as an act of abject subservience, and thought, 'Kneel to God if you like, or to the Saints, but not to mortal man!' Mother St Paul could have explained it all from her own point of view, emphasising the virtues of humility, obedience and duty voluntarily undertaken, but the opportunity did not arise, and Nikki had to acquire this symbolic understanding through later experience. She recognised instinctively the coercive power of the Church over spirit and imagination, and, at a subconscious level, resisted it, just as she had resisted the possessiveness of her own parents, and would, in due course, resist the domination of political ideologies.

One notable exception to her passionate individualism was her love of choral singing, in which she surrendered herself completely to being a member of a group, which in this case represented no threat of domination or control, but existed solely for the production of pure harmony. With her initiation into plainsong, choral work became for her a spiritual experience inspiring and elemental. At least three times a year the school provided the choir for the sung Requiem Mass in the Cathedral. After some years as an ordinary member of the choir, she was selected in her 5th form year as one of the four Cantors who were required to perform sequences of the Mass by singing contrapuntally. She recalls vividly an occasion when she was so transported by the sound of a certain passage in the music that she found herself singing with tears streaming down her face.

The choral experience in which she took so much delight was in marked contrast to the sadly abortive efforts her parents made to involve her in family music-making at home. It was paradoxical that Frank and Meg, whose instrumental and vocal skills enabled them to entertain their friends and neighbours, should have been incapable of joining with their daughter in the production of music for their domestic pleasure. However, whenever they tried to draw her into either trios or duets, it invariably ended in discord. Tension mounted over timing and missed cues; disputes broke out over interpretation of the score, and, as tempers flared, performance declined, to the point when their collective efforts had to be abandoned. Nikki was reduced to misery by Frank's constant fault-finding, and to silent hysteria by Meg's Romantic style of expressive singing. They were soloists trying, with the best intentions, to be an ensemble and it did not work.

But there were other sources of music in the home - the radio and the gramophone - and she had access to an exceptionally fine collection of classical records accumulated by her parents over the years.

In the early 1930s the musical soirées were largely but not entirely superseded by meetings of various friends from the wider community whom Frank and Meg invited to the house for discussions on social and political affairs. It was a period of world economic depression and of ominous political events, prominent among which was the rise of the dictators Hitler and Mussolini. These developments produced a growing demand for information and an escalation of public discourse on political issues. In the provision of mass communication the monopoly of the press had for several years been gradually eroded by the advent of radio, at that time under the control of the dictatorial Sir (later Lord) John Reith. Talks on major topics of public interest were a regular feature of BBC broadcasts, and it was an established practice that the public response to these should be monitored by a national network of regional groups of listeners. Groups had to listen to the broadcasts, discuss their contents along lines suggested by Corporation leaflets, and send in reports. Meg, with Frank's agreement, volunteered to organise such a discussion group and to provide the venue for its weekly meetings at Goldney Road.

During the same period, always eager to make up for lost educational opportunities, Meg had been taking lecture courses and tutorial classes variously provided by the Bristol Co-operative Society, the Workers' Educational Association, and the University Extension Department. In the process, she studied economic theory, world religions, moral philosophy, introductory psychology, and Marxist theory.

Her introduction to Marxism gave her the added satisfaction of feeling she could meet Frank halfway in the discussion of this branch of philosophy. Her own interpretation of the Marxian concept of 'praxis' was more down to earth than Frank's, being concerned more with the social conditions of the poor in Bristol than with prospects of revolutionary change at the macro level of society.

One of her initiatives was an appeal to the Church authorities about the shocking state of the slum dwellings they owned in the older part of Bristol. She succeeded in arousing strong public feeling on the matter, and, with the help of Canon (later Bishop) Dudley Narborough, induced them to have the slums demolished and replaced by new houses. As joint Honorary Secretary of the Bristol Public Welfare Committee, she helped to organise a housewives' campaign against profiteering and the excessively high prices currently being charged for food and household commodities, prices which disproportionately burdened the poorer classes least able to afford them.

The sum of Meg's activities at this time brought a succession of visitors to the house, representing a wide range of occupations : factory workers, artisans, academics, ecclesiastics, and political activists. The latter were Left-wing and ranged from members of the Communist Party to moderate social reformers. The names of some of those who visited the house stand out in Nikki's memories of those years : Harry Pollitt, Arthur Horner, Palme

Ahead of her Time

Dutt, Professor Campion, Emeritus Professor of Philosophy at the University, John Pilley, the first Professor of Education, and Canon Dudley Narborough, already mentioned. There was Harry Toogood, one time Reader at Uppsala University, whose political convictions and wide reading had led him to a quiet life as a boot mender in Clifton. His shop was the meeting place of a mixed and fascinating group of people of all ages and opinions, and it was here that Nikki always found a ready welcome and the opportunity for long talks on a seemingly limitless range of subjects. The multi-talented Charles Hobbs (whose family became lifelong friends) self-taught philosopher, political thinker, and skilled craftsman, introduced her for the first time to the principles of three-dimensional design. Then there was John Flynn, a newsagent, who lived in a house known to his friends as 'the bomb shop', and boasted that the seat of his outside toilet had been sat on by Lenin. Another visitor was Ivan Maisky, the Soviet Ambassador. Learning that Nikki wanted to be an actress when she grew up, he offered her parents the chance of sending her in two years' time to Moscow, where she could at the age of eleven have started a five years' course of training at the Theatre School. It was an opportunity that had no equivalent in Britain at the time, but Frank and Meg had no hesitation in coming to the joint decision that it had to be declined.

Both shared the ideals of those intellectuals who had welcomed the Russian Revolution of 1917 and the subsequent creation of the USSR.

> 'And out of the red, red flood shall arise
> a new society where men are brothers'

wrote Frank in 1932,

> 'where non are idle, where all can work
> to build anew the earth, and gather
> the fruits of its munificence
> for all to share.'

In spite of their radical sympathies and their communist friends, neither of them ever sought membership of the Party, and indeed broke off their connection with it after the Hitler-Stalin Pact of 1939.

Much of Nikki's life at home was thus spent in the company not only of her parents but also of other adults many of who were actively involved in the social and political events of the period. It was neither a salon, in the sense of a 'cercle littéraire', nor was it a 'think tank', yet it partook of some of the characteristics of both. She responded eagerly to the constant flow of intellectual stimulation, and steadily accumulated a knowledge of national and world affairs far in advance of her years.

Most of the meetings, and invariably the BBC discussions, were held in the evenings, and both Frank and Meg would usually be present at these. Other study groups were held at the house in the daytime when he was at work; she did not always take part, and Nikki, in termtime, was at school. All these occasions involved Meg in providing hospitality and it is doubtful whether Frank knew how many of these there were. It is certainly likely that he did not know of all the spontaneous lunches, and, in view of his parsimonious ideas it was just as well that he was not present to witness them. It has to be said that Meg conscientiously limited her expenditure to the minimum and provided only the most simple fare. Some measure of this can be gauged by the time when Meg got the curate drunk on her orange wine. 'It's really only fruit juice!' she had assured him.

As she grew older, Nikki still found it difficult to understand her father's shifting moods and often unpredictable behaviour. One instance of this was when several friends had been invited to the house for an evening meal. One of these, the octogenarian Professor Campion, was known to have become interested in spiritualism, so it was no surprise when, before dinner was finished, he excused himself from the table, saying that he had to leave for an appointment in Bristol. After he had left, Frank said, 'He must be going to one of his séances.' Nikki, thinking that, as a self-confessed atheist, he would approve, replied, 'perhaps he'll raise the Holy Ghost this time!' But, to her consternation, far from being amused by a repartee of the kind he usually encouraged, he reacted with furious indignation and gave her a severe ticking-off for blasphemy.

Not all her role conflicts arose out of her father's inconsistencies; she experienced the uncertainties common to all adolescents in western society at the stage when they are no longer children, yet are still not accepted as adults. In this intermediate position, although she met and talked to individual members of the groups who came to the house, she was regarded nevertheless as too young to be present, once the discussions began. Fascinated by what was going on, and eager to learn what the discussions were about, she used to sit on the staircase in the hall, and listen to the proceedings from there.

One afternoon in the school holidays she was settled in her usual place on the stairs, listening desultorily to a discussion of no particular interest to her. Neither Frank nor Meg was involved in the meeting, except in the provision of hospitality. Frank was out at work, and Meg was in the kitchen preparing refreshments. A sudden lowering of voices focused Nikki's attention, and from what ensued it appeared to her that she was listening to a communist plot to incriminate, for 'the good of the cause', one of their own party, for a penal offence he had not committed. The full implication of what she had heard became clear only some time later, when she heard that the man concerned had been sent to prison. It was an object lesson in 'realpolitik' which she was never to forget, and which formed the basis of a lasting distrust of communism and of total systems in general. She felt that she had witnessed the essence of something far more inimical to personal liberty than ecclesiastical dogma, for here was evidence of a will to distort the truth in the supposed interests of an arbitrary 'greater good'. It was her first experience of political pragmatism divorced from moral or ethical considerations.

Ahead of her Time

Frank's chronic ill-health had led him between the wars to collect potential therapies as assiduously as he collected religions. He had reached the point of losing his faith in orthodox medical practice and limited his investigations almost entirely to the field of alternative medicine. He read innumerable books and experimented with a series of different therapies, but to little effect. In 1932 he read a new book which was to change not only his life but also the lives of the other members of his family. Written by a Swedish dietician, it was about the dietary treatment of illness, and included specific reference to the colitis from which Frank suffered. That summer they travelled to London to meet the author, and learned that Frank could be cured in three years by adherence to a prescribed vegetarian diet, which, it was assumed, would be followed by the whole family. They spent two weeks at his establishment, during which they were initiated into the diet, and Meg was instructed in the correct methods of preparing and cooking the food. It would be easier to say what the diet allowed than what it prohibited. It was unappetising, monotonous, and almost totally lacking in flavour, and it became the regular diet of the family for the next three and a half years.

'Morning ritual - no-one could have called it breakfast -' Nikki recalled, 'consisted of a gritty poultice made of two cupfuls of bran (the sort horses eat), one of raw oats and one of boiling water, eaten after two minutes' soaking, with black treacle or sour milk.'[1]

She could only suppose that her meek acceptance of such a regime arose from a desire to live up to her father's definition of intelligent judgment, a belief that his survival depended on their support in sharing the diet with him, and the notion that it was going to be good for all of them.

The consequences for her social life were disastrous. She felt herself an outcast among her contemporaries, for, when she was invited to their homes, she always had to take a list of things she could not eat, which usually comprised the whole of the meal provided. Conversely, none of her friends came to tea with her a second time, as they were subjected to the same rules.

She was permanently hungry and, eventually, as her longing for the 'wrong' things grew, 'my adherence to honesty weakened, and the guilt-ridden ice cream devoured secretly, the pork pie bought with my sixpence pocket money, ceased to be occasional symbols of a depraved nature, and became ordinary occurrences.'[2]

In 1935, three years after the diet had begun, Meg caught undulant fever; her weight dropped to four and a half stone, and she nearly died. The direct cause was not the diet, but contaminated milk from a Bristol dairy which was later prosecuted. The doctor had to insist, in spite of

---

[1] Extract from 'Bran Mash for Breakfast'. BBC Radio, Woman's Hour Talk (1960) reproduced in full in Appendix A

[2] ibid.

Frank's objections, that she should be fed with meat jelly if she was to survive. In the event, her life was almost certainly saved by the fortunate chance of her doctor's having access to some of the first antibiotics, then only in the early stages of development.

Meg convalesced for six months in Italy, while her mother, Elizabeth Ann, took over the management of the household, with the result that Nikki, much to her relief, came off the diet. Frank continued but with minor modifications of which he was unaware; as, for example, the occasional spoonful of meat gravy poured over his nutmeat rissole 'to make it taste nicer'.

Soon after Meg returned from Italy, glowing with health and in high spirits, she resumed her former way of life with renewed energy. She no longer had responsibility for the BBC discussions, but in the late 1930s she became involved with a group which brought political refugees out of Hitler's Germany. The house became a reception post for many individuals and families on their way to a new life in Britain and the United States of America. On one occasion she discovered that a supposed refugee was, in fact, a Nazi informer; challenged him with it and treated him to a blistering denunciation in her most forthright North Country manner. She never saw him again but made sure that he was immediately reported to the refugee agency.

It was not the first time that she had interested herself in the affairs of German refugees, for, in 1936, she had taken Nikki, then aged fifteen, to spend two weeks with the Bruderhof Commune in Cirencester. This was a community of earlier refugees who had fled from persecution in Germany after the First World War. They were organised on the principles of self-help and self-sufficiency, preserved a low profile in relation to the indigenous population, but had some interaction with it, mainly economic. The life of the commune made a deep impression on both of them. All the members contributed to the welfare of the group without any status distinction between mental and manual work. A former history professor was employed on hedging and ditching, while an ex-judge helped with the local harvest as well as dealing with legal affairs. A wide range of craft skills was represented, and included violin-making and ivory-carving. Money earned was held in common and some of it was used to send members to London and elsewhere, selling their products and buying new equipment and materials for their work.

Nikki remembers that she and her mother entered into the division of labour while they were there, joining in a variety of domestic tasks as and when required. One agreeable memory was sitting in a sunlit courtyard shelling peas, while someone read aloud from a philosophical textbook, the content of which was subsequently discussed. She was to reflect with some nostalgia on this experience when, in the 1960s, sporadic and less authentic versions of the commune system were formed as an expression of the so-called counter-culture of that time.

Ahead of her Time

Meg, impatient after her long illness to return to her academic studies, and in spite of the fact that she had not matriculated, managed to convince the authorities at Bristol University that she was capable of following a three-year course in philosophy for her own personal interest, though she was never allowed to take the degree examination. Grateful for the opportunity, she became a model student in respect of regular attendance and conscientious application. Her natural ebullience, however, proved too much for some of the academic staff. It had always been her way to challenge everything with which she disagreed or which she did not comprehend and she saw no reason to modify her behaviour in the context of the university lecture or seminar. Her challenges were never of an aggressive kind, and were invariably motivated by a desire to learn and understand. Suffice it to say they did not find favour with those of her tutors who felt threatened by them or simply did not approve of their students exercising this degree of freedom.

When Meg finished her course in 1938 Nikki was sixteen, and had recently passed all the five requisite subjects of her School Certificate examination, obtaining credits in four of them. Frank's response on hearing the results was predictable: rather than offering congratulations, he focused on the one subject in which she had not gained a credit and remarked drily, 'I see, so you've failed'. He was clearly unaware of the counter-productive effects that can be generated by negative suggestion, and probably thought his words would spur her to greater effort in the future. Whatever the case may have been, two years later, Nikki, who admits that she did no real work until the last six months before the examination, gained her Higher School Certificate in English, French and History, with a subsidiary paper in Biology, gaining an especially high mark in English. 'I never knew', said her English teacher, Mother St Christopher, 'if you were going to fail or to do brilliantly!' She was obviously delighted it had been the latter, but her comment found echoes amongst other members of the teaching staff who had found Nikki an exceptionally intelligent pupil, but at times unpredictable, disturbing to their moral certainties and perceptions of social reality.

In retrospect, Nikki thought she must have been a trial to the nuns and that they were probably greatly relieved when she left the school for the university. She felt they had been far nicer to her than she deserved, or, at any rate, than they might have been in the circumstances.

It is an equally plausible hypothesis that, since they were not into the breaking of spirits, there were those among them who missed her vitality and spirited independence.

In spite of her frequent and sometimes long periods of absence through ill-health, they had tried to remedy all the tuition she had missed and had succeeded in providing her with an excellent preparation for higher education.

She left without regret, but with a strong sense of gratitude for all the nuns had done for her. If La Retraite was a quieter place following her departure, it was probably a less animated one.

4   The University Years

Nikki spent the last two weeks of the school holidays in the summer of 1939 at a drama school in Dorset. The course ended on a Friday and she returned to Bristol on the same evening, being surprised to find that the train in which she was travelling had been entirely blacked out. Two days later, on Sunday the third of September, she listened with her parents to the Prime Minister's announcement on the radio that Britain was at war.

It had been apparent for some time that the Government's policy of appeasement towards Hitler had broken down, and that, in spite of the hopes for peace raised by the Munich Agreement of 1938, military conflict between Britain and Germany had become inevitable.

Frank and Meg had seen it all coming and wisely took the precaution of moving Meg's mother, Elizabeth Ann, out of Bristol and into the country, correctly anticipating that the city would become the target of enemy air raids in the event of war. They found residential accommodation for her in Blagdon, a village situated at the foot of the Mendip Hills, some twelve miles south of Bristol. Soon after the war began they left Bristol themselves and went with Nikki to live in Compton Martin, a village only a short distance from Blagdon, and here, in due course, Elizabeth Ann was reunited with them. Another change affecting family life at this time occurred when Frank was transferred by the bank to a new appointment in Blackpool, and was thereafter able to be with the family only at weekends.

As an extension of her work on the Public Welfare Committee, Meg was involved in setting up a new organisation concerned with civil defence: the Bristol Air-Raid Precaution and Protection Committee. The aims of this organisation were to alert the public to the state of unpreparedness and lack of protection in the event of air attacks on Bristol, and to exert pressure on the City Council to take urgent remedial action. 'Dear Friend,' read a leaflet she and her joint honorary secretary circulated widely in August, 1939, 'We should like to draw your attention to a Mass Meeting to be held on October 22nd at the Co-operative Hall, Castle Green, to hear Professor Haldane, who will put the case for real protection. Our Council must have the united, ungrudging help of all workers if we are, at this late hour, to save the lives of thousands of Bristol citizens, for whom there is as yet no protection. We shall be glad, therefore, if you will send a delegate to our next General Meeting at the Co-operative Education Centre, Broad Weir, on August 18th at 7.45 p.m.'

During the so-called 'phoney war', when, for nearly eight months, the expected military engagement abroad and aerial bombardment at home failed to materialise, life continued very much as before, except for the obligation to observe air raid precautions, carry identity cards and gas masks, and adapt to the rationing of food and clothing.

Ahead of her Time

When the land war in Europe began in earnest in the spring of 1940 and the German Army finally launched its assault on the Western Allies, the situation changed dramatically. The enemy air raids which followed the fall of France and the evacuation of Dunkirk by the British Expeditionary Force were only the first of many which were to cause devastation and loss of life in London and other cities, including Bristol. Since these raids were for the most part nocturnal, Nikki ran a calculated risk in making her daily bus journeys to school in Bristol. There was, of course, always the possibility of daytime raids, and, if the alarm sounded, it was necessary to interrupt the journey and take cover in the nearest air raid shelter.

Bus services became less reliable as the war progressed but when they failed to run she was usually able with others in the same predicament to obtain transport in the Army lorries which made the journey to Bristol on a regular basis. This was only one of the many instances of spontaneous mutual support and communal interdependence fostered by the war; a precedent of the widespread practice of hitch-hiking which developed after it was over.

Paradoxically, the Mendips did not prove to be the absolutely safe haven her parents had anticipated, for they were on the flight path of the German planes returning from their raids over Bristol, and these frequently jettisoned their surplus bombs in the surrounding countryside.

In June she was due to take her Higher School Certificate examinations and, as the time drew nearer, to spare her from the fatigue involved in making daily journeys to school, arrangements were made for her to stay for three weeks in an hotel in Bristol. It was a wise precaution, for she had been showing signs of nervous strain as a result of war-time conditions and these were compounded by anxiety over her forthcoming examinations or, more precisely, over the possibility of disappointing her parents' expectations.

The arrangement did nothing, however, to prevent her coming out in a widespread nettle rash, accompanied by severe itching, which persisted for nearly three months, including the period of the examinations. So acute was the eruption that she had to be bandaged extensively, in order not only to treat the condition but also to prevent her from scratching the affected areas of skin.

The examiners were apparently not informed, as they would be in such circumstances today, that she had been obliged to write her papers with arms bandaged to the wrists and wearing white cotton gloves. And it is uncertain whether, if they had known, they would have made any allowances for her condition. Whatever the case, to judge from the marks awarded, they were well satisfied with her performance in the examinations, and her admission to the University was secured.

There had been no question of entering any university other than Bristol. Unlike the present system of multiple applications through the Central Clearing House, it was assumed that school leavers with the necessary qualifications, unless they had gained specific exhibitions or scholarships elsewhere, would attend their local university. One variation of this procedure which affected Bristol in the 1940s was the evacuation of undergraduates from King's College, London University. The latter came with their tutors ostensibly to escape the London Blitz but were soon to discover that they had exchanged one perilous situation for another, though with a reduced level of risk. This amalgamation proved beneficial to undergraduates of both universities, providing cross-fertilisation through the interaction of students and the exchange of tutorial staff.

In general, one of the least satisfactory aspects of the transfer from school to university is the lack of any systematic preparation for the role of the undergraduate. Bristol was then no better and no worse than other universities in this respect. The independent public schools and local authority grammar schools with long-established and close connections with the universities provided some form of preparation, but, for the rest, it was assumed that either the university would provide the necessary induction or the students would find out for themselves. It was manifestly bad psychology to place any reliance on the latter, for it ignored the frame of mind of the individual at such a time, and the difficulty of obtaining all the information needed at the beginning of an academic year. Nikki was not alone in coming from a school which had provided her with no form of anticipatory socialisation in this respect. Since the university disclaimed any responsibility in the matter, she was left to find her own definition of the undergraduate role. First it was necessary for her to relinquish the character of school pupil, at that time viewed conventionally in terms of waiting to be told what to do, and to a great extent passively receiving transmitted knowledge. Now, regarded as a young adult, she was required to assume the personal responsibility involved in reading for a degree, and for the detailed organisation of her studies, actively making decisions on the processing of information and the selection and use of learning resources. She adapted quickly, but in the process of adjustment valuable time was lost in her first year. It served to show that the consequences of expecting too much of undergraduates can prove as serious as expecting too little. To do either is an error of judgment, as well as a disservice to students, and is only one example of the necessity for university tutors to have some formal qualification in the theory and practice of teaching.

With her simultaneous release from conventual seclusion and the constraints of family life, she might be supposed to have entered this new phase of her life with a sense of liberation and excited anticipation of what the future had in store for her. For various reasons, this was not the way it worked out. In accordance with normal practice she was accommodated at Clifton Hill House, a women's hall of residence, during her first year, and, although this meant removal from home, it still involved other restrictions of a kind commonly found in boarding schools. Students were expected to return to hall from their daily lectures not later than 6 p.m. and to remain there, unless they had special leave of absence, until the following morning. The manifest function of these limitations was to know the whereabouts of all the resident students in case of air raids, but none doubted the existence of a latent purpose as much concerned with their moral as with their physical welfare. There was an effective hidden curriculum which seemed to belong more to a young ladies' finishing school than to a university. This involved her in learning by observation certain new codes of language and behaviour which everyone else appeared to know already. With this disadvantage, and the sense of traversing a minefield, she suffered embarrassment on several occasions during her first few weeks, being either told directly or left to infer that she had offended the proprieties in one way or another.

Nikki was disappointed to learn that the Honours course in English and Philosophy for which she had been accepted was no longer available. It had been cancelled because enrolments had fallen short of the minimum number required. To be able to take the subjects for which she had opted, she was obliged to follow a combined degree course which included English, History, Philosophy, Psychology, and subsidiary French. At first discouraged by this turn of events, she gradually came to appreciate the structure and content of the alternative curriculum. Liberal rather than exclusive, it comprised a range of subjects in all of which she took great interest, with the exception of the Old Norse, Icelandic, and Anglo-Saxon sections of the English component, which she detested.

It was not entirely an advantage to have followed her mother through the same department within the memory span of the lecturers she had worked with. And, after several puzzling encounters, she concluded that Meg's lively but untrained mind had proved a challenge in seminars, and her unorthodox approach to authoritative statements had not always been appreciated. That her warm and friendly openness of character had won her many friends at the university and elsewhere cut no ice with the academic staff. This was brought home to Nikki at her first lecture in Philosophy. It transpired that the professor was one of those who had taught her mother when she had been a student two years before.

Seeing Nikki's name on the register, and identifying her among the assembled students, he said, as if searching his memory, 'Greenall? Let me see - ah yes, I remember your mother well', and proceeded to recall with some irony the exceptional circumstances of Meg's university career. Had his tone been less ironical, it might have appeared that he was attempting, however tactlessly, to make her feel at home. As it was, sensitive and lacking self-confidence, she was acutely embarrassed and made to feel publicly humiliated. Later experience convinced her that the professor's underlying motivation was a not uncommon prejudice, amongst male academics, against the study of philosophy by women, a prejudice by no means insubstantial even today.

One of the first events of the academic year was the presentation of new undergraduates to the Vice-Chancellor of the University. Nikki learned only when it was too late that, in addition to wearing gowns, female students were required to wear white gloves for the ceremony, which involved shaking hands with the Vice-Chancellor. It struck her as an absurd ritual to have been preserved in time of war, when clothes rationing was in force and money, especially for students, was scarce. It also discriminated against women, since wearing gloves was not required for the male freshmen. Something, however, had to be done, and a solution presented itself when a colleague who had succeeded in obtaining a pair of gloves offered to share them with her. It was not possible to transfer both gloves from one to the other, so it was agreed that the owner had an ipso facto claim on the right-hand glove and that Nikki should make the best use she could of the other. In the event, her friend was able to conceal the gloveless hand under her academic gown, but Nikki had to hold her glove in one hand and offer the other to the Vice-Chancellor, feeling herself trapped in a breach of etiquette only marginally less serious than having no gloves at all. Whether or not it was viewed in this way by the authorities, she herself was made to feel maladroit and somehow in the wrong. This accumulation of adverse circumstances in her first months at the university, together with the lack of any clear idea of what she was supposed to be doing, reduced her to a state of hopelessness and a sense of personal failure. Now, surely, was the time to run away and join the circus or, more realistically, the Navy, since the Women's Royal Naval Service was calling for recruits, and Nikki gave it more than a passing thought. She even went as far as attending a preliminary interview with the WRNS. But there were constraints on her freedom of action of which she was aware yet which, as a result of her depression, she had temporarily glossed over. Meg was still in a state of acute distress and to have left her at such a time would clearly have aggravated her suffering to an intolerable degree. Prompted by these reflections, Nikki went to see Mother St Paul to talk the matter over and was advised, predictably, to remember her duty to her mother. So, with some reluctance, she withdrew her application and resumed her academic career.

Gradually things began to fall into place, and she was able to develop a coherent understanding of the organisation of the university and of her own particular role within it. She became increasingly familiar with the routines of student life, and more confident in her ability to distribute time systematically between academic studies and social commitments. Within this more stable conceptual framework she was able to take an objective view of her new social environment, and in the process discovered a degree of freedom that her first impressions had not led her to expect. It was a new kind of freedom, in her experience, involving independence of action and providing opportunity for the exchange and exploration of ideas with tutors and fellow students drawn from a wide range of social backgrounds. It was a revelation to her that university education comprised more than the content of a specific degree course, and that it could derive as much from interaction with fellow students as from the academic curriculum. She found herself in an exciting new world of cognitive opportunity, and became aware of the existence of new social realities to be explored and understood. She appreciated for the first time the epistemological truism that knowledge is a continuum and, in this sense, indivisible, in spite of its necessarily differentiated cultural organisation. And the validity of this important insight was illustrated by the particular structure of her degree course, with its complement of overlapping academic disciplines.

The sex ratio of the student population in the universities underwent a distinct shift during the war, and women began to outnumber men by an increasing margin as the latter were called up for service in the armed forces. Bristol, with its medical, engineering, scientific and theological faculties, was an exception to this general trend and had a sizeable proportion of male students destined for reserved occupations, and these were augmented by others who had been evacuated from London University. Nikki thus found herself a member of a community of undergraduates in which the sexes were evenly represented, and where the relatively large number and the behavioural expectations combined to allow the free choice of friends and the avoidance of incompatibles.

It was at exactly this point that Nikki discovered men, and men discovered her. As she had been brought up to regard men and women as equal though different, this discovery showed every indication of generating problems of adjustment on both sides. Apart from her adolescent infatuation with the young communist who had been killed in Spain, and her friendship with Peggy Scully's brother Ray, her knowledge of the opposite sex was based largely on the older men she had met in her parents' social circle. It was partly because of this that she had hitherto found little in common with young men of her own age, and sometimes found it difficult to take them seriously. Since the relatively mature young men she met at the university were at first something of an unknown quantity, she needed time to find out more about them. She enjoyed the new freedoms associated with mixed groups; the conversational exchanges, the intellectual fencing, and the spontaneous fun, but these were all conducted at the level of quasi-sibling relationships, and she was content that for the time being this involved nothing deeper in the way of emotional commitment.

'Not from any motive of shyness, I tended at first to shelter behind my girl friends, summing up from a safe distance the nature, characteristics, and possible dangers of the genus 'Man'. I had not been brought up with the customary view of myself as a woman which many of my contemporaries evinced. Injunctions such as 'Don't let them see how clever you are' or 'Always wait for the man to make the first move' had not figured largely in my expectations of social life, and I was inclined to regard men as just the same as women, only different! I had observed Peggy flirting, and thought it must be wonderful to be able to do it, but I didn't know how. I enjoyed the mixed company of men and women and spent most of my first two years at university in a group of people without attaching myself particularly to anyone, though I had three or four close women friends. We supported each other; exchanged news, views, gossip and clothes with careless abandon, and I rather suspect embroidered our accounts of relationships with the opposite sex according to the expectations of the person we were talking to. Again, just like men; the same but different.'

Outside the academic curriculum, social activities revolved around the Students' Union and a range of clubs and societies of a bewildering variety. According to the choice and number of activities undertaken, it was possible to enter into either a simple or a complex network of relations in which the individual could try out different roles, self-inventions, and reinventions. It was a social framework which facilitated getting to know others and, through a succession of mirror images, learning more about oneself.

For all that she remained uncommitted, as time went on, she came to develop closer associations with individual men with whom she shared interests and already felt at ease. Neither she nor they had any intention of early commitment at a time when the future was uncertain and, anyway, most women students did not rush into sexual encounters, 'for the simple reason that we feared pregnancy more than virginity.' Nevertheless, 'I fell in and out of love with alarming regularity, and with remarkably little discretion.'

There were grounds for optimism in her growing self-confidence, sense of identity, and knowledge of being accepted as a member of the community. There was also objective evidence to show that she had the ability to attain the intellectual and academic standards demanded by her tutors, and, in due course to obtain a good degree. However, contrary to appearances, all was not well. She was still prey to the intermittent doubts and apprehensions that had undermined both her confidence and her self-image from early childhood. The effect of these was to inhibit that concentration of mental energies which could have maximised the achievement of which she was capable. As it was, these energies were often expressed in outbursts of activity which focused on a variety of projects tangential to the subject concerned. Sometimes she would swing from one activity to another, as if from some negative thought that she would fail if she went any further, and would return to the discarded activity sometime later. 'As my enthusiasms were universally directed, and capable of being aroused at any moment by some new or stimulating idea, I found the temptation of alternative paths more irresistible than the straight road to scholarship I was expected to follow.' This did not mean, in consequence, that her learning was superficial, because she mastered new knowledge with exceptional rapidity, and imposed on herself standards of achievement so rigorous as to border upon perfectionism. Whilst she acknowledged the value of the academic disciplines, and conformed, in time, to most of the requirements of her degree course, she never allowed them to suppress her omnivorous appetite for knowledge in its widest sense. There was no reason, in her view, to regard what she learned from the social interaction of daily life as intrinsically less valuable than the content of the academic curriculum. She thought her neuroses were probably at the root of this way of perceiving knowledge, and she may have been right. Neurosis and creativity have often been bedfellows, and, in any case, her extra-curricular activities provided a lively counter-balance to academic study.

Thus her leisure pursuits were chosen with an emphasis more on physical recreation and the expressive arts than on pure intellectual stimulation.

Although equipped by her background and upbringing with a high level of political sophistication, she took little interest in student politics. She had seen and heard enough of politics at home to have developed a healthy scepticism about ideologies and the power they are capable of exercising over the minds and thoughts of men and women. Her critical faculties had been sharpened in the stimulating atmosphere of radical socialism, and she had always managed to preserve her intellectual autonomy and resistance to indoctrination.

Studies of Socrates and Plato gave her a keen appreciation of the dangers of political rhetoric. 'I never go to political meetings', she said, 'because, if they are good (i.e. effective), they are dangerous, and, if they are bad, they're boring'. If Roman Catholic dogma had appeared to her to threaten individual freedom of thought and personal integrity, how much more so did she apprehend the dangers of Marxist determinism. She could appreciate the political idealism of individual Marxists, and identify with the basic ethical principles of Marxism, but she abhorred the unethical means often adopted to achieve its goals in the real world.

'I was all for social justice, and felt deeply about it; and I dare say many of my friends judged me to be an out and out radical. Two things, however, prevented me from joining a political party: one was my dislike of submitting my considered judgments to predetermined political evaluations; secondly, as a woman, I had observed with a certain cynicism that, if you give a man an inch in politics he builds an empire, never the promised utopia'. She found her distrust of utopian social philosophies confirmed by the writings of Karl Popper, in particular 'The Open Society and its Enemies', published in 1945, a year after she had left the University. And she identified strongly with the freedom of mind and spirit expressed in the poetry of William Blake:

'In every cry of every man,
In every infant's cry of fear,
In every voice, in every ban,
The mind-forg'd manacles I hear'.

One of her favourite recreations was dancing, which she loved inordinately and with a feeling amounting to passion. She was an instinctual dancer, and dancing was for her a creative activity in which she invested enormous energy and imagination, and from which she derived a sense of great joy and emotional release. Dances were held at regular intervals both in the University and elsewhere, and she attended these whenever she had the opportunity. Much as she enjoyed these occasions, there was one drawback:

'The men I liked were bad dancers, while the good ones, with some exceptions, rarely possessed any other attractive qualities.'

Film-going was another of her leisure activities. In addition to her periodic visits to the local cinema, she became a member of the students' film society, run at the time by Roger Manville, and, in consequence, developed a strong and enduring interest in the film classics to which this introduced her for the first time.

The theatre, to which she was devoted, was usually too expensive for more than the occasional visit. She preferred not to go at all, rather than queuing for cheap seats or seeing the performance from the gallery; so it was a great joy when she was taken from time to time by relatives or family friends, either in Bristol or in London, for this invariably guaranteed her a good seat.

The financial allowance she received from her father had been calculated at subsistence level, and, as it had to cover the cost of food and transport, there was little left over for even the smallest luxuries. Spare-time avocations which were either free or entailed only nominal, often subsidised, charges were well supported by students. The lively café society which flourished in the immediate environs of the university was attractive precisely because it was possible to spend hours in the coffee shop or tea room for no more than the price of a cup of coffee.

She supplemented her allowance by voluntary firewatching duties and, at Christmas, by sorting parcels at the Post Office. One Easter holiday period, Frank, in a fit of pique because she had not written to him, stopped her allowance temporarily and told her to get a job. She found work at the Duncan House Hotel, a small establishment which had formerly housed the senior department of her first school. She remembered having been taken there as a junior pupil to see the entrance to a passage which led by a labyrinthine network of underground tunnels down to the water's edge. According to local history, this had been used long ago as a secret route for the transfer of smuggled goods. The entrance was concealed behind the wall of the dining room and the hotel owner made a feature of it, opening it up for guests at periodic intervals, and inviting them to peer through a grille into the dark passage beyond.

Nikki was conscientious to a fault in the performance of her domestic tasks. All went well until one morning a young man of about her own age walked into the dining room where she was working. As he entered, she was kneeling under a table with a cloth and a bucket of water, trying to remove a stain from the carpet. 'Did I leave some books in here?' asked the man abruptly, in a tone that was both insolent and accusatory. Not having seen any books in the room, she replied that she did not think so, and suggested that they had probably been taken to his room. 'Well, go and get them!' shouted the man angrily. To which Nikki retorted, 'I suggest you go and get them yourself, I am busy'. The young man spluttered with rage and stormed out of the room, slamming the door behind him. She fully expected this to be followed by a summons from the owner, demanding an explanation, but nothing happened, and she was left to conclude that either he or the hotel guest had decided not to take the matter any further.

Frank restored her allowance before the beginning of the next term, presumably unaware of the precious study time she had lost as a result of working throughout the vacation.

One day, Nikki was sitting in a café with a group of friends when the conversation turned to the question of whether people liked their baptismal names. She expressed dislike for her own name on grounds of euphony and negative historical associations: 'Audrey Barbara Greenall has too many r's in it. It sounds all hard, square, and peculiar'.

The name of Saint Etheldreda had been gradually corrupted to Saint Audrey and the shoddy goods associated with Saint Audrey's Fair had come to be described as 'tawdry'. Somebody suggested that she ought to be called 'Nikki', which met with immediate and unanimous approval, especially by Nikki herself, who snapped her fingers with delighted recognition of a name she would much prefer to her own. By way of comment rather than dissent, a colleague of Russian parentage mentioned that it was commonly a man's name in Russia, whilst a mischievous Scot observed that the Gaelic 'nikkum' translated as 'small devil'.

Like many other undergraduates during the war, she had volunteered for firewatching duties, and, for nearly three years, contributed to a service which became increasingly important, and often dangerous, as the scale of the German air raids intensified. Volunteers attended a preliminary training course, which included extinguishing fires, and simulation exercises conducted in smoke-filled rooms. On the completion of this, they were allocated to various prominent buildings in the neighbourhood, such as the university tower or the Red House (home of the Savage Club).

Normally, the firewatchers worked in pairs, alternating their observation and rest periods throughout the night, but at times they were obliged to work alone. There was nothing to do unless the air raid warning had been given. Once the sirens had sounded the alarm, the student had to patrol the inside of the building, prepared, in the event of incendiary bombs, to warn the nearest fire warden, and attempt to put out any fires with extinguishers and buckets of sand. On the peaceful nights when there were no raids they were simply required to be present at their stations, and were free to pass the time as they chose. This usually took the form of reading, studying, or playing cards. Nikki soon became adept at poker and pontoon, and played for small stakes, but never hazarded more than her pay for the night's firewatching. The place she liked most was a lofty room under the bell chamber of the university tower, where the acoustics were so good that she spent much of her time singing the Hebridean and Russian folk songs she loved so much.

In spite of all the risks in which she had been involved, she was only once in real danger. This was on a night when she was knocked down by the blast of a high explosive bomb, and fell down a flight of steps, injuring the base of her spine, fortunately, with no serious repercussions.

It would be fanciful to suggest that these indirect contacts with the wartime enemy had any connection with her desire to learn something about the use of firearms. But she did find common cause with a group of colleagues who were interested in forming a women's rifle club, on similar lines and using the same facilities as the only existing club of this kind, which was for men only. It transpired from their inquiries that there was no objection to this, and, with the support of the regimental sergeant-major, who was responsible for running the men's club, they duly constituted themselves as the first Bristol University Women's Rifle Club. The RSM provided them with the necessary rifles, targets, and ammunition, and volunteered his services in training and supervision. They fired once a week with small bore rifles on an enclosed miniature range in the university precincts, and made several excursions to an open range in the hills near Bristol, where they used Lee Enfield rifles with .303 ammunition. On one occasion in a match at Westbury-on-Trym they defeated a team of American servicemen.

But, of all the various clubs and societies, it was the Bristol University Dramatic Society which commanded most of Nikki's time and energy, aside from her academic commitments. Her joining this was something of a foregone conclusion. The histrionic gifts which had prompted Ivan Maisy to suggest dramatic training in Moscow had developed as she grew older; she never forgot what he had said, and often talked of being an actress when she grew up. She acted at school and, in her last two years at the convent, appeared several times with distinction in performances of the Bristol Co-operative Dramatic Society.

Because of the prevailing conditions, BUDS during wartime was an informal organisation, lacking any continuity or stable bureaucratic structure. Whilst performances were given at regular intervals, they were of an ad hoc nature, and, from an accounting point of view, conducted as separate ventures, production expenses being paid for out of the proceeds of ticket sales. The standard of production and the quality of the acting were consistently high, in spite of the regular turnover of available players, directors, and backstage workers.

If Nikki ever had any thoughts of using her experience with BUDS as a starting point for a career in the professional theatre, they were destined for disappointment. Unlike those graduates who, after the war, went on to stage careers from Oxbridge, she was faced on leaving university with a choice of service in the armed forces, factory work, teaching, or some other reserved occupation. Her regular appearances on the stage gained her a considerable reputation in the university; her characterisations were intelligent and spirited, and her versatility enabled her to take parts in tragedy or comedy with equal success. Not all productions were 'all right on the night'. On one occasion, playing the role of the heroine, she had just begun a dramatic oration marking the climax of the play when a stage hand calmly and absent-mindedly walked off stage with the flat immediately behind her, depicting a fireplace and an overhanging mantelpiece. Unaware of this, she was puzzled by the laughter of the audience but continued with her speech. During this, the stage hand, realizing what had happened, tried to make amends by returning the scenery to somewhere near its former position. Somehow, by a supreme effort of self-control, and against all the odds, Nikki managed to hold the attention of the audience right up to the end of the scene. The curtain came down, and, according to one observer, she stormed backstage, boiling with indignation, and vented her anger on everyone in sight.

The academic interests of undergraduates studying English Literature were reflected in the selection of plays, so that she found herself more than once performing in the more sanguinary tragedies of the Elizabethan era. 'The play', read a programme note to Thomas Kyd's Spanish Tragedy', 'is, frankly, a melodrama - an Elizabethan shocker. It is full of blood, murder, and sudden death. It would, perhaps, be going too far to describe Kyd as the Edgar Wallace of his age, but such an analogy may assist a modern audience to appreciate the spirit of the play.' John Webster's 'The White Devil' followed in quick succession, and Nikki owed it to the casting director that, although 'beaten to the floor', she was not among the numerous corpses carried off the stage in that grisly piece of *grand guignol*.

Productions were not always in this vein, and, in Bristol Warship Week in 1942, the company presented the naval comedy 'The Middle Watch', by Ian Hay and Stephen King-Hall. According to the programme, the performance had the dual function of amusing the audience and contributing to 'the magnificent effort of the Warship Week organisers to build, equip, and absolutely own Bristol's own battleship, HMS Jamaica'.

Judging by the impression she made on her friends during this period, something of her stage persona clearly spilled over into everyday life. An appearance of affectation and theatricality in both behaviour and dress invested her with a glamour, sophistication, and worldliness of which paradoxically she herself remained largely unaware. Faced with the challenge of wartime clothes rationing, she responded with her usual practicality, and enjoyed improvising variations in dress, and did so with remarkable ingenuity and style. She would, for example, vary the use of a scarf by wearing it on successive days, first round the waist, then the neck, and finally, on the third day, as a dashing turban with one end hanging down at the side. Marjorie Wood (later Baroness Chanteau) recalls her 'archetypal chic', and being impressed with her vivacity, flair, and elegance.

Reflecting on this phase of her life, Nikki interprets the pattern of her behaviour at that time in terms of the continuing quest for self-knowledge and identity.

'Having been brought up to treat men as equals, I observed, a little late, that certain behaviour patterns were associated with being female, and I started trying them on for size, in the hope of finding one that fitted. Hence, I suppose, the somewhat contradictory range of character types I adopted probably struck my friends as bizarre, if not downright peculiar. My behaviour must have seemed to indicate a worldliness and sophistication that was far from the truth.'

The capacity for friendship, in which she took after her mother, had little opportunity for development during her schooldays. With the exception of Peggy Scully, she had few friends of her own age before going to university, but here she found herself in a social milieu which positively encouraged the accumulation of friends. Partly because of the paucity of close relationships in the past, she had come to place a great value on friendship, and the friends she made of either sex tended to become lasting ones. Those who know her well and who have direct experience of this quality in her nature are agreed on its constituent elements: empathy, loyalty, moral and often practical support, and the conscious effort to maintain communication. Margot Holbrook, a fresher from King's College when Nikki was in her final year, remembers being a little in awe of 'this grown-up young woman', watching her for tips on behaviour, and being impressed by the confidence with which she would talk on equal terms with the lecturers. 'She jollied along the German professor; the sort of person we would have dodged past, ducking our heads. One summer morning I was walking along Queen's Road and happened to pass them going in the opposite direction. Nikki told me later that the Herr Doktor had made a comment about me, saying, 'Now that's what I call a pretty girl!' I mention this because it was so nicely generous to pass the compliment on - not every woman would have done so. 'Years later, when she was appointed to an important post at Cambridge University, Margot remarked again on this quality of generosity: 'She was totally delighted when I was appointed - unlike many so-called friends. Indeed she was never petty and never stooped to belittle other women's achievements, but made the most of them. As a woman friend, she was and is incomparable'.

Nikki's friendship with Margaret Keith (later Brook) began when they were both first year students living in the hall of residence. Margaret, a striking dark-haired young woman, was the daughter of a distinguished London pathologist, and had been educated at the prestigious Kensington High School for Girls. The blend of unconventionality and traditional upbringing in her character appealed to Nikki, although she was at first somewhat overawed by the self-assurance she attributed to her friend's public school background. It was one of those friendships which develop against the odds between people who have apparently little in common. Margaret invited her home for tea, in order to meet her mother. It was not a success; her hostess clearly thought her, or at least made Nikki feel that she thought her, an unsuitable friend for her daughter. One or two other mothers were subsequently to perceive her as some kind of threat to their offspring, but it was to their sons and not their daughters. If Margaret's mother had hoped to undermine the relationship, she was disappointed in the event, for her prejudiced behaviour served to reinforce rather than weaken the bond between the two friends.

Their main point of contact was as co-residents in the students' accommodation, but a mutual interest in acting brought them together in several productions of the Dramatic Society. With her natural ebullience, Margaret was very good in character roles. In one of these, as a hearty extravert known as 'Bounding Julia', she performed with such spectacular success that afterwards the name was adopted by her friends as an affectionate nickname for her. This she took in good part, but it is unlikely that she was flattered by the designation, however well intended.

After graduation, she spent a further year working for a post-graduate diploma in education, and, on completion of this, went into full-time teaching. Her first marriage ended in divorce after three years, and she joined the Colonial Education Service, teaching for several years in Ghana before it became independent in 1957, at which time her contract was terminated. She returned to Britain but was soon on her way back to West Africa, this time to Nigeria, where she took up an appointment in the training of teachers. This was the beginning of a long and distinguished career which culminated in her promotion as principal of the training college. During her time in Nigeria she was made a chief of the Yoruba tribe in her own right, and it was as Mrs Chief Brook that she married and became the fourth wife of Chief Justus Akerodulu, curator of the Benin Museum of Antiquities. They became widely known throughout the country, and together made a very considerable contribution to Nigerian life.

Being an established figure in society by the time of national independence in 1960, Margaret avoided losing her job again, as in similar circumstances she had done in Ghana. This time she merely resigned from the Colonial Education Service, whose remit had come to an end, transferred to the new Nigerian Education Service, and resumed the work she had been doing before.

Justus Akerodulu was not only responsible for the curation of ancient artifacts but was himself a consummate artist in wood carving and sculpture. On one of the periodic visits he made with Margaret to London in the 1960s and 1970s he gave Nikki a present of a set of chessmen he had carved out of wood. Each piece was a masterpiece of design and execution, as well as being a portrait of a member of the Yoruba tribe.

Margaret's wide knowledge of fairy tales and legends and her interest in their value in education led her to collect a great many of the stories and myths of the Yoruba, and she later used these as material for plays and broadcasts in Britain, as well as publishing others in book form. She had an enormous zest for life, while her warmth and generosity earned for her the lasting affection and respect of the tribe of which she had become a member. She changed remarkably little as the years passed, and was unspoiled by her experiences in Africa. Even when Nikki met her last, there were residual traces of 'Bounding Julia', and she still employed the phrase she always used at Bristol when expressing sympathy: 'Poor toad!'

Another friendship was that which Nikki contracted with Peter Godwin Willows, a spastic who, after obtaining an arts degree, went on to study law, and later qualified as a barrister. Peter's achievements, and those of others like himself, have their place in the social history of modern Britain, for it was their struggle against the ignorance and prejudice of their time which paved the way for subsequent changes in public attitudes and government policy towards the disabled. He spent much of his life challenging, and refuting by his own example, the traditional assumption that virtually every spastic was mentally defective or subject to what psychologists called 'behaviourial difficulty'. The medical and social sciences appeared to be united in regarding spastics as a homogeneous category and not as a group of individuals with different symptoms, capacities, and behaviour patterns. As he was to point out in his autobiography.[3] Peter had to fight from childhood onwards against the negative discrimination supposedly legitimated by what he called 'pseudo-scientists' and embodied in the law, medicine, and public administration. One of the earliest instances of this was the doctor who told his parents he could not possibly go to a public school. However, Peter, with his parents' support, had already decided that he was going, and did so. Later, after he had passed his first degree at the university, another doctor told him he was not capable of becoming a lawyer and that he could never expect to earn his own living in the normal surroundings of office life. Both of these objectives he succeeded in achieving. He came to terms with his inevitable dependence on the help of others, and never thought of accepting this as anything to be self-conscious or ashamed about. This meant that his friends were tacitly expected to anticipate his needs and, as a matter of course, to offer help when required in an unfussy manner, without wanting to be thanked every time they did anything for him. He wanted to avoid becoming arrogant as a result of being waited on hand and foot, but was not always successful in doing so. Even his friends found him a difficult person at times; opinionated, hypercritical, and acerbic, yet capable of a dry wit and sardonic humour. It was a disposition which tested friendship to the limit, but at least had the advantage of showing him who his real friends

---

[3] Willows, P.G. Human Tortoises. Max Parrish & Co Ltd, 1960

were. Nikki got on well with him because she could understand and accept his anger, realizing that it not only provided him with an emotional release but also that it was the source of his determination to go on fighting.

Peter was fully aware of his irascible nature and explained it in terms of the frustrations and humiliations to which the spastic was constantly exposed in the course of everyday life.

'It is thus comprehensible that a spastic who has overcome some or perhaps most of the difficulties besetting him should be of a forceful disposition, accustomed in every respect of life, to succeed only as a result of assault on opposition, whatever it may be.'

Comparing himself with those who had abandoned the struggle, he once wondered if perhaps, by passivity, dependence, and seeking less, they were happier than he, but he knew that he could never have acted differently.

Nikki met him in her first year. They were fellow members of the same history group, and she was among those who gave him the kind of spontaneous and unostentatious help he sometimes needed. Although he was provided with full-time care and attention at home, he tried on principle to be as independent as possible at the university. He was brought in by car, and, once inside whichever building he was attending, he would make his own way to the lecture rooms, using the lift to reach upper floors, and manoeuvring himself slowly and with difficulty along the corridors.

His disability did not prevent him from writing, but at times affected his speech, so that he was unable to read his essays aloud in seminars and tutorials when required. With any other tutor this requirement could have been waived, but it was not possible in the case of the history professor, because he was totally blind. On one occasion Nikki volunteered to read Peter's essay for him. This was so well received that she subsequently undertook the role of his unofficial amanuensis and performed the service on a regular basis. The discussions which followed her reading of the essays often made her acutely uncomfortable because of the unusual degree of acrimony they generated between Peter and the professor. It is true that Peter was hypersensitive and unwilling to accept adverse criticism, but this alone did not account for the intensity and bitterness of their disputes, and she sensed the existence of a latent animosity which had more to do with their mutual condition of disability than with their academic differences.

The moral was not lost on her that a disabled person should no more be expected to be sweet-tempered and reasonable at all times than anyone else; and that disabled persons are not obliged ipso facto to like all others in similar circumstances.

The support of his friends was self-evidently of paramount importance to Peter, though he was far too vulnerable to have ever acknowledged this openly, and was more likely to scold them for failing to correspond or keep in touch than to admit to any sort of dependence. 'Your reputation as a correspondent was never gilt-edged,' he wrote to Nikki on one occasion, 'but in all other respects stands very firm.' His friends, for their part, never gave him cause to doubt their loyalty. They were compassionate, but too sensitively aware of his needs to disclose their compassion to him. They recognised the fundamental kindness, the damaged self-image, the strength of character and will underlying the public self he presented to the world; as well as respecting him as a person and paying tribute to his extraordinary achievements.

In 'Human Tortoises' Peter himself paid tribute to 'Mary', who, having been employed by his parents as a governess when he was ten, became his nurse and mentor, and stayed with him until the end of his life.

'Tea at Peter's,' Nikki recalls, 'was rarely a comfortable experience. Sometimes it was a family gathering in the drawing room, where his father polluted the atmosphere with clouds of cigarette smoke, and his mother fixed me with an unnerving stare as if she suspected I had designs on her son. At other times it was in Peter's room at the top of their multi-storeyed house, either talking, or listening to Mahler on a very powerful radiogram, which he always played at full volume, without the slightest consideration for friends or neighbours.' As her aim at this time was to remain just a chess-playing friend, without any emotional involvement, his mother's attitude was a particular cause for exasperation.

Prevented from practising as a solicitor or barrister, he spent some years of unremitting frustration employed in the legal branch of public administration. In this he was engaged in tasks below the level of his qualifications, paid less than the value of the work he did, and systematically denied promotion. However, as some consolation, he was able by shrewd financial investment to accumulate enough capital on which to retire and devote himself full-time to writing, a second career on which he had for a long time set his heart. In the event, this was not the success he had hoped for; and, of his three published works, two (a novel and a book of short stories and poems) were published at his own expense, and only one, his autobiography, was taken up by a professional publisher.

Advances in drug therapy and the accessibility of new remedies greatly enlarged his capacities and quality of life in the years following his graduation. Concerned to increase his mobility in any way open to him, he managed in the face of opposition, and through sheer determination, to obtain a driving licence, first for a powered invalid tricycle, which he rode for fourteen years, and later for a car which he drove for an even longer period before he was finally obliged to give it up.

At the time of her first marriage in 1947, Nikki invited him to the wedding, in London. In his letter of acceptance he said that he would be arriving with 'Mary' several days before the event and wanted to arrange a meeting. 'But can you arrange for some form of transport back at the appropriate hour?' he wrote. 'Or I'll have to stay the night with you, and then what will the neighbours think? I will do anything but walk, tube or bus.

Ahead of her Time

If it's all you can manage, I don't mind you pushing me back in a wheelbarrow.'

She kept in touch with him intermittently as the years passed, exchanging letters, visiting him occasionally at his home in Bristol, and, finally at the nursing home where he spent the last two years of his life.

Marjorie Wood, author of the felicitous expression 'archetypal chic', mentioned earlier, was one of the evacuated King's College undergraduates, reading French, and a year ahead of Nikki. They met casually through mutual friends, took an instant liking to each other, and quickly established the kind of rapport which leads to mutual confidence and lasting friendship. Marjorie recalls sitting alone one day in Berni's drinking coffee and studying her notes when she was addressed by a man sitting at a nearby table. He was in his mid-forties, had silvery curling hair and bright blue eyes. Not wishing to encourage his attentions, she responded courteously but with an air of finality and returned to her papers. Undeterred, the man introduced himself and disclosed that he was a psychology lecturer at her own college, and, like herself, evacuated to Bristol. This put her in a delicate situation, but, after they had conversed for some time, she reluctantly accepted an invitation to have coffee with him on the following day. After he had left, Marjorie decided she would need someone to chaperon her at the arranged meeting, and was leaving the café wondering whom she could ask when Nikki suddenly 'breezed around the corner' and provided the solution to her problem.

Marjorie's first impression of Nikki was her attractive personality, and elegance of dress: 'Two colours of grey, and a kind of turban head dress.' She found her very slightly but not unpleasantly affected, reserved and quiet. Recalling the occasion in question years later, Nikki recognised the affectation as role-playing and thought the reserve and quietness probably resulted from the fact that the subject under discussion was rowing, about which she knew nothing, but which was, together with caving, one of Marjorie's special interests.

For her part, Nikki found Marjorie attractive, vivacious, and exceptionally intelligent, with enormous charm and self-possession. She was intrigued to find later, when she visited her family at their Derbyshire home, that Marjorie seemed to become a very different person from the sophisticated and worldly young woman she knew at the university, and she found it difficult at first to reconcile these two sides of her personality. The Woods came from a long line of gentlemen farmers dating back to the 16th century and Marjorie was brought up on conventional lines and according to traditional values in a farming community. The youngest of three daughters, she had been protected by her parents from all except the domestic aspects of work on the farm, but was no stranger to the vicissitudes associated with agriculture. She had a deep spiritual affinity with the country, and it was doubtless the combined influences of this and the presence of her conventional family that evoked the change in her which Nikki had noticed.

Sensitive to the feelings of her relatives, Marjorie kept them largely unaware of her life style and amusements when away from home, irreproachable though they were. Whatever her two elder sisters might have thought, it is almost certain that her parents would not have understood the contemporary mores of undergraduate life. As a result, Nikki was always careful to modify her own behaviour when staying with the Woods.

She greatly admired Marjorie's obvious efficiency and capacity for organisation:

'She was educated in an excellent co-educational grammar school in Derbyshire, and had been very well taught what I had notably missed out on, namely how to work with only the minimum of instruction. This was a skill which I had belatedly to acquire during my first year. She was capable of organising her work and her social life most efficiently, and, unlike myself, seemed entirely unencumbered by any expectation that 'authority' would disapprove of her ideas or opinions.'

Never, during the two years they spent together at Bristol, did Nikki cease to wonder at the apparently magnetic powers of attraction Marjorie exercised over the opposite sex:

'She was attractive, with a tall, slim figure and long legs, and a capacity for gathering men around her which was quite unrivalled in my rather limited experience. Time after time I watched, fascinated, and tried to learn from her, without, I may say, much success. If she travelled by train, there was always someone, stranger or friend, waiting to lift her case onto the luggage rack or carry it for her. On one rare occasion when there was no-one around, I performed the service myself without thinking about it, and never realised that it was precisely this attitude which prevented me from receiving the attention she took for granted.'

It was a kind of attention whose days were numbered and one which ultimately very few women were able to enjoy, let alone regard as a privilege due to their sex or legitimated by cultural heritage.

Marjorie, like Nikki, was perhaps still exploring roles and seeking identities at this time. Her love of the French language and literature which she was studying, and everything connected with them, had begun at this stage to dominate her choices in life, and were to lead in time to the pattern which the rest of it was to assume.

She graduated in 1942 and left Bristol to commence a nine months' course of training for war service in the Aeronautical Inspection Directorate remaining in this important work until the end of the war in 1945.

In the summer of 1941 Nikki had just finished her first year, when two events followed in quick succession: her grandmother, Elizabeth Ann, died, and her father arrived home on a visit from the north, where he had been working, and announced that he had fallen in love. He proposed forthwith to share his presence between the conjugal home and a love-nest which had yet to be purchased in London. He asked them to share his problem, which was that he wanted Meg as well as his inamorata, and thus had a difficult decision to make. 'He was', observed Nikki, 'like a little boy with two lollipops who couldn't make up his mind which one he wanted.' She records this sequence of events with a clinical detachment due to the passage of years, but this was far from being her state of mind at the time: 'My mother had hysterics and my father, puzzled as usual by the unreasonable behaviour of the human female, asked me to find his new pyjamas and pack him a lunch for the journey back to the north. Mother's hysteria continued unabated for several weeks and my father came and went in a frenzy of exasperation. It was painful, tiring, and socially embarrassing, for, when his marital eccentricities became common knowledge in the village, we were classified as irretrievably mad, and otherwise ignored. The rest of my summer vacation was spent in absorbing as much of my mother's excessive emotion as I could, and I returned to Bristol with a sense of relief when the new term began.

'My father was always a vigorous supporter of the right of women to work, often maintaining that no female should be able to obtain a permanent 'meal ticket' by the simple expedient of getting married. Whether this influenced his choice of a mistress is hard to say, and it was not a matter on which I felt able to question him. It must, however, have been a source of moderate satisfaction that his new companion was then at the peak of a successful professional career as a civil servant. She owned an agreeable flat, lived in comfort on a steadily improving salary, and looked forward to a generous pension. She was also a lifelong militant socialist, which alone, in his judgment, was evidence of her superior intelligence. When, despite my mother's vehement disapproval, I was introduced to her, my reaction was one of mild surprise that anyone with this amount of freedom, financial security, and an independent life, should allow my father to complicate it.'

'The only thing which my parents were able to reach any kind of agreement on was that I was the obvious person to take my father's place and act as my mother's prop and support for the rest of her life. As I was not actually consulted on the matter, it was taken for granted that I was happy to concur. He advised her kindly that she should look for paid employment as soon as possible, as he would now have two homes to keep going. He felt it was essential for me to obtain a good degree in order to ensure a better than average post, and suggested that his lover might be the best person to counsel me as she had been so successful in her own career and would know more than my mother, who had no academic qualifications.'

'This last piece of inspired rationality did what no sensitivity could have achieved: it aroused my mother's temper to a point where she felt compelled to fight back. After years of depending totally on his role as husband and breadwinner, she set about getting a training as a catering organiser in the Government service and subsequently earned her own living (even, much to his chagrin, equalling his own salary), which was not bad going, as she was forty-nine when they separated. She held a number of appointments during the war, spending an average of five to six months in different parts of the country. She set up a catering establishment at British Oxygen, went on to do the same in Coventry, and, finally, ran an underground works canteen in Wiltshire, where the quarries had been converted to the production of aircraft engines. Characteristically, she campaigned relentlessly against every form of petty theft.'

'Whilst I loved and admired her, I was nevertheless driven by the running battle she conducted with my father after the separation to a level of distraction that seriously interfered with my studies. In between bouts she was the same loving, caring and generous person she had always been, but his manipulative behaviour turned her into a childish woman as far as he was concerned. In the crucial years of my degree course they pursued me all over the place in order to carry on their quarrels in front of me. They appealed to me as an adjudicator: I was the adult and they were a pair of demanding children, each wanting of the other the one thing they could not have. The scale of their quarrelling was such that I was asked to leave one set of digs because of their behaviour.'

'Towards the end of my last year I finally summoned the courage to give them an ultimatum: either they ceased their visits and left me alone to try and get some sort of degree or I would throw the whole thing up before the final exam. This actually worked, and so did I, but I suffered a good deal of inner guilt over what they called my selfish and inconsiderate behaviour, 'after all their loving care'.'

Predisposed to accept their opinion as justified, Nikki could not in the last analysis blame herself for what she had done. Neither of her parents had ever graduated and had little idea of the pressures of a degree course, especially in the final stages. Had they done so, they would never have jeopardised her chances of success, as they nearly succeeded in doing.

Somehow, despite what seemed impossible odds, she sat all her examinations and in due course obtained her degree.

The previous autumn she had been obliged to make a decision about her future career. The options were restricted by the conditions of war, and by her mother's dependence on her after the separation. This dependence was in no way lessened by the new career which Meg herself had undertaken and which involved spending long periods away from Bristol. She still looked forward to the time when she could lead a more settled existence and they could be together again. 'It wasn't that Meg expected me to be with her,' Nikki observed, 'but that she was going to be with me; together versus the world!' Meg had left the rural retreat of Compton Martin by this time, let the house in Bristol, and rented a commodious flat in London, in Emperor's Gate, South Kensington.

Ahead of her Time

Nikki had long since abandoned any ideas of joining the Women's Royal Naval Service, or any other kind of work which might have separated her from Meg for an indefinite period. As a last resort, she opted for teaching.

This meant spending another year at the university, in the Department of Education, where she studied for a teaching qualification - the Postgraduate Certificate of Education (PGCE). The course was divided between educational theory and practical teaching, and was assessed on a continuous basis, with only one formal written examination, in hygiene. The main components of the theory were the physical and psychological aspects of child development, the history and philosophy of education, and some consideration of related social perspectives. Speech training was provided because of the high proportion of students with regional accents, but Nikki was one of three for whom this was not considered necessary, and who were thus exempted. As graduates were normally expected at this time to be employed in secondary schools, teaching their specialised subjects, the main teaching practice was spent in a grammar school, and took up the whole of the Easter term. However, each student was required additionally to spend three weeks in observation and teaching at an elementary school in the summer term before the commencement of the formal PGCE course. This provided a valuable orientation to the wider context of the educational system and an opportunity for active involvement in the education of younger children.

This assumption made moderate sense in relation to the main teaching practice, but was far less tenable in the case of the preliminary attachment. Mr Penberthy, head of the elementary school to which Nikki was appointed on the first practice, appreciated and made due allowance for her inexperience and lack of training, and gave her encouragement, practical advice and instruction. 'What is your worst subject?' was one of the first questions he put to her. 'Maths!' she replied, without hesitation. 'Right', he said, 'seven periods a week as long as you are here!' He followed this up by systematically giving her before each period a set of sums, which, if necessary, he corrected before she went into the classroom. She accepted gladly, and with his guidance soon lost all the fear of mathematics she had learned at school. She made rapid progress under his tutelage, and, judging by the written comments he made on each of the lessons he supervised, he came to regard her as an exceptionally promising teacher.

This was not a view shared by the principal supervising tutor from the Department, who made no allowances for inexperience, and concentrated exclusively on criticising all the faults she could find. This negative attitude appeared to Nikki to contradict the most basic principles of teaching, in which her tutor might have reasonably been expected to set an example. Insofar as the teaching practice involved being thrown into the deep end, to sink or swim, the supervisor's conduct, in contrast to that of the head, seemed both arbitrary and unjust.

The discrepancy between the assessments recorded in her lesson notebook was so conspicuous at the end of the term that they might well have been written about two different people.

Mr Penberthy found her lesson notes 'very full, well thought out, and excellently arranged', while her supervisor 'could not understand her notebooks at all, and thought their contents disorderly.' The head stated that her presentation was well organized, her explanations clear and concise, and the content of her lessons imaginative and well adapted to the needs and interests of young children: 'They responded willingly and obviously enjoyed working with her, with the result that there were no problems of control. They did their best work for her.' It would appear either that the tutor did not read these notes, or, if she did, that she chose to disregard them. There was certainly no indication that she ever sought to consult the head or to reconcile the widely divergent opinions they held about the same student. 'All you succeeded in doing,' she commented on a lesson in simple proportion, 'was to confuse the children by drawing ideas from the class. You did nothing to make them think about the meaning of proportion.' This, in fact, was precisely what Nikki had intended by inviting ideas, but her tutor would not have it: 'You were merely instructing them to juggle unintelligently with figures, which is not education!' There was more to come: 'Avoid that superior, impatient voice when the children do not give you the answers you want (largely as a result of your own faulty teaching).' If the voice in question had an edge and a suggestion of tension on this occasion it is hardly to be wondered at, but it was the same voice which Mr Penberthy had described as 'pleasant yet decisive, capable of waking up a sleepy class, enthusiastic and sympathetic, depending on the situation, with a wide and expressive range.' Nikki would have been the last to suggest that there was not any substance in the adverse criticisms of her teaching. Her objection was to the manner in which they were expressed and the latent messages they conveyed. These were more to do with the attitude of the tutor towards her personally than with any objective assessment of her potentiality as a teacher. She knew that her tutor disapproved of her as a person and, in spite of the fact that the formal PGCE course had not yet begun, had already decided that she was unsuited to teaching. The trouble was that Nikki herself was coming to the same conclusion. With the notable exception of Mr Penberthy, she had met very few teachers who were capable of awakening in her any sense of vocation. Her experience of schools and teacher training was making her increasingly aware of the extent to which the educational system was permeated by an authoritarianism with which she could not identify. All too often she had seen what she regarded as the abuse of authority at all levels of education, legitimated by tradition and only slowly responding to the challenge of more enlightened ideas about learning and teaching. The misuse of authority appeared to be as deeply entrenched as ever; it was a kind of 'theatre of the absurd' with teachers exacting the compliance of their pupils by means of a range of negative motivations: fear of failure, exposure to the ridicule of their peers, and punishment, both corporal and symbolic. It was a process of inducing sometimes lasting anxiety in others; frightening children and expecting worthwhile learning to ensue; dictating what pupils should think rather than encouraging the free play and imaginative exercise of ideas.

If, to obtain a professional qualification, she was required to passively accept this model of education and to suppress her own passionately-held liberal theories about learning and teaching, she did not see how it was possible for her in principle to continue with the course. Finally, she had to acknowledge that she had been insensibly following in a family tradition set by her mother - and with just as much innocence - viz. offending the proprieties by her unconventionality, outspokenness and independence of thought. She took her self-doubts to the professor of education and found in him a sympathetic and encouraging listener. It was fairly certain that he knew the state of affairs in the Education Department and had a shrewd idea of the actual reasons for the difficult time she was having with the senior tutor.

He appreciated her scruples but assured her that they were baseless, told her that she could make a valuable contribution to the teaching profession, and recommended her most cordially to continue with the course.

For her final teaching practice she was allocated to a grammar school, the head of which she described as the rudest man she had ever met. It transpired that he was vindictive as well. Badly needing someone to whom she could let off steam, Nikki had trustingly confided her opinion of his intolerable behaviour and of aspects of his conduct of the school to one of her tutors, who had promptly passed it straight on to him. Shortly after this he arranged for her to be visited by an external school inspector, but warned her of this only half an hour before his arrival. If he had expected her to be disconcerted by this he was to be disappointed. The inspector was greatly impressed with her work and gave her a first-rate report and told the head she was really someone who ought to be in teaching, a comment strongly suggesting that he had previously been invited to find exactly the opposite.

Any consideration of whether there had been collusion between the senior tutor and the head might seem far-fetched and savouring of the worst form of conspiracy theory. Whatever the truth of the matter, there is no doubt that there were those in positions of influence and power who had set their minds against her entering the teaching profession. In the light of the evidence, their reasons could hardly be expressed in objective terms of intellectual, academic or pedagogic criteria, so they were obliged to justify their opposition in terms of personal qualities. These of course were far more difficult to evaluate because of the subjective element in the process of assessment, and the tendency for judgments to be often as much statements about the assessor as about the assessed. Thus, although objectively there was nothing about Nikki's personal qualities to which exception could be taken (on the contrary, from a liberal point of view, they would have been celebrated), they found in them a threat to the status quo, to their own sense of authority, and by extension to authority in general, Nikki was painfully aware of the similarity between these circumstances and the reactions she had encountered with the nuns at La Retraite. The difference was that the nuns, whilst temporarily disconcerted by her challenging ideas and independence of thought, accepted them with a love and tolerance born of deep spiritual resources, whilst the academics had responded with anger and hostility. It was the difference between mature and immature behaviour.

'I was probably an unsatisfactory student in their terms,' she reflected some years later. 'I challenged practically all the shibboleths current at the time, and this doubtless upset the conventional expectations as to how a student should behave.' Apart from the senior tutor, no real doubts had been expressed in the University Department of Education about her ability as a teacher, and, in due course, she was awarded her Postgraduate Certificate of Education. If it had involved a struggle, it was because she was not prepared like some of her colleagues to simply coast along, taking the line of least resistance. The effort was productive, however, for it had focused her attention on the conflict between educational ideologies in the teaching profession and had reinforced her own conviction that the hope for the future of education lay in the gradual dissemination of the liberal and democratic principles which had inspired her own early education at Duncan House.

5   Alternative Futures

Newly-qualified graduate teachers employed by the Bristol Education Authority had little say in the choice of their schools. They were deployed in accordance with a quota system in which there was no guarantee of appointment to grammar schools, so that, if there were no vacancies in the latter, they could at the discretion of the Authority be assigned to other kinds of school for which they had received no specific training.

Thus it was that in October, 1944, Nikki, who had reasons for remaining in Bristol, came to join the staff of a special school for boys and girls aged 7-16 with severe learning and behaviourial difficulties, a category then designated educationally subnormal.

Up to a year before, the school had provided also for several categories of physically disabled children, but these had been segregated in another establishment where their special needs were catered for.

It was a challenging job, facing her with problems of a kind she had not previously encountered, and demanding specialist skills with which the relatively short PGCE course could not have been reasonably expected to equip her. Like her colleagues on the staff of the school, she was therefore obliged to learn by experience. It was not even a case of 'sitting with Nellie', for there was nobody to learn from by observation; she had to do the best she could on her own with a mixed class of twenty-eight adolescents aged 13 - 16.

She was the only university graduate on the staff, and one of only three possessing a teaching qualification. The head was a woman possessed by religious mania and seemed to be well on the way to certifiable lunacy. She believed fervently in corporal punishment and used the cane with medieval enthusiasm, determined to drive out original sin if this were humanly possible.

Most of the children were of low measured intelligence and needed the amount of individual attention that the size of the class rendered impracticable. This in itself contributed to, even if it did not entirely explain, the frequent incidence of disruptive behaviour in the classroom. Children who had been brain-damaged at birth were capable of behaving adequately for long periods but were liable to sudden outbursts of uncontrolled aggression, if not actual violence, when frustrated and angry.

Learning was retarded in some cases by single and easily identifiable factors like poor eyesight or partial hearing, in others by a complex of interacting genetic, physical, intellectual, emotional and social factors.

There were several epileptic children in the class whose periodic seizures were almost invariably accompanied by vomiting and incontinence. Dealing with the initial symptoms was the responsibility of the teacher who, when these had abated, was expected to take the afflicted child to a member of staff qualified in first aid. Cleaning up afterwards was usually done by the caretaker, but, if he was not available, Nikki had to do it herself. Some of the epileptics were syphilitic, a condition inherited from the mothers of the children concerned, who were known to be local prostitutes and thus especially vulnerable to sexually transmitted diseases. Some families of this kind were trapped in a cycle of disease and deprivation in which handicapped daughters became pregnant at an early age, sometimes while still at school, and were a few years later bringing their own offspring to the same special school which they, and in some cases their mothers, had themselves attended.

The heterogeneity of special needs represented in the classroom led Nikki to realise that, despite all her efforts, her function was in effect custodial rather than pedagogic. There was clearly a limit to the number of special needs that could be accommodated in one class, and years were to pass before educational legislation finally led to the introduction of a wider range of special schools and the specialised training of teachers to staff them.

Shortage of time for individual pupils was her greatest problem. Nevertheless she learned a great deal about the causes of backwardness and retardation, and, by a process of trial and error, refined her skills of diagnosis and knowledge of remedial teaching techniques. Typically, she disregarded her successes and dwelt on the failures which, in the circumstances, were inevitable and would have been equally the lot of the most experienced teacher. She numbered among her 'failures' a boy of low intelligence whom she despaired of helping with arithmetic, yet who helped his father on a market stall and, using his own methods, apparently managed cash transactions without ever making a mistake.

She concluded that teaching the educationally subnormal at that time required very special qualities and a sense of vocation, and these she did not in all honesty feel that she possessed.

At the end of the Easter term in 1945 she contracted measles, and resigned from the school shortly afterwards, only a few weeks before the national victory celebrations marking the end of the war in Europe. The global war, however, was not yet over, and it was uncertain how long it would continue in the Far East where the Western Allies were still engaged in military conflict with Japan. This uncertainty was resolved quite suddenly in August of the same year when the United States Air Force dropped atomic bombs on Hiroshima and Nagasaki, leading to the capitulation of Japan a month later.

The advent of peace and the gradual conversion of the war effort into national recovery and reconstruction eliminated the obligation to continue teaching, so that Nikki was able to review the career she had so recently undertaken and consider whether this was what she really wanted to do.

Although the special school was, for reasons already disclosed, far from being an educational environment in any real sense, she had learned many invaluable lessons about teaching children with special needs, and these were to stand her in good stead in her later career. She came to understand through experience the infinite patience required in the diagnosis of learning difficulties and the adaptation of remedial techniques to the needs of individual children. She was able through her own spontaneous empathy to appreciate the difficulties encountered from the point of view of the learner. And she knew the excitement and satisfaction (probably greater than in any other branch of teaching) to be gained when prolonged experimentation is rewarded by the sudden dawning of a child's comprehension. This was as near as she came to a sense of vocation, but the negative aspects of her initial teaching experience in schools far outweighed any attractions, with the result that she decided to suspend any final decision about a career in education. In the meantime she awarded herself a sabbatical of indefinite duration, during which she could explore alternative options, not excluding possibilities outside education altogether.

This was a wise conclusion in any case because it served to break the pernicious cycle of school-university-training college-school, which came to be recognised some years later as conducive to parochial attitudes and an impediment to the social and emotional maturation of young teachers.

Twenty years later, in the post-colonial sixties, she would have almost certainly been tempted into some kind of short-term voluntary service overseas if this could have been reconciled with her mother's circumstances. However, in 1945 no such opportunities existed and her vision of the immediate future had to be restricted accordingly.

Meg was at this time in charge of catering at the Brompton Hospital and living in the flat at Emperor's Gate in Kensington. Here Nikki, who was quite ready to exchange the provincial life of Bristol for the more cosmopolitan world of the capital, joined her in the late spring. In the meantime Marjorie Wood had come to the end of her service in the Aeronautical Inspection Directorate and had herself decided on a career in teaching. This brought her to London, where she joined Nikki and her mother in Kensington. Shortly after this, Meg left them both in charge of the flat and went down to Polperro in Cornwall, where for the next two years she ran a small hotel called Killigarth Manor.

Marjorie spent her first year in London studying for her Postgraduate Certificate in Education at Maria Grey, one of the constituent training colleges of the University. After qualifying, she was appointed as a lecturer in French at Ealing Technical College where, later in her career, she became Head of the Languages Department.

During her year at Maria Grey Training College Marjorie did one of her teaching practices at Twickenham Girls' Grammar School. On the staff was a young French teacher called Geneviève Sanua Seymour whom she met in the first instance through a shared professional interest in language teaching. Subsequently this relationship developed into a close and enduring friendship, which later expanded to include Nikki, as Geneviève became a regular visitor at Emperor's Gate. Geneviève's father had been a military engineer officer of mixed Franco-Egyptian parentage, while her mother was a Seymour of Scottish-American descent, one of her 19th Century ancestors having been a State governor in the U.S.A. In 1945 after the war they had both been honoured with the Legion d'Honneur for services in the French Resistance during the German occupation of Paris, taking enormous personal risks providing information and intelligence reports to the underground movement. Against all the odds they managed to escape detection, living unknown to the Gestapo in an apartment they owned on the top floor of a building in the Rue de Laborde. This had been partly achieved because they were registered by the German authorities as having only one address which was at their house in Crosne, some twenty-five kilometres outside Paris in the district of Seine et Oise. Edith Sanua-Seymour had been honoured before, receiving an award from General Pershing at the end of the first world war for her voluntary work for American servicemen in Paris at that time. Her achievements were crowned in the 1950s when she was elected to the presidency of the French branch of the Daughters of the American Revolution.

Geneviève had only been on a temporary engagement for one year at the school in Twickenham and when this came to an end she returned to her parents' home in Paris, but the three friends remained in close touch with one another, in the years that followed, through correspondence and the exchange of visits.

Soon after her arrival in London Nikki took a job as a private detective. It had nothing of the excitement or personal risk usually associated with the life of the 'private eye' in crime fiction. The opportunity arose when a woman friend employed by a solicitor in this capacity gave up her job and recommended her as a temporary replacement. The work was mainly concerned with divorce and involved finding out where the parties were living and obtaining depositions from them. As the law stood at the time, divorce was still relatively difficult to obtain, but she was not required to practise any form of deception in order to gain information, nor to act out the farcical role of surprising 'guilty' parties in 'flagrante delicto'. Because of the war most of the people she visited had been waiting for years, and were eager to provide the information she required. She was glad when, after four weeks, her contract expired and she was free to look for more congenial employment.

Her mother had a contact in Spitalfields Market, a businessman who, on hearing that Nikki was looking for work, offered her a job in his company. Situated east of the City and bounded by Shoreditch and Whitechapel, the market was at the centre of London's commercial life and at the heart of cockney culture. Petticoat Lane, the street market of which it was said that your watch could be stolen from you at one end and sold back to you again at the other, was just around the corner. To Nikki it was a new and exciting social environment bustling with life and purposeful activity, and she felt herself as far from academia as it was possible to be.

Her work involved being something of a general factotum: cleaning, sweeping up, running errands and making tea, but also managing the telephone exchange and performing minor clerical duties.

She learned about the wholesale fruit and vegetable trade, took driving lessons and qualified to drive a motor vehicle, subsequently acting as a chauffeur for her employer on his periodic buying excursions.

It was in the role of telephone operator that, in all innocence, she committed her first blunder. She had explained to a caller that her employer was away on account of Yom Kippur, the Jewish Day of Atonement, a statement which was nothing less than the truth. It was not good enough for her boss, however, and he went to some pains when he heard about it to initiate her into some of the basic principles of business diplomacy. 'Never, but never,' he admonished her, 'tell anyone I'm not there, or that there's a Jewish festival of any kind!'

She had been warned about the peculiar uses of language in the great London markets: the argot, the cockney idiom, the rhyming slang and the liberal use of the taboo four-letter word. Whilst the latter could frequently be heard in the market halls, it was seldom in the immediate presence of women. It was Nikki's observation that, where this tacit code of restraint was breached, it was usually because some of the women were themselves prone to swearing or because the men had some reason to regard them with contempt.

When the wife of the café owner next door fell ill, Nikki, with the consent of her employer, helped out during her lunch hours. She made omelettes and acquired a local reputation at the same time for her culinary skill, using a recipe she had picked up years before on a holiday in France. For her own part, she could not get over her amazement at the supply of eggs to which the café owner had access at a time when food rationing was still in force.

At the end of every week, in accordance with their status in the organisation, employees were given a parcel of goods as a bonus in kind. This would usually contain vegetables and fruit, and sometimes included bananas, supplies of which, having been cut off during the war, were once again appearing in Britain, albeit still subject to rationing.

She made a number of friends in the market and the neighbourhood, and was invited home to meet their families. It was an enriching experience, and she was deeply affected by the warm sense of fellowship and interdependence she found everywhere, and by the courage and cheerfulness manifested often in circumstances of extreme adversity. What also impressed her was the way in which living and working were indivisible, fostering the social cohesion which is the 'sine qua non' of any genuine community.

Some months previously Nikki, one of whose many interests was photography, had joined the Photographic Society in Manchester Square. This was open to both amateur and professional photographers, and

77

offered a range of activities including lectures, discussions, practical workshops and organised theatre visits during which members could practise their technical skills.

Professional models, some of whom were also aspiring actresses, were employed to pose for photographs at some of the practical sessions. On one of these occasions a young girl posed in the nude, having given her age as seventeen, the minimum legal age for work of this kind, but was found after the event, when suspicions had been expressed and inquiries made, to have been only fourteen. She was later to become a film actress of international renown.

Periodically, parties of members attended special productions at the Windmill Theatre, where they were allowed to take stage photographs of the performers, subject to the legal stipulation that nudes, like those of the Folies Bergères in Paris, were motionless.

A chance meeting while on holiday with Meg in Cornwall led her to consider the possibilities of a professional career as a photographer. One of the people they met at the hotel where they were staying, learning of her interest, and concerned to use his influence on her behalf, gave her a letter of introduction to Angus McBean, the photographer, then already an established figure in the theatre world, and in the early stages of creating an international reputation.

A meeting was arranged, the result of which was that she was taken on for a trial period as his personal assistant. What she had not been told by her sponsor was that Angus McBean had only recently been discharged from prison, after serving a sentence of two and a half years for homosexual offences. Not that this would have concerned Nikki in any way, as her ideas on homosexuality, like her ideas on other moral issues to do with personal autonomy, were characteristically libertarian. In the event, the fact of his sexual orientation did indirectly give rise to complications, affecting the length of time she was to spend in his employment.

When she began working for him he was in the first phase of rebuilding his professional career. He had acquired a studio near Covent Garden, and, with the assistance of his brother-in-law, Cecil Paul-Jones (Paul), was in the process of refurbishing it according to his own design. Paul spent many hours converting Angus's detailed plans into drawings from which he could work, and then proceeded to implement these by himself doing the necessary building, painting and decoration. There were malachite sconces, plaster swags and gilded detail everywhere, in a style which Paul described as 'Lost Empire'. 'The finished product was amazing to an eye starved of colour during the previous years of war,' Nikki recalled. 'The extravagant excitement of Angus's designs and his use of colour and shape came as a welcome surprise; rather like the moment when the curtain rises in the theatre and you see the whole magical presentation of the set designer's background for the first time'.

As a relatively unskilled novice, her duties included arranging photo calls and accompanying Angus to these, carrying equipment and doing anything required to set up what he needed for the assignment, for example, moving furniture or holding a light or reflector in different positions and at different angles. She also glazed and polished his finished work, cleared up, made coffee, and answered the door and telephone to a succession of theatrical personalities, many of whom were household names.

Angus did all his developing and printing himself and would in no circumstances allow anyone to interrupt him when he was working in the dark room. His skilled retoucher, who had her own room upstairs, was the only person allowed to add to or subtract from his photographs, and then only under his instruction and supervision.

This was, of course, long before the invention of the airbrush, regarded as such an indispensable, even commonplace, article of photographic equipment today. He once told Nikki that, to his great surprise, the only portrait which had not required any retouching to improve the skin quality was the one he had done of Mae West, then in her sixties. He had expected a lacquered layer of makeup and found instead a faultless skin.

For Nikki his extreme professionalism was an education, and his meticulousness and dedication made a lasting impression on her: 'His portraits for the theatre', she observed, 'initiated a new style which was to make everything we knew before in the way of theatrical photography seem flat and stale'. As he was later to say himself in the context of his pioneering work in photographic surrealism, 'I had a passion to make the camera do things it was not designed for.'

By the end of the trial period, which had lasted five weeks, it was clear to both of them that she lacked the obsessional concentration on detail which was such an essential part of his own artistic genius. Whilst she had enjoyed her time at the studio, she realised she was not going to be able to stay. For one thing, her friendship with Paul, who had been widowed a few months earlier, did not altogether please Angus. Added to which Paul was already looking out for a more permanent job which his temporary sojourn at the studio could not provide.

Nikki found that she was missing the pursuit of knowledge in its widest sense and the intellectual stimulus of the limitless world of ideas to which university life had accustomed her. The theatre still exerted its fascination as it had always done, but she realised that it was no more than an infatuation. Having initiated inquiries about employment opportunities in the field of educational administration, she finally applied for the post of assistant secretary at the Association of Teachers in Colleges and Departments of Education (ATCDE) and Training Colleges Clearing House.

In preparation for her first interview with the secretary, Edith Atherton, at the ATCDE office in Victoria Street, she had gone to some pains to appear as conventional in dress and appearance as possible, and to this end had chosen to wear a pale lipstick instead of her usual bright one. 'Teachers were still dressing like poor relations in those days; partly for financial reasons, and partly because they were expected to set a good example to the girls and not look unsuitably smart or - God forbid - sexy.' Unfortunately she had not reckoned on the fact that a pale lipstick can be more noticeable than a more vivid one if the colour is wrong, and, as a result, Edith's first reaction was to say that she wouldn't be able to endure looking at such an awful colour day in and day out. At that point Nikki thought she had lost the job. It was only later she realised that the mock serious tone and gentle irony were among Edith's many amiable personal characteristics, and that she would have been incapable of assessing anyone on a purely subjective basis. In spite of the lipstick, she was appointed on a month's trial.

6   Marriage and Family

Nikki and Paul were married in September, 1947 at the Register Office in the Royal Borough of Kensington, and set up their first home together at the flat in Emperor's Gate.

Mother St. Paul wrote from La Retraite: 'and you, my dear little girl, are doing good and useful work, and doing it well; but much more worthwhile and important will be the founding of your own home. Paul's work sounds very interesting. Anyone who creates beauty is a benefactor to mankind and a pointer towards God, the Supreme Beauty.'

Paul had been twice married before, the first marriage ending in divorce in 1936 and the second with the death of his wife (Angus's sister) in 1944. When Nikki first met him he was picking up the traces of his pre-war career, working free-lance, and tentatively considering the courses open to him. As both his father and great grandfather had been doctors, there was an expectation in the family when he left St. Pauls School in the early 1920s that he would follow suit. His father arranged for him to attend the medical school in Vienna, without realizing that Paul had no interest in medicine and wanted to become an artist. His relationship with his father was unfortunately not of the kind where dissent on his part would have been tolerated, with the result that he said nothing and spent most of his time in Vienna studying at the art school instead. When eventually the truth came out his father instructed him to return to England at the end of the college term. Whilst he was highly displeased by the discovery, he could see that Paul was determined on his future career, and grudgingly accepted the *fait accompli*'. In the years which followed, Paul had several jobs in which he was able to exercise and develop his artistic talents. He spent one year with a water colour painter and picture restorer, and later joined a company which specialised in the construction and painting of theatrical scenery.

Having a small financial allowance from his father, he was not obliged to work for a living, and this enabled him to devote much of his time during the 1930s to the kindred of the Kibbo Kift, founded by John Hargrave[4]. This was a woodcraft and camping movement which had branched out from Baden-Powell's Boy Scout organisation and was destined to play an important role in the social and political life of Britain between the wars. Far from being merely a 'back to nature' movement, its aims were diverse, and encompassed recreational, educational, ethical, economic and political objectives. Residues of the Boy Scout image were eventually blurred by the active propagation of its reformist economic policy on Social Credit. A Green Shirt Movement constituted from members of the Kibbo Kift was

---

[4] Hargrave, J. The Confession of the Kibbo Kift. Pub. McLellan (1927)2nd Ed. (revised) 1929).

started in order to take the message to the people, and this was later to enter the orthodox political field as the Social Credit Party of Great Britain.

The Kindred was suspended during the war, and, in spite of attempts to revive it afterwards, went into a decline from which it never recovered. During the war, Paul worked in an aircraft factory near Weston-Super-Mare and served as a fireman in the Voluntary Fire Service, though, because of his remote location in the country, saw far less of the action than Nikki, who was a mere firewatcher in Bristol. As a first step in the reconstruction of his life in 1946 he had taken the job with Angus McBean as a stopgap while looking into the prospects of a permanent career more suited to his experience and capabilities. This quest took on a greater sense of urgency once he and Nikki had decided to marry, and, later in the same year, he was appointed by the British Rayon Federation to establish and develop, as its first director, the new Rayon Industry Design Centre in the West End of London. His achievement at Rayon was an unqualified success and the reputation of the Centre remained as a tribute to his efforts long after he had left. However, once it had been instituted, his work became increasingly a matter of routine management and decision-making, with the genuinely challenging tasks being performed by others. Consequently, three years later, he resigned from the Federation, having been offered another job for which his interests and abilities especially qualified him. This was as chief editorial officer at the British Standards Institution, a post he filled with distinction until his retirement twenty years later. In recognition of his exceptional record of achievement, the Institution seconded him for the last six months of his career as codification consultant to the International Organisation for Standardisation in Geneva.

Having successfully completed her probationary month at ATCDE, Nikki was confirmed in her appointment as assistant secretary and settled down to a period in educational administration which was to stand her in good stead in her subsequent career. The Association functioned not only as the professional organisation of lecturers in Teacher Training Colleges and University Departments of Education in England and Wales, but also the central Clearing House for the applications of students seeking admission to the training institutions concerned.

Post-war economic recovery was only in its initial stages and many of the privations of war were to persist for several years to come. The shortage of housing and business accommodation meant that most categories of office workers had to adapt to restricted space and severely limited resources. Considering all the responsibilities of the ATCDE, it is remarkable how it managed to function in the cramped accommodation made available to it in Victoria Street.

The office consisted of two rooms on the top floor of a very high building. 'There was no lift,' Nikki recalled, 'which was very good for us all, except when later on, as a pregnant ex-employee, I came back part-time for a special job of work. The smaller of the two rooms, made smaller still by filing cabinets, was where Edith Atherton and I worked at desks facing each other. I think it was probably due to her calm and pleasant manner, which seldom varied, and her good humour, that we were able to sustain a working relationship month after month with a minimum of disagreement, and that never serious. The other room, in which there were more filing cabinets and three desks, was occupied by the two hard working and friendly members of the clerical staff. The roof leaked, and, on one unforgettable occasion during a period of exceptionally wet weather, we processed hundeds of applications(under umbrellas for two days)without losing or spoiling one of them.'

The atmosphere was co-operative and authority never became an issue. 'Edith was my first and best experience of how to obtain good team work without coercion or intrusive regulations. At the time it seemed to me that she behaved with courtesy to everyone and expected the same in return. I assumed it was mainly a question of personal quality, but I now know that, in so doing, I was underestimating her skill and understanding of the art of management. She taught me my first lesson about not passing projected anxieties down the line to one's subordinates. It was a lesson which became the basis of my whole management strategy at King Alfred School.'

'When I started we did very little personal interviewing of applicants who had failed to gain entry to the college or department of their choice. Later, when we moved to new premises in Oxford Street (only one floor up this time, in a former ballroom dancing studio decorated in two hideous shades of salmon and blotting paper pink), more people found their way to us. 'Remember', said Edith Atherton, 'that 90% of those who don't get the college of their choice will be contacting us to complain and blame us for what may well be their own failure. Never let anyone go until you have got them to smile at least once, even if it is your lunch hour! Also ensure that all letters and telephone messages are answered immediately'.'

Edith herself always gave people the impression that she had all the time in the world for them, and this, oddly enough, did not result in lengthy interviews, partly because they felt they were really being listened to. I always tried to do this, and I never sat behind my desk to interview people. She was a remarkable and exceptional woman who changed my life in many ways, particularly my ideas about women in authority. I had had so many experiences of negative female authority that it was a revelation to meet a woman capable of exercising control without resorting to status games or personal domination.' For her part, Edith Atherton recalled that, 'although I was her boss, I always thought of Nikki as the brains! She had the priceless quality of being a good listener - invaluable in administration as well as in friendship'.

Nikki became pregnant in July, 1948 and continued working at ATCDE for about eight weeks, at which point she notified her employers of her intention to resign. During the first week of December she received a letter of appreciation from the Chairman of the Association, Professor Fletcher, Director of the Bristol University Institute of Education. 'The Executive,' he wrote, 'really have been immensely struck with the way in which you have carried out your duties and so often put in a good deal of extra work over and above what might have been expected of you. We all hope very much that your retirement into family life will be a very happy one. Perhaps at some time later on you may think of returning to help us again, in which case nobody would be more pleased than I, and I know in saying this I speak for all my colleagues on the Committee.'

In the event she did help them again in the early 1950s on a part-time basis when, thanks to the flexible arrangements made possible by Edith Atherton, she was able to spend much of her time working at home. It was during this period that she undertook the major task of compiling the first ATCDE Handbook.

April, 1949 was the expected date for confinement and. Nikki prepared for the event by consulting the Harley Street specialist Doctor Grantly Dick Reid, under whose tutelage she was given dietary prescriptions as well as being introduced to antenatal exercises and relaxation techniques calculated to ease the process of childbirth.

As the period of gestation drew on, complications arose, and, at twenty weeks, she was rushed into the Obstetric Unit of the University College Hospital and prematurely confined. A miscarriage ensued and she lost her twins, a boy and a girl, shortly afterwards. Although heartbroken by this personal tragedy, she fortunately sustained no internal injury and was able to go home ten days later, as she said in a letter to a friend, 'prepared to start again as soon as possible.'

Towards the end of the following year she was again pregnant, and badly in need of some means of relieving the tedium of her enforced inactivity. 'If you care to send me any more translations, or rather if you can trust me with them' she wrote to Geneviève, 'I shall be pleased to do them. My waist more than my wits is affected by pregnancy and I require a little mental work now and then.' Geneviève taught English at the Haute Ecole Commerciale pour Jeunes Filles in Paris and depended on Nikki and, later, Paul, to monitor the English translations she made from French texts for use with her students. It was a measure of her thoroughness that she continued to send translations for their approval throughout her teaching career, even when her own excellent command of English barely rendered it necessary. As Nikki once pointed out to her, 'You are getting so good that all that remains for me to do is to indulge in nuances and subtleties of idiom and meaning.'

The baby, a girl, was born on the twenty-second of February, 1950. 'She is very pretty,' Nikki reported to Geneviève, 'and will have grey eyes and chestnut hair if she continues as she has started. We have called her Miranda Beatrice, the second name after Paul's stepmother. I love the name Garance, but know that in this country the pronunciation would make a mockery of it and a misery of her life at school, so we dared not risk it.'

In 1951 Frank Greenall died in hospital in Hastings, when Nikki was eight months pregnant with her second child (Richard). The cause was renal failure induced by the cumulative effects of the phenobarbitone which had been prescribed for his emotional condition. Meg was in Cornwall at the time, which meant that, as she could not be told until she had access to medical attention, there was a delay of five days before she received the news. She had herself nearly died two years before and the doctor was afraid that a sudden shock without access to the support of her relatives and friends might bring on another attack.

In retrospect, it was as well that events took this course, because it made it possible for the funeral to be held without the fear of awkward situations arising between the official and non-official widows.

Nikki had visited him in hospital towards the end of his terminal illness, and had been distressed by the visible evidence of his physical decline. His spirit, however, was undiminished and he made no attempt to modify his habitually acerbic manner, resisting all pressure to conform to the conventional sick role. Where she had anticipated the possibility of some change in his nature she found that he was still at odds with the world, fighting rather than accepting his circumstances, expressing fortitude in his own way.

Years before, at the University, she had once written to thank him for fostering in her a love of English and philosophy. It was thus a deeply moving experience for her when, a few days after the funeral, she was disposing of some of his personal effects and found that he had kept her letter, even though he had never replied to or otherwise mentioned it.

After Frank's death in July, several events affecting Nikki and her friends followed in quick succession. In the same month Marjorie Wood married Baron Yves Chanteau and they took up residence not far away in the vicinity of Emperor's Gate. Geneviève, who with Nikki's encouragement had been thinking for some time of returning to teach in England, obtained instead a post in Gillespie High School in Edinburgh, where she remained until 1953, the year, she recalled, when George VIth died and 'the school all went into black.'

'On Monday night, the third of September, Richard Alexander arrived,' Nikki reported, 'after a four and a half hour journey, and he is very sweet. He has red-copper hair and is big-boned. I think he may have grey eyes but at present they are dark, clear and blue.'

Earlier in the year it had transpired that the apartment blocks at Emperor's Gate were scheduled at some indefinite date for redevelopment, in which event the continuation of Meg's tenancy could not be guaranteed. As Nikki and Paul had already decided that the city was not a healthy environment in which to bring up young children, this seemed to them the right time to look for accommodation further afield, not in the depths of the countryside but within commuting distance of London. In the spring they found a large house in Carshalton in Surrey which they liked and which appeared to meet their requirements. Negotiations continued throughout the summer, contracts were signed, and in December, two and a half months after the baby's arrival, the family including Meg, moved into their new home.

Nikki was unwell for much of the first two years in Carshalton. The discovery that her blood was rhesus negative had led to the administration of counteractive drugs during her pregnancies, and these had upset the chemical balance of the body, in particular affecting the kidneys, and had left her in a state of chronic debilitation. A doctor at the University College Hospital, to whom she had gone for advice, told her she was clearly not strong and that she should resign herself to the fact that she was going to be a permanent semi-invalid. Fortunately, subsequent events were to disprove this unconditional diagnosis. In 1953 she was introduced by Yves and Marjorie Chanteau to Doctor Chandra Sharma, a homeopathic practitioner, who had recently migrated to Britain from India, and was then practising in London. It was a meeting that changed the course of her life, for as a result of his treatment, she gradually regained the health and strength which had been thought unattainable by means of conventional medicine. It was, in fact, a reintroduction to homeopathy, because both her parents had been interested in alternative medicine, and the family doctor throughout her childhood in Bristol had been a homeopath. However, on reaching adulthood she had become responsible for her own medical care, and being unable to afford homeopathy, she had been compelled to register with an allopathic panel doctor.

Dr Sharma had in addition to his qualifications in homeopathy an Indian medical degree in orthodox western medicine. For this to be acceptable in Britain, he was required to spend a year as a hospital intern, after which, subject to the approval of the British Medical Association, he was eligible for enrolment on the Medical Register and legally entitled to practise.

He was a natural healer and an intuitive diagnostician, and Nikki had no doubt in her own mind that she owed him, if not actually her life, then at least a life worth living. With the revival of alternative medicine and the increase in its popularity in the 1960s his practice grew rapidly and with it his reputation. He was regularly in demand as a lecturer at medical schools and international conferences, and patients came from all over the world to see him at his London clinic.

Miranda and Richard had not been well in Carshalton, suffering from periodic sore throats and chest infections. Chandra Sharma, whose diagnoses were frequently surprising to the uninitiated, attributed these recurrent symptoms to the presence of a cemetery in the immediate vicinity of the house. He recalled the opinion of an elderly doctor he had once known to the effect that the 'graveyard cough' was so called not, as popularly supposed, because it portended the grave, but because it afflicted mainly people who lived in close proximity to burial grounds, where the nitrate content of the soil was exceptionally high. His prescription for the children's ailments was simple but impracticable: sell the house and move to another location. Nikki and Paul, who had by this time implicit faith in his judgment, attempted to implement his advice but the housing market was at a standstill and their agents were unable to find a buyer. However, on the doctor's recommendation, they did the next best thing, which was to look for a private school with boarding facilities on a weekly basis. It was a hard decision to make, for they were both against boarding education in principle, but they agreed that the children's health constituted an overriding factor.

Near Epsom, several miles from Carshalton, they found a school which provided the reassurance they were hoping for. This was New Sherwood, run by John and Irma Wood in accordance with the same liberal principles which had become central to Nikki's own philosophy of education. Prior to this, Miranda and Richard had had some experience of nursery and infant day schools in Carshalton but in both cases they had been unhappy. But they enjoyed New Sherwood, greatly improved in health, benefited from the more congenial social environment, and came home for the weekends and holidays.

Nikki's circumstances at this time confronted her with a problem shared by many women in modern societies, that of reconciling the traditional roles of wife and mother with an economic role outside the home. Informed public opinion, supported by the findings of social research, was moving towards acceptance of the idea that the two roles were not incompatible and that women should be left to make their own choices in the light of what was best for their families and themselves.

Nikki was disposed by upbringing and experience to concur with this opinion, having been influenced not only by her mother's example but also by socialist and feminist ideals, with their emphasis on women's personal freedoms, including integration into the productive and political systems.

Although Paul's occupation carried managerial status, his salary was not sufficient to support the family without the additional income Nikki was able to contribute. Thus, so far from having the choice of remaining at home in the roles of wife and mother, it was imperative for the sake of the family that she should resume her career as soon as possible, and earlier than she would have preferred.

The kinds of difficulty they shared with other dual-career families came under investigation some years later and were reported in a study of women in professional and managerial jobs, published in 1971.[5] In this a distinction was drawn between the dual-career and the two-job family. In the latter the wife keeps up her primary commitment to the home and interrupts her work whenever the interests of her husband and children

---

[5] Rapoport, R & R. Dual-Career Families. Penguin 1971.

require it. In the former, since a career demands specialised qualifications and experience, there is not the same degree of flexibility, and continuity is an essential condition of employment. For this reason, much harder thought and circumspection is needed by the dual-career couple than by other kinds of two-worker family, and they need to examine all the implications of their present situation and future contingencies. 'For mothers who are educated and of high ability, 'noted the study,' a half-baked compromise between the claims of work and the family will not do. They tend to be conscious and conscientious mothers. Most are likely to slow down or drop out of their careers during the time when they have young children, and then need to accelerate back.'

Nikki's return to teaching had necessarily to be more gradual than the term 'accelerate' would suggest. At first, poor health prevented her from doing more than her maternal and domestic responsibilities required, and these taxed all her available strength. As her health improved, she was able to undertake progressively more work, adapting this to the successive stages in the children's development and to their changing needs. She resumed working at home for the ATCDE, did some supply teaching, filling in for absent teachers, and taught part-time in order to be with Miranda and Richard in the afternoons.

Domestic help was essential in these circumstances, and Paul and Nikki were fortunate enough to have someone on whom they could depend to provide this. 'We had a marvellous helper all the time we were in Carshalton,' her name was Kitty Purchase, she was a woman of great character, though she had little confidence in herself at that time and I do not know how I could have survived the first four years without her.'

The orderly pattern of family life established by these arrangements were soon to be disrupted when changes which could not have been anticipated followed one another in quick succession.

In 1952 Paul's step-mother died, and his father at first insisted on staying on alone in his large, rambling house, but was finally persuaded to come and live with them. His health began to deteriorate rapidly, and he became increasingly dependent and in need of care, which resulted in a great deal of extra work for Nikki until he died in 1954.

Then, not long after this, Meg invited her sister Con to join the household, a decision fraught with problems, for, much as they loved each other and could not live apart, they were unable to live together either, quarrelling much of the time and trying to involve everyone else in their disputes. They also interfered in the day to day running of the home, were more critical and demanding together than they would ever have been apart, and contested with Nikki and Paul the right way to bring up children.

This explosive situation was made worse when Con's son-in-law, Bruce Main, and her daughter Mary, who was expecting a baby, came to stay temporarily whilst they were looking for a house of their own. Undertaken in a spirit of goodwill, this further enlargement of the household proved to be a disaster. Tensions were generated, between the two generations which seriously threatened the stability of the family, and, for the sake of the children as much as for their own, Nikki and Paul declared that it was a state of affairs they could tolerate no longer. The outcome was that Meg left in offended indignation and went to live in the Isle of Wight,. Con, Mary and Bruce with their baby daughter Frances, decided to live in London where they found alternative accommodation pending their final removal to Kent, where they ultimately settled..

When the crisis with Meg was at its height, Nikki, nearly at the end of her tether, wrote to Geneviève with the request: 'Please write and offer me some practical Gallic advice.'

This sequence of events demonstrated what the experience of some socialist countries had already shown - namely that two-income families can signify in practice one job for the husband and two jobs for the wife, who still finds herself obliged to carry the greater part of the domestic load, even when, as in the case of Paul, the man is willing and makes a genuine attempt to share it.

With the departure of the relatives, life in the nuclear family recovered its equilibrium once more, and Paul, who had been concerned by Nikki's total exhaustion after the recent upheaval, urged her to accept an invitation from Geneviève (The Gallic response) to spend a week with her in Paris. He was himself due for a holiday and wanted to do some interior decoration at home. With the domestic help that had been arranged, he was sure he could manage to look after his father and the children in her absence. Thus persuaded, she agreed to go, and wrote to Geneviève, suggesting dates: 'It only remains now for you to tell me that none of the dates is convenient and I shall burst into bitter tears and enter a repentant order!'

Geneviève had suggested the inclusion of a coach tour in the holiday scenario but Nikki had to warn her 'that coaches are alas the only vehicles in which I cannot travel without immediate nausea. So I am afraid it will have to be train or motor-powered roller skates.'

It was a concomitant of their exchange visits that each of them ascertained beforehand what the other needed her to bring in the way of commodities from abroad which were not easily obtained at home. For Geneviève this usually meant articles of clothing, cigarettes, tea, and books, the latter principally but not exclusively related to her English teaching commitments in Paris. For Nikki it was mainly clothing, sometimes pharmaceuticals, and perfume (neither too sweet nor too heavy).

'You can if you will bring me a pair of grey leather gloves,' she wrote on one occasion, "and another like the pair that was stolen, black with leather palms and suede backs.....remember?'

This was not the first time she had experienced difficulties with gloves. Once, Geneviève had sent her a pair which met with the anguished response by return of post: 'Greatly to my regret, the exquisite gloves you sent are too narrow in the palm and I did not dare to use force, for fear of damaging them. They are really lovely, but unfortunately my housewife's hands outrage them.'

The projected holiday went according to plan and Nikki was able to recover her energies in the stimulating atmosphere of Paris. There were visits to the theatre, art exhibitions, the grands magasins, and excursions to some of the great châteaux on the outskirts of the city. She returned to England after a week of hectic activity refreshed, full of high spirits and optimism about the future.

Carshalton was not entirely without its own amusements and, a few weeks after her return, she went with Paul and two friends to a fancy dress dance, representing 'the Night Life of the Gods'. She went as Venus, 'most respectably dressed in pale yellow with a head dress of wings'. Paul was Jupiter, in gold, red and white, while the others portrayed Mercury and Diana. 'In all we won three prizes out of the six awarded. Paul designed the costumes and I made them, so we felt rather proud of ourselves.'

It was at one remove from the theatrical work in which they had both been involved for several years, and it was a foregone conclusion when, not long after this event, they became members of a local dramatic society - the Carshalton Players. Together they constituted a welcome and valuable addition to the company. Paul applied his professional skills in the areas of scenic construction and costume design, and Nikki contributed her talents as an actress, make-up artist, and sempstress.

The level of production was high, as, in a sense, it had to be in the face of sophisticated audiences whose critical standards were sharpened by frequent exposure to both television drama and the easily-accessible London theatre. As it was, the society's performances compared favourably with those of the better professional repertory companies, and they enjoyed the well-deserved support of a regular local audience who were both appreciative and discriminating.

At about this time amateur acting was the subject of controversy in the correspondence columns of one of the national daily newspapers. It had started with a feature article written by the distinguished theatre critic W.A. Darlington in which he expressed the opinion that all too often amateur dramatic societies disliked any criticism which did not consist entirely of praise.

Nikki entered into this correspondence, writing to the editor of the newspaper concerned, making known her agreement with Darlington's opinion and offering her own tentative explanation for the behaviour in question:

'Perhaps the explanation for their attitude is bound up with the fundamental reasons for which people join these groups, and which are rarely understood. We tend, I think, to join them because we want something which we cannot find elsewhere - a wider emotional experience, a sense of achievement, a brief glow of limelight, a feeling of importance in a social pattern.

There is, in my opinion, nothing wrong with these reasons; on the contrary I think they are excellent reasons as long as they are realised and admitted. Unfortunately most amateur actors are only just sufficiently aware of their motives to be vaguely ashamed of them (our Puritan background is much nearer than we think) and therefore cannot face anything which seems to threaten the mainly illusory picture they have built up in their minds. They tend, in fact, to act to themselves first and to the audience second, if at all. The fact that an interest in the drama is a very secondary motive in their wish to take part in plays is amply proved by the almost universal lack of response which any suggestion of professional coaching, lectures, or even the minimum training in make-up and costume evokes.

They tend to boast: 'We try to avoid being theatrical', as if it were a virtue in them, and do not realise that what one offers the public in exchange for its money must inevitably stand comparison with other commercial entertainment. One meets the odd society which has a true interest and deep delight in the theatre. Its members as individuals have undoubtedly joined for the same unconscious motives as in any other society, but through a real desire to improve have come to realise more about their work and themselves and have used drama for their own satisfaction, at the same time giving to it their time, skill, discipline, and emotional energies. The by-product of this exchange is often a first-rate company and one which can take criticism, informed or not, at its true value and use it to its own advantage.'

With Miranda and Richard settled at New Sherwood school it was possible for Nikki to think of changing from part-time to full-time teaching. A suitable vacancy occurred at the time at the nearby Wallington County Grammar School for Girls and she was appointed at the beginning of the following term as a teacher of English and Drama.

Wallington was a very good school in the formal tradition, manifestly successful in achieving its aims of intellectual excellence, moral integrity, and disciplined behaviour. With an effective system of pastoral care, it was a well-integrated academic community in which staff, parents and children appeared united in pursuit of a common goal, under a regime which could be aptly described by the term 'benevolent autocracy'. And if the school was not perceived by Nikki with her more liberal philosophy as an alien environment this was largely due to the headmistress, Miss Amy Bull, a woman she admired, respected, and genuinely liked as a person. If there were frustrations and unresolved conflicts in the school, they were remarkably few and far between. Although privately sceptical about the formalism of the system Nikki at no time felt out of place and was content during the years that followed to teach in the conventional manner expected of her. Any thought of initiating reforms in her class teaching she instantly put aside, feeling that it would be an unwarranted presumption and, in a sense, savour of disloyalty to the Head personally.

Ahead of her Time

This resolve was perhaps made easier by the fact that English and Drama allowed some latitude for the legitimate use of informal methods of teaching and she made the most of the opportunities that arose.

She learnt a great deal from Amy Bull, and took to heart some of her more memorable precepts, for example:

'The most selfish people you meet are those for whom everything has been done'

'The more you expect of children, the more they achieve;
The less you expect, the less they are capable of achieving.'

Like all such maxims the latter was subject to qualification. As Nikki later observed, it is possible to demand too much of children as well as too little, and the skill of the teacher rests in knowing where to draw the line.

In 1958, her final year, in spite of some initial resistance from a conservative senior English mistress, she obtained Miss Bull's permission to organise a drama festival for the first time in the history of the school. This innovation aroused great excitement and curiosity because, as people remarked, nothing like it had ever been done at the school before.

With Paul's help, she drew up plans for the construction of a classical proscenium to frame the platform in the school hall. These were implemented with remarkable efficiency and inspired improvisation by staff and pupils in the Art Department. The stage was flanked by simulated columns made out of hardboard and topped by Grecian urns. Splendid winged angels cavorted in the centre of the proscenium arch, and the whole edifice was embellished with painted wreaths, garlands and festoons.

The festival took place at the beginning of the summer term in order to be well out of the way before the school examinations. This meant that the organisation and rehearsals had to be done in the previous term and towards the end of the Easter holidays.

Five short plays were enacted and produced from the fifth and sixth forms over a period of two days and followed by an adjudication. For Nikki it was a tour de force; she was involved in every aspect of the festival, from the overall plan to the smallest detail of each individual production. She advised on the choice of plays (but left all the main decisions to the older members of the school who were delighted to take the responsibility on instead of being directed by staff), casting, direction, make-up, stage management, backstage and front of house administration. The plays, in which all the male parts had of necessity to be played by girls, were The Affected Young Ladies, by Janet Dunbar, two plays by Shaw: The Dark Lady of the Sonnets and The Trial Scene from Saint Joan, Ophelia (derived from Hamlet), by T.B. Morris and I Was a Stranger, by Kathleen Stafford.

The festival was an enormous success, and Nikki's reputation was greatly enhanced as a result. 'Our thanks are due to Mrs Paul-Jones', wrote a correspondent in the School Magazine, 'for her untiring encouragement and enthusiasm which have brought new life to our

Dramatic Society.' She was gratified to feel that her innovation had contributed something of lasting value to the school. As she remarked later, on learning that the drama festival had been instituted as an annual event and that the proscenium was still in place, it was one of those rare occasions in a teacher's career when it was possible to see the results of one's efforts.

Congenial and in many ways rewarding as she found her work at Wallington, Nikki knew that it could never be more than a temporary stage in her career. Her potentialities were only partly fulfilled and she was eager and ready to undertake greater responsibilities, preferably in a school with aims more closely identified with her own ideas on education.

Sam and Elizabeth Holiday with their children:
Meg (centre back), Alan and Constance

Frank Greenall

Meg and her brother Alan (right)
with Tom Howarth (head groom)

Nikki aged three, summer 1925

Lucy Greenall, nee Brambles
Frank's Mother

At University of Bristol, 1942

First year at King Alfred School
Easter 1959

Competition photograph entitled
'The Bistro', 1942

Paul with (L to R) Meg, Richard, Nikki, Miranda and Dr Walter Paul-Jones

Detail from KAS photograph, summer 1966. Nikki with her co-head Alan Humphries and school secretary Margaret Bassett

Nikki with teaching colleagues from Bhalgar School, Ahmedabad, 1983

With John in Venice 1980

At King Alfred School, 1983

Part Two

7   Debut at King Alfred School

John and Irma Wood, who ran New Sherwood, had seen an advertisement in the educational press for a deputy headship at King Alfred School in Hampstead, North London, and convinced that Nikki would be a suitable candidate, urged her to apply for the post. The King Alfred School, to employ its full title, was well-known as one of that small group of independent progressive schools which have done so much to shape the course of education during the present century. Her credentials were impressive: a graduate of Bristol University, she had taught children of different levels of ability in primary and secondary schools and in a school for children with special needs. Her educational philosophy was congruent with the ethos of the school for which she was applying, an earnest of which was that her own children were in a school broadly predicated on the same principles. Finally, by means of part-time study, she had added to her professional teaching qualification by obtaining the Guildhall School of Music and Drama Certificate in Drama, passing the examination with distinction at the highest grade.

As the due date for applications had expired, Nikki rang the school to ask if it was too late and was told to apply nonetheless. The date and time of the interview, she was informed, would be notified shortly. There had been fourteen applicants for the post; five of these had been shortlisted and included two from the teaching staff of the school. Some time passed and there was no sign of the expected communication telling her the date of the interview. It transpired later that the interviews had taken place without her and that she was on record as having failed to put in an appearance. This might well have been the end of the story, had it not been for the fact that the selection board had decided not to appoint any of the other candidates. Also, the headmaster, Mr B.H. Montgomery, known as 'Monty', curious to know why Nikki had not come for her interview, rang her up and found out what had actually happened. The result of this was that a special interview was arranged to take place soon afterwards. Nikki had not been prepared for what seemed an uncommonly large selection board, comprising all K.A.S. Councillors and certain other persons making a total of twenty-five. This procedure was obviously more to do with the school's democratic tradition than with any assessment of reactions to stress, but there can be no doubt that the collective pressure of such a committee must have been formidable. She found the best way of dealing with the situation was to think of her examiners as an 'audience' and this worked well, with the result that what for many people would have been a daunting experience was perceived by her as a challenge. Once over the 'first night nerves', she was in her element, responding with her usual directness and lucidity to the questions addressed to her, confident in her professional knowledge and experience. The Council was favourably impressed and duly appointed her as Deputy Head for one year, starting in the summer term of 1959, with a view to a co-headship thereafter.

It was only after her appointment that she was told of the factional dispute which had divided the school for a year following the resignation of Mr Montgomery's former co-head, Mrs Hetty Barber. The central issue in the conflict was the succession to Monty himself on his retirement, which it was anticipated would take place within the next few years. As it was represented to Nikki, it appeared that a deliberate campaign had been mounted by one faction to induce the Headmaster to accept early retirement, thus making way for the appointment of a senior member of staff and his wife as co-heads. This met with considerable opposition and the political in-fighting which ensued affected parents, staff and pupils to a degree which threatened the stability of the school as a whole. Members of the Council canvassed a wide range of opinions on the basis of which they resolved to settle the dispute by making an appointment from outside the school. Apprised of this background at her preliminary briefing, Nikki was enjoined to support the Head in attempting to restore the unity on which the welfare of the school depended. It was a task which long outlasted Monty's time at King Alfred's but which was eventually in great measure achieved.

During the first few weeks in her new job Nikki felt as if she was being rushed off her feet. Every moment of her waking hours seemed to be taken up by the affairs of the school and she ended each day in a state of near exhaustion.

Paul wrote from Carshalton:

'You are in a bit of a bewilder at the moment, wondering if you and sanity and King Alfred can ever live together. If there is anything that can save KA it is you who can make it happen. You have never had any but positive thoughts and that quality cannot fail to bring about change. You have always had the ability to help people to be more themselves, and better selves at that.'

The summer holiday at the end of her first term was not restful by any standards, for there were continuing responsibilities to do with the school, and matters to be dealt with such as selling the house in Carshalton, finding a property in London and another school for the children. At first they took a large house in North Square in the Hampstead Garden Suburb, within easy reach of the school, and nine months later moved into a small property they had bought round the corner in Erskine Hill.

The household was now reduced to Paul, Nikki and the children; although Meg, who had rejoined the family in 1958, accompanied them to London, she stayed only for a short period and soon left for the Isle of Wight, where once again she shared a house with her sister, Con.

8 Progressive Education: Historical antecedents

In common with other Heads, Nikki had always deprecated the label 'progressive' as applied to schools like King Alfred. It had been introduced in the early years of the 20th Century to designate a small but growing number of independent schools dedicated to a new and more liberal form of education than was then available in either the independent or maintained sectors of the educational system.

The term is beset with problems of definition, having a wide range of connotations not exclusively to do with education itself. In the political context it has been appropriated by the Left and is regarded as ipso facto suspect by the Right, despite the fact that the Right have generated policies they would not hesitate to distinguish by the self-same epithet 'progressive'.

In the educational context it has been applied variously to comprehensive secondary and primary schools and to several enterprises collectively known as 'alternatives in education' comprising 'free' or 'community' schools in inner urban areas, 'schools without walls', and children's rights workshops. Confusion is worse confounded by the grouping of these variants under the same umbrella as the independent progressive schools, since the latter themselves represent a wide range of educational philosophies, albeit sharing certain aims in common. This range was suggested by W.A.C. Stewart[6] as extending from the liberal to the anarchic, and it is an unfortunate legacy of the labelling process that it is the excesses of the anarchic end of the continuum that have done some harm to the public image of progressive schools as a whole.

The image itself has several versions but usually includes the suggestion that schools run on a 'do-as-you-please' basis, that there is no formal curriculum, classes are optional, academic standards are correspondingly low, and there is a lack of respect for authority. Whilst this stereotype may have no parallel in any actual school, some of its components do exist in a very small minority of schools.

The conflicting ideologies of progressive educators are part of a larger conflict between progressive and traditional schools. This, in turn, is a special case of the inveterate conflict between freedom and authority, between individual self-determination and social control.

The question of the degree of permissiveness that is optional and the degree of restraint that is necessary in the raising of children, whether in the family or in the school, is one of the most important in education today and one which remains largely unresolved.

---

[6] Stewart, W.A.C. New Society. 13 Feb., 1964.

Many of the ideas about education that are today called progressive long antedated the progressive school movement, which had its beginnings towards the end of the 19th Century.[7]

In the ancient world Socrates used inquiry methods to enable his students to 'discover' knowledge through their own efforts; Plato and Aristotle were concerned with recognition of the child's integrity and attention to the individual child's needs and interests; Plato in particular recognised play as a means of learning.

Humanists of the Renaissance, doubtless to some extent influenced by their ancient mentors, stressed the enjoyment of learning, the study of the needs, capacities and characteristics of individual pupils, and advocated 'mild discipline' and 'the absence of fear' in the education of young children. Comenius in the 17th Century wrote of the need for gentleness and love in teaching, rather than cruelty, and like Francis Bacon before him, prescribed sensory experience as the basis of learning. The 17th Century philosopher, John Locke, emphasised individual development, experiential learning, and deprecated punishment and rewards on the grounds that 'these led to deceit and to good behaviour for the wrong reasons.' He also recommended instruction in a variety of crafts in later adolescence as part of a rounded education.

The French philosopher Rousseau, a disciple of Locke, was probably the greatest single influence on English progressive education. In 'Emile', his published views on education, Rousseau asserted that the aim of all education should be the freedom and happiness of the child.

Childhood, he argued, was not simply a step to adulthood, but an important stage in its own right. All learning should be based on experience, on self-initiated discovery, and should not come from books or from a teacher. He further argued that, since original sin did not exist and children were all innately good, children should never receive punishment in their early years: it should always follow as the actual consequence of their faults. This was a view of freedom far beyond anything Locke would have approved. Nikki had reservations about Rousseau and felt that the freedom of which he spoke with such conviction was only part of the story. She could not forget the selfish and heartless way in which he was said to have treated the mistress with whom he lived for twenty-five years, offering her no help or support with her five pregnancies and leaving her with no option other than to have their children delivered in the Foundling Hospital.

'His freedom, it seemed to me, was an excellent example of a theory following and justifying the desire to act in a particular way. I was to meet this phenomenon quite often during the '60s and '70s when it was used to

---

[7] Curtis, S. Boultwood, M. A short history of Educational Ideas, U.T.P. 1965; and A History of Educational Ideas Since 1800, Chs. 6, 10, 11. U.T.P. 1970.

explain, defend and sanctify every conceivable self-indulgence of living both in education and in society at large.

'I believe that unless the freedoms which are sought are based on and shaped by a basic philosophy which includes and recognises the rights and needs of others, those freedoms can become a form of tyranny. There is no more potent force than that of the totally dependent baby whose desires are his whole universe. The self-discipline needed to hold to the underlying principle must eventually be developed if the energy which drives the desire is to be harnessed. It cannot be effective and positive until it is controllable, instead of being impelled by passing whims, unrecognised emotions, and instinctual needs.

'Recognition of and acceptance of 'the other' as equally important must be at the heart of growth to adulthood and therefore of education.

'Unfortunately the spinners of ideas who evolve impracticable theories for others to carry out are all too often found in the world of professional educators. Not infrequently they are people who, having disliked the need for self-discipline which a teaching career demands, escaped into an easier life as philosophic ideas-men/women, sniping at the people who actually do the work and avoiding any contact with the children for whom they prescribe new and untried methods which end up by becoming fashionable.

'But, yes, Rousseau's ideas were seminal, and, by positing the extreme view of personal liberty possible in an educational context, he established the parameters of a debate that is still going on.'

Educational ideas from the ancient Greeks onwards had limited influence at the time they were enunciated, unless their authors were actively associated in some way with the practice of teaching, as was, for example, the case with Colet, Ascham and More in England. The impetus required for any real dissemination of more liberal ideas on education came mainly from the continent, where a number of educators enjoying the advantage of patronage were starting to put their ideas into practice in small experimental schools.

The Swiss educator, Pestalozzi (1746-1827), one of the first observational psychologists, insisted that early learning must be based on sensory experience, and paid close attention to the individual development of children. On the principle that 'life educates' he sought ways of fostering natural learning processes, encouraged exploration of the environment and learning by the direct experience of actively doing things. He graded the sensory experiences of his pupils just as he graded their intellectual experiences, and introduced them to stages of learning only as and when they were ready for them. He ran his school as a family and, as far as possible, as a self-supporting community, and included in the curriculum a variety of crafts which made a practical contribution to this endeavour. Pupils tended their own small gardens and went on walks of observation which related to their studies in natural history and geography.

Ahead of her Time

J.F. Herbart (1776-1834), an original thinker and prolific writer on education, visited and was greatly influenced by Pestalozzi, and later founded a teachers' training college in Germany, where he regularly taught in the demonstration school.

In the conviction that experience is the basis of all education and development, he believed that it was possible not only to build up the human mind by deliberate teaching methods but also to devise effective instruments of mental measurement. He placed great emphasis on the systematic presentation of curriculum subjects in a form which stressed the underlying unity of all knowledge, by this means facilitating the learning process.

It was the mechanistic quality of his teaching methods and the authoritarian assumptions of Herbart himself that were later found alien to progressive educational thought, but his ideas on the correlated curriculum were adopted with enthusiasm.

Friedrich Froebel (1782-1852) was inspired to adopt his career as an educator by the example of Pestalozzi and worked with him in Switzerland for two years. Froebel believed in the innate capacity of young children to learn for themselves, a capacity which could be fostered or stunted in the course of experience. He thus envisaged the role of the teacher as one who should provide the freedom and the direct experience of the environment, interfering as little as possible, but always being available to provide guidance when needed. Play he regarded as an integral part of the learning process, and lessons were based on the experiences of the children's own lives. Learning topics were interrelated, referred directly to their own environment, and took account of different levels of understanding.

Froebel stressed the need to reconcile individual and group interests, towards which end he ensured that the curriculum which children followed included both individual and collective experiences. At the heart of his educational philosophy was his respect for the uniqueness of each individual child, who 'must be recognised, acknowledged and fostered as a necessary and essential member of humanity'. Froebel's legacy to the world was the enormous influence of his work on nursery and infant education. In particular, the international movement which grew out of the kindergartens he invented and first established in Germany.

Maria Montessori (1869-1952), like Froebel, greatly influenced by Pestalozzi, developed the latter's work on sensory learning as the precursor of abstract thought, and followed Froebel in stressing the direct and active involvement of children in their own learning, with the minimum of intervention by the teacher. She rejected group activities and concentrated her attention on the individualisation of learning. Teaching materials or apparatus were devised by the teacher to be 'not only didactic but also self-corrective, that is, capable of correct solution by trial and error.'

The methods of Froebel and Montessori were not identical in spite of a considerable measure of overlapping. Montessori encouraged, with the use of apparatus, self-activated discovery learning of what was already known. Froebel encouraged the more scientific discovery of what was not known.

Another major influence on the progressive education movement was the American professor of philosophy and education John Dewey (1859-1952). Whilst Dewey's philosophy was libertarian, he provided at the same time a salutary corrective to the wilder flights of progressive enthusiasm. He was quick to emphasise that the cult of individuality did not mean licence. Freedom of activity, by the same token, did not mean that nothing worthwhile would be learned. The disciplining of the self through the experiences provided by the school he felt was an essential part of the educational process. The ideal aim of education for Dewey was 'the creation of power of self-control'. The individual exercises in problem-solving he gave his students were the inspiration for the subsequent development of the Project Method. Dewey also believed that the principles of democracy should be learned in schools not simply by precept but also by example.

The work of the early pioneers - Pestalozzi, Froebel, Montessori - came to fruition in England in the nursery school movement launched by Margaret and Rachel Macmillan in the early years of 20th Century. 'The Macmillans,' writes K. Watson, 'stressed the importance of the physical well-being of children, creative activity and the need to sustain the emotional and intellectual growth of children simultaneously.'[8]

All these liberal educational theories and practices of the last two millennia have in their time stood in marked contrast to the prevailing ideas of the role and status of children in the contemporary world. In this view children were perceived as adults in miniature, to be tolerated, filled with knowledge, and moulded in accordance with the wishes of their elders, a process reinforced where thought necessary by punitive sanctions.

The historical explanations of this phenomenon usually begin by citing the centuries during which the Church exercised a monopoly over all forms of education. This ensured general acceptance of the Christian doctrine of original sin and thereby legitimated authoritarian systems of control in both schools and families, supplemented by the widespread use of corporal punishment.

'Make him do as he is bid,' advised John Wesley, 'if you whip him ten times running to effect it. Let none persuade you it is cruelty to do this: it is cruelty not to do it. Break his will now.' Progress towards spiritual growth was thought to be enhanced by the mortification of the flesh.

There was also the political consideration that doctrines of individual freedom were perceived in autocratic societies as threatening to the social

---

[8] Watson, K. The Growth of Progressive Education in the 20th Century. UCCF Associates. 1980.

order. The introduction of popular education in England in the 19th Century met with resistance in the early stages because of fears that it would enable the poor to read subversive literature and make them dissatisfied with their condition.

A new pressure towards authoritarianism came with the economic changes associated with the industrialisation and urbanisation of Britain and the eventual introduction of universal education towards the end of the 19th Century. This involved a minimum of education and a large element of training in the docility and obedience considered essential to a large industrial workforce. It necessitated large classes and strict discipline, and allowed no opportunity for individualised teaching or learning.

It was these conditions in the elementary schools of the time and the authoritarian character of the independent public schools that instigated the progressive or New Education Movement, as it was alternatively called, which began in the last decade of the century. It was a challenge to educational orthodoxy and an implicit critique of the existing educational provisions.

The movement developed in three distinct stages.[9] The first of these was in the nineties which saw the foundation of Abbotsholme (1889), Bedales (1893), Clayesmore (1896), and King Alfred School in Hampstead (1898). The second stage followed the first World War, during which ten new schools were opened: St Christopher, Letchworth (1918), Bembridge (1919), Rendcomb (1920), A.S.Neill's Summerhill (1924), the Malting House School, where Susan Isaacs worked in Cambridge (1924) (now closed), Dartington (1925), Frensham Heights (1925), Rudolph Steiner's first Anthroposophical School, now Michael Hall (1925), Bertrand and Dora Russell's Beacon Hill (1927) and Bryanston (1928).

The third stage came in the period leading up to and including the early days of the second war (1939-45): Gordonstoun (1934), St Mary's Town and Country School (1937), Wennington (1940), and Monkton Wyld (1940).

The basic and most significant difference between King Alfred and the other schools in the group is its function as a day-school. From its inception, this determined its special ethos, aims and objectives. In particular, one of its most valued traditions has always been the close co-operation between parents, governing body and staff in the life of the school. The boarding schools, on the other hand, have equally valued the relative remoteness from parents as the best guarantee of achieving their educational objectives. It enabled them to gain more control of the child's environment. It was because of the boarding element that co-education, with all its associated problems of sexual morality, came to be regarded as perhaps the most radical innovation of the progressive movement. These were problems that did not affect King Alfred School to anything like the same degree.

---

[9] Stewart, W.A.C. op cit.

There were, of course, many other differences not only between King Alfred and the boarding schools themselves. In both cases they were united by a common culture within which there existed a wide range of diversity. This culture was constantly revivified by the cross-fertilisation of ideas and the periodic migration of individual members of staff, in particular Heads, to other schools within the group. (C.E. Rice, King Alfred's first Head, for example, came from Bedales). At the conservative end of the continuum was Abbotsholme under its founder and reforming Head, C.H. Reddie. The latter had no time for co-education and ran the school according to his own ideas of what an ideal public school should be. There was no corporal punishment; the curriculum included a wide range of subjects all of which were systematically related to modern life, with science (a novelty in 1889), modern languages, music and the arts. Religious education was based on an adapted and highly selective use of the Bible and 'an idiosyncratic chapel liturgy.'

Like the public schools, he saw Abbotsholme as a training establishment for leaders of nation and empire, but had radically different ideas on how this should be done. Estate work and other manual activities were encouraged to inculcate respect for the dignity of labour, and to a large extent replaced traditional games. Much of the school day was spent out of doors, and the pupils wore a uniform of shorts, open-necked shirts and berets.

Unlike some of his peers, Dr Reddie was an autocrat where his own educational theory and practice were concerned, and his intention was to mould his pupils in accordance with a prescribed ideal.

To A.S.Neill, whose Summerhill represented the more radical end of the continuum, the idea of moulding children was anathema. He would, he said on one occasion, no more try to mould a child than he would try to mould a dog. At Summerhill the individual freedom and happiness of children was given absolute priority. Attendance at classes was optional, and the preparation for adult life emphasised the development of well-integrated personalities rather than the acquisition of knowledge and skills. Pupils and staff were on first name terms, and decisions affecting the school, including the formulation of rules, were taken democratically at the weekly meetings of a parliament in which all were represented.

In between Abbotsholme and Summerhill came all the other schools, each with its own variations on the progressive ethic. One writer,[10] in a sample survey, summarised the trends of particular schools in the following way: Abbotsholme 'mainstream'; Bedales 'world outside'; King Alfred School 'parentwards'; St. Christopher 'Do it Yourself' and 'vegetarianism'; Dartington 'education for sanity';[11] Town and Country 'spiritual

---

[10] Nicholson, Caroline. The Observer, June 23, 30, July 7, 1963
[11] Vide Curry, W.B. Education for Sanity. Heinemann. 1947.

completeness' and 'the group process'; Monkton Wyld 'anti-rat race'; Wennington 'individual'; and Summerhill 'permissive to screaming point'.

A small number of schools incorporated in varying degrees some of the ideas and values of Theosophy. Based on a philosophy of ancient Indian origin, the Theosophical Movement proclaimed acceptance of the universal truths common to all religions, the immanence of God, the brotherhood of humanity, reincarnation, and the identity of man with nature. The growing internationalism of the movement was marked in 1921 by the creation of a world-wide educational forum - the New Education Fellowship. John Russell, Head of King Alfred School from 1901-1920, and his successor Joseph Wicksteed were leading figures in the movement, of which the latter's father, the Reverend Philip Wicksteed, was one of the founders.

A common interest of the progressive schools was the development of psychology. Whilst this had been implicit in the work of the continental educators, it had not developed as a coherent and established science until the late 19th Century - almost at the same time as the beginning of the progressive movement itself.

The first objective tests of mental ability and motivational characteristics were introduced in the 1880s and Freud commenced his clinical studies in psychoanalysis in 1886.

With the spread of psychology, the progressive schools, with their child-centred principles, were among the first to understand its educational implications, and to interpret and apply its findings. Intelligence tests were useful in the diagnosis of learning difficulties, but the new 'theologies' of psycho-analysis were welcomed with even greater enthusiasm because of their potential disclosure of the unconscious sources of motivation. Inevitably, mistakes were made. Psycho-analysis was not always fully understood and not infrequently misinterpreted. For example, the idea that any form of suppression was wrong gained currency in some schools and was implemented in excessive forms of freedom which threatened to damage the reputation of progressive education as a whole. A.S.Neill, who started by accepting the value of Freudian analysis at Summerhill, eventually concluded that it was not analysis but freedom that was 'curing' disturbed pupils. 'It was just as well,' he added, 'because we can't analyse the whole human race.'

In his valedictory speech as Headmaster of King Alfred School in July, 1920 John Russell intimated that in his retirement he was proposing to write a history of the school, adding the proviso 'unless my heart fails me'. For whatever reason, his intention was never realised and the question of a history was not raised again until 1963, when the Headmaster, Mr B.H.Montgomery, and the school secretary, Miss Else Hibburd, both of whom had recently retired, were invited to undertake the task.

It was suggested by Roderick Garrett, the Chairman of Council, that the history should be regarded not as a full-length literary work for general publication but simply as a chronological file of relevant documents, annotated where necessary, for retention in the school's archives.

By the winter of 1965 the co-authors had completed their long and arduous task. It had involved the rationalisation of a mass of archival material and the systematic perusal of documents going back to the foundation of the school in 1898. These efforts culminated in a consecutive historical summary together with a file index which facilitated access to original abstracts and other documents.[12]

During her own time at the school, Nikki, who was aware of the limited objectives that had been given to the writers of the short history, resolved to design her annual reports in the hope that, if a definitive history were eventually to be written, these would present the author with as orderly and complete an account of the ensuing years as could be managed in a limited space. Towards the same end she began in her spare time to write an expanded version of the Montgomery/Hibburd summary - in effect attempting a more exegetic treatment of the same material than had been contained in the brief of the co-authors. Through lack of time this undertaking was only partially completed. The abridged version which follows draws substantially on the admirably clear and succinct account prepared by Mr Montgomery and Miss Hibburd, and includes some critical interpolations derived from Nikki's own unfinished writings on the subject.

---

[12] Montgomery, B.H., Hibburd, E. A Short History of The King Alfred School Society. KASS archives, 1965.

9   Outline history of KAS

In July, 1897 a group of distinguished Hampstead residents, the foundation members[13] of the King Alfred School Society (K.A.S.S), issued a circular entitled 'Proposed Rational School' in which their basic educational principles were set out. It was signed by Mrs White Wallis and Mrs Roscoe Mullins who for years remained honorary joint secretaries, the former described by a co-founder as 'the moving spirit and inspiration of the Society all through its earliest years'.

Many of their recommendations, thought revolutionary at the time, have subsequently become normal aspects of contemporary - particularly primary - education, and their aims were expressed with commendable clarity. Their object was to secure a 'rational education' for children, including their own, based on principles enunciated by educational reformers like Pestalozzi, Herbart and Froebel, and implemented by selective application of scientific methods of teaching and learning. They were fortunate enough to obtain the support and guidance of a figure distinguished in the educational world of the day - Doctor J.J.Findlay, later Professor of Education at the University of Manchester. He was responsible for the formulation of the school's policy and was for many years its general consultant. He was responsible for the choice of King Alfred the Great as patron, and the approaching millenary of the king's death (A.D.901) must have been a major factor in reaching the decision. Sir Hamo Thorneycroft, a founder member of the Society, and himself the sculptor of the statue of Alfred erected at Winchester in 1901, named his

---

[13] The foundation, members who subscribed their names to the Articles of Association were:

F.W.Miall. Journalist. (Brother of Prof.L.C.Miall, FRS., biologist and educational reformer of Leeds University, who became the first President of the Society 1899-1908).

Cecil J.Sharp. Principal of the Hampstead Conservatoire of Music, Collector of Old English folk songs, and founder of the English Folk Dance and Song Society.

Alice Mullins. Wife of Roscoe Mullins, the sculptor. She was the mother of Claud Mullins, a pupil at King Alfred School, later a London magistrate and writer on law reform.

Sir Hamo Thorneycroft, RA. Sculptor. His wife was President of the Society from 1951 to 1958.

Isobel White Wallis. Wife of E.White Wallis, a distinguished scientist.

Gerald C.Maberly. Barrister-at-law. Hon.Treasurer of the Society, 1910-1924.

J Godfrey Hickson. First Hon. Solicitor to the Society.

(Vide Montgomery, B.H., Hibburd, E)

daughter Elfrida after one of the king's daughters whom he had 'caused to be informed in the liberal arts', ranking her claim to education equally with his sons.[14]

Before the end of 1897 the Society was fully incorporated and membership was open to parents and others interested in educational reform. Plans to open a day school for the co-education of boys and girls from 4 to 12 years of age were set in motion; premises were found in Ellerdale Road, Hampstead and, on May 2nd 1898, six pupils - four boys and two girls - attended for the first time. The occasion was marked by a formal ceremonial meeting at which Mr Cecil Sharp, the collector of folk songs and dances, took the Chair, and Mrs (later Dame) Millicent Fawcett gave an address. C.E.Rice, M.A., a scholar of Caius College, Cambridge, left Bedales School to become the first headmaster, and his wife accepted the post of lady superintendent and teacher of art.

Thirteen children enrolled in the following term, and by 1901 the total number of pupils was fifty-two.

The first prospectus, dated 1898, was quite specific about the pattern of education which was to be followed, but qualified this by saying that, in working out a detailed teaching scheme, priority had to be given to the actual attainments of the pupils and not to theoretical schemes. The object of the education to be provided was 'to develop faculty in all directions and draw out the self-activity of the child', and the approach to learning was to emphasise the concrete rather than the abstract. The principle of co-education was applied in all areas of school life - (a later headmaster excepted football from this) - and classes which were limited to 12 or at the most 15 children relied a great deal on oral methods. French lessons were conducted entirely in French, and whenever possible education was carried on out of doors 'in garden, field and hedgerow'.[15]

There was to be no religious instruction or observance, but teaching was to be conducted in a religious spirit, and the Bible studied as both literature and history and as a source of moral training.

The child's energy and interest were directed to 'learning for its own sake and for its value in training and development'. From this it followed that the curriculum was to be based on the needs and interests of the children and not on the demands of examining bodies. Since the value of education was intrinsic, and learning its own reward, prizes, scholarships and honours were avoided. After the age of twelve, however, pupils could be prepared, apart from the regular curriculum, for entrance examinations to other schools; and those over fifteen could be prepared to compete for scholarships at institutions of further or higher education.

---

[14] Montgomery, B.H. Hibburd E. A Short History of the King Alfred School Society. K.A.S.S. Archives, 1965.
[15] Ibid.

Character training, according to the prospectus, was attempted 'by a friendly and courteous relationship between the staff and the children ..... by giving honour to all service rendered for the public good and by providing opportunities for such service'.[16]

The Society saw themselves as the spearhead of a missionary enterprise committed to disseminating the principles of the New Education. This they sought to achieve by opening a chain of K.A.S.S schools which they proposed to support initially by means of loans until such time as they were able to finance themselves. The plan was that these, like the parent school, would act as 'demonstration' schools and would be staffed from a special teachers' training college to be established for this purpose. These ambitious plans were to be supplemented by a vigorous propaganda campaign conducted through the press, by conference, public lectures and meetings.

The publicity campaign was immensely successful and the time devoted to its various aspects indicates that daily life in the school must have been infinitely less demanding than nowadays. The records evidence an extraordinary number of conferences and meetings, and the Council encouraged a constant flow of visitors to see the 'rational school' at work. It seems not to have occurred to the members of Council that so many visits might have been an intrusion both on the children's education and on the professional responsibilities of the staff. The head had eventually to make a plea for such visits to be made by appointment only.

The original plan of opening a number of similar schools and a training college had eventually to be abandoned for want of financial backing. There were no endowments and the first twenty years of the school's life were punctuated by monetary crises and the threat of closure.

These crises might well have been avoided if the Society had been prepared to surrender a measure of its autonomy in exchange for public subsidy, but this it resolutely refused to do.

It was for this reason that generations of K.A.S parents, staff and pupils were recurrently involved in self-help activities, estate work and fund-raising enterprises.

Independence was also the reason why for a long time there was reluctance to apply for recognition by the Board of Education, and why the Society reserved the right to invite outside authorities 'sympathetic to its aims' to inspect the school at periodic intervals.

Charles Rice soon realised that a small school, dependent on its fees, could not continue to do justice to the education of the under-14s and at the same time provide specialist tuition for older pupils. When a demand arose for the extension of the upper age group, he offered to co-operate in the division of the school into two sections: a senior school at Ellerdale Road and a new junior school elsewhere in the locality.

---

[16] Ibid.

Regrettably, his offer was refused by the Chairman of Council without even the courtesy of a formal discussion, and he quietly resigned, 'to avoid further controversy and prejudice to the cause of education'. This was by no means the only time when members of the Council, informed by conviction rather than by practical sense, led the school into difficulties from which it later had to be extricated. On the evidence of minutes and letters of the period, they thrived on stormy meetings and dramatic confrontations. This would have mattered less had they had any conception of the proper function of a headmaster. Significantly, it was not until two and a half years after his appointment that the head was first invited to attend a Council meeting and to give a report on the school. Communications between him and that body took place by letter, with an occasional visit from a member appointed by them to convey and explain their decisions to him. His modest and reasonable requests for school necessities, whether concerned with equipment or maintenance, were often curtly refused and his decisions in minor matters were frequently overruled.[17]

Cecil Sharp, Chairman of the Society, was one of the four members of Council who resigned with him in protest, and it was he who commented in a letter 'I find among a considerable section of the Council a tendency to interfere with what I conceive to be the function of a headmaster which would inevitably wreck any school'.[18]

Half the children left the school when Charles Rice resigned in 1901, and of those who remained two were subsequently known as 'Charlie's Champions'.

That the school survived at all was due in considerable measure to an unusual and gifted man. A theologian turned rationalist, John Russell had the advantage of varied teaching experience in England and France, backed by good academic qualifications including a degree in theology. It seems clear from all the documents of the time, as well as from the recollections of those who knew him personally, that Russell, or 'J.R.', as he was usually called, did more than any other single person to establish the character and atmosphere of K.A.S.

During his headship of nineteen years he laid stress on everything which could contribute to providing for every child the fullest possible measure of freedom within a carefully designed framework of social responsibility.

Education towards social maturity was fostered not only by example in the course of daily interaction but by the democratic institution of a 'School Parliament'. This provided a forum and a 'court' for the discussion of actual conflicts of interest affecting the school population, and those who were judged to have helped or hindered the communal process were accordingly commended or called to account. Girls had the same voting rights as boys

---

[17] Montgomery, B.H. Hibburd, E. Op cit.
[18] Ibid.

at a time long before the introduction of women's suffrage in the adult body politic.

Daily assembly was run like a large family gathering at which all present were encouraged to express their opinions on matters of common interest. It was a consensual ritual which encouraged in each individual child a sense of belonging and supplemented the expressive functions of the 'Parliament'.

At the time it must have been an unusual experience for many of the children, but it was the start of what has always been one of the school's most notable characteristics - a capacity to produce children of all ages who can speak easily in public without either self-consciousness or over-confidence.

Although the school was small in these early years, the curriculum was wide and varied in content. The academic subjects included physics, chemistry, French and Latin. The modern approach to geography teaching had been adopted, with the guidance of two of its promoters, as early as 1903, long before it became known generally in other schools. Woodwork, metalwork, pottery, basketwork, bookbinding and printing were given a generous allocation of time in the afternoons, when there was a 'free choice' timetable. The standards of achievement were high and on several occasions specimens of work were sent to exhibitions in London and Paris.

Russell was ahead of his time in recognising the importance of sex education in the upbringing of young children. Introduced in progressive stages by means of informal discussion and treated incidentally in relevant curriculum subjects, it was calculated to develop natural and healthy attitudes towards sexuality and to establish 'beautiful and honourable relations between the sexes'.

Practical nature study was an important part of the curriculum, and for many years a detailed record was kept of the work done by children who had cultivated the kitchen garden and the flower garden. Several parents were interested and joined in the periodic nature expeditions that were frequently undertaken to places such as Hampstead Heath, Northwood and Child's Hill Fields. 'Parties of children, staff and parents went regularly for rambles and picnics in the Chilterns. In 1903 and 1904 John Russell took school holiday parties to Wimereux in France for a week'. The propaganda movement gathered pace under Russell and the many meetings and conferences held at the school and elsewhere attracted speakers of distinction, for example Bernard Shaw, Flinders Petrie, Lowes Dickinson and Marie Stopes.

Shaw, according to a report which appeared in an issue of 'The Author'[19] took part in a discussion on the question of whether the study of literature was decaying in schools. Predictably, he took the unconventional view that, if this were the case, it was a very good thing too, as there was a

---

[19] Article entitled 'Schoolboys and Literature' in 'The Author', 1901.

great deal too much reading done anyway. No-one had any right to force any education upon a child, except useful education. Every other form should be the spontaneous outcome of a child's character. The report noted that the King Alfred School Society did not as a body accept his views and that John Russell spoke in support of teaching literature, saying, in particular, that 'if a master approached the subject in a spirit of sincerity and not of convention or dogmatism - guiding taste rather than dictating to it - he would have no difficulty in interesting young people'.

By 1910 when the number of pupils had reached seventy an adjoining house was bought in Ellerdale Road; the premises were extended, and by 1915 the numbers had been increased to a hundred.

Unfortunately, before the first World War too many parents still regarded it as a suitable school for younger children, but were apprehensive about its capacity to provide for the academic needs of older children. Even today the remnants of this curious legend linger on, despite the school's solid and consistent record of sixth form and university successes. Margaret Basden, one of the first university graduates from K.A.S. was the first woman to qualify for a primary Fellowship of the Royal College of Surgeons and to take her M.S. degree. Her success was ascribed by her examiners to her 'having been taught to learn', an assessment echoed many years later by another K.A. graduate who went on to do a Ph.D. and told Nikki of his own sense of discovery during his time at Cambridge: 'When I first went up I wondered what K.A.S. had really done for me by comparison with all the high-powered, well-trained first year students I met. By the second year, I knew. They found it hard to work unless someone made them. I had been taught to work by myself and on my own initiative.'

During the first World War various co-operative war-work efforts were made by staff and children, and clothes and food were provided in response to national appeals for the relief of distress. Over fifty Old Alfredians had joined the Armed Forces before conscription was introduced; nine were killed, or died, on active service, and at least seven were decorated for gallantry.

In 1919, after the war, the number of children at Ellerdale Road was over ninety and, as accommodation was stretched to the limit, a search began for larger premises which would allow for growth in the size of the school and space for all the outdoor activities which could not be catered for on the existing site.

A suitable site which had lain derelict for years but which had great possibilities for development was found near the edge of the Heath between Old Hampstead and the newly developed Hampstead Garden Suburb. This was the Manor House Estate and it was purchased jointly with the Industrial Orthopaedic Society, the boundary between the school and the hospital being agreed after discussion in the autumn of 1919,. The school acquired six acres of woodland, a lodge, driveway and coach house together comprising half of the former estate which became known as Manor Wood. The successful negotiations owed much to the efforts of Sir Patrick Geddes,[20] President of the Society from 1919 to 1925. Between 1910 and 1912 the Society had opened two open-air nursery schools, later called Garden Schools, for children aged 3 to 7. One was run on Froebel and the other on Montessori lines, and it was the latter which moved into the coach house at Manor Wood in 1919. Montessori methods continued to be used for some years after this, but were gradually superseded , because of their rigid theoretical premises, by Froebelian methods. The school was first designated as a Preparatory School, and later incorporated into K.A.S. as the nucleus of its nursery department.

John Russell had been actively engaged in the plans to move to Manor Wood, but, as he was approaching retirement, the main burden of establishing the school in its new premises fell to his successor. Under J.R.'s leadership the school had evolved in very much the way its founders had envisaged. It was largely due to his personal charisma that the only changes requiring some modification of the traditional ethos - viz. homework and preparation for the examinations of older pupils - were effected without the kind of disruption that had led to the resignation of his predecessor. Also, he must take a great deal of the credit for changing the hierarchical relationship between Council and Head which had existed when he first came to the school. By the time of his retirement he was held in great affection and esteem by the whole community of councillors, parents, staff and children.

During Russell's last two years at the school A.S.Neill was an assistant master on his staff, having been demobilised from the Army in 1918. Neill had obtained J.R.'s permission to run his own class as a 'democracy', but, predictably, the experiment was a failure, as it was almost certain to be, in isolation from the rest of the school. When he left K.A.S. to start his own school, first in Lyme Regis, and shortly afterwards in Suffolk, the school journal recorded 'the loss of Mr A.S.Neill, who washed his hands of us at Xmas, being unable to persuade Mr Russell to be as revolutionary as the 'Dominie". At a farewell meeting held in his honour on July 16th, 1920 JR summed up his long career at K.A.S. by saying that he had done his imperfect best. Whilst he was more than certain that many of the old ways in education were utterly wrong, he was less certain than he used to be that the new ways were all (as yet) utterly right.[21]

There were two candidates for the succession to the headship: George Earle, who had been at the school since 1901 and had the solid backing of

---

[20] Sir Patrick Geddes (1854-1932). Professor of Botany (Dundee) (1883-1920). Also achieved distinction in town planning, social, academic and economic reform.

[21] Report of a meeting celebrating the retirement of Mr John Russell, 16 July, 1920. K.A.S.S. Archives.

the staff; and Joseph Wicksteed, who had taught at K.A.S. in 1904 but was currently a master at Bedales. Wicksteed's influential referees (including Russell himself), his reputation as a scholar and literary critic, and his active involvement in the broader education movements of the time, led Council to decide in his favour. His appointment was greeted with a storm of protest, and Earle and all the other full-time members of staff resigned. In consequence, when Joseph Wicksteed took up his appointment in September, 1920, his first task was to find a new staff. It was a tribute to his judgment, also to his luck, that all those he appointed both then and in the next few years were teachers of high calibre, who made an enormous contribution to the development of the school in the inter-war years, when the numbers were effectively doubled. Thus the crisis passed and the school weathered the storm, even if it had sailed perilously close to the rocks. K.A.S. still had to treat seriously the question of its survival, and could ill afford eruptions of the kind that had attended the change of headmaster. By the time Manor Wood was acquired, ambitious building plans had been drawn up by Charles Voysey[22], an Old Alfredian, who was then the school architect. After the purchase of the site little money remained for building and development, and any idea of constructing a new school permanently in brick had to be postponed indefinitely. A number of wooden ex-Army huts were bought and erected in the grounds between the trees. The siting of the huts provided the nucleus of an open-air school and established the decentralised plan which became the pattern for all subsequent building development. Out of these developments there grew a tradition of working out of doors whenever possible and this lasted for twenty to thirty years. In keeping with the same idea was the construction of Squirrel Hall, the log-built open-air meeting place which Wicksteed designed and, together with parents, staff and older children, helped to build. It was situated under a magnificent Spanish chestnut tree (reputed to be about four hundred years old) which formed part of the structure, and lasted until 1971, when the supports were found to have rotted at ground level and to be in a dangerous condition. A new Squirrel Hall was built largely by staff and pupils with a small but devoted group of parents under the supervision of Cecil Lush, the Honorary Architect. It was constructed of telegraph poles, the only form of inexpensive wood available in the 1970s.

The building of the King's Cross to Bank extension of the London Underground Railway produced large quantities of excavated soil, and arrangements were made to have this dumped and spread over the lower northern part of the estate to make a level area for a games field.

A stream which flowed through the grounds from a natural spring was piped and diverted under the new ground, nevertheless still emerging at the

---

[22] Son of C.F.A. Voysey (1857-1941), described in Chambers Biographical Dictionary as 'perhaps the most important architect and designer of wallpaper and textiles of the generation after William Morris.'

southern end of the field, to render the area waterlogged in wet weather. The natural amphitheatre made by the spring was adapted and shaped to make an open-air theatre in 1924.

Wicksteed replaced the School Parliament by an Advisory Council composed of staff representatives and pupils, the latter elected by the upper school. A new constitution gave the Council legislative, executive, and judicial powers, subject to the veto of the headmaster. It was intended to deal with matters of common interest outside the curriculum, and the teachers' sphere of influence in the classroom. It was one of a number of innovations which aroused the disapproval of certain parents, some of them on the Council of the Society, who felt that Wicksteed had carried the idea of freedom too far, and possibly further than was intended in the original principles and ideals of the school. Fortunately, a majority voted in favour of Wicksteed and recorded a vote of absolute confidence in the changes he had made and in the soundness of his methods. Relaxation of the taboo on examinations had led insensibly to a measure of stereotyping in the curriculum, and steps were taken to counter this tendency by the introduction of a new timetable incorporating a modified version of the Dalton Plan, then becoming popular in the United States. This obviated the worst effects of mixed-ability teaching and provided more opportunities for individual work, the use of learning resources, and correlation of subjects of the pupil's own choice.

From 1926 onwards the financial position of the school began to improve. Gifts and loan conversions had averted closure, but extreme care in expenditure was essential for many years to come. The wooden huts were either dismantled or re-erected elsewhere, and the programme of building a more permanent brick-built establishment continued steadily: the new school hall (1926); the library block, with a science laboratory and art and craft wing (1930); and a nursery block in 1933.

Some teachers were still giving unpaid or underpaid services, and fund-raising events were a regular and necessary part of the life of the school.

The Board of Education first inspected the school in 1922, and again in 1928 when a full-scale inspection was carried out, as a result of which K.A.S. was for the first time granted recognised status. This had been achieved without prejudice to the founders' principles and the school was henceforth included in the Government's Superannuation provisions under the scheme of 1926. This situation continued until 1955, when it became possible to afford the more expensive Teachers' Pensions Scheme (1948).

In 1934 the Society agreed a firm scale of teachers' salaries, but these were well below the official Burnham Scale. They were raised to 90% in 1948, but it was not until 1952 that they could afford to pay the full Burnham salaries.

These developments were of vital importance to the school, for its survival increasingly depended on attracting highly qualified teachers, and a precondition of this was to be able to offer at least the same salary scale as the maintained schools.

In 1933 Joseph Wicksteed retired. He had presided over a period of recovery, growth and development, in which academic standards had been raised, the number of pupils nearly doubled, the estate improved beyond all recognition, and a number of permanent buildings erected. The school was relatively well-equipped, had its own playing field, and, thanks to the prudent management of its Honorary Treasurer, was in a sound financial position.

Remembering the turmoil which had accompanied Wicksteed's appointment in 1920, Council was cautious in its approach to the choice of his successor. They were fully aware of the danger to which the school would be exposed if there were any occurrence of a similar kind.

There was a wide choice of well-qualified candidates for the post of head, but finally the Council set a precedent by appointing from the teaching staff Violet Hyett and Hugh Birkett as joint heads. There is little doubt that this solution was influenced by a petition, organised by seniors and signed by all pupils in the upper school, supporting their candidature. The appointment also introduced what seemed to many to be a more logical pattern of headship for a co-educational school, and thereafter co-headship remained the organising principle until 1970, except for the period 1945-1949.

During the 1930s the number of children rose from 160 to 220. The main increase was in the upper school and was partly attributable to an influx of refugee children from the continent. Traditionally open to all nationalities, K.A.S. welcomed the arrival of these newcomers as a cultural and educational enrichment of the community. Larger numbers made possible an expansion of curriculum options and an extension of team games, while the decade as a whole was notable for the burgeoning of music and drama. Additional staff were appointed during these years, and advanced courses were established in the sciences and arts subjects. As a result, an increasing number of pupils went from the school direct to university, and the standard of academic work was raised throughout the school - an achievement duly acknowledged in a Board of Education inspectors' report in 1938.

Faithful to the traditions established by their predecessors, Violet Hyett and Hugh Birkett made special efforts to keep the school community informed about the outside world, both at the national and the international level. Excursions were made to factories and to public works, newspapers were studied and discussed, visiting speakers came to talk of their specialised knowledge, and visitors came from other countries because they had heard about the school and wanted to see it for themselves.

In 1939, plans were well advanced for the next stage in the building programme, but these had to be abandoned, as the war, which had been threatening for some years, became imminent.

Two years before, Violet Hyett and Else Hibburd, the school secretary, had bought Flint Hall Farm in Royston, Hertfordshire as a holiday and ultimate retirement home. They also planned to invite the school to make use of the land, some two hundred acres, for camping and rural studies. Another factor which had affected their decision to purchase the farm was the possibility that it could provide a temporary home for the school in the event of war.

Council considered a number of evacuation schemes and, in spite of some objections, the decision went in favour of Royston. Some parents observed that it was near two aerodromes; others that it was at exactly the distance from London where air battles were likely to take place.

Work started at once. Adaptations were made to the farm buildings, extensions were carried out, and equipment was transferred from London. By the outbreak of war on the 3rd of September the accommodation was ready for occupation, and shortly afterwards the move took place, leaving Manor Wood to be subsequently requisitioned by the War Office. At Royston there were 32 boarders and 18 day pupils, whose parents had obtained local accommodation. Local recruitment later raised the total complement to 91 pupils. The logistics of the whole operation is a story in itself. Suffice it to say that it was one of extraordinary achievement, in which staff, pupils, and parents all contributed to the re-establishment of part of the school at Royston, and managed to keep it running for most of the war without any significant diminution of standards. The physical conditions were rugged but rewarding and, at first, their lives followed a pattern familiar to Alfredians, that of self-help in many aspects of estate work. There were practical tasks to be undertaken: building construction, conversion and repair, in which Hugh Birkett, applying his exceptional mechanical skills, led by example. Household cleaning and everything to do with the provision of meals were in the early stages the responsibility of the community and organised on a rotary basis. In time, as the derelict farmland was restored to agricultural production, and stock management was introduced, staff, pupils and parents were once again involved in the division of labour.

All the members of staff who could afford it accepted a salary reduction of 50% and paid the same cost price sum as the children for board and lodging. New rules applicable to boarding conditions were drawn up jointly by staff and pupils, following thorough discussion; team games were organised, and a programme of weekly Saturday evening entertainment was introduced.

Academic work continued without serious interruption, as air raids were mostly at night, and public examinations were taken as usual from 1940 to 1945, with very satisfactory results, and several pupils obtained university places.

An excellent corporate spirit prevailed and the educational benefits of farm life were very evident. Actually, no bombs fell in the area of Royston proper, but the neighbouring aerodromes were attacked.

D-day (6th June, 1944) and the advance of the Western Allies in Europe raised the spirits of the British people and generated widespread optimism that the end of the war was approaching.

As early as 1943, due to the initiative of Mrs Renée Soskin (née Beloff), an Old Alfredian, a nursery school was opened in Holford Road, Hampstead. The success of this venture led Mrs Soskin and others to contemplate further development of a K.A.S. revival in London. Following discussion with Council representatives and the co-heads at Royston, she was delegated to write a letter of invitation to Mr B.H. Montgomery, a former assistant master at the school (1932-1940), then teaching in Devon, asking him to re-establish a senior K.A.S. in London. He agreed, and the school opened in Branch Hill, Hampstead on 2nd October 1944, with Mr Montgomery as headmaster. As the war did not end in 1944, as anticipated, bombing continued during the first six months of the school's existence, and air raid precautions were necessary.

Throughout 1945 there was a gradual filtering back of staff and pupils from Royston and a corresponding winding down at Flint Hall Farm School, which closed finally in July, 1946. In January, 1945 the two London schools amalgamated, and by the following Spring, when the end of the war was imminent, negotiations with the War Office about de-requisitioning the Manor Wood Estate were in progress.

Violet Hyett and Hugh Birkett announced their intention of retiring at the end of 1945, so that the plan for re-uniting the Royston and London outposts of the school at Manor Wood presupposed that B.H. Montgomery would be the overall head.

The devastation and neglect left by military occupation would have been daunting to anyone; to those returning from Royston, scene of their pioneering achievements, it must have been cause for dismay.

Records describe seriously damaged buildings, smashed windows, inoperative heating apparatus and removable articles like taps, door-handles and linoleum stolen or destroyed. 'Tons of hardcore had been spread over half the field to make a parking ground for military vehicles and the other half was pitted with trenches. Barbed wire lay around and one of the cloakrooms was filled nearly to the ceiling with sand'.[23]

The rehabilitation of K.A.S., like the colonisation of Flint Hall Farm, was a story of phenomenal endeavour involving the combined efforts of enthusiastic and willing helpers, and supplemented by paid workers of various kinds from outside.

The school reopened officially on 26th September, 1945, with a total of 157 pupils, and the process of rehabilitation continued throughout 1946.

---

[23] Montgomery, B.H. Hibburd, E. Op. cit.

The playing field was restored and again in use by the summer; outdoor play apparatus was repaired, and new equipment was installed.

Apart from the renewal of the physical environment, there was the urgent problem of rebuilding a community which had been dispersed by the action of war. About half the school population - both staff and pupils - were new to the culture and ethos of K.A.S. Many of the children had been evacuated in far less favourable circumstances than the Royston evacuees, and had had unsettling experiences which left their mark on them. It took a great deal of tact, patience and understanding, but, with the energy and determination of a core of experienced staff, parents and senior pupils, the school gradually evolved into a cohesive whole.

The organisation of the school as it affected staffing, accommodation, curriculum and learning resources was well enough established by 1949 for an inspection by the Ministry of Education, and in that year a full-scale review was carried out. The H.M.I.s report expressed appreciation of the post-war difficulties that had been overcome, commended those activities in which K.A.S. invariably excelled, and criticised the methods they found unorthodox, albeit recognising their inherence in 'rationalist' pedagogy.

It was regarded as a fair and encouraging assessment, and the general effect of the inspection was to stimulate a re-examination of the principles and aims of the school in relation to modern standards of comparison, and to re-affirm its educational ethos. A familiar theme that had appeared in the report concerned the tendency for many pupils, especially boys, to leave before the age of twelve. A growing waiting list now made it possible to adjust this anomaly by screening entries more carefully and offering preferential places to children whose parents intended to keep them at the school until at least sixteen. This policy, together with the growing belief in the value of co-education for boys, produced the desired effect, and, by 1955, the number of boys and girls was approximately even throughout the school.

The pattern of joint headship was reintroduced in 1949, when Mrs Hetty Barber, a senior member of staff, who had formerly taught at Roedean and Christ's Hospital, was appointed as co-head with Mr Montgomery. A period of development followed in which public examinations exerted an increasing influence on the curriculum of the upper school, and there was a steady expansion of the Sixth Form. What had been a mere trickle of scholastic distinctions - some of the highest order - in the inter-war years became a continuous stream, and the rising number of G.C.E. entries qualified the school to have its own examination centre. And the myth that K.A.S. was anti-academic and not suitable for boys after the age of twelve was finally laid to rest by the record of the period 1950-1960, when Old Alfredians gained three 1st Class Honours Degrees, a Balliol Scholarship, and fifteen other scholarships or exhibitions.

All these developments raised the perennial question of whether the emphasis placed on examinations was diverting attention from the main purpose of the school - namely, learning for its own sake and not for the sake of extrinsic rewards. The answer was the same as it had been when John Russell won concessions from Council in the past - namely that the survival of the school depended on its being prepared to respond to changes taking place in society. The changes initiated in the school in no way infringed the spirit of the founders' principles. Nor did they threaten the interests of the various categories of non-academic children, whose needs had never been subordinated to the business of preparing others for examinations.

In 1952, moral concern surfaced again when the school population reached a total of 280 children. Now it was feared by some staff as well as parents that the special 'family' character of K.A.S. could easily be lost if the community became too large. It was concluded, however, that the advantages of having a larger top to the school more than compensated for the disadvantages of greater numbers. As a result of the favourable staff-pupil ratio (which remained at about 1 to 13), by means of various organisational expedients, and, most of all, because of the interest which each member of staff took in every child, it was possible to deal satisfactorily with such difficulties as developed.

By 1957 the financial position of the Society, owing to the shrewd management of its successive Treasurers, had become stronger than at any time in its history. Many improvements were now made to do away with the old inconveniences that had been endured for so long; for example, less than satisfactory heating and lighting facilities, improvised accommodation, makeshift and inadequate storage space, insufficiency of books and teaching aids.

Building development continued, providing more classroom space to meet the needs of rising numbers of pupils, and the school gradually became a more comfortable and convenient place in which to work.

The enlargement of the school had greatly expanded the range and quality of activities available, both in respect of curriculum options, and of extra-curricular clubs and other interests.

Art, music and drama flourished, and there were innumerable excursions to places of historic interest and to exhibitions of all kinds. There was camping at Royston, and many school holiday parties were taken abroad. The numbers interested in team games multiplied, and the standard of play in cricket and hockey improved to such an extent that matches could be undertaken with other schools on a regular basis.

If the school appeared to be taking on some of the attributes of conventional public schools, this was only because it had adapted successfully to the changing demands of both society and its parent body, nevertheless consistently preserving intellectual continuity with the progressive ethos of its founders.

In 1957 Mrs Barber, after playing a central part in the post-war period, left K.A.S. to take up another appointment. Mr Montgomery remained as sole head until 1960, when Nikki, on the conclusion of her year as deputy, was appointed as his co-head.

10 Conservation and change: The perennial problem

Nikki began her long career at K.A.S. at the beginning of a period of accelerating social change. 'The '60s were more of a shock than the '70s,' she observed, 'probably because by the '70s adaptation had become second nature.'

The period of post-war recovery was over, and developments in science and technology, fuelled by research in industry and the institutions of higher education, were transforming the economic system of production in ways which radically affected the entire social structure.

By 1962, New Commonwealth migrants of Afro-Caribbean and Asian origin, many of whom had made an invaluable contribution to Britain's economic recovery, represented some 3% of the British population. Although only a small proportion of the whole, their concentration (in the face of appreciable local prejudice) in several of the main conurbations caused problems of race relations and integration. These have still not been resolved, in spite of attempts to settle them by parliamentary legislation.

Public consciousness about the extent of racial discrimination gradually widened to include other categories of perceived injustice, so that the rights of women, children, the disabled, and the aged became subjects of public discussion and eventually, in some cases, legislation. These events were the precursors of the current debate on 'political correctness.'

The relatively affluent 'consumer society', liberated from war-time austerity, was now offered a vast range of commodities, services, and leisure activities from which to choose, while choices became increasingly difficult, owing to the growing sophistication of the advertising media.

Television, more influential than film and radio, and combining elements of both, was rapidly establishing itself as a new agency of socialisation, partly reinforcing, partly challenging, the traditional agencies of family, school and peer group.

The spectacular development of transport and communications brought greater mobility and, with it, new motorways, atmospheric pollution, and an increase in the pace of everyday living.

The greater openness of society which evolved after the war encouraged a proliferation of sub-cultures and alternative life-styles. Some of these were a source of cultural enrichment; others were less so. Either way, their combined effect was to measurably weaken the influence of the central value system, and to give pluralism a solid foundation in the realm of ideas. This in turn reacted adversely upon family life, where parental roles were already the subject of uncertainty because of changing theories of child-rearing.

125

Ahead of her Time

Medical science and the health and welfare services were well advanced in the process of creating a healthier population in Britain. But, paradoxically, the same drug therapy that benefited the sick and the disabled was to generate the socio-pathological manifestations of drug abuse and addiction.

Finally, the exponential growth of knowledge and its contingent obsolescence appeared to cast doubt on the conventional assumptions regarding the aims of education. If present facts were to be rendered obsolete in a few years by the appearance of new knowledge, most of the existing school curriculum would become an irrelevant anachronism. This suggested the curriculum should be more future-oriented and that priority should be given to learning how to adapt to rapid changes in knowledge - in effect 'learning how to learn' - something in which K.A.S. pupils could be said to have a head start.

The 1960s, characterised in the press as 'swinging' and 'permissive', were perceived by many people as symbolising an advance in the democratic process towards a more egalitarian and caring society. Nikki was as caught up in the excitement about this prospect as anyone else. What gave her pause for reflection, however, and consequently a certain unease, were the prevailing sense of euphoria, the flight from reality, and the potentially destabilising trends towards excessive novelty, over-stimulation and anomic stress.

It was a decade in which youth and youthfulness were celebrated to an exaggerated degree. A new breed of teenagers appeared to think they had invented sexuality, whilst some their elders appeared by their behaviour to be seeking an adolescence they felt they had been denied. Militant trade unions and newly politicised student unions were taking to the streets, challenging the government and the forces of law and order. The social system was overheating and threatening to run out of control. It was a situation which called for a clear and objective appraisal of the future role of the school in relation to the profound changes taking place in society.

'My own feeling at that time,' Nikki recalled years later, 'was that we had to assess what these new freedoms would do to and for education, and what they would do to and for our children. We were not there to reform society, nor were we the agents of revolutionary change. Our traditional role was to stand out against extremism at both ends of the political spectrum, not in the sense of compromise, but as an expression of independence of judgment. Children had to live in the world as it was going to be, and be prepared for it, but not sent into it either with blind acceptance or with an attitude of total rejection of what was happening. It was all to do with respect for children as individuals and enabling them to develop faith in their own judgment; and this was what we tried to do'.

Whilst her appointment in 1959 as Deputy Head had been approved unanimously by the Council, it was clear that the same degree of unanimity was not represented amongst members of staff. The factional disputes over the succession to Mrs Barber had, of course, not been resolved by Council's decision to appoint a candidate from outside the school. The long and bitter conflict of the last two years had prompted a representative group of parents to express grave concern about the strained relationships at K.A.S., urging Council to make the greatest possible efforts 'to solve the problems that were strangling the school.' They went on to say that, as a result, academic performance had suffered, and both morale and standards of discipline had deteriorated.

This was the state of affairs presented to Nikki by the Chairman of Council, together with an earnest appeal to join with the Headmaster in attempting to remedy the situation. It was a daunting task, and one that was not going to be resolved overnight. Whilst appreciating that one of the first tasks before her was to develop good personal relationships with all members of the school community, she saw that, in the circumstances, relations with staff should be her first priority.

An intimation of what she might be up against in the early stages was suggested by a Job's comforter who told her that one of the teaching staff had objected to 'the appointment of this middle-class female' - a curious argument to hear in an unequivocally middle-class progressive school, even if some of its members did represent the political Left.

That some members of staff would harbour resentment at the frustration of their own plans for the succession was inevitable, but they could not, in all conscience, focus this on Nikki. Thus it was that with time, patience and goodwill, she was able eventually to develop co-operative relations with most if not all of the staff, based on genuine liking and mutual respect.

There were few such problems with the pupils. They were accustomed to informal relations with teachers and, finding that she in no way disappointed their expectations, but that on the contrary she was a friendly and sympathetic person, the majority accepted her into the K.A.S. family with a readiness not evinced by some of their elders.

She made early contacts with the parents on Council, and those who daily brought and collected their children or who had business in the school; but first encounters with other parents had to wait for the periodic gatherings like parent-staff meetings, open days, or the annual general meeting.

The parent body, as might be expected from the school's situation in London, and particularly in Hampstead, included a relatively high proportion of parents in business and professional occupations, together with an unusually large number working in the arts, entertainment and the communications media. In all these categories there were those who had achieved eminence, but it was self-evidently those employed in the arts and the media whose celebrity was known to the public at large, and many of these were household names. It was an unique body of parents, gifted, creative and successful, united by a common interest in the education of their children and in the particular form of education offered by King Alfred School.

Moreover, they exercised a number of positive functions in relation to the school, providing children with occupational role models, and influencing others to send their children to the school. While not the least of their functions was, as it had been for their predecessors, the contribution of their time, effort, and special abilities towards the preservation and development of the school, whether in the form of practical work or of the perennial activity of fund-raising. It was not, after all, every school that could call upon Albert Finney to play auctioneer at an Open Day, Erich Gruenberg, Emanuel Hurwitz or Humphrey Lyttelton to give performances of their music, or Alan Bates to take part in an end-of-term revue, but all these events at various times took place with resultant benefit to school funds.

Nor did every independent school have the good fortune to number amongst its parents a few wealthy philanthropists, the generosity of whose financial donations contributed so much to the modernisation of the school; or exceptional parent-Treasurers like Gerd Weiss, Teddy Epstein, and Bernard Igra, without whose foresight and prudent management the school might not have survived.

Nikki's gradual initiation into the ways of the school was by no means a leisurely process. Any desire she may have had of maintaining a low profile during the first few weeks, observing, listening and learning, had to be accommodated to an intensive schedule of administration and teaching.

To one with recent experience of grammar school organisation and office procedure the laissez-faire attitude at K.A.S. to staff accommodation, domestic arrangements, and the basic principles of bureaucratic organisation, came as something of a shock. She wondered momentarily whether this attitude was a tacit expression of the culture of the school, but dismissed the idea and resolved that it was something she would have to deal with in due course. In the event, her first impression proved to be not so far from the truth.

The problem with the staff room was, aside from its acute discomfort, the virtual impossibility of having any discussion without constant interruptions by children coming to the door and (though not supposed to) into the room, to speak to members of staff. The door was never closed for more than a few moments, even in the coldest weather, and the struggle was soon given up as it became too much of a nuisance to keep closing it. Some of the staff seemed to be troubled by an access of conscience if it was suggested that the room might be made more comfortable, or that the children might be kept out. There were, after all, other and better opportunities for them to communicate with their teachers. There appeared to be an unspoken assumption that the staff should be available at any and every moment, apart from actual lessons, and at no time separated from the children.

10 Conservation and Change: The perennial problem

Nikki remembers being told in the hushed tones of one who admires but can never emulate, that one ex-member of staff was entirely against having a staff room at all, as it was incompatible with the family atmosphere of the school. 'This seemed to me to be based on a very muddled misconception, and I was sure our happy feeling that children wanted us all the time was an unjustifiable conceit. But the serious aspect of the supposed dilemma was the loss of opportunities for valuable informal discussion about individual children and their problems, and the occasional clarification of basic educational principles.'

One day she decided to investigate the regular complaints of the Lower School staff about the standards of cleaning in the classrooms. In order to be able to speak with authority, she visited the nursery and, after clearing up and tidying things away, she cleaned the floor with wax and an applicator, and then, much to the amusement of the members of staff who were present, timed the whole operation. She found that less than half the time had been spent in actual cleaning, and more than half clearing up untidy equipment, hanging clothes on pegs, and putting belongings away - the job for which the teacher, not the cleaner, was responsible. What sounds like a classic example of the new broom was far from being the case. The whole affair was conducted as a light-hearted time and motion study, amidst gales of laughter; the cleaning problem was resolved and there were fewer complaints in the future..

Another domestic issue was the question of the cloakrooms. Open to wind and rain, these were a constant source of annoyance and frustration, as clothes were left all over the floors, and no-one took any responsibility for their own or other people's property. Conceding that this sort of behaviour came only too naturally to children, she nevertheless felt that indulging their irresponsibility by doing nothing was in fact an abdication of the teacher's own responsibility. Putting senior pupils in charge of the cloakrooms - a normal practice in other schools - was amongst the taboos at K.A.S.; the staff had not the time (and some did not approve of doing it anyway), with the result that supervision went by default.

When she first arrived at K.A.S. Nikki was given for her own use a small room in the office complex. This was known as the Visitors' Room and, while not frequently used for its stated purpose, was liable to be used by other people at various times. She included a description of the room in a letter written to Geneviève in Paris in the summer of 1959: 'The room has a chair, a rickety table, and is full of cardboard boxes bursting with papers. There are a number of musical instruments including two large drums and a double bass. I have decided that anything larger than 6 feet tall has to have a name, so I am calling the 'cello 'George'. The other day the Secretary and the Head complained that so many people were using the room that it was impossible for them to have a private conversation (the Secretary's room and mine have a common ceiling and only cardboard over the corridor which divides them). I pointed out gently that I had merely accepted the conditions presented to me, and that I personally would be very glad to have the room to myself. A fiat has gone forth; my name is to be put on the door, and it is now my own room.'

Shortly afterwards, the boxes and the musical instruments were removed elsewhere, 'George' being the last to go, because of the difficulty of finding secure accommodation. Next to Mr Montgomery ('Monty') the most influential member of the staff was Miss Else Hibburd (known to everyone as 'Hibby')), who had been at the school since 1920, first as a mathematics teacher and, from 1927, as administrative secretary. With a longer association than anyone in its history, she had understandably something of a proprietorial interest in K.A.S. She it was who, with Violet Hyett, had bought Flint Hall Farm in Royston and had it converted with such labour into a wartime home for the school. It was largely her skill and dedication in the day to day use, investment, and distribution of the school's money, under the supervision of the Honorary Treasurer, that had kept K.A.S. afloat both during the war and later through the difficult years following its return to London.

It in no way detracts from her achievement to say that, by 1959, within less than three years from her retirement, the years of struggle had left their impress on Hibby, albeit not indelibly. If she found adaptation to change more difficult than before, it was not that she was incapable of changing, but she did so more slowly. Careful financial management and consolidation, saving by every means possible, had for her become habits of thought, persisting long after the need for stringent economies had passed.

The implications of Hibby's policy for the development and efficiency of the school became cumulatively more apparent to Nikki during her first few months at Manor Wood. The purpose-built library suffered from the lack of money and still largely consisted of discards from parents and a very small number of books purchased for special subject areas. Most were second-hand and some, particularly in the sciences, obsolescent or otherwise of doubtful value to pupils. When Nikki suggested the introduction of an annual book-purchasing allowance it was greeted with alarm by Hibby, but, fortunately, both the Head and Treasurer were in favour of the idea and she was induced to give her approval.

Members of the teaching staff were expected to supply their own teaching material, and some of them, particularly those teaching in the Lower School, had had specific training and were therefore capable of producing a wide and imaginative range of teaching aids. By no means all the Middle and Upper School staff enjoyed this advantage, so that their products were of uneven quality and effectiveness. As the paper and paint supplied for these purposes were strictly rationed and of the poorest quality, teaching methods lost something of the stimulus they might otherwise have had.

Another form of economy, which had its origin in the financially-perilous years of the school's history, was the individualised negotiation of staff salaries. Whilst Nikki fully appreciated Hibby's selfless devotion to the survival of K.A.S., she was unhappy about methods which she felt the current situation no longer justified.

'She put a certain degree of moral pressure on some of the staff to persuade them the privilege of working at K.A.S. was really quite enough to compensate them for a salary which was less than the Burnham level to which they would be entitled elsewhere. In certain cases the person concerned was of independent means, and she induced more than one of these to give their services without remuneration. Usually this was in the case of part-timers whom it suited to act as patrons of the school in this way, and there was clearly no objection to this, provided they were academically qualified and up-to-date in the subjects required.

'As the Council had recently decided that it was in a sufficiently stable position to offer its staff Burnham salaries, albeit at a basic level in most cases, I took the view that we should use this to ensure, when appointing staff, that we had the best available choice, and I was concerned lest an applicant with the right qualifications and experience might be rejected in favour of a less suitable teacher purely on the grounds of cost. I believed strongly and made no secret of my conviction that the strength of any school lies not in its impressive buildings, shiny floors, or expensive equipment, but in the quality of its staff.

'Another device which Hibby employed was to delay the payment of staff salaries until she felt that the balance in the bank was good enough to permit the outlay. I challenged this on the grounds that, if she was obtaining interest on what was not her money, this was every bit as bad as usury - a practice to which she had the strongest moral objections. But, to do her justice, I must also add that, in more than one case I knew of, she herself lent money without security, and entirely interest-free, in cases which she felt deserved help, and never told anyone what she had done. We agreed to differ on principle, but I insisted that staff salaries must in future be paid on time, unless we were absolutely bankrupt.

'It seemed to me that her almost obsessive loyalty to the school prevented her from realising that what amounted to unfair treatment of staff, most of whom were considerably less well off than the majority of the parents, was against the very principles for which the school was supposed to stand.

'On the lighter side, as a person trained in office procedure by three years under a most efficient woman boss, I was appalled by her filing system, which consisted of bundles of paper tied with salvaged string, which were piled on open shelves and gathering dust year after year. This was a battle I never won, and dear Hibby was still accumulating bundles until the day she retired. I knew when to give up. My real respect and admiration for her quality as a person overcame my exasperation with her foibles, provided I got my own way when it really mattered.'

When applying for the post at K.A.S. Nikki had been struck by the fact that no matter when one rang up there was always an inordinately long wait before it was possible to speak to anyone except Miss Hibburd, who never gave her name unless directly asked. On visiting the school for her interview, she still had not discovered the reason for this, but when she arrived to take up her job she could hardly believe the procedure that attended the process, and had done so for years. There was only one telephone and this, of course, was in the Secretary's office. If a caller wished to speak to the Head, Hibby would do her best to persuade him/her to leave a message and only if she failed would she say curtly "wait", and, putting the telephone down, go to her cupboard and take out her coat. She would then leave the office and walk up the slope to the next building where Monty's room was situated on the first floor behind the library. He would then put on his coat and scarf and return with her to the office where, if the caller had not by then rung off, he would take the call. Nikki watched this repeated over a period of time with growing amazement, and finally asked him whether he would not prefer to have a switchboard and his own extension. He admitted that it had often occurred to him that it would be more convenient but, as Hibby felt it to be an unjustified extravagance, he had not pressed the point.

Nikki suspected that one of Hibby's motives was to ensure that nothing happened in the school without her knowledge, and found later that she managed by various strategies of a similar kind to circumvent decisions of which she disapproved. 'The school's interests were her overriding concern, and I never doubted the genuine impulse which underlay her decisions. On the other hand, I felt that education in general and administration in particular should be based less on personal power and more on the overt use of reason between responsible people, and time after time I challenged her on these grounds. It took a month to get her agreement in principle, but another four months before the switchboard and extensions were finally installed.'

Dress was optional at K.A.S. as a matter of principle. The voluntary green uniform of the pre-war years fell out of use with the seniors after the war, but retained its popularity with the younger children and their parents until well into the sixties. When jeans swept the market, they quickly became, and have remained ever since, the unofficial uniform of the vast majority of children. Amongst the staff, a few of the women tried to follow the fashion, but the nature of the grounds and the fact that, for most of the year, there was almost as much mud on the classroom floors as outside, owing to the lack of proper paths, meant that skirts, sweaters and strong shoes proved to be the most sensible wear. Men opted for the casual and informal or the semi-formal, aware that clothing had to be capable of withstanding the wear and tear of daily life in the classroom.

10 Conservation and Change: The perennial problem

Nikki had always had a keen interest in dress. She gave it the same careful and thoughtful attention as any other expressive activity in which her creative imagination was involved.

Fully aware of the practical implications of her choice of clothes, she took into account the fact that, as deputy head, she had to meet parents, prospective parents, official visitors and members of the public of various kinds. For this reason her dress was semi-formal, functional, and elegant, whilst her grooming was impeccable. She considered that taking the trouble to be well turned out was in the interests of the school and good for public relations, which indeed it was, as many people were later to testify. One such person was Margaret Maxwell, senior mistress and second generation old Alfredian, who said that her stylish and well-groomed appearance, quite apart from her personal qualities, was one of the aspects that built the school 'into a professional-appearing place, rather than a progressive one in the outré sense.'

Nikki quickly became aware that her view of suitable clothes was not shared by some of the staff, who held that all attention to dress betrayed a non-progressive absorption with personal vanity. 'The lingering puritanism', she remarked, 'which had been present from the first days of the school's existence, was still active. The only day in the year on which conscious dressing-up was not frowned upon was Open Day in the summer term, when even the 'boots and bombazine brigade' sported hats'. Among the more important recollections of her first year was the favourable impression she formed of the school's academic performance. This she was surprised to find was of a remarkably high standard, particularly in view of a non-selective entry and the fact that, as a result of this, less than a third of the children would have been eligible for grammar school education had they been in the state system. Examination results were well above the national average, and this she attributed to the efficiency of the teaching methods and the individual attention given to each child which a low staff-pupil ratio made feasible. It was possible for the same reason to operate a less cautious policy than other schools on entering pupils for examinations. No-one was ever prevented from taking a subject in the General Certificate of Education if he/she seriously wanted to do so, and, although sometimes a reduction in the number of subjects was recommended, this was never done arbitrarily. In an extreme case, a pupil who had taken six subjects in the G.C.E. 'O' Level in the summer of 1959 and failed five of them had nevertheless worked extremely hard and refused to be discouraged. It brought down the school's average, but the boy had done what he wanted to do, and it had finally convinced him and his parents that he was not suited to an academic career. At Wallington and other grammar schools, Nikki reflected, the reverse of such a policy would have prevailed, on the principle that failure often discourages further effort and can induce in the learner the formation of a negative self-image.

Ahead of her Time

At K.A.S., on the other hand, it was claimed that, because no-one was considered any less worthy as a person by reason of failing, negative reactions to failure seldom ensued, and the examination was perceived in a more positive light as merely a useful diagnostic instrument.

She reserved judgment on the validity of this claim because of the hypothetical or, at best, anecdotal nature of the evidence. She was too familiar with the widespread and exaggerated veneration of the IQ as the 'measure of the man' both in education and society at large; too aware of the attitudes of many teachers towards children in the low streams of schools, not to be sceptical about the supposed insulation of K.A.S. children from the negative meaning of failure. As she saw it, some children lost confidence as a result of failure; others found in it the motivation to succeed. Such individual differences were not reducible to general solutions, and this was why knowledge of each individual pupil was so essential if the right decisions were to be reached.

Another aspect of the academic performance of the school was the standard of teaching. This, doubtless as a reflection of the selection procedure, showed an unusual degree of variation, and the level of competence ranged from the inspired and highly professional to the relatively mediocre.

Of one master she wrote to a friend: 'He makes no attempt to keep his classes quiet because he does not want to be unpopular. So others are disturbed. In spite of his ability, he can't see that all it leads to is loss of respect for the subject and chaos in the classroom. There is little sign of preparation or organisation of the work. He tells me that he considers his value as a teacher is enhanced by the fact that teaching is only one of his many interests, and not a 'trained set of tricks'. If he were an effective teacher with some real self-discipline , I would agree that other interests are a decided advantage, but teaching must come first. All this has produced an irresponsible outlook in his classes, and their room, which has to be shared with others, is left in a mess. I refused to teach in it yesterday until it was cleaned and tidied up, and the noisome experiment which had been left in one of the cupboards was removed to the laboratory.'

This was the first instance of a problem that became familiar to her in subsequent years - the teacher with unresolved and woolly ideas about the theory and practice of progressive education or, worse still, with woolly ideas about which she/he was prepared to be inflexible and dogmatic.

The arts, which had always, on principle, been accorded equal status with academic subjects were in temporary decline. This had started a few years before in the unsettled period following the departure of Hetty Barber. There was practically no music in the school apart from recorder classes and the activities of the constant and dedicated few invariably to be found at any time in K.A.S. history in choir and orchestra. A notable exception was drama which, following its successful revival after the war, had enhanced its reputation with a series of excellent productions under the direction of Mrs Renée Soskin. Nikki herself, together with one of the parents - the actor David Kossoff - adjudicated a K.A.S. Drama Festival during this period. For the rest, music classes had become scenes of trouble-making and disruption, with disorderly children being excluded, as a regular occurrence. Staff in the Lower School, who had been less involved than those in other departments in the disturbing events of the last two years, felt that they were to some extent cut off from the rest of the school, and that no-one was interested in the work they were doing. Nikki re-established contact and arranged a programme of regular meetings with them, including weekly visits during the lunch hour.

At the end of her first year she was left with a sense of something accomplished but twice as much still to be done. This was to be a characteristic refrain of every subsequent year she spent at the school. It had also seen the initiation of a critique of the theory and practice of progressive education which she was to develop during her years at K.A.S. into an informal action-research programme. This served to promote a periodic revaluation of the aims, objectives and performance of the school in the context of a rapidly-changing social environment.

It would be difficult to exaggerate the private dismay and disillusionment she had suffered in the first term. Dismay because of the cool reception she had received from many of the staff, ranging from veiled resentment to reserved neutrality; disillusion because of her expectations of a school ostensibly dedicated to progressive ideals, priding itself on a caring and familial self-image. What had most sustained her will to carry on in the early stages were the children, the governors, and several members of staff and parents who had made her feel welcome in the school from the first. However, the suspicion and reserve with which she had at first been received gradually diminished and people accepted her for herself instead of treating her like an unwelcome stranger.

'There have already been noticeable changes in the school', she wrote to Geneviève, 'but I am sometimes daunted by the thought of all there is to do. One most encouraging thing is the changed atmosphere in the staff room, which is far nicer, more 'intelligent' and friendly than it had been for years, according to some of my colleagues. I am still waiting for my new desk and then I shall be able to make a real improvement to my room. I have curtains now at both windows, a nice cupboard from home, and I want to bring an armchair for visitors, and a small carpet, but I can't afford it yet.'

This suggestion of continued austerity at King Alfred School prompted Geneviève to ask: 'Do your puritan, cheerless cold rooms uplift the children's souls or do they merely make them feel uncomfortable? There is one place in Paris where I teach, namely the College Sévigné, which is - due to the lack of money - the most cheerless, ugly and drab, though not cold, school I know, and I also know that I would on no account send a child there. You can have a mind attuned (?) to beauty, capable of seeing it, loving it, creating it, only if you let it grow amidst beauty, and not in porridge, oatmeal, rust and brown ugliness. You might lecture your Parents' Association on that. After all, Ruskin and William Morris were English.' To which Nikki replied some weeks later: 'As regards the puritan aspect of our school, no, it does not improve the children or their minds. I am trying my best to make changes in the whole aspect of the school, but I don't know whether I shall get anywhere, as so many people appear to be very set in their ways.'

An official announcement was made in March, 1960, that, in view of the approaching retirement of Mr Montgomery and Miss Hibburd, the deputy head, Mrs Paul-Jones, was to be appointed headmistress from the beginning of the summer term, thereby reviving the dual headship and ensuring continuity in the administration.

There followed two years of consolidation during which the school recovered its equilibrium and saw the kind of comprehensive progress which becomes possible when forces are united and not pulling in different directions.

Pupil numbers grew to nearly three hundred - a figure which owed more to a spectacular increase in the size of the Sixth Form than to any other cause. Competition for university places in general had become more intense and examination qualifications at GCE Advanced Level were now required for an increasing number of careers. These pressures revived the historic dilemma of K.A.S. - the threat of an unbalanced curriculum disproportionately weighted in favour of academic at the expense of non-academic subjects. The Open Room System came in for prolonged discussion, the outcome of which was a reaffirmation of its value in self-directed study and the resolution to preserve it by means of well-co-ordinated organisation.

Nikki's transition from deputy to joint headship had been facilitated by Monty's encouragement and understanding, and the steady progress towards the restoration of unity owed much to their successful collaboration during his last two years at the school. 'Co-headship is a curious relationship', she wrote to a friend at this time, 'and it requires a great deal of give-and-take on both sides, but I have never experienced any real difficulties during the past two years, and I very much hope that things will go on as pleasantly from that point of view as they have done up to now'.

Monty and Hibby officially retired at the end of the summer term 1962, marking thereby the end of an era. It had been arranged that Hibby should continue to come in several times a week, for as long as necessary, to conduct a thorough handover to her successor.

At the Open Day in July the Chairman expressed the gratitude and appreciation of children, staff and parents for their many years of work at the school. Tribute was paid to the enormous contribution each of them had made to the advancement of the school in accordance with the ideals of its founders and especially to its restoration and development after the war.

On the same occasion it was announced that Alan Humphries, a senior master at Frensham Heights, an independent progressive school, had been appointed as Nikki's co-head in the autumn term, and that Mrs Margaret Bassett was to replace Hibby as secretary to the Society. The appointment of Alan Humphries created another of those 'incestuous links' by which Ron Brooks so memorably suggests the schools maintain 'the purity of their progressive pedigree'.[24]

'Monty is leaving at the end of this term' Nikki wrote to Geneviève, 'and we are to have a new co-head from a school very much like our own. I think he will be good, and I like what I have seen of him very much.

'Did I tell you that I have redecorated my room at the school? It is terracotta on three walls and white on the fourth; white paint everywhere and new modern curtains, with broken bars of yellow, coffee, light and dark, black, white and the same terracotta. I have Chinese rush matting on the floor, two modern basket arm chairs, a new lampshade in white, and a new glass-fronted bookcase in waxed mahogany to match my desk. There are cushions in black and also lilac, which may sound odd but looks lovely. I keep flowers in the room and people come and sit and talk to me now because the room looks so inviting. I know it has taken three years to do it but it would have been impossible when I first came here, so I didn't hurry it. I got the staff room done first and then attended to my own, and I shall now do one or two other rooms.'

The changes to which she referred were not only of a physical kind, as was attested by Denise Gibbs, later Head of Middle School, who said Nikki had changed the whole quality of relationships in the staff room, which became more open and relaxed, bringing laughter to a place where it had formerly been a surprisingly rare commodity.

The new co-headship got off to a good start.[25] She found Alan Humphries to be a very able and energetic man whose ideas on education marched with her own. He was lively and constructive in his approach, as well as agreeable to work with, and she felt that together they ought to be able to sweep away some of the cobwebs that had accumulated during the last twenty years. She sensed that he was apprehensive at the notion of shared power and the lack of final authority; indeed he had told her that in principle he disapproved of the system of co-headship, but at the same time fully acknowledged that in the present instance it was working very well. In 1966 Nikki wrote a paper for the information of Council and parents entitled The Functions of the Heads in which she included a rationale of co-headship, extending some original ideas of the child psychologist, D.W. Winnicott. In this she emphasised the function of the school as an analogue

---

[24] Brooks R. King Alfred School and the Progressive Movement (1898 - 1998). University of Wales Press. 1998.

[25] Child, H.A.T.(Ed.) The Independent Progressive School (includes contributions by Nikki Archer and Alan Humphries).

of the family in providing 'the circle of love and strength' which a child needs as a stable framework if s/he is to learn what it is to feel free and at the same time secure. 'Among the adults in the school', she went on, 'the women staff represent - particularly for the younger child - the feminine principle which is so important to his/her whole pattern of future relationships with both men and women, and which is met with first through the mother. The male staff represent the stability, through strength and protectiveness, which the father provides in the home. The heads, each in loco parentis, represent the complementary relationship of men and women which should, but unfortunately often does not, exist in society as a whole. The woman has a particular value in her quasi-maternal relationship to the boys and the man in his 'paternal' relationship to the girls, in addition to the particular sympathy and understanding which each can show for the younger members of their own sex.

'The Heads in addition must stand, when the occasion demands it, for the external control which children need. When the unconscious conflict between impulsive behaviour and the wish to control themselves becomes too strong to be borne, anti-social behaviour acts as a kind of danger signal. It is then that the authority of the Heads must function. It must not function punitively, but with certainty and understanding.'

Both Heads were sensible of the problems inherent in a joint headship. These had been mentioned but not made specific in the Montgomery/Hibburd history of the school, where it was noted that 'In the frank and free atmosphere of King Alfred School the advantages of this innovation have outweighed the disadvantages'.

How the co-heads in 1933-1945 and 1949-1957 interpreted their mutual roles in the historical context of those times is matter for speculation; but it is certain that in the egalitarian climate of the 1960s the complementary relationship between Nikki and Alan Humphries called for exceptional sensitivity on both their parts. The ambivalence in society about women in authority was reflected to some extent in the school itself, despite the Alfredian ethos, and not all its members, either parents or staff, could quite reconcile themselves to changes in authority relations.

Nikki recalled the occasion when a parent rang the school, asking to speak to the Head. It was on a matter which either she or Alan could have dealt with equally well. He was told that Mr Humphries was not in but that he could speak to Mrs Archer. 'No', the caller replied, 'I'll ring again tomorrow when the Head is there'. She was amused rather than irritated by this, for, being little concerned with the pursuit of personal power, she accepted the incident as symptomatic of all social reform, namely that it is usually prolonged and invariably conducted against considerable resistance. She considered the attitude of this parent far less important - since it concerned only herself - than that of those parents who still thought it right to promote their sons' education at the expense of their daughters' education.

10 Conservation and Change: The perennial problem

As her convent education in the thirties had been directed by staff who maintained that women could and should perform any job of which they felt themselves capable, she was horrified by such attitudes in the seventies.

She was, however, not prepared to waste effort on matters over which she could exercise no direct influence, and reserved her energies for the primary task of collaboration with her co-head in tackling the problems that lay ahead. In a decade marked by the escalation of sexual politics co-headship called for the adoption of new and more sensitive attitudes towards joint leadership and shared authority. It was by dint of imagination, tact, regular consultation, and consideration of each other's interests that Nikki and Alan Humphries achieved a harmonious and effective working partnership, against all those residual social forces calculated to make it otherwise.

Tension between conservation and change has been a constant feature in the history of King Alfred School, and examples of this have appeared at several points in the foregoing text. This tension has principally arisen where changes have been apprehended by some members of the school community as a departure from the school's original ethos. Periodic reviews of progress in relation to the founders' principles have therefore been a regular occurrence in the life of the school. However, the social conditions arising from the accelerating pace of change in the 1960s confronted Council, Heads and staff with a rapid succession of additional educational and philosophical problems, some of them entirely new and others old and familiar, yet under new aspects, calling for reappraisal in the light of altered circumstances.

11 Democracy and Education

The developing critique in Europe and North America of the actual as distinct from the notional progress of democracy was gathering momentum during this period. Discussion of concepts such as equality of opportunity, human rights, freedom and authority had entered the public arena and was no longer regarded as the sole prerogative of academics and politicians.

Like other progressive schools, King Alfred was in an unusual position with respect to this public debate, as they had all since their inception represented an implicit embodiment of the democratic principle.

For KAS it was a problem of relativism and situational ethics: had the school been relatively less democratic in the past? Was it today a model of democracy for other schools to emulate? Or did it fall short of some supposed ideal of the democratic process? In any case, how far in practice can democracy go in any school if it is to carry out its prescribed functions?

The school had certainly become a more democratic organisation in the years following the Second World War. There was a wider distribution and sharing of power, including more effective procedures for consultation and transmission of information, and these changes involved the whole school community. There was no room for complacency, however, for there were those who argued in favour of more democratisation and their claims had to be addressed.

If discussion was to be anything more than assertion and counter-assertion and the exchange of what R.S. Peters[26] calls 'catchwords in the ideology of democracy', certain basic principles had to be established.

First, popular rule in small face-to-face communities, as typified by some of the ancient city states, was necessarily superseded in modern societies by representative government. By the same token, self-government in a boarding school of some fifty pupils like that of A.S.Neill's Summerhill cannot be realised in a day school numbering several hundred. Few, if any, schools can properly be described as democratic institutions in any absolute sense. Even Neill believed that democracy was impossible unless it was 'dictated' and that 'it had to be fought for' under the guidance of a benign dictatorship.

Second, the head, according to Peters, is appointed to organise a community of mainly immature people and has to decide how far authority can be delegated. Any consideration of the limits of school democracy must, therefore, be prefaced by a realistic appraisal of the formal position and responsibilities of the head. Failure to do this can lead to cynicism and disillusionment if what is thought to be a democratic process is perceived to be more apparent than real. It is thus essential that the limits be clearly defined and understood, taking into account the role of the head, the

---

[26] Peters, R.S., Ethics and Education (Chapter 11). Allen & Unwin, 1970

school's aims and objectives, and the legal framework by which it is bound.

Participation by pupils in the management of the school dates back to 1902, when John Russell introduced a 'School Parliament', with equal voting rights for boys and girls, long before the advent of women's suffrage. His successor, Joseph Wickstead, created an Advisory Council, elected by the Upper School, with legislative, executive and judicial powers (subject to the head's veto) to deal with all matters of common interest, excepting the curriculum and the teacher's sphere in the classroom.

The School (pupils) Council of the 1960's was composed of members of staff, together with pupils elected as form representatives from the Upper and Middle Schools. Only during the period of Russell's headship was the school (like Summerhill) small enough to allow the direct participation of all the children. In both of the latter cases the growth in the number of pupils had made representation unavoidable. The constant factor in all three stages was the constitutional provision of the head's veto, the inevitable corollary of the responsibility with which he/she was invested.

Children at KAS were able to vote on matters within their sphere of competence, but these were self-evidently more restricted in scope than was the case in the boarding progressive schools. In consequence their participation in school management was minimally executive and almost entirely limited to advice and consultation.

In Nikki's view the actual limitation of their powers and the reasons for this should be clearly explained to the pupils. To do otherwise would be morally indefensible, pretending the existence of a power that had no basis in reality.

By 1969 a sequence of events had combined to produce a change in the climate of student politics at King Alfred School. Following parliamentary legislation arising from the recommendations of the Latey Report.[27] The age of majority had been reduced to eighteen. The ensuing change in the legal status of senior pupils made little difference at first because members of staff had adapted to the maturation of 6th formers, and had long since ceased to regard or treat them as young children.

Universities and polytechnics had barely recovered from the tempestuous events of 1968, when students in the capital cities of Britain and Europe staged mass protests, occupied campuses and threw down the gauntlet to authority.

A radicalised National Union of Students had promoted the formation of a junior wing, or affiliated union, of school pupils - the National Union of School Students (NUSS). Not surprisingly, the latter organisation soon succeeded in recruiting some of the senior pupils at KAS, and it was as a result of their activities that a new and in a sense alien confrontational aspect entered into the relations between the pupils' Council and the Heads. The irony of the situation lay in the fact that the school had from its

---

[27] The Latey Report - The Age of Majority - HMSO 1967

inception always enjoyed most of the more sensible rights contained in the NUSS Charter. Consequently, the petition presented to the School Council contained a number of demands of an extreme nature which could not be accepted. The Heads conceded, however, that 6th formers, subject to parental consent, need not henceforth be in school except for timetabled lessons.

It was later, in the 1970s, that a senior boy interested in political action, with a small influential backing among fellow pupils, tried by unconstitutional means to bring in an alternative school constitution. It had clearly been influenced by what was thought to be the theory and practice of A S Neill, but was at the same time quite adamant about what was pupils' business and what was not. The draft constitution was comprehensively flawed, and infringed the rights and responsibilities of Head and staff in such a way as to flout all staff authority, leaving final decisions with the pupils' Council. Nikki and the staff sought some response that would avoid humiliating the leader but in the event she had no alternative but to veto the proposed constitution. The whole affair was concluded by a letter from the Chairman of the KAS Council to the School Council stating that they could not dictate policy over such matters as discipline without nullifying the basic conditions necessary for the conduct of the school.

Some years later Nikki was to tell a Times' correspondent, 'The pupils' Council had won all the main arguments many years ago. There is only a small area left where they can make decisions. But it's a very good way of introducing young people to the democratic process. Although they should be listened to with respect and given explanations if something is not possible, lack of experience inevitably limits their ability to be able to make decisions about the future.'

'Despite the genuine openness of the forum, there were always complaints about the lack of democracy and the dictatorial behaviour of the Heads and staff. We suffered occasionally from visiting journalists, educational authors and other experts who were certain that secret censorship of a sinister and hypocritical kind was being exercised by the adults in defence of their own position. One of these engaged in conversation with one of the middle school groups who were indignant at having been outvoted in council by peers who disagreed with their argument. Finding a receptive, not to say gullible outsider willing to listen to their story, they filled him with some interesting 'facts' about the repression of true democratic opinion in the school. Without checking with anyone, this expert swallowed the story whole and went happily away. The indignation of children's council and staff when the book came out was both real and heart warming, but the author was not easily forgiven.' [28]

It was considered important that democracy should be manifested in the

---

[28] Skidelsky, R. English Progressive Schools, Penguin 1969

everyday life of the school - experienced as a reality - and not merely talked about in the abstract. The discussion of moral issues, whether in the pupils' council or in appropriate classroom situations, often centred on concrete events arising from the daily life of the community.

Whilst teachers were, by definition, in authority, their relationships with the children were informal and non-authoritarian. The practice had grown up soon after the war for teachers and pupils to be on first name terms, with the result that children tended to regard their teachers as friendly, supportive adults, more experienced and knowledgeable than themselves, concerned for their welfare and the facilitation of the learning process. This was conducive to the creation of a learning environment free from the negative distractions of fear and anxiety so often found in more conventional schools.[29]

It is a truism that democracy has to be worked at and depends for its survival on constant vigilance. This was well illustrated in 1967 in connection with the organisation of school meals. Some members of staff had recently taken to sitting on their own at a separate table, and not, as was the usual practice, with the children. This had developed innocently enough because the number of teachers taking school meals had risen to a figure exceeding that required for the supervision of individual tables. The matter was raised at the next KASS Council Meeting and, after discussion, the principle of non-segregation at meals was unanimously confirmed and democracy was subsequently restored to the dining hall.

Another traditional principle was put to the test at about this time, when a new member of staff rebuked a child for some misdemeanour in a manner so excessively scathing and contemptuous that the astonished victim reported the matter to his parents. The latter, in turn, complained to the Heads, representing the teacher's behaviour as a violation of both the rights of their son and of the progressive ethic of 'being on the side of the child'. The teacher concerned had come straight from an autocratic state school and, in spite of an initial briefing, clearly had a great deal to learn about the democratic ethos of KAS and its implication for the relationship between teachers and pupils.

Some social commentators during this period deplored an increasing selfishness in public behaviour and complained that everyone was obsessed with rights but apparently little concerned with responsibilities. And, with a narrower focus, there were those who criticised the progressive schools for their preoccupation with freedom and individuality, considering such goals as conducive to egotism and self-indulgence, Nikki felt that such criticism was based on a misconception and was always at pains to correct it whenever the occasion arose. In her view, individualism, like non-conformity, did not necessarily tend to selfishness. On the contrary, it was

---

[29] Holt, J. How Children Fail, Pelican 1965
   Holt, J. How Children Learn, Pelican 1970

conducive to independent thought, judgment and responsibility, in contrast to the thoughtlessness and irresponsibility which so often accompanied compliance with custom, group prejudices and ideologies - what Charles Voysey called 'collectivist dogma'.[30] The development of an independent mind was the precondition of character formation. As to the interpretation of freedom and the definition of its limits, she echoed the constant response of progressives through the ages, 'Freedom is not licence'. And because freedom was not licence, it followed that it was always subject to the limits represented by the interests of other members of society.

As Anthony Storr pointed out in 'The Integrity of the Personality', 'A society of individualists each pursuing his own ends regardless of the needs of others is an impossibility'.[31]

The aim of KAS was, in the words of John Russell, 'to provide every child with the fullest possible measure of freedom within a carefully designed framework of social responsibility'.

In a discussion paper on 'The Framing of Policy', written in 1966, Nikki made the following observations on individualism:

'Sociologists have provided us with abundant evidence that a society which is too successfully conditioned to conformity, risks the submergence of individual freedom and the dangers of state tyranny. On the other hand, the work of social psychologists exposes the dangerously self-centred attitude which can be engendered by an extreme preoccupation with individual wishes and demands. We believe that any successful education must achieve a measure of reconciliation between the claims of the individual and the needs of society, where they are at variance. We are a part of contemporary society and we are obliged to participate in it. That obligation does not lie, I believe, in submission to our society but in co-operation with it. We must look at its values and decide which we should conserve and which oppose. We have to contribute, but in a way which is the result of conscious and deliberate choice, and not just by accommodating ourselves to the 'mores' of our particular social or national group.'

In practice, concern for the individual child was expressed in several ways. There was the pedagogic interest in individual differences of ability and achievement, and in the teaching methods suited to particular needs. There was respect for the individual as a person, and the reassurance of being accepted as a valued member of the school. This sense of belonging was enhanced after 1945 when teachers and children addressed one another by first names. Nikki recalled being told by an Old Alfredian how 'it became a matter of pride both for the children and the staff that it was possible to depart so radically from the normal practice in schools, while retaining the courtesy towards teachers that grew from real respect for the

---

[30] Voysey, C.F.A., Individuality, Nadder Books 1986
[31] Storr, A., The Integrity of the Personality, Pelican 1964

qualities of the individual'.

There was also a greater understanding than in the past of the psychological - in particular, emotional - needs of individual children. This did not imply any encroachment on the territory of the professional psychologist, but simply indicated an extension of the teacher's observational role and a new sensitivity to the emotional factors underlying children's behaviour.

An example of close observation is provided by an anecdote recorded in the short History of KASS.[32] A small boy was working in the garden, engaged in his "chosen" activity, when he was overheard muttering to himself, "I hate my hobby, I hate my hobby...how I hate my hobby!" Nikki had always enjoyed this story and thought there was a lesson to be learned from it: that, depending on age, level of maturity and self-confidence, being offered a choice can be perceived as a compulsion to make choices prematurely. It was something the experienced teacher had to bear in mind when creating opportunities for the development of decision-making ability.

The degree of individual caring involved called for altruism and empathy on the part of the teacher, qualities which, in fact, Nikki herself particularly exemplified. Her door was always open as far as possible to staff, children and parents needing to talk. And she was as concerned with the problems of gifted children as with those of children with learning difficulties; with the well-adjusted, achieving child as with the unhappy, disturbed, or disruptive child.

Margaret Maxwell, Senior Mistress and Old Alfredian, recalled a staffroom discussion when a colleague remarked that a particular physically-disabled child never expressed gratitude for help received. Nikki, remembering her spastic friend, Peter Willows,[33] asked why the child should do so. Disabled people, she said, 'obviously appreciated their dependence on the help of others, but their positive self-image rested on the extent to which they could be independent. Their dependence made 'patrons' of their helpers, while they themselves were reduced to being 'patronised'. Not that this excused arrogance, discourtesy or never giving thanks in any circumstances. Obviously, in the company of strangers thanks would be appropriate, but with friends and equals in the school, there is no particular need for thanks to be either expected or given.' It was an unconventional argument at the time but became more familiar years later as the campaign for the rights of the disabled gathered momentum. Another Old Alfredian, the novelist Jenny Diski[34] recalls coming to KAS at the age of fifteen when she was 'a permanently disturbed person,

---

[32] Montgomery, B., Hibburd, E., Short History of KASS, KASS Archives, 1965.
[33] Peter Willows, op cit., (page 61)
[34] The Ham and High, 20 September 1991, and letter from Jenny Diski to the author, 8 January 1992

potentially disruptive and not ideal pupil material', and being treated by Nikki with 'enormous sensitivity'.

'It's always easier in an institution to have blanket rules that have to apply to everyone, but I've always had the feeling that the easy way is not what Nikki is interested in. She wants the right way - the one that allows individuals to benefit from what is on offer. Her sensitivity to my particular psychology at the time meant that she pushed me only to the degree that it was useful, and was able to turn a blind eye to my difficulties in coping with the more social aspects of school life.'

Doris Lessing, who had approached Nikki on Jenny's behalf to obtain the place at KAS, was struck by her remarkable insight into the needs and interests of individuals and the appropriate ways of treating them - her capacity for 'accepting children as they are'.

The goals of individual development, individuated teaching, and pastoral care depend on a high staff-pupil ratio, and the preservation of this has always been a *sine qua non* in the history of King Alfred School. School numbers have risen periodically as a condition of economic survival, but the size of classes has remained, on principle, a constant factor.

The co-heads and staff were not unaware of the negative aspects of individualism - these were apparent in the everyday behaviour of children implicitly acting out their own ideas of what progressive education was all about.

The emphasis on individual freedom and the absence of undue pressure could, at worst, lead to a lackadaisical and sometimes irresponsible attitude to co-operation with the purposes of the school. Some pupils would make little effort in the pursuit of their studies; others would appear late for or miss play rehearsals, or fail to learn their lines. Yet others might not turn up for team games voluntarily undertaken, or fail to practice skills in music, art or tennis, in all cases unconcerned with improvement and indifferent to standards.

Such instances underlined the progressive teacher's dilemma, namely how to reconcile the twin goals which were to some extent mutually incompatible:

(1)   happiness and fulfilment and
(2)   productive work, becoming an active moulder of culture, not a passive consumer.

Liam Hudson[35] goes so far as to suggest, as does Robert Skidelsky[36], that making children happy, secure and independent may be counterproductive, reducing intellectual potentialities instead of increasing them, thereby 'blunting the cutting edge of their capabilities'.

To resolve the dilemma and to elicit the self-activity of the child in these circumstances required not only all the motivational skills of the teacher but

---

[35] Hudson, Liam in M.Ash et al "Who are the Progressives Now?" RKP 1969
[36] Skidelsky, R., op cit.

also the active support of the parents concerned.

Concern for the interests of others, an integral part of the KAS ethos, was bound to find expression in a wider social context than merely that of the school itself. Within a short distance were some of the most derelict inner city neighbourhoods in London, representing in their most acute form the whole range of problems associated with poverty and deprivation. Former generations of Alfredians had been no less concerned with the conditions in these areas of the metropolis and the school had reason to be proud of its contribution by various means to the social welfare of the community. Socialist parents and teachers, united by a common interest in social justice, had always been substantially represented at KAS. Of these, a large proportion were in the Fabian tradition, believing in gradual, constitutional reform, state action to ensure greater equality, and the elimination of poverty. The remainder constituted a broad chapel of those holding more radical views to do with overturning the status quo by means of basic political and social changes. The 1960s marked the development of a new and more critical attitude amongst some of the senior pupils, suggesting the influence of the resurgent Marxism currently pervading institutions of higher education. Their ideas were less concerned with class antagonism than with the more recent critical analysis of power structures. And the stamp of Marxist doctrine was already discernible in the adoption by the pupils' Council of a more active and confrontational role in the promotion of change. Some 5th and 6th formers, from family backgrounds with far more affluent material standards of life than any of the teaching staff, challenged their teachers with being "agents of privilege" and thought that a wider cross-section of society should be represented in the school. The KASS Council expressed sympathy with the second of these propositions but had to inform the pupils concerned that because of inflation and constantly rising prices, the fees were already high, and Council did not feel that it would be practicable to raise them further at the top end in order to subsidise parents who could not afford to pay the economic rate.

The incursion of radical ideas into the Upper School curriculum did not occasion the alarm or misgiving that might have been the case in more conventional schools. The attitude of the Heads was that Marxist thought was free to take its place in general discourse and in the academic evaluation of current value systems. Freedom of thought for the staff was part of the pattern of freedom of thought for their pupils. The checks and balances of an open system were calculated to avert one-sided presentation or indoctrination. The accent in discussion and debate was one of rational and dispassionate inquiry, tolerance for opposing ideas, wit and good humour. The tone was well expressed by an essay set on the general course by Margaret Maxwell which read "Consider whether Marx and Engels or Marks and Spencer have done the greater good for British Society".

Nikki, who alternated with Alan Humphries in drafting the Heads' annual report, noted in the report for 1968 that 'some of the teachers and students who visit KAS refer to us as a school for the privileged few, and there is usually an implied suggestion that, however lucky our children are to have such opportunities, privilege is socially undesirable and will soon become obsolete. Looking at our far from luxurious physical conditions and comparing them with those of the state schools we visit, the description may seem absurd. Nevertheless, there is a sense in which we are privileged. The freedom we enjoy here to try and teach our children, without the use of fear, something of independent thought and judgment, of concern for the dignity of the individual, of involvement in their community, which includes both the young and the old, of the equal and complementary function of men and women in society, of compassion which encompasses, but is not restricted to specific religious beliefs, all these are privileges which, even today, comparatively few enjoy'.

The foregoing discussion of democracy has to some extent pre-empted consideration of authority and leadership, both of which came under review at this time. Traditional autocratic forms of authority were everywhere being challenged, and demands for accountability increasingly insisted upon. Just as the meanings of democracy and progressive education were being re-evaluated, so were authority, leadership and the role of the heads coming under closer scrutiny. Some progressives were advocating the abolition of authority structures and hierarchies and, by logical extension, the abdication of authority by teachers. A growing emphasis on children's rights[37] unsettled and weakened the resolve of some parents to exercise authority over their own children.

It became necessary for the heads, staff and Council to revivify the norm of accepting authority as an enduring function of society and essential feature of organisations, which schools inevitably are. It was stressed, however, that the form and exercise of authority should be in accordance with the traditional democratic ethos of the school. That this act of reaffirmation had been required was ascribed to the failure to distinguish the concept of authority (the function) from that of authoritarianism (one form of implementation) - presumably the true object of rejection.

The problem as it was seen at KAS was one of striking a balance between the exercise of authority - the inescapable concomitant of the teacher's role - and the cultivation of non-authoritarian relationships. To a large extent this was achieved by understatement and the playing down of authority in such a way that it was latent rather than manifest. This in no sense involved manipulation or 'playing a part'. It was a spontaneous expression of the genuine commitment of teachers to the progressive ethic and the desire to maintain the informal relationships upon which the personal development of children depended. But this development also

---

[37] Adams, P et al Children's Rights. Elek Books, 1971

depended on teachers being in authority and being prepared to assert this in case of need, for there were always some children ready to test the reality of both the system and the teacher's role.

The anarchic nature of abdicating authority whether in home or school was thus seen as not only a betrayal of responsibility as an agent of socialisation but also a grave disservice to the children themselves. For the child's capacity to develop individuality and separate identity is largely dependent on having someone, be it parent or teacher, to oppose, challenge and differ from, in a secure and caring environment.[38] In Nikki's view, 'The child to whom nobody has ever said no' is well on the way to becoming a tyrannical monster'.

Whilst the styles of leadership adopted by the joint heads were to a considerable extent prescribed by the culture and ethos of KAS, these were constantly evolving in response to the rapid changes taking place in society.

In the first place, the school was in terms of head-staff relations far more democratic than it had been in the days of John Russell and Joseph Wicksteed. Progressives though they were, each in his own way was capable of authoritarianism where the realisation of his own educational ideas was concerned.

Another change was that schools in general had adopted more bureaucratic procedures of administration. In the case of KAS, this had involved an expansion of the heads' responsibilities, while in no way changing the democratic style of leadership to which they were unanimously committed.

The notion of 'bureaucracy' struck a discordant note in the context of progressive education, but was made acceptable to KAS culture by minimising its impersonal and emphasising its humane aspects.

The changing role and status of women had opened the way to more opportunities in employment at executive level and the gender role implications of this incursion into a hitherto exclusively male preserve were by no means clear.

It has often been suggested that the price women pay for executive power is to surrender some of their femininity and to emulate the traditional model of male authority. To Nikki this had always appeared to be a betrayal of the role of women, for it implied that male leadership was the standard of all leadership, and, by implication, disvalued the leadership qualities that women uniquely possess. She had no inclination whatsoever to imitate the management style of 'company man' with what Katharine Whitehorn [39] so memorably refers to as 'an unattractive manifestation of testosterone'. It was quite alien to her philosophy to be anything other than herself. She took seriously the symbolic meaning of the co-headship and accepted the

---

[38] Storr, A., op cit.

[39] Whitehorn, Katharine, Woman as Company Man, Observer Article

complementary relationship between male and female this implied with the proviso that this in no way excluded her from an equal share in all areas of decision-making, and did not restrict her to those areas traditionally regarded as the prerogative of women.

Her leadership style was the outcome of years of experience in teaching and administration, and a total dedication to the broad principles of the progressive movement. She was averse from all authoritarianism, seeing it as the source of all the most negative elements in education. She did not view herself as a leader in any charismatic sense, and in this respect leaned some way towards the Steiner principle of collegial management, without going to the extreme of doing without heads, except in the smallest of schools. Thus she was non-hierarchical, predisposed to consultation, and concerned to arrive at decisions only after the fullest discussion with colleagues. Tough-mindedness and tender-mindedness were well blended in her personality, so that she was caring, supportive and empathetic as well as being entirely capable of taking difficult decisions when required - 'Rebecca of Sunnybrook Farm I am not'. Abhorring negative and destructive confrontation, she delighted in genuine heuristic disputation, always provided that it was conducted in accordance with civilised rules of procedure. Nikki was a teacher and also an inveterate learner, her interests seeming to be limitless and her tastes catholic. An original and lateral thinker, she shared her knowledge with others, and challenged received ideas and unexamined assumptions. She encouraged the free exchange of ideas and regarded it as a source of innovation and change. And, because she had seen so much achievement and endeavour wasted through fear and inhibition, her idea of freedom included being allowed to make mistakes, as a legitimate and positive aspect of the learning process. As an earnest of this she displayed over her desk an elegantly lettered inscription: 'I have given myself permission to be wrong', which was probably less a statement about herself than a philosophical observation about the folly of unreflective certitude in human affairs. The following extract from her paper 'The Functions of the Heads' gives expression to some of her thoughts on authority, leadership and the positive as distinct from the negative functions of conflict in relation to the making of policy:

'Our policy, by which I mean the policy agreed by members of the Society, the heads and the staff, must be realistic and significant in the world as it is today. We shall never agree on every aspect of our policy but we can hammer out a working agreement on the priorities and principles involved, and our differences of opinion are valuable, even vital, to a living and growing school. The idea of complete unanimity of opinion among the staff is one which would alarm me if I did not know it to be impossible. A vigorous, dynamic community, aware of itself and its responsibilities, must include differing viewpoints and constant questioning of values. The staff and the heads spend many hours thrashing out principles and practice, and criticising as constructively as possible their own beliefs and those of others. This is healthier and more rewarding in terms of the school's future than any unanimity could possibly be. We hold the same principles, generally speaking, otherwise we should not be working here; but putting them into practice is a complex and difficult business, and we often disagree about how it is to be done. I sincerely hope we shall continue to do so as long as I am connected with the school. No one is right about everything all the time, and, if we accept this, we can compromise with one another's views more readily.

'Those people who make a certain field of work their particular study may be expected to have something to offer in that field. King Alfred School provides its own safeguards against authoritarianism in its heads but no one would deny that they have a vital function of leadership.

'There is a growing tendency to regard the word 'leadership' with disfavour because of the wide range of meanings, some regrettable, which it has acquired. On the other hand it is hard to find a realistic substitute which has no pejorative associations. The heads have been appointed because they are (or should be) authorities - that is specialists - on education. It is they who must be aware of current trends of thought and research in their field. It is they who must assess the value of these trends; advise the King Alfred School Society about them through its elected Council and interpret them in relation to the school. If the parent body does not consider the heads capable of leadership in this sense, they should replace them. If they are capable of it, then they are entitled to general support and should be allowed freedom to deal with the practical problems, of interpretation and implementation of the policy which the Society has agreed.'

One of the most remarkable examples of how far she was prepared to go in fostering co-operative relations between head and staff was her decision in the early 1970s to arrange and to take part in a symposium at Brighton Polytechnic along the lines of an encounter group. This was organised on an optional basis for members of the teaching staff of KAS of whom, in the event, one third - twenty members - attended. There were two facilitators who, for most of the time, acted as non-participant observers; the theme for discussion was up to a point open-ended but broadly concerned with the problems of inter-personal relations within the school, and there was a tacit understanding that the discourse would be free from any constraints which might inhibit the genuine expression of people's feelings.

According to one observer, most of the group were at first uneasy in this novel situation, suspicious and reserved. 'They thought there was a hidden agenda', Nikki recalled, 'and I knew that there wasn't one. I had good reasons for not wanting to be the person who opened the discussion but, in order to get things started, I eventually felt obliged to do so.'

That there were frustrations among some members of staff became quickly apparent. One young man took the lifting of sanctions quite literally and addressed her in an unnecessarily discourteous and aggressive manner, expressing dissatisfaction with what he saw as the hierarchical aspects of the school. And what had been hitherto generalised discussion turned to the exercise of authority by the head and a personalised attack on Nikki herself by the young man and two other members of the group who accused her of being a 'dictator'. Because of the suddenness of the assault, the wildly exaggerated epithet that had been applied to her, and the injustice of their criticisms, she was unable to keep back her tears, but this did not stop her from replying to the charge.

The cause of frustration had been exposed, based on a failure to understand the nature of authority, and not for the first time, she found herself trying to explain the principle that some of those drawn to progressive education find so difficult to comprehend - that authority is the inescapable concomitant of responsibility. She had taken an emotional battering, but had known at the outset that she was placing herself in a vulnerable position and was prepared to take the consequences, in the hope that good would follow from the collective experience. If the younger staff had acquired a better understanding of the meaning of authority as applied at KAS, and more readiness to co-operate with what they understood, Nikki felt that the experiment had been justified. There was no doubt that her relations with staff improved and that respect for her leadership and personal integrity was enhanced.

There was an occasion in 1964 when a deeply disturbed and unruly boy, who had been a constant source of trouble to both staff and children for a long time, had to be asked to leave. Summary expulsion at KAS did not exist, and the boy was present at the end of term ceremony when it was the custom for either Nikki or Alan to make brief valedictory remarks about the school leavers. Nikki, in this instance, made a point of not differentiating the boy publicly from the other leavers, and made whatever positive comments she could about his time at the school. This so incensed one member of staff, who had borne the brunt of the boy's disruptive career, that he wrote to her during the ensuing school holidays, deploring what she had said at the farewell ceremony. In reply, she wrote the following letter:

'I did not reply to your letter earlier because I wanted time to think about it, not only from the point of view of the incident, but also from that of the principles involved.

I was sorry that you felt I had let you down or appeared to contradict your opinion of the boy by what I said. My intention was to make it clear that whether he was being good or bad, he did not indulge in half-measures. This is my personal opinion of him, and I think I am entitled to it, however mistaken I may be. I agree that he rarely wanted to work, and therefore evidence for his being good in this direction is very slight, but his conscientious practice for the leavers' concert showed that he was capable of putting his whole heart into the process, when the motivation was there.

All this is a matter of personal opinion and I am willing to accept that my judgment may be at fault. The fundamental principle, however, on which I based my remarks is one in which I believe firmly, and from my knowledge of you, I would have thought it expressed your own view. It is that one should never willingly or deliberately damage a child's personality by final and public condemnation. Therefore I wanted to find something which I could honestly say would leave him, as it were, intact and able to face the sufficiently shocking fact of having to leave school. I think it was Homer Lane who said that it is not enough to love the sinner though you hate the sin: you must try to love the sin because it is part of the child whom you are trying to educate. I know this sounds far more idealistic than any of us are prepared to support and yet I have seen you putting it into action on many occasions and felt that it was part of your very real conviction about children and education.

I seem to have gone more deeply into this than perhaps you wanted me to when you wrote your original letter, but I was concerned about it and I think the point involved is of fundamental importance. I am so glad that you will be coming to our little party at the end of term.'

If the tone of this letter and the manner of her dealing with the incident appear conciliatory, this is exactly what they were, for they reflected her rejection of the negative, confrontational approach to problems, and her positive search for solutions which left participants with their self-esteem intact.

She believed it was a moral strength and not a weakness to be able to admit mistakes, and to acknowledge that one might at times be wrong. But, of course, it was possible to find, even at KAS, a small number of authoritarian personalities[40] whose conventionality led them to perceive in such beliefs the weakness and ambiguity they could not tolerate in themselves. To people of this kind she and her co-head, Alan Humphries, were to some extent vulnerable, just as Nikki by her own decision was vulnerable at the Brighton seminar. It was the vulnerability of the democratic process itself when it is exploited by those few problem teachers and problem parents who seek by its means to further their own as distinct from the common advantage.[41] Other members of staff were exposed to this risk but to a lesser extent than the heads, who saw it as part of their responsibility to shield them from it as far as possible.

The type of problem teacher has already been indicated in the discussion of the events of Brighton Polytechnic; the type of problem parent is concerned with the exercise of power, either for idiosyncratic reasons or ostensibly in support of children's educational interests. In either case it can demand a disproportionate amount of staff time which should be at the disposal of children, or it can interfere to an unacceptable degree with the

---

[40] Adorno, T.W., et al The Authoritarian Personality. (NY) 1964
[41] Neill, A.S., The Problem Parent, 1932, The Problem Teacher, 1939.

responsibilities of the heads, not to mention the added drain on the physical and emotional energies of both. But these problems should not obscure the positive contributions of generations of KAS parents who enabled the school to survive, to expand, and achieve the educational standards for which it is renowned. The harmonious relationship obtaining between the majority of parents, Council, staff and pupils has been part of that achievement; and it has come about in spite of the negative forces which have periodically threatened to undermine it since the foundation of the school.

The discussion of various aspects of democracy in education which had excited so much attention during this period culminated in the summer of 1968 in a one-day conference at KAS on 'Notions of Authority in Education'. There were four speakers: the psychoanalyst and educational psychologist, Doctor Robert Shields, Katharine Whitehorn of the Observer, and the two heads. Doctor Shields emphasised that a child needed to see the mother as a really feminine figure and the father as a completely masculine one. The mother represented an 'all-embracing kind of love', and the father, while strong and loving, represented authority and a demand for responsibility. Deviation from these gender role expectations could affect the child's learning ability and sex role identification.[42]

Katharine Whitehorn reduced her subject - Do we need Authority? -to the proposition that there were three reasons why people obeyed: habit, force and because they decided that it was the right way. A democratic society needed authority but only the third reason was morally acceptable.[43]

Alan Humphries addressed the question "How far towards freedom in education could those in authority go?" The right relationship between teacher and learner was fundamental to the learning process, so the question of how much freedom was necessary to achieve that relationship was the main issue. The extremes were patently wrong: both the absence of freedom and the absence of authority. The attempt to find a compromise or a mean could not lead to a satisfactory answer because freedom was a relative concept qualified by different and changing circumstances. Another important question was "freedom for what?". Freedom was not an end in itself, but a starting point for positive progress. The struggle for freedom had in the past been 'freedom from' e.g., fear or want. The key to the right relationship between teacher and pupil lay in 'freedom to do'. The real job of the teacher started at this point, and his skill should be directed to leading the pupil to the best possible use of his freedom. The problem of how much freedom was certainly answerable, but it would provide material for another conference, the theme of which would surely be that the role of authority was to create, maintain and defend the freedom from which real

---

[42] Express & News, July 5th 1968
[43] ibid.

education started.[44]

Nikki, in conclusion, dealt with authority as a socio-cultural construct and considered some of its educational implications.[45]

'There should be a category of words defined in the dictionary as potentially explosive - handle with care! The list would probably require editing every few years as current fashions of thought were outgrown, but I suggest that one of the perennials would be that harmless and necessary abstract noun 'authority', which today arouses as much heat in higher academic circles as it once did in the self-absorbed world of the progressive schools.

'On the principle that, even if we can't agree, it's helpful to know what we are fighting about, the following definition might clear enough space to give us a meeting ground. Authority - the permission accorded by one group or individual to another group or individual to give orders in any situation in which both are involved. Please note that I have specifically avoided drawing any distinction between the kind of situation where A obtain B's obedience by force, overt or implicit, and that in which there is an amicable recognition by both that in this particular set of circumstances A is better fitted than B to make decisions. Take it one further: when we talk of 'an authority' we mean someone who has become recognised as an expert in his field and might be expected to know a good deal more about it than the average person. Whether or not this gives him a better right to speak on his subject than anyone else might make interesting discussion material for a philosophy seminar, but it does give others a comprehensible reason for listening. There is a lot to be said for learning by doing but if your chosen topic happens to include pyrotechnics you are likely to learn more happily from someone who knows the properties of gunpowder than by dabbling with potassium nitrate and sulphur in the back parlour.

'A society with fairly stable patterns of authority is likely to reflect this stability in the province of education, and in our social history the implicit connection between 'an authority' and 'in authority' has been accepted with very little dissent until fairly recently.

'Granted it is difficult for young children to present any really effective opposition to an idea held almost unanimously by the adult section of their community, even if it occurs to them that someone, somewhere, is being got at. But when the adults themselves start to question, challenge, and generally make hay of the traditional hierarchies of authority, the ensuing uncertainty spreads to all ages and groups and we in education have to make a swift and unsentimental review of our assumptions.

'Having concluded that, whatever the purposes of education and the social framework in which it exists, we are going to need people who are

---

[44] New Era, Vol.49, No.9, November 1968 (Now New Era in Education, Journal of The World Education Fellowship)
[45] ibid.

'authorities on' and also (for particular purposes such as physical safety and psychological security) 'in authority', where do we go? Presumably we need people who, while being 'authorities on' and capable of taking authority, in the sense already mentioned, are also able to establish and maintain genuine relationships with the young. It sounds simple enough and perhaps it would be in some societies. Unfortunately for teachers our ideas of authority figures are part of our cultural pattern and it is this which so often gets in the way.

'Roles, in the social psychologist's terminology, determine to a great extent our conscious or unconscious expectations in our relationships. They form a kind of pattern into which we expect others to fit and even into which we would ourselves expect to fit. From early childhood through adolescence we respond to others and to situations according to expectations based on past experience. Once we have formed an idea about how something should be it becomes part of our frame of reference and is difficult to be aware of, let alone change. So, the parson's wife, the downtrodden husband, the patient Griselda can gradually obscure the real person until even they no longer know which is real and which is role. Roles have, of course, been part of the equipment in schools for a long time and very useful too. If you can get your young to identify with the right roles - Head Boy, Pride of the Sixth, the Girl who Saved the School, etc., you've gone a good way towards social control now and later. Sometimes they get the wrong idea and identify with the Terror of the Fourth; you can't always win.

'When the logical educationalists of the twenties decided that legends and myths had no place in the upbringing of children they probably threw some very powerful pieces of social equipment out, along with the fairy-tale bath water. One of the results of this game of role expectation is that it delays, even hinders, the formation of relationships. We don't see X as a person, we see him as a bank manager, the policeman, or the man who comes to look at the gas meter, and only after that do we get to know the person behind the image. In the case of the teacher this process gets even more complicated by the fact that our basic father and mother figures become involved, so we have at least two layers to get through before coming (if we ever do) to the person himself. None of this would matter so much if our authority images of teachers were more attractive or, to put it more bluntly, based on less repellent prototypes. Who in their senses would want to make a real relationship with Messrs Brocklehurst and Squeers or have anything but mild contempt for the depressing cavalcade of undervalued and exploited creatures who were misnamed 'governesses'? As for the terrifying female authority figures who dominated so much of our 19th century literature, they would have frightened even Freud.

'Things have changed a great deal in the last twenty years but we still meet parents who see a head through the eyes of an apprehensive youngster and resent the fact without really knowing it. The respective sex roles don't help either. We still haven't much idea as to whether women really are a different kind of animal from men, although it is fairly clear that if your tribal culture demands warlike tendencies in its women and attributes what we think of a feminine traits to its men, both parties will develop the appropriate role responses in spite of the physical characteristics and child-bearing. Ever since St Paul, and later St Jerome, decided that women would be less troublesome if they were less attractive to men, the Virgin Mother, who had after all very little to smile about, became the pattern of Christian womanhood.

'She stayed that way through the Middle Ages, with depressing results, suffered a brief eclipse in the Eighteenth Century, was revived most oddly by Queen Victoria and, by a process of symbiosis, merged into the social image of schoolmistress which persisted until the second world war. The long period of female subservience in economic and other fields has affected the way in which both girls and boys respond to the female teacher. Boys can still be deeply affronted by being expected to accept a woman in authority, and girls can be overawed or disappointed when they confuse the male teacher with the dominating father figure. Each generation of children takes some of these role images into adulthood with it and perpetuates their influence. Perhaps the time is coming when we can begin to perceive the complementary roles of men and women in terms which neither denigrate nor patronise either sex. We might then find it possible to establish teaching situations in which authority could be recognised and related to the needs of children and adults...and perhaps we could cross it off that list.'

12   Conservation and Change Revisited

Demands for more democratic procedures at King Alfred School had been voiced by a small number of parents two years before - in 1966. In particular, they wanted a greater measure of participation in the running of the school, as a means to which they sought an improvement in the system of communication. This, it was thought, would give access to more information, thereby making both their elected members of Council and the joint Heads more accountable to the parent body as a whole. These same parents had expressed dissatisfaction with certain aspects of educational policy and this gave added point and a sense of urgency to their demands. The situation was not unlike that which had arisen in the case of the Pupils' Council and caused the same kind of *frisson* amongst those who thought it was not quite the accepted way of doing things at KAS, not on account of the substance of the representations but because of the confrontational manner in which they had been expressed.

'Most of the parents', observed one member of the Parent-Staff Committee, 'were satisfied, but the radicals were militant.' It was said the radicals had introduced an air of bitterness into discussions about the school and its future and that they were venting their discontents on the Heads instead of taking them to Council in accordance with the normal procedure. 'The spectacle of the Heads being attacked and harassed at meetings was degrading and sickening', said an observer, 'no self-respecting Head could put up with this for any length of time'. Indeed, Alan Humphries was said to have threatened resignation if the parents concerned did not stop interfering in matters concerning the staff.

Predictably, Council and Heads decided that it was necessary to examine the reasons for the attitudes and behaviour of the parents concerned, and then to issue an educational policy statement for the information of all parents. On this basis parents would have the right to (a) accept the policy (and thereafter support the Heads and staff in implementing it); (b) reject it and remove their children from the school; (c) remain in KASS but seek to influence or alter policy by democratic procedures; (d) express views at Society or Parent-Staff meetings.

In the statement which ensued an undertaking was given to examine ways of further improving communications in the Society. A clear distinction was made between the constitutional rights of all members of the Society to express their views to Council and the Heads on questions of broad policy, and the right which granted the Heads power, subject to the approval of Council, to implement policy and control staff without interference. It was open to parents to seek policy changes through the normal democratic procedures of the Society, at annual general meetings or at specially convened statutory meetings. Discussion - even controversy - was welcomed, but it was hoped that this would continue to be conducted in a friendly and constructive atmosphere. Otherwise, the wrong kind of public debate would result, with the possibility of impairing good relations throughout the school, 'stifling the very purpose and spirit which brought our school into being - a willingness to experiment with new educational ideas and methods.'[46]

The statement went on to express confidence in the ability of the Heads and Staff to implement the aims and principles on which the curriculum was based, with due regard for the pressures of social change, and fully endorsed the methods currently being pursued towards the achievement of the goals of the school.

In particular it addressed the central issue in the litany of complaints advanced by the disaffected parents - namely the decision of Council and Heads to initiate a major reorganisation of science teaching, incorporating the new Nuffield methods and resources. Existing facilities were obsolescent and methods out of date, conditions which were unacceptable if the school were to prepare its pupils for the modern world. Nuffield methods, it was stressed, were closely in harmony with the educational principles of the school, involving pupils in practical 'hands-on' activities and experimentation, and enabling syllabuses to be adapted to the specific needs of individuals.

The crucial importance of adaptation to change was re-emphasised by the Heads in their next annual report.[47] 'The education of human beings', they said, 'must be seen in terms of growth. Therefore we must recognise the nature of growth and the extent to which growth involves change. Change, involving past, present and future in a continuous process, is different from the kind of change in which the old is scrapped and replaced by the new. As King Alfred School evolves, the new aspects grow out of and are related to the old; new parents and children, new staff, buildings, equipment and techniques are all assimilated and become part of it, and the essential character of the community which made it remarkable in 1898 is just as recognisable and vigorous in 1966.'

One sceptical member of Council, who was disposed to reserve judgment on the proposed innovations, posed the question, 'What are the specific functions of KAS generally? In what fields can it be a pioneer?' It was a question Nikki regarded as problematic, for it seemed to assume that KAS was obliged by its 'progressive' cognomen to be in a constant process of invention, striving to remain ahead of the field. The reality was that, like its peer schools, it had done with pioneering and, insofar as its distinctive principles and methods had still not been fully adopted by schools in general, it was still ahead in this particular respect, and able to claim the title of 'demonstration school'. This did not preclude KAS from active experimentation, responding to social and educational change in the same

---

[46] KASS Relations between Council, Heads and Parents. September 1966
[47] KASS Annual Report No.55 December 1966

way as other schools, evaluating and selectively adapting the findings of educational research and methodology to its own use.

This flexibility of response was of special importance in the 1960s because of the accelerated pace of change in science and technology. A Labour Government under Harold Wilson had committed itself to building socialism 'in the white heat of the scientific and technological revolution'. The educational implications for the future were self-evident. It meant that no-one could claim to have had a comprehensive education without some minimum level of scientific knowledge, both pure and applied. All would need to develop, in the words of the Newsom Report,[48] 'some measure of mechanical intelligence'.

Nikki at this time drew up a discussion paper on science at KAS, in which she outlined the current and future developments of the Nuffield Science Project, and the logistics and estimated cost of introducing the scheme at Manor Wood. The paper included a factorial analysis of the options open to the school and concluded with her own recommendations.

'There seem to be four possible choices open to us', she wrote. 'First, we could continue to teach science as we are doing at present with somewhat improved laboratory conditions and as much equipment as we are able to afford. As I foresee it, the result would be that within five years we should be unable to compete with the state schools and we should, therefore, lose those children who showed, or whose parents assumed that they might show, a scientific bent. We should also be likely to lose our science staff for the following reasons: if the new teaching of science becomes the general practice, any teacher using the old method would find it difficult to get another job, having spent years isolated from the latest methods. No first-class teacher would wish to do a job in conditions which were hopelessly inadequate, using methods which were no longer in current use.

'Second, we could cease to teach science altogether above the junior level in the school, and try to negotiate some arrangement with other local schools or technical institutes for those of our children who had shown an aptitude at the primary stage. Even if this were possible, the disintegrating effect on the school and the children would, I think, outweigh any possible advantages. It would be very different doing the whole of one's science education in another school from just going to another building for a particular lesson. The physical arrangements necessary would, of course, be complicated and difficult, and I doubt whether this really is a feasible alternative.

'Third, we could cease to teach science at any but the most elementary level, which I think would result after a certain time in the disappearance of our senior pupils, for reasons which are obvious enough to need no further

---

[48] Central Advisory Council for Education (England) Report: "Half our Future" (The Newsom Report) HMSO (1963)

amplification at this point. It is abundantly clear that science and technology are becoming increasingly dominant factors in our lives, and it seems likely that the next twenty-five years will see greater changes in the pattern of civilised life and education than in the past two hundred years. This may be a conservative estimate.

'In the past, King Alfred School has tended to assume that it was possible to educate children within the disciplines generally described as the Arts without depriving them of any important or significant aspect of cultural growth. It was assumed, rightly or wrongly, that an intelligent person educated in literature, with a sense of historical perspective and an ability to obtain information and make judgments, could take his place in modern life according to his inclination and abilities, and that any further training he might require if he decided on a change of direction would be no more than he could easily obtain.

'This is no longer true, if it ever was. Within a few years, technological knowledge, at what is now regarded as a comparatively advanced level for most of us, will have become a necessity for a very large number of people, if they are going to earn an adequate living in a fast-changing world. If King Alfred School is to continue to exist, it can only do so within a framework of reality. If we cannot offer an education which takes the changes of modern life into account, we shall not attract parents who are willing to pay for the education we provide because they will realise that by following a one-sided educational path they may prejudice their children's future. In a short time we would become a school for emotionally maladjusted children and those whose ability was so low as to make it difficult for them to go through the normal school pattern. I take it that such a future is as undesirable to the members of the Society as it would be to me and to the rest of the staff.

'The fourth and final choice is that we should decide on a new direction for our energies and beliefs, by the expansion of our science facilities on a scale proportionate to the new demands for a technologically-educated population. If we cannot, because the world is no longer shaping that way, continue to educate humanists who are capable of doing a little science, we can, on the other hand, aim at educating our potential scientists and technologists to be both literate and morally responsible.'

This latter course of action was the one which Nikki and her co-head recommended and which was ultimately approved by Council.

In advancing her views she had absolute confidence that the proposed changes were in accordance with the traditions of the school and was at pains to clear up any misunderstandings resulting from the contemporary Snow v Leavis debate on 'the two cultures'.[49] Some parents appeared to think domination of the curriculum by science was being advocated, whereas the actual intention was to maintain a balance between the claims

---

[49] Snow, C.P., The Two Cultures and the Scientific Revolution. Rede Lecture, Cambridge (1959)

of science and the humanities which had always been integral to the philosophy of KAS. The innovations in prospect could be simply summarised as acceptance of the principle of science for all children and the modernisation of science teaching.

Nuffield science, involving new purpose-built laboratories, equipment, storage space, augmented staffing and the in-service training of existing staff, was by far the most ambitious project of its kind in the history of the school. In the interests of curricular balance, it was combined with a plan to expand accommodation and resources for arts subjects in a new building to be called the Arts and Science Block.

It is remarkable in the light of all these developments that Robert Skidelsky[50] who visited the school prior to the publication of his book 'English Progressive Schools', should have by implication included KAS in the following comments on the schools in general: 'Progressive education stopped growing after 1940...' and 'The progressives entirely failed to foresee this further evolution of the industrial system, with its need for a highly trained labour force and a highly skilled managerial elite.'

The technological society was at this time no longer a distant prospect but a growing reality of everyday life, the television set in the majority of homes being its most obvious manifestation. During the 1960s the impact was beginning to affect education. BBC radio programmes for schools were quickly overtaken but not displaced by their TV equivalents. By the early 1970s digital calculators were becoming part of the equipment of many of the children and the school was soon to obtain its first computer.

Contrary to popular expectation, the Heads and staff treated these innovations with cautious scepticism, being concerned to discriminate between those which enhanced the learning process and those which did not. Like others in the teaching profession, they foresaw the subsequent expansion in gadgetry and the dangers in the proliferation of ephemeral and relatively expensive novelties, quickly exhausted and of negligible educational value. Programmed learning texts, whether in book or computerised form, had obvious advantages in terms of individualised learning and instant response, as well as the facility of self-diagnosis and correction. They were effective methods of learning in some subjects but not in others, and could be a useful auxiliary in remedial education. As such, they were clearly not in the category of gimmicks but had much to offer as aids to learning, as long as they were not treated as having any wider function than this.

Nineteenth century ideas of 'human capital' and the factorial organisation of state schools were of too recent origin for teachers not to be suspicious about innovations suggesting the treatment of individuals as units in a mechanistic process.

---

[50] Skidelsky. R., op cit.

Ahead of her Time

Writing in 1969 to Geneviève, now a university lecturer in Paris, Nikki voiced her own feelings on the subject: 'I suspect the disadvantages of mechanical systems have yet to be discovered and that they will not prove as efficient as their inventors hope, if only because of the unpredictability of human beings, whether adults or children. Machines taught by machines might be foolproof, but...You can't make a blanket assumption that a system can be applied effectively to all children. Learners are individuals, and there are many ways of learning, some better than others for particular individuals, according to what motivates them. All these different learning styles are threatened by mechanistic processes, and extreme care needs to be exercised lest the teaching machine, if adopted, becomes 'the only way'. This is doubtless what the commercial entrepreneurs would like to see - classrooms full of pupils working in a 1:1 relationship with computers, the teacher being reduced to a non-interventionist role, but available as an adviser when required, one of a number of different learning resources. It takes little imagination to envisage the results: the increasing isolation of the child from social interaction and co-operative activity with peer group and teacher and all the consequences that would flow from it. It is a scenario that I cannot really take seriously, for I think it would almost certainly be averted at some early stage when pupils revolted against the insufferable boredom of it all.'[51]

One of the messages conveyed by the technological revolution was that life was to be made easier and more comfortable as a result of modern inventions. Welcome though this was in contexts of home and work, it could be deceptive in the context of education. Here some of the inventions were tools designed to make learning easy and pleasant by means of a variety of props, electronic technology, and short cuts to knowledge. These could be used as positive variations of the play-based learning activities of early education, but could also induce in some older pupils the negative expectation that learning did not necessarily involve effort. This in no way meant that pleasure and enjoyment had no place in the more serious academic studies of the middle and upper schools, but it was felt necessary to correct the illusory notion that there were easy routes to genuine learning, and to re-emphasise the old precept that nothing worth having is gained without effort.

By the same token, basic mathematical skills continued to be taught at KAS despite the advent of digital calculators, thus facilitating understanding of the symbolic processes involved.

The influence of the new technology was felt primarily in the area of teaching methods, and not, with the exception of the natural sciences, in that of the curriculum. The latter was affected by the growing accumulation

---

[51] The more efficient electronic learning aids which entered the toy market in the 1990s have still not disposed of the boredom factor, for which reserve software packages are the suggested remedy.

of new knowledge and the demands of a rapidly changing society. Every subject came under close scrutiny and discussion during these years and was assessed in terms of the relevance of its content and methodology, as well as its relation to the rest of the curriculum.

Every subject was affected in some way by the climate of change, and it was typical of KAS that the review and the discussions which followed ended in a workable compromise in which a balance was struck between conservation and change.

In September 1963 a new method of teaching reading - the Pitman Initial Teaching Alphabet (ITA) - was introduced in Lower School. It had gone through all the conventional stages of research and development, and spectacular results had been reported from the sample of primary schools in which it had been tested.

'Kindergarten pupils at King Alfred School', announced the Express & News in 1965, 'are learning to read with forty-three symbols instead of the usual twenty-six letters of the alphabet. The school was one of the pioneers of the ITA scheme, which it introduced in 1963. Before adopting the method, Mrs Nikki Archer, who is joint head of the school, visited Leicestershire schools where the system was in progress and was impressed by the way in which children were learning how to read.' The account went on to say that both staff and parents were pleased with the results. Pupils showed no difficulty in 'graduating' from Pitman symbols to the traditional alphabet, one reason for this being that the classroom posters were written in both styles. The new method was found to help juniors, first with pronunciation, and ultimately with spelling. If parents had taught their own children to a fairly advanced stage by orthodox methods, it was not usual to introduce the latter to ITA.

The sequel was less gratifying, and illustrates well the reservations and confidence limits which necessarily have to qualify research findings. In the short term, ITA appeared to justify all the claims that had been made for it. But the longitudinal reality, exposed by some five years' experience of using the method at KAS, was that for a small but significant number of children it had failed to work. Those who had had difficulties in learning to read continued to have difficulties, and those who could not spell continued to find difficulty in spelling. Yet all of these proved capable of improvement when exposed to alternative traditional methods.

The Reading Research Unit at London University, with which Nikki and Alan Humphries had established a connection, found that the negative results of the experiment were largely replicated in other trial schools, a finding later confirmed by the National Foundation for Educational Research, and the scheme was comprehensively phased out shortly afterwards. The Lower School was also the test bed for the change from chronological age grouping to the new method of 'family' grouping, a recent innovation in some of the more progressive state primary schools. The rationale was based on the premise that age was increasingly less relevant to different levels of maturation and achievement. Research evidence showed that groups comprising a three-year age span not only experienced a stimulus to learning but also improved markedly in social behaviour. The younger children acted more maturely in the company of their elders, while the latter became more responsible and protective towards their juniors. The success of this structural variation led to discussion of possible extension to the Middle and even the Upper School, but this was found to be impracticable on academic, organisational and social grounds.

Another experimental venture was the introduction of colour factor as an aid to learning mathematics. A review of this scheme after the first year of its operation reported encouraging results, showing its capacity for enhancing the children's understanding of mathematical principles. The report added the reservation, perhaps with the history of ITA in mind, that final assessment would have to wait until the experimental cohort had reached the higher levels of mathematics.

A further important curriculum change resulted from the decision to discontinue Latin as a subject for all children and to replace it by Spanish as a second foreign language. It was a decision that, in the words of the Heads' annual report in 1965 'was not taken lightly and certainly not in any fervour of anti-Latin excitement'. It had been decided that majority needs determined the issue with the proviso that minority needs had to be catered for, and those who needed Latin as a qualifying subject for entry to university must be taught at some stage, probably in the sixth form.

One of the more complex problems of the 1960s was that of moral education. The erosion in post-war Britain of a central value consensus and the ensuing uncertainties about moral standards had been the cause of public concern and a demand for more resolute action by schools and other agencies of socialisation to remedy the situation. One of the first official responses to the public disquiet was the inauguration of a ten-year research project under the auspices of the Farmington Trust at Oxford. The terms of reference were to conduct research on the topic of moral education and to seek answers to the following questions:

(a)   What is moral education? Who can be said to be morally educated?

(b)   Which findings of psychology and social science are relevant to it?

(c)   How can children at school be morally educated?

Moral education, being inherent to a greater or lesser degree in all education, was not regarded as a subject in itself but as permeating the curriculum in its wider sense, to include the culture and ethos of the whole school.

It might have been thought that KAS, by virtue of its progressive ethos, had little to learn about moral education, but there was no room for complacency. The multidisciplinary approach of the research unit and the conceptual discussion contained in their preliminary report[52] raised new issues of which the school had necessarily to take account. As an earnest of intent, a day conference was held at Manor Wood in April 1966 on Ethical and Moral Values in Education at which the philosopher, John Wilson, Director of the research project, was one of the main speakers. The Farmington Report found widespread confusion on the subject, and identified conflicting ideas that urgently needed resolution. It was claimed, for example, that cultural pluralism rendered impracticable the transmission of an unequivocal set of moral absolutes. The notion that, in practice, morality was 'caught' rather than 'taught' was widely accepted. The confidence of teachers in being able to fulfil their traditional role as agents of moral authority had been undermined by moral relativism, whilst much of what was assumed to be moral education was in fact indoctrination. Altogether less controversial was the assertion that authoritarian approaches to moral education were an anachronism in democratic society. Nikki concurred with the identification of the problems and the conclusion that much of the current uncertainty stemmed from conceptual confusion. The most serious consideration was, in her opinion, that some teachers had justified the abdication of moral authority on the basis of misconception and unexamined assumptions. Whilst there were conflicting values in society - many of them relatively superficial - there were also many fundamental and enduring values over which a broad consensus existed. The degree of moral relativism in no way warranted the renunciation of moral authority by the teacher. Education was to be preferred on principle to indoctrination, but there could be justifiable cases of indoctrination, e.g., very young children or any persons demonstrably incapable of thinking for themselves. It was a truism that morality was often caught by the example of others, but moral education could not be left to chance, and for moral development to occur there had also to be some deliberate intervention by responsible adults towards the transmission of values.

Not all members of staff were persuaded of their inescapable responsibility towards the children in their care. 'It's the name of the game', said one teacher, 'we don't pass on values'. Nikki challenged this: what did he think children were learning when a teacher ignored swearing and cheating on the football field? To do nothing passed on a message of acquiescence, weakening sanctions against the undesirable behaviour and reinforcing the likelihood of its being repeated.

Towards the definition of a morally-educated person, the research unit drew up a tentative list of suggested moral components with 'some chance of being assessed in neutral terms'. Profiles of this kind, it was suggested, could be used for diagnostic purposes to gain some idea of the moral

---

[52] Wilson, J., Williams, N., Sugarman, B. Introduction to Moral Education, Pelican, 1967.

'rating' of a school and of the kind of moral curriculum that it might be appropriate for it to follow. The context of the school and whether its ethos and organisation served to exemplify moral values, was considered as important as the content of its academic curriculum, and in this respect KAS could claim an exemplary record.

The psychological perspective in the Farmington research included reference to the important seminal work of Jean Piaget[53] on developmental stages in moral thinking and to the extension of this by the Harvard psychologist Lawrence Kohlberg.[54] Teachers were already aware of Piaget's stages of cognitive development, but the salutary effect of Farmington was to alert them to the significant application of this learning theory to moral development.

The report suggested a variety of methods which schools might find appropriate to their own particular circumstances, based on the aim of passing on a way of thinking which would enable the learner to respond with sensibility to any situation involving moral decision, however new or unprecedented.

A similar aim was expressed subsequently in the Schools' Council Moral Education Curriculum Project, which referred to the adoption of 'a considerate style of life', implying a pattern of behaviour which took other people's needs and interests into account as well as one's own. Both these aims and suggested methods accorded well with the educational philosophy of KAS, which had always discouraged indoctrination and stressed autonomy, compassion and social responsibility.

In the time of John Russell, when the school had been relatively small, the rule had been that the discussion of moral issues should never be in the abstract but should always be concerned with the actual problems arising in the daily life of the community. With the growth of the school, and the increasing tendency for older children to stay on, the needs of senior pupils required less restrictive measures, and discussion was obliged to range more widely, underpinned in the 6th Form by taught elements in moral philosophy.

Study materials from various School Council Projects bearing on moral education were tested, evaluated, and fed into appropriate subjects of the curriculum. Methods usually involved the pupils in studying texts, discussion, simulations and role-play, and all provided opportunities for them to arrive at their own individual conclusions without direction by the teacher.

---

[53] Piaget, Jean, The Moral Judgement of the Child, Routledge, 1932

[54] Kohlberg, L, 'The cognitive developmental approach to socialisation', in Goslin (ed) Handbook of Socialisation: Theory and Research, Rand McNally, 1969.

Whether teaching 6th formers or younger children, Nikki often used the Socratic method, challenging and questioning them, encouraging them to think for themselves.

'I didn't want them just to accept what I said', she observed, 'anything was open to question and could be discussed, provided it was never at the expense of other people.' She found that one of the most effective media for discussion was the moral dilemma, in the form of 'what would you do if...?' The value of the method was revealed in a letter she wrote to a Belgian academic - Professor Christiane Brusselmans - who had been specialising in moral education:

'One of my favourite dilemmas for 12-14 year olds goes as follows: you have two friends of whom you are equally fond. One of them does something wrong for which the other gets the blame. The culprit does not own up and the other friend is going to be punished. What do you do? The different responses to this are remarkable. Girls nearly always say something like 'you could not be real friends or you would not let someone else take the blame.' Whereas boys tend to take a more legalistic point of view. Both boys and girls, with what I would call developed moral feelings, end up by saying that they could not leave the situation exactly as it stands, but would have to try and persuade the culprit to face his wrong-doing and accept his punishment. No-one ever suggests informing the authorities as to the identity of the culprit, and, if I ask them whether they feel this would be an appropriate action, they invariably say 'no'. Older children will occasionally comment that 'if it is very bad, like murder, perhaps we should tell someone'. More girls than boys say that they would go to their parents and ask for advice. Without exception, in the sessions I have done, they finish up by asking me what I would do, and it usually starts a new round of discussion when I say that I think I would do this or that.'

In retrospect, the review of moral education at KAS had not necessitated any fundamental changes in the curriculum. Reaffirmation of the responsibility of all teachers towards the moral education of their pupils was timely and necessary; the methodology of creating an environment conducive to development of moral responsibility underwent some modification in response to new ideas; there was a greater awareness of the developmental stages of moral thinking; but the greatest change was, of course, in the content of moral education, reflecting the multiplication of new and unprecedented moral problems in society.

Some would include the radical change in sexual mores amongst the problems of the 1960s, but this is in its turn a problem of value judgment. Certainly it was a change which had a less traumatic effect at KAS than in society at large. Sex education was not an instant curriculum innovation but a spontaneous development of an existing provision which now required expansion in the light of new demands. The co-educational tradition had always been carried to the utmost limit, and school life was therefore much the same for girls and boys alike. As a result of this, neither sex could be said to hold any sense of mystery for the other, and both sexes could relate to each other in a natural and unaffected manner. John Russell, in an interview with the Daily Chronicle in 1906 remarked that 'each sex influences and modifies the other, so that the girls shame the boys out of cruelty, untidiness and thoughtlessness, and the boys shame the girls out of false sentiment, and the helplessness which is more often than not assumed because it is thought to be a ladylike characteristic.' It was 'JR' who sought to promote 'natural and healthy attitudes to sexuality and establish beautiful and honourable relations between the sexes'. With this kind of tradition behind it, sex education could take place in a matter-of-fact way either in the course of informal daily contact between teachers and pupils or in the more formal context of curriculum studies.

A theme by now familiar to the reader is the periodic concern expressed by a small number of parents in each successive generation about the supposed threat posed by innovation to the ideals of progressive education. If asked, the Heads at any stage of the school's history would have said these ideals were quite as precious to them as they were to the parents concerned, and that no change was ever entertained without reference to the conservation of traditional principles. It was the expansion of the school and the increasing concern with examinations that most set the alarm bells ringing and pricked the progressive conscience.

The first, it was argued, would undermine the close-knit 'family' structure of the school, and thereby reduce the amount of time teachers could devote to the needs of individual children. The second would serve to divert attention from the main purpose of the school - namely learning for its own sake and not for the sake of extrinsic rewards.

The answer given by the Heads and the Council remained the same; the school would not have survived if it had not responded to change, or, if it had survived, it would not have been as it was as present, but in the form of a therapeutic institution catering almost exclusively for children with learning or behaviourial difficulties.

As for learning for its own sake, there was nothing to suggest that examinations and intrinsic learning were of necessity mutually exclusive. It was the role of the teacher, by the provision of intrinsic motivation, to ensure that they were not. Current school numbers left considerable room for expansion before there could be any threat to the 'family' network, or deterioration of the close staff-pupil relations which had always characterised KAS. On the contrary, since the increase in numbers went *pari passu* with a proportional increase in staffing, conditions improved measurably, for additional specialists could be employed, extending the range of optional subjects in the curriculum and introducing new services, for example, remedial education and counselling.

Towards the end of the decade Council announced, in connection with the forthcoming building programme, an increase to be phased over the period 1969 to 1979 from 350 to 480 pupils.

Another myth which sprang from the examinations issue was that there might be a concentration on the needs of the academic at the expense of the non-academic pupils - a suggestion of a discriminatory two-tier system quite alien to the ethos of the school. This too had to be dispelled by reassurances to the contrary.

It was pointed out that KAS was comprehensive in intake, and that its pupils were taught in mixed-ability groups. Each child was recognised and treated as an individual, valued as a member of the community with a unique personal contribution to make to it. The success of any one child was recognised, irrespective of whether the achievement was in academic studies, arts, crafts, drama or sport.

If there had ever been any suggestion of elitism, however fleeting, at KAS, it was not on the basis of academic achievement, but quite the converse. Anecdotal evidence of this transpired in an attitude survey of Old Alfredians conducted in 1989. One respondent recalled being made to feel inferior and excluded by 'an elite group of hippy, arty, 'in' people'.

Nikki, whose first teaching appointment in Bristol had been in a special school for children with learning difficulties,[55] had a vested interest in children with special educational needs, and was largely responsible for the introduction of specialist remedial tuition at KAS as well as the employment of a school counsellor. Her experience of exceptionally intelligent, creative or gifted children had led her to the view that many, if not all of their number, belonged by definition in the category of those with special educational needs. So far from gifted children requiring no special consideration, some, as a result of physical, psychological, or social factors, were functioning well below their intellectual capacity, while others were bored and frustrated because teachers lacked the knowledge of how to provide for their special needs, and to optimise their special abilities.[56]

Doubtless the relaxed atmosphere and the child-centred curriculum of KAS served the gifted child well enough before the Second World War, but during the 1960s a growing body of research became available on the nature of giftedness and the conditions most favourable to its development as well as those likely to frustrate it. This research received a considerable amount of attention both among interested members of the public and in educational circles. Campaigners promoting the interests of gifted children recommended the introduction of special facilities in schools and of supplementary extra-curricular activities to enhance the development of their exceptional abilities. These efforts culminated eventually in the foundation of the National Association for Gifted Children (NAGC) whose aims included the raising of public consciousness, the dissemination of

---

[55] q.v. Chapter 5
[56] Appendix B. Case study of a gifted child under the pseudonym 'Karl' by Nikki Archer

information, and the improvement of communications between those engaged in the work.

The latter organisation acted as a moderating influence on those elitists who appeared to be thinking in terms of segregating gifted children and exposing them to some form of pressurised treatment. Margaret Branch, one of its founders and first chairperson, showed herself to be in sympathy with the ideals of progressive education when she wrote of the need to view child development as a whole - physical, intellectual and emotional.[57]

This was akin to KAS philosophy, which stressed not only the education of the whole person but also the discrete nature of childhood. A child was not an adult in miniature, and childhood was not merely a stage in the progress towards adulthood. The chauvinistic notion of selecting gifted children and separating them from their peer group as an elite, implicitly 'different' from 'normal' people, was alien to their most fundamental beliefs. While the idea of some kind of hothouse treatment, some kind of express course of education calculated to accelerate development was regarded as a denial of the childhood which formed an essential part of the normal pattern of growth. In the words of Friedrich Froebel: 'The boy has not become a boy, nor the youth a youth, by reaching a certain age, but only by having lived through childhood and further on through boyhood, true to the requirements of his mind, his feelings and his body'.

The combination of individualised and group learning at KAS was well adapted to meet the special needs of gifted children. It provided opportunities for both self-directed studies at the child's own level of ability and for collaborative learning with other children in mixed ability groups.

The demands of the teacher's role were complex. Not all gifted children had been identified as such: some were underachieving to such an extent that their giftedness remained undiscovered. Intelligence tests, with all their limitations, were still found useful in providing a preliminary indication that some children might have unrealised potentialities. Once identified, this category of pupils required diagnosis and remedial treatment before further progress could be made.

Where the gifted child was clearly identified, the teacher was involved in the deployment of different sets of skills for individual and group learning situations.

In the first of these a high degree of sensitivity to the child's needs was required, and the ability to act as a facilitator, devising individual projects and assignments calculated to stimulate learning and stretch capacity, as well as providing access to learning resources.

In the group situation the teacher became less of a learning facilitator and more of a social facilitator, involving the child in classroom interaction, encouraging him/her to participate in discussion where all were equal and

---

[57] Branch, M and Cash, A. Gifted Children. Souvenir Press, 1966.

able to express themselves freely, on condition that they did so with respect and consideration for others.

Also required was the maturity to be able to accept that a child might be and probably was capable in many situations of more intelligent behaviour than the teacher. Conversely, the immaturity of other dimensions of the child's personality left many ways in which the teacher could reinforce the process of development. Whilst any extra-curricular activity in which the child expressed special interest was encouraged, it was not done in a way suggesting undue pressure. On the other hand, everything was done to create a learning environment in which he/she could live as normal a life as possible, as an accepted member of the peer group and the school, valued for personal qualities which conferred no extraordinary status or special privilege.

On one occasion Nikki received a letter from a parent whose son had recently gained a First Class Honours degree and a research scholarship at Cambridge. 'There were many people who said the relaxed atmosphere at KAS was all very well', he wrote, 'but the children's future will depend more on getting ahead in the rat race, which usually means getting into a university. My reply was always that if children can have their first eighteen years spent in happy school days, that amounts to a quarter of their life and, with such a happy foundation, it must be a good idea that, if they are relaxed and happy, they are just as likely to win the prizes as those who are breaking their heads in crammer schools. It is nice that I can say I told you so with both my children. One other point, when Anthony was about seven, you thought it was a good idea, from a social point of view, that he should stay down one year. This idea met with strenuous opposition from all our numerous friends and relations, who thought this step would put him behind for the rest of his life. Fortunately, although I am a democratic socialist, I run my home as a benevolent dictatorship and I decided that King Alfred knew better even than Anthony's grandpa. As I understand that Anthony had got one of the best firsts on record, it would appear that has been vindicated too.'

Feedback of this kind was rare, but welcomed by staff for the reassurance it provided that their efforts were broadly on the right lines. And it was, in Nikki's view, to the staff that credit was due for the relative successes of individual pupils, whether gifted or not, in whatever aspect of school life they had excelled. 'It was always the class teachers who took the main burden of responsibility for the children in their groups each year, and their professional skill and personal commitment to the ethos of the school was of paramount importance. It was their personal knowledge of individual children based on daily contact that provided the most reliable and positive picture of each child's needs and capabilities. Many children came to us with damaged self-confidence as the result of earlier experience and needed all the expertise and reassurance that staff could give them before they were able to develop their own abilities and feel recognised and valued for what they were rather than for what they might one day achieve.'

13 New Threats to Survival

In the mid-1960s, with a Labour Government in power, two political events occurred which had implications for King Alfred School. First was the promulgation of Circular 10/65, in which Anthony Crosland, the Secretary of State for Education, sought to accelerate the reorganisation of all maintained secondary schools on comprehensive lines. The second, complementary but with a view to change in the longer term, was the setting up of a Public Schools Commission[58] under the chairmanship of John (later Sir John) Newsom, to recommend how the public and direct grant schools could be integrated into a national comprehensive school system. Both measures were concerned with Labour's ultimate goal of establishing a single national system of schools through which all children would pass, irrespective of ability, gender or social origin.

A number of comprehensive schools already existed, having been the preferred form of implementing the 1944 Education Act in some Local Education Authorities (LEAs), both Conservative and Labour-controlled. Support for comprehensives was thus not strictly polarised on party lines, but while Conservative policy allowed choice, universal comprehensivisation was an essential feature of Labour ideology.

At KAS the expectation was that 'push' and 'pull' factors would probably operate in response to the gathering momentum of the comprehensive school movement. Some parents might find the new schools attractive, and certainly more economical, for the same kinds of reasons that had brought them to King Alfred; for example, non-selective entry, mixed-ability teaching, wide choice of academic and non-academic courses, new curricula, backed by generous learning resources, and the research and development functions of the Schools' Council.

Conversely, such parents might be off-set by a contra-flow of parents from the new comprehensives, apprehensive about real or imagined problems of learning and behaviour associated with the sheer scale of these organisations. It had to be faced that they were still largely an unknown quantity and of enormous diversity, some in modern purpose-built premises, others amalgamations of existing schools; some relatively liberal and progressive, others still bearing the authoritarian imprint. In addition, however 'progressive' they were, this was almost invariably defined in terms of what was acceptable to the LEA, school governors, parent body and teaching staff. Which is to say that it fell short or was a misapplication of orthodox progressive educational principles. Exceptions to this were so few that they effectively proved the rule.

---

[58] Public Schools Commission Report, DES 1968

Ahead of her Time

Risinghill,[59] a large comprehensive school in a working-class district of London, was one such exception. Michael Duane, the Headmaster, following his appointment in 1960, abolished corporal punishment and ran the school on progressive lines until 1965, when it was closed down by the Inner London Education Authority. The experiment had shown how far it was possible to translate progressive educational principles and methods into a state secondary school. His transformation of the school provoked both hostility and enthusiastic support. What was greeted as an unqualified success by his supporters was regarded as a failure by his more numerous and influential opponents.

The official reason given for the closure was that the premises were urgently needed to accommodate Starcross, a secondary school for girls. Several months before this, Nikki, who had visited Risinghill and knew of its achievements under Michael Duane, wrote to Anthony Crosland, making a plea for reversal of the decision: 'I am aware of the need for accommodation which has made the proposal to transfer Starcross School an understandable and apparently reasonable one. What concerns me is the even more vital need of the children who at present attend Risinghill and those who should go there in future.

'All schools which, forsaking the traditional sanctions in education, attempt to establish a free and direct relationship with their pupils, encounter temporary crises. The stage which Risinghill has reached is precisely this. If support were forthcoming now, a new life and vigour might be given to that movement in education which finds expression in the progressive schools, and which must be the basis of any really successful attempt to implement the Newsom Report[60] in spirit as well as in letter.

'Our juvenile courts are full of potential young criminals who, from a deep conviction that they are up against authority in all aspects of life, probably cannot now be helped. Mr Duane and his staff, by their policy of personal concern for each child's problems and by their refusal to take the easy way out which corporal punishment offers teachers, would continue gradually to reduce the numbers of children who reach the courts.

'If Risinghill becomes a girls' school there will no doubt be many people who will feel relieved at the prospect of less trouble with discipline. But for those boys and girls who are now likely to be denied an education in which discipline by fear is forbidden this decision will constitute a very real setback.

'I feel confident that, with the power to implement the progressive policy of education which it outlined while in opposition, the Government will not be guided solely by material considerations and expediency in such a case. There is so much more at stake here than simply a matter of administrative

[59] Berg, L. Risinghill: Death of a Comprehensive School, Penguin 1968
[60] Central Advisory Council for Education (England). Report 'Half our Future', HMSO (1963)

convenience. If Starcross and Risinghill were to join forces as a truly comprehensive and co-educational school, and the present conflict were to be lost in the new process of growth, the whole of the educational world would be the richer for it.'

In January of the same year as the closure of Risinghill, Alan Humphries, Nikki and A.S.Neill appeared with Michael Duane in an ITV documentary called 'Sunday Break'. The theme of the programme was whether progressive education could become a reality in the state system. Duane gave an account of the social environment of his school and of the reforms he had introduced since his appointment in 1960. Neill commented favourably on the school, describing it as 'giving out love' and as having far greater handicaps than Summerhill, 'where the parents believed in freedom and what the school was doing'. It was left to Alan and Nikki to give their accounts of different aspects of KAS, its history, philosophy, and the characteristics distinguishing it from more conventional schools.

These individual contributions established the existence of much common ground between the participants, but the difficulties peculiar to Risinghill became increasingly apparent as the programme unfolded. A councillor and member of Risinghill's parent-teacher association praised Duane's initiative; and a parent expressed respect for him but did not think the system worked: 'he treats all the children as 'problem children' when he should treat them as normal. To do otherwise is to exonerate the child from all responsibility'.

A probation officer thought the approach was correct and liked the emphasis placed on the development of originality and independence, adding, 'You can't really expect a boy from a deprived background to conform to the rigid pattern of conventional schools'. At this point a voice-over announced, 'Risinghill is to close in July. Michael Duane's efforts will not go unnoticed. Progressive education brought some benefits to Risinghill.' And the final word went to the principal of a teachers' training college, 'I think we should see more experiments of this kind in state schools'.

The fate of Risinghill should not be allowed to obscure the fact that a number of progressive comprehensive schools, typified by Countesthorpe[61] and Stantonbury, survived and flourished in spite of opposition, an achievement largely due to LEA support and other favourable circumstances unfortunately lacking in the case of Michael Duane.

The subsequent development of the comprehensive school movement, whilst it included the emergence of a number of outstanding schools, was qualitatively so unequal that it was not surprising to find only a very few parents removed their children from KAS, whereas the number of pupils transferring to the school went on increasing well into the next decade.

---

[61] Watts, J. The Countesthorpe Experience. Allen & Unwin (1977)

The Public Schools Commission had been mandated to conduct their inquiry in two stages. First, they were to consider the boarding schools and only on the completion of this stage to turn their attention to day schools. The matter was not therefore as urgent for KAS as it was for the other members of the progressive school community. Nevertheless, a close watch was kept on events, and discussions took place on the future role of the school in the event of integration into a unified system of education. Nikki's view was that, if integration proved to be a serious possibility, a pre-emptory case should be prepared for submission to the Department of Education and Science, recommending the designation of KAS as a special 'centre of excellence'. It could fulfil the role envisaged by its founders as 'a demonstration school', collaborating with training colleges and university departments of education in the dissemination of progressive educational ideas and teaching methods. To do nothing and simply wait for the school's role to be arbitrarily imposed could lead to the extinction of the school in its present form, and the dissolution of seventy years' specialised experience.

By the time the Commission reported, it was apparent that the fears of the independent schools could be laid to rest for the time being. For all that Anthony Crosland had wanted to integrate them into a unitary system, he made it clear he would not countenance their abolition as this would have been an unacceptable curtailment of democracy.

The Report contained detailed recommendations on the ways in which integration could be effected, but the financial estimate of the cost of such an operation to the LEAs was so prohibitive that the Government was compelled to shelve the policy indefinitely.

Some three years before the Commission had been set up, a series of articles by Caroline Nicholson[62] appeared in the Observer, posing the question of whether the progressive schools were still progressive or whether they had been compelled by the struggle for survival to compromise, and thereby change the kind of education they had set out to achieve. The question itself was prompted by the curricular innovations of the new primary and secondary comprehensive schools and their claim to be the new progressives. In the course of her investigation Caroline Nicholson visited eleven of the schools concerned. At KAS she was impressed by the welcoming atmosphere which was discernible not only in the reception of visitors 'but also in the welcoming of children in all their diversity. All people matter and all people matter equally.' The survey concluded that most of the schools had had to make compromises but these had not necessarily involved the sacrifice of traditional principles. The openness and informal relationships remained, the child-centredness, and the emphasis on the education of the whole person. Compromise over examinations, always the subject of heart-searching, had shown that higher academic standards and humanity were not mutually exclusive.

---

[62] Nicholson, C. op cit. Chapter 8

Another compromise was over finance. Insolvency might at one time have been a mark of ideological purity - 'we'll avoid corruption by avoiding proper budgeting' - but it could not last.

The KAS balance sheet, she noted, was in a healthy condition. Also, in some schools, there had been a marked compromise in relation to the democratic process, more particularly in children's participation in the regime. On this the author commented, 'Any form of democracy in schools can be abused or become phoney, but I feel uneasy that so many heads say this with relief'.

As to the claim that the progressive impulse had passed to the state schools, she acknowledged that this was true of some but by no means all such schools. Some of the progressives had resisted compromise more than others, but perhaps at the cost of isolation from the world outside. Growing points in education, she asserted, could not be pinned down to any type of school or system. 'It happens where there is diversity and integration. Here is progressive education.'

The establishment of the Public Schools Commission, the 'progressive' aspirations of the state schools, and, possibly, the reverberations of the Nicholson inquiry persuaded the trustees of Dartington Hall School to convene a conference in 1965 'with a view to establishing the position of progressive education in the contemporary world.'[63] These terms of reference were in effect an enlargement of the kinds of discussion taking place at KAS at this time, and motivated by the same considerations.

The intention of the trustees had been to arrange for 'a meeting of minds', drawn not only from the progressive movement but also from the educational world in general. To keep the numbers within reasonable bounds, only a few of the progressive schools were represented, and these did not include KAS because, as a day school, it was presumably thought to be less closely involved with the agenda than the boarding establishments. Apart from the trustees and joint heads of Dartington, the other delegates included representatives from the maintained system of education, universities and research departments, together with several eminent psychologists.

What had been intended as a fruitful exchange of ideas between groups sharing a common interest in progressive education turned out to be a confrontation between irreconcilable attitudes and assumptions. The common interest was quickly shown to be more apparent than real, whereas the basic reality was a conflict between traditional and modern progressives.

Speakers from the traditional progressive schools collectively presented a retrospective view of progressive education - stressing in particular the importance of psychology - and a survey of contemporary practice.

---

[63] Ash, M et al Who are the Progressives Now? An account of an educational confrontation, RKP, 1969.

Ahead of her Time

Whether they had had early warning of what was to follow is not known, but the vehemence of the critical attack to which they were subsequently exposed must have taken them by surprise.

It started with a concession. Whilst credit was due to them for pioneering progressive ideas in education, these had now been adopted in the state schools. 'So what', asked a former chief education officer from Devon, 'have they got that the national system has not, or won't have shortly?'

It was claimed that progressive schools created a protected environment 'against harmful relationships and the supposedly terrifying curricular requirements of the state system'. This arose, in the opinion of Professor Harry Ree of York University, 'out of ignorance and an outdated Boys' Own Paper image of modernised state schools'. They insulated children from the real world outside, 'keeping them away from immediate and immense social problems, whereas state schools are right up against them'. For all their claims to social integration, for example through voluntary social work in the community, this was usually 'at a distance' , self-consciously condescending, short-lived and not genuinely 'of the community'. They might turn out many well-balanced people but only within the narrow social context of people like themselves. This comment was of a piece with the observation that education in progressive schools should not be only for the privileged few whose parents could afford to pay fees.

It was left to Doctor D.Cook of the Devon LEA to deliver the final broadside, drawing an analogy between the progressive schools and the denominational schools in the past, 'their pioneering work finished, dragging along in the wake of the maintained system where all the progressive things were happening, and gradually by a series of compromises entering the national system themselves'. Was it not time, he asked, for the independent progressive schools to do the same?[64]

This expressed the 'modern' progressive's case in a nutshell: the traditional schools had fulfilled their purpose and should now be considering what role they could play when incorporated into a national system; the 'new' progressives, representing the state and the scientific approach, had superseded them.

There was little direct and no co-ordinated response to all the above points by the progressive school representatives. It was as if the suddenness of the attack had left them temporarily speechless. The silence did not last, however, and was broken eventually by a series of spirited rejoinders. L.C. Shiller, who had shown in a paper on progressive ideas in state schools that these had influenced the primary more than the secondary sector, now scorned the irrelevance - 'the little bits of research' - being conducted in the new comprehensive schools. Kenneth Barnes, Head of Wennington, stressed the goal of producing originality (in its widest

---

[64] Ash, M. et al op cit.

sense), especially in personal relations, implying that comprehensive schools provided little time for this. While Maurice Ash commented that when it was claimed in the state system that all children were now regarded as equally important, this was not the same thing as considering each child as a person.[65] Notions of this kind might have contributed to a substantive answer to the question 'what have the progressive schools got that the national system has not?' But, unfortunately, a lasting impression had been made by the comment of one of the heads to the effect that 'it was something intangible, so far not identified', and this confirmed the 'modern' progressives in all their prejudices.

Clearly the irreconcilability between the protagonists arose from different interpretations of the meaning of progressive education. When the state schools claimed to be in the vanguard it was on the basis of widespread research activity taking place into testing, teaching, learning, methodology, school organisation, etc., and of concern for individual differences and related needs. When they claimed to be as concerned with the individual, and as child-centred as the progressives, it was not the same thing at all, being concerned with children as units and not as persons. In the state schools the concern was still predominantly with society and its demands, whereas in the progressive schools the main concern was with the child.

Aside from the confrontation, valuable contributions were made by the research psychologists who were present at the conference. In addition, one of the trustees, the social scientist Doctor Michael Young (later Lord Young of Dartington), spoke on 'Progressive Schools and the State'. Predicting that these schools would not be compelled to enter the national system, he suggested for discussion the options open to them if they should wish to do so. This overlapped to some extent with discussions that had been held at KAS when considering the objectives of the Public Schools Commission. In due course, those schools which had not been represented at the conference obtained reports of the proceedings and Nikki expressed her thoughts on some of the main issues. On the underlying causes of the confrontation, she thought there was some truth in the claim that ignorance and prejudice could be found on both sides of the argument. Relatively few educationalists ever visited schools in the opposite camp. It was therefore 'not a fruitful exercise to throw bricks across the divide, and I always felt we should be looking for those aspects of child development on which we could agree, and try to explain what we thought was essential in the perspectives and methods of the two different approaches'.

She felt that the modern progressives at the conference had made the mistake, possibly with intent, of stereotyping the progressive schools and thus glossing over their actual diversity. It was salutary to remember that

---

[65] ibid.

there were also variations between the comprehensive schools, for example between those in socially-privileged suburban areas and those in the inner city. The degrees of 'protectedness' and 'insulation from the real world' were manifestly different. 'In such contrasting social situations, protectiveness is, after all, a variable. Parental attitudes can range, in my experience from the excessively protective to the almost unbelievably casual, and teachers also have a wide range of standards when it comes to defining what is essential protection and what is overdoing it. In responding to the charge that our children are insulated from 'real' problems, I must acknowledge that our position as a day school is different from that of our boarding school colleagues. But I would say that, while the children of the progressive movement may not have had their noses rubbed in the compost heap of poverty, they have had to deal from an early age with the problems which an 'open system' involves. Insularity is far from being a typical descriptive feature of progressive school children. On the contrary, the success of our methods was described by one Cambridge don as the production of really sane young adults who could and did take responsibility. I think it was the assumption that progressive educational ideas had been so fully established in the state schools that I found particularly objectionable. Pioneering ideas require two things for their implementation: first they must be genuinely understood, and secondly they must be supported by proper financial and other provision. If either of these is lacking, no more than lip service can be paid to them in practice. At KAS we had always had a struggle to work on the lines we believed were right for children, and the very survival of the school owed a great deal to the self-denial of those teachers who in the early days worked for very low salaries, and in some cases for no salary at all. The state system certainly adopted some of the ideas of the early educationists in the progressive field, but the most important idea, which was the high ratio of staff to children, was never implemented. This is the fundamental reason why the state schools have not been able to achieve progressive education in the sense in which we understand the term.

'At the time when money appeared most plentiful in state-funded education, priority was given to prestigious buildings, fittings, audio-visual aids, etc., and not to reducing class numbers.

'The result was seen later when it was found that many pupils in beautiful and well-equipped comprehensive schools were neither grateful for their new surroundings nor inspired by their opportunity to learn new and exciting skills. The large scale of the comprehensives reduced the opportunities for the development of genuine pupil-teacher relations, with a resultant growth in the influence of the peer group. All education is a process of change which arises through relationships with other people, and children learn about being adults through their contact with older people and not with their peers. No teacher, however skilled and conscientious, can balance the influence of the dominant element in a group of youngsters who are determined not to learn. Even in small classes there are problems, and immense patience is needed to overcome the resistance manifested by children who don't enjoy a particular subject.'

Financial estimates relating to the programme of expansion scheduled for the late 1960s had risen sharply as a result of increased building costs. Once again the Society was faced with the economic reality that its income from fees was barely sufficient to cover current expenditure. Any major projects of the kind in question had to be funded by alternative means. As so often in the past, the Society had to rely on its own efforts and on the generosity of others, but on a scale much larger than ever before. 'The difference between the sixties and the twenties and thirties', observed one Council member, 'was that magnificent things could be done then, without money, but not now'.

The urgency of the situation prompted Council and Heads to invite help from a wider range of parents than hitherto, in particular to call on the influence and expertise of those in business and management. The Appeals Committee, for example, included four businessmen, a theatrical impresario, and an eminent civil servant, while its patrons comprised three Members of Parliament, including two of Cabinet rank. Parents who had not hitherto done so were encouraged to covenant their school fees; approaches were made to firms and charitable institutions, and donations were canvassed. The Parent-Staff Committee were indefatigable in organising drama festivals, music recitals, and a variety of fund-raising events in which Open Day featured as the high point of the year.

The Press was on the whole a valuable ally in the campaign, publicising, as it had done so often in the past, noteworthy events in the daily life of the school in exchange for news items of usually more than common interest.

If KAS was to some extent ambivalent towards the Press it was because of unfortunate experiences in the past when they had found individual journalists capable of gross irresponsibility harmful to the school. These instances demonstrated the readiness of some journalists to seek out and emphasise, if not to actually manufacture, sensational news. An early experience of this was when a reporter, whom they had welcomed to the school on what was understood to be a bona fide fact-finding assignment, induced a child to be photographed climbing out of a classroom window. A few days later the photograph appeared in a newspaper with the caption: 'The way to get out of lessons at King Alfred School'.

Far less objectionable was a feature article in the Daily Mail with the headline: 'When they wear what they like, just look what they wear'. This was illustrated by pictures of three young girls wearing an assortment of clothing, including a mini dress, a maxi skirt, jeans, a cartwheel hat, and 'a sweater borrowed from a tall male.' The photographs were well posed and of considerable charm, and, while they almost certainly pleased the initiated, they also doubtless confirmed all the worst prejudices of the intolerant.

But John Izbicki, a KAS parent, more than compensated for cases like this, which were exceptional and relatively few. As Education Correspondent of the Daily Telegraph, he made an invaluable contribution to KAS through the medium of his influential column, regularly publicising the school's educational ideas and values, praising its achievements, and correcting many of the wilder rumours it inevitably attracted.[66]

The effects of this kind of publicity were palpable but usually indirect, long-term, and not easily measurable. The same could be said of the Heads' intermittent appearances in radio and television feature programmes and of their not infrequent correspondence with the newspapers. Like the regular coverage of events taking place in the school, they had the function of attracting public attention, disseminating KAS philosophy, and recruiting new pupils - one good reason for not courting bad publicity.

Granada TV had filmed at King Alfred in connection with a series on progressive education in 1965, and followed this up with another series for 15 year olds dealing with Human Relations, in which they again sought the school's collaboration. Elaine Grand, the producer, wrote to Nikki about this: 'As an admirer of your school and its principles, I would be most grateful if I could see you at some time about the preparation of the series'. Two senior pupils, Gavin Wright and Stacey Tendetter, were particularly asked for 'because they were good in discussion and wanted for further appearances'. In January 1968 the Golders Green News bore a headline: 'New Block in Action', and went on to announce the official opening of the new £60,000 Science and Arts Building. While readers of the Hampstead & Highgate Express (the 'Ham & High') were informed that a new voluntary activity called 'The Young Music Makers' had been started at KAS on Saturday mornings 'for mothers and musical children'; and, in another issue, 'unlike many private schools, KAS tends to try new experimental methods, such as Cuisenaire Rods, Colour Factor, and the Initial Teaching Alphabet'.

From time to time, the national dailies would be attracted by newsworthy items relating to the school, especially when they had to do with celebrities. One instance of this occurred in 1969 with a report in the Sunday Telegraph that Peter Sellers's son, Michael, was part of a team which had entered a £1,000 short film in Britain's first National Film Festival for students. 'Fifteen 6th formers from KAS which runs a production unit recruited Michael to edit the film, financed by their parents. Part of the film was made in Peter Sellers's former home in Elstead in Surrey, now occupied by Ringo Starr. The 16mm film was shot in Eastmancolour.'

---

[66] See also Izbicki, J. Education A-Z. Collins, 1978

13 New Threats to Survival

One important outcome of the efforts of the Appeals Committee was the introduction of a new and more profitable means of fund-raising - that of the theatrical or film benefit performance. One of the first ventures of this kind took place in 1965, when the theatrical impresario John Gale, KAS parent and member of the Committee, presented Rupert Davies in Georges Simenon's 'Maigret and the Lady' at the Strand Theatre. It was billed as 'a preview, performed in aid of the King Alfred School Building Development and Endowment Appeal'.

A few years later, the Daily Express announced that the European film premiere of Stanley Kubrick's '2001 - a Space Odyssey' was to be shown at the Casino Cinerama in London's West End. What the report did not say was that Stanley Kubrick was also a KAS parent.

Not all such ventures, however well-intentioned, ran as smoothly or were so well organised. One parent, not on the Appeals Committee, knew a pop singer who had suggested making a short film at KAS. It was to feature a performance of his own work, and he had asked if volunteer pupils could be enlisted to act as 'teeny-boppers'. The whole operation was to be completed during the lunch break and a reciprocal contribution was to be made to the Appeal Fund. The parent obtained clearance from the Heads, accepted full responsibility, and went ahead with the organisation of the event. With the sequel that, since the role of the children had not been made sufficiently explicit, they ended up over-excited, completely exhausted, and in no fit condition for afternoon school. What had started out with the best of intentions had gone badly wrong and, although no serious harm had been done, it was difficult to escape the feeling that the children had in a sense been made the victims of exploitation. In the light of this experience, it was not surprising when, shortly afterwards, an opportunity arose to benefit from a special performance of a Beatles' film, the Heads turned it down. It would not, in their view, have been good for KAS to be associated with the kind of mass hysteria that usually surrounded the public appearances of the Beatles. The new breed of school development directors of more recent times would understand the reasons for such a decision, knowing the care and integrity that are necessary if they are to preserve the good image not only of individual schools but also that of the independent sector as a whole.

14   New Directions

In 1970 an important change took place in the school which was to have far-reaching effects. Soon after the start of the January term, Alan Humphries informed Council that he had applied for and been offered the post of Headmaster of the new British School in Brussels, and would be leaving at Easter to take up his new appointment. As a result of this, it became necessary to give urgent consideration to the responsibility structure of the school, in the light of present and future needs. After exhaustive discussion, the staff decided to put before Council the view that positions of responsibility should be filled, where possible, from within the school. Experience suggested that it took about two years for teachers joining KAS to succeed in making their full contribution, and positions of authority tended to be most successful when they were allowed to grow. The beginning of a period of expansion and development seemed an appropriate time at which to reorganise the responsibility structure in a way that would make the most positive use of staff experience. Council's decision, therefore, to appoint Nikki as sole Head, Roy Greenfield as Deputy Head, Margaret Maxwell as Senior Mistress, and Malcolm Manwaring as Head of Middle School had the clear support of all members of staff[67]. Self-evidently, these changes had involved a review of the question of co-headship. In retrospect, it had acquired more the status of a longitudinal experiment than a permanent institution, and, as such, it was open to revaluation in the light of changed circumstances. At this critical stage in the history of the school the disadvantages were more apparent than the advantages. For example, the acceleration in the pace of change and the extension of the Heads' responsibilities severely curtailed the time available for consultation, and seriously delayed the process of decision-making. Also, regrettably, there were those individuals, fortunately few in number, who were not above playing off one Head against the other, a phenomenon not uncommon in the best-regulated families.

Nikki had not forgotten the ideal of co-headship envisaged in the paper 'Functions of the Heads' which she had circulated several years before.[68] However, experience had shown that it was an ideal not to be achieved merely by the willing efforts of the individuals concerned, but that it depended also on the social and cultural context. Equivocal attitudes towards sexual equality and, in particular, to women in authority, persisted in society, and even KAS could not claim to be entirely free from them. The co-headship of Nikki and Alan Humphries had been as effective as it could be in the current stage of social evolution.

---

[67] A few years later, Gordon Davies, Head of Science, was appointed as an additional Deputy Head.
[68] op cit. Page 137.

Ahead of her Time

The KASS Annual Report for 1970 contained a foreword by the Chairman, W.A. (Alan) Wood, in which he said on behalf of the Council how happy they had been to put their confidence in her as sole Head. 'She has taken over', he added, 'at a critical time in the history of King Alfred School and things were not made any easier for her by the fact that all the changes had to happen in the middle of the school year. We must all be grateful for the way she has set about the job and for the splendid support she has secured from the whole staff.'

In the mid-1960s, contingencies affecting the relationship between Nikki and Paul led inexorably towards the breakdown of their marriage and to an eventual divorce. In a legal context which still made it difficult for couples to end their marriages amicably, they retained for each other the genuine respect and affection that had always hitherto characterised their relationship. It was the kind of marriage breakdown which the Divorce Reform Act of 1969 would have particularly addressed, for, although not without pain, it was free from the guilt, shame and bitterness which the Act sought to alleviate. And, in the years that followed, what was inherently a warm and caring relationship endured and remained a constant source of enrichment in both their subsequent lives.

The divorce proceedings were thus easier for all concerned than they would otherwise have been. The case was undefended, and the Court's arrangements relating to the custody of the children, disposition of property, and financial provision, were settled without disagreement.

Nikki set up a new home in Woodside Park Road, North Finchley, and Paul continued to live at the former family home in Hampstead Garden Suburb.

Miranda and Richard, who had been weekly boarders under a supposedly progressive regime at the Town and Country School, had become unsettled and miserable. They were therefore relieved when Nikki and Paul found places for them at Monkton Wyld, a progressive boarding school near Charmouth, in Dorset. It had been a difficult decision to make, but one which seemed in the circumstances to be for the best. The children had been accustomed to progressive education from infancy onwards and would have been unhappy in a state school. 'Miranda had lost confidence in her abilities when she was at day school where her dyslexia had been neither recognised nor helped, and she probably suffered more from the change than we realised at the time. She was deeply unhappy at being away from home - the only place she felt really secure. Would not King Alfred School have been the obvious solution? Paradoxically, no. The inadvisability of children's attending a school where one of the parents is Head had been so widely corroborated as to become, in the educational world, a part of received wisdom. The permutations of role conflict which can ensue do not require elaboration here. Nikki summed up the more important implications with characteristic succinctness: 'Miranda and

Richard would have suffered if I had taken unpopular policy decisions. I was not willing to see them become 'hostages' for my 'good' behaviour'.

In the early sixties, Nikki's mother, Meg, lived on the Isle of Wight with her sister, Constance. For a time, they ran a small hotel in Ventnor, but eventually, and not for the first time, agreed to part company and go their separate ways. Con returned to the mainland, and Meg moved to Carisbrooke, a village near the centre of the island, overlooked by the ruins of its ancient castle, where Charles I was imprisoned prior to his trial and execution. She came to London and stayed with the family at regular intervals, and members of the family spent several holidays at Carisbrooke during the years she was there. During these years also, a number of KAS teenagers had reason to be grateful for Meg's kindness and hospitality, when getting away from London provided a welcome relief from problems which had threatened to overwhelm them.

She had been reminded periodically that, whenever she felt she could no longer continue living on her own, she would be welcome to rejoin the family in London on a permanent basis. She eventually decided that this time had come, and in 1966 moved into 2 Woodside Park Road in Finchley, where Nikki had converted the whole of the ground floor into a self-contained flat for her accommodation.

By this time Nikki and I had been married for two years. Pat, my former wife, who had custody of our children, had during this period remarried. We all tried to put the children's interests first, while accepting that no change of this kind can occur without pain and regret. Our children were all inevitably affected in their own individual ways by the change but, with the passage of time, gradually adapted to it. In this, they were helped by the reassurance of parental love and care, and by the co-operation of the adults in maintaining a cohesive albeit an extended family structure.

In 1968 my mother, Dorothy (Dorrit) Archer, retired from the Royal School, Bath where she had worked as a house matron since 1954, the year of my father's death. We talked with her about the possibilities of coming to live with us, but she was afraid of being a burden and insisted on preserving her independence. We were able to find her a flat in the house of Mrs Peggy Mitchell, a friend who lived only a short distance from us in North Finchley.

15   Selection and In-Service Training

Amongst the many problems facing Nikki at the school in 1970 were those concerning the recruiting, selection and in-service training of new staff. The programme of expansion that lay ahead, the curricular innovations, and growing demands of social change and new legislation made it imperative that staff should be of the highest professional competence and personal quality. Council had acknowledged the importance of this by entrusting the primary responsibility for the appointment of staff to the joint Heads, a responsibility that now fell to Nikki as sole Head. The school's distinctive aims and objectives required of its teachers not only exceptional pedagogical skills but also a high degree of empathy, understanding and maturity. By the same token, the achievement of its goals required the close co-operation between school and home that had always been a characteristic feature of KAS.

In the light of these criteria, it was an irony frequently observed that progressive schools appear to have a singular attraction for immature teachers. There are those who go through a developmental process similar to that of some children who transfer to progressive schools at an advanced stage of their education and experience initial difficulties of adjustment. A causal factor in both cases appears to be the existence of an authoritarian background, typically involving family, previous schools, or both. Often, like most apostates, they go to extremes of enthusiasm, embracing unrealistic ideas of what progressive education is about.

Caroline Nicholson's Observer articles attracted a number of letters expressing apprehension about teachers of this kind.[69] 'I hope your account', wrote one correspondent, 'has not made it all sound so twee and easy (teacher-pupil ratio 1:9) that teachers with personal problems will be tempted to seek an easy way out in progressive education. Children getting to know themselves in a permissive situation also bring teachers up against their own personalities with a much heavier bump than in the set-up where adults can protect themselves with a screen of discipline.'

Another, more acerbic, writer commented that 'we who scrape harder than we can afford to send our children to progressive schools do so happily if we know we are giving the opportunity to mature, skilled, teachers to educate more fully and generously than would otherwise be possible. But our intention to finance amateur neurosis centres for lost adults at the expense of our children is strictly limited'.

One summer in the 1960s Nikki received the following letter in response to an advertisement which had appeared in a number of newspapers: 'Dear Friend, I am writing about your advertisement in the New Statesman. if I have passed my finals, I shall have a BSc (Special) degree in physics in a

---

[69] Nicholson, Caroline, qv Chapter 8.

few weeks. I am a pacifist, anarchist, and vegetarian. I should like to visit the school informally, so long as no-one else has applied to teach, this is because it is against my principles to compete with anyone else because clearly this means taking the bread out from another's mouth, etc., and in any case the world is big enough for a physicist elsewhere. I am a keen supporter of CND, anti-apartheid (sic), anti-vivisection, etc. I oppose the penal system, the Conservative central office and the concept of punishment. If I come to see you there is no obligation for me to teach and there is no obligation for you to have me teach. However, if I were to teach at King Alfred's, I would expect to have small groups of say four to seven pupils so that I would be able to give the personal love and the tuition in the subject of physics (and the mathematical methods in physics) as per the syllabus of the University of London (or another syllabus if any pupils are studying for other exams). I believe it is also essential that those who will be members of my little seminar should come of their own free will because of their interest and love of physics. There are other things in the world other than physics and I would very strongly recommend that those who are not genuinely interested in physics stay well away from the subject of physics for life.

'There was mention in the advertisement of the Burnham Scale. I do not want the Burnham Scale in fact I do not want any salery (sic). This is because salery is subject to income tax (i.e., State thievery). The Welfare State is spending money on military preparations which I will not support with one penny. I am also opposed to the idea of the national insurance stamp, part of which goes to the so-called health service. I am a supporter of nature cure (or rather prevention) and cannot subscribe to orthodox medicine, although I respect the views of those who do. So in so far as money goes it had better be pocket money or a gift if you want to. I am a total abstainer and a non-smoker.

'Please do not bother to answer this letter if someone else has applied or is applying or if I am not the type of person you are looking for.'

This was clearly an idealist without very much knowledge or experience of progressive education, perhaps in many ways less of a problem than the experienced teacher with an unshakeable commitment to some unrealistic misconception of the principles in question.

Eleanor Urban, a former Head of Monkton Wyld, spoke with feeling at the Dartington Conference in 1965 of 'the very foolish and unrealistic anarchy going on in progressive education'. 'It was', she said, 'individualism run riot - we don't want that. Half-baked adherents who don't quite understand progressive education. It's not just mixing up children and materials and hoping for the best; or a teacher's conscientiously believing she should not suggest anything. Children resent teachers who won't teach.'[70]

---

[70] Ash, M et al, op cit. Chapter 13.

Nikki's view was that those teachers who had extreme notions of freedom in education tended, like A.S.Neill, to confuse what was possible in therapeutic institutions with what was possible in schools. Neill himself was aware of his own weaknesses and how much his ideas lent themselves to misinterpretation. He wanted to criticise 'his sillier disciples' but without, as he said, 'handing a gift to the Thatcherites'.[71]

Nikki found that some new teachers confused being friendly and informal with children with being friends with them. It was a significant semantic distinction with important professional implications. 'Friendship', she pointed out, 'is a reciprocal relationship . A friend is someone you take your troubles to. While children are encouraged to bring their troubles to teachers, it is not expected that teachers will take theirs to the children. If teachers and pupils were to be friends in the literal sense, there would be many ways in which this could effectively undermine the role and function of the teacher. Just because staff and pupils call one another by their first names, it doesn't mean there isn't a certain objectivity in the relationship.'

In contrast to those new teachers who came to the school with preconceived ideas, later modified through observing colleagues, and the advice of senior members of staff, there were others, usually from traditional schools, who did not understand the conventional forms of staff-pupil relationships at KAS and still retained vestiges of an authoritarianism to which they had become habituated. Notwithstanding the initial briefings given to new members of staff, habits persisted at first, and some new teachers found that what were perceived by children as discourtesy and lack of consideration had been the subject of unfavourable reports to their parents.

Nikki felt that the relatively long process of initiation and acculturation ideally experienced by teachers in progressive education raised important considerations relating to the appointment of senior staff. These she imparted to the Chairman of Council in support of proposed changes in the staffing structure necessitated by her appointment as sole Head: 'I am aware of the suspicion and apprehension with which new members of staff tend to be viewed in this school by both parents, children and, to some extent, other members of staff. This seems to have been a characteristic of the school throughout its history, and certainly my experience bears this out. I think it may well be due to the fact that a small, and to some degree, inbred community responds to changes rather in the way that a village does, and with perhaps something of the same justification. It is also observable that, when people have been members of this community for about a year, they begin to change and to allow aspects of their character and personality to come to the surface which hitherto have perhaps not been so noticeable. Where children coming to us from other schools are

---

[71] Hoggart, R. Review of Neill of Summerhill, by J Croall, RKP 1983. Times Educational Supplement, 10th June 1983.

concerned we call this 'the lid coming off' and it is a process we have come to recognise and accept during the first six months after their arrival. With adults it is often delayed, but nonetheless inevitable. The atmosphere of greater freedom here permits people to explore and experience those sides of their own development of which they have hitherto been only partly conscious.

'The result of this is that it takes at least two years before we can be certain of what a person is really like and only the most mature people are the same at the end of the second year as they were when they joined us.

In a school in which authority is viewed with as much distrust as it is here, you can envisage the strength of adverse reaction likely to greet the appointment of external candidates to senior posts on the teaching staff. For this reason I have come to the conclusion that, wherever possible, no-one who has been in the school for less than two years should be appointed to a senior post, accepting, of course, the fact that circumstances may not always make it possible to act in accordance with this principle. There are plenty of examples of the nearly disastrous results of departing from it.'

It was a recommendation well calculated to serve the needs of the school, and one which underlined the distinction between KAS and the average state school. It provided for organic growth, stability and continuity, essential conditions for the achievement of genuine progressive education. Where promotion of staff in the maintained system usually entailed transfer to another school, because of status and authority considerations, promotion in an almost non-hierarchical organisation like King Alfred's could take place without affecting individual status or personal relationships.

The principle had been exemplified by the redistribution of responsibilities following Nikki's appointment as sole head. The newly-created posts were all allocated to senior members of staff, whom she described as 'admirably qualified to fulfil the functions we are looking for, and all with the great advantage of being known and trusted by everyone'.

The in-service training of staff went on continuously, taking several different forms. There was experimental work in classrooms, trying out and evaluating new teaching methods and materials, and testing new types of organisation. Specialists kept themselves abreast of developments in their subjects through membership of professional associations, and most teachers attended refresher courses from time to time.

On the basis of existing arrangements whereby students were enabled to do their teaching practices at KAS, Nikki initiated a productive reciprocal relationship with certain training colleges, which as a *quid pro quo* shared their expertise, offered information and advice, if required (e.g., with reference to Nuffield Science), and encouraged staff to attend short courses or day conferences that might be of interest to them.

Nikki, for her part, made a number of visits over the years to training colleges, lecturing to student teachers and attending seminars; spreading the gospel in the propagandist tradition of her predecessors.

Some members of staff worked extra-murally in order to obtain further academic qualifications. Nikki herself had done this during her early years at KAS, attending part-time the London University Institute of Education, where she studied philosophy for the Academic Diploma as a preliminary to a Master's Degree in Education. 'My last two years of study at the Institute', she wrote to Miss Bull, her former Headmistress at Wallington,[72] 'have been rewarding in every way. They have deepened my understanding and widened my outlook, and I am sure the discipline of work has been good for me. Most of my reading had to be done at 6 o'clock in the morning and I went into the examination with the rather shamed knowledge that I had not done as much as I should have done. However, when I rang my professor to ask whether I had passed, he said 'with flying colours', so I felt much better after that.'

Her degree course at Bristol University in the 1940s had comprised a conventional linear history of philosophical ideas and doctrines, couched in the older view of philosophy as a teleological process towards personal growth, enlightenment and wisdom, what Socrates termed 'guiding the soul'. By contrast, the dominant paradigm represented at the London Institute was linguistic analysis. In the empirical tradition, this regarded the interpretation and understanding of language meanings as a precondition of conceptual analysis or the discussion of abstract ideas. This narrower discipline had important insights to offer teachers, since, for one thing, it disclosed the extraordinary number of educational concepts like motivation, interest, etc., which were shown to mean widely different things to different people.

Unfortunately, the course, which Nikki had at first found stimulating, failed to live up to her expectations. Her original professor, an eminent and well-respected member of 'the old school' of philosophers, retired. After this, seminars were conducted along tutor-directed lines and resolved themselves into brilliant virtuoso performances by the tutors, with only in her view a perfunctory concession to the participation of students. 'Philosophical analysis was transformed into a kind of game', she recalled, 'with rules of procedure which could not be departed from. It was like a form of licensed verbal aggression, reminiscent of the ancient Sophists, where the purpose was to win the argument rather than to seek the truth. When some of us intervened to ask questions or enter the intellectual game, we were dealt with incisively and dismissively, and few ever ventured to participate again. It was an object lesson in how not to teach, and had nothing whatever to do with real understanding.'

---

[72] Miss Bull qv Chapter 6.

Ahead of her Time

For a year she continued to work on her MA thesis, but a steadily growing workload at KAS, especially after her appointment as sole Head, finally obliged her to abandon the enterprise. Some time afterwards, she came across the following poem by Bayard Clayton and noted with some amusement its pertinence to the style of teaching then current on the philosophy course.

<u>Lyric for a Linguistic Analyst</u>

God give me strength to leave you, to deny
The message in your analytic eye,
The cold brain searching for the reasoned laws,
The ritual worship of determined cause,
The calm denial of the power of will
Which, while denying, you exhibit still.
Damn your philosophy! and let me be
Of your too barren cerebration free.
Search out my meaning, and when all's been said
You yet may find me...in a Poet's bed.

An entirely new kind of problem to do with the in-service training of staff arose in 1970. It was without precedent in the history of the school and involved two successive cases of dismissal affecting ethnic minority teachers.

Under the terms of its original constitution KAS was open to teachers, as it was to children, irrespective of race, ethnicity or religion. It was, in effect, an equal opportunities employer long before this designation had been invented. An active theosophical and humanitarian tendency persisted in its inherited culture, generating in the school a strong internationalist outlook. When, in response to the growing evidence of racial prejudice and discrimination in Britain, the maintained schools had introduced anti-discriminatory policies, KAS had with justice not felt any need to follow suit. For these reasons, the cases of the teachers concerned came as a shock to the school, in particular to the Head and the Council, who were required to make the painful though unavoidable decisions.

In each case, after a trial period in the school, the two teachers had proved, for personal and cultural reasons, to be incapable of maintaining classroom discipline and effective communication with their pupils. Both were graduates, highly recommended by their universities, and had made a favourable impression in their interviews with the Head and other members of staff.

One of them was sometimes to be observed in the grounds pursuing his pupils and appealing to them to return to the classroom. The other had a highly excitable temperament and, although he could make himself understood in his calmer moments, became incomprehensible when excited, which, in the classroom, was not infrequently.

While both teachers had been educated abroad, one had had teaching experience there, but the other had obtained a post-graduate certificate in education in England, obtaining a distinction. They clearly regarded traditional and formal methods of teaching as the norm, and appeared to have little patience for or understanding of the largely informal, individualistic and interactional methods of KAS.

Matters went from bad to worse. Children complained to their parents that they could not understand what the teachers were talking about and that they were incapable of keeping order. The parents, in turn, demanded action from the management. Every effort was made to help the two teachers overcome their individual difficulties, but with little success. At Nikki's instigation, one of them agreed, albeit reluctantly, to undertake a part-time course in speech training, half of which she paid for out of the Head's allowance for staff courses. After the first few sessions, he stopped going, without mentioning it to anyone except the tutor, making it clear that he did not think there was anything wrong with his English or that he was in any need of such a course. When it became clear that in neither case was there any hope of improvement, all the usual procedures were followed. Oral and written warnings were issued, together with detailed accounts of the circumstances which necessitated their resignations.

It was perhaps inevitable, in the sensitive climate of race and ethnic relations at this time, that, in spite of all the patience, tact and consideration that had been shown, both teachers should have appealed against their dismissal.

It proved a traumatic experience for Nikki who was obliged to defend herself and the school first before an Industrial Relations Tribunal and later before the Race Relations Board, against allegations of unfair dismissal. This was claimed in the first instance on the grounds of insufficient evidence and in the second of racial discrimination under the terms of the Race Relations Act of 1965.

In both events judgment went in favour of KAS, the Tribunal ruling that there had been no wrongful dismissal, the Court that there was no case to answer. Exoneration did little to console Nikki or Alan Wood, the Chairman of Council, who had been with her on both occasions. For, although there had been no alternative to the action they had taken, they would have taken the same action had it been the case of any other teachers, it was clear that the plaintiffs believed they had been the victims of discrimination. It had been an unhappy sequence of events, both for Nikki and the Council and the school. More particularly was this the case because there had been non-Europeans at KAS before, all of whom had been integrated and highly successful members of the teaching staff.

Shortly after these events Nikki was grateful and to some extent reassured to receive a letter from a former KAS pupil, Bruce Pitt, son of

Ahead of her Time

Lord Pitt of Hampstead, the first West Indian Chairman of the Greater London Council. Bruce had recently been published Barrister-at-Law, having also graduated from London University with the degree of Bachelor of Laws. Having congratulated her on becoming sole Head, he went on to say, 'You know I have always told people that if you had not come to KAS when you did (1959) I would never have been given the opportunity to prove my worth. I have never forgotten being told when I was fifteen that the only subject I was thought capable of passing at 'O' level was Art. It was your decisive action in placing me in the 6th Form which raised my outlook to beyond meagre qualifications, together with Ian Carnegie's constant concern and encouragement. I am glad that now your inherent good will is available to all. The school cannot but progress. You may not know, but had you not come when you did, my father would have taken me away at sixteen.'

Encouragement had always been given to members of staff to pursue activities outside their school work, thereby keeping in touch with the outside world, widening interests and revitalising energies. The typical forms of extra-mural activity were evening classes or lectures and vacation courses. There were, however, precedents for the award of sabbaticals to senior members of staff who had completed relatively long periods of service at the school. For example, Miss Hyett, Headmistress from 1933 to 1945, spent a term visiting schools in Russia, an experience which gave her, as she said, 'a new lease of educational life'. In 1966, Alan Humphries was awarded a Walter Hines Page scholarship and passed a month of the autumn term studying education in the United States. In December 1969, Council agreed to Nikki's having a sabbatical term at a time of her own choosing within the next eighteen months. She had initiated inquiries about possible educational projects with organisations like UNESCO, VSO and UNICEF. When it was learnt that Alan Humphries would shortly be leaving to take up his appointment in Brussels, her plans had to be indefinitely deferred.

Three years later, when she was able to consider the matter again, she found that the overseas projects involved more time than she could give, and concluded she would have to find something within the United Kingdom. The outcome of her inquiries was that she was offered - and accepted - a Schoolmistress Fellow Commonership at Churchill College, Cambridge for the Michaelmas term of 1973.

An announcement appeared in the national press under university news, and the Sunday Times did a short feature article on the event under the heading 'A Suitable Case to Examine'. 'What she gets', wrote Atticus, the correspondent, 'is accommodation at the College, with access to its facilities and its people, teachers and taught, with no obligation beyond that. It is, however, usual to use the time for study of a special project and Mrs Archer has chosen - not unnaturally, coming from a progressive school like King Alfred - to consider alternatives to the present system of O and A level examinations. Nikki Archer is known for a remarkable tolerance and understanding: perhaps her questioning of the timed examination system exemplifies that, since she herself is one of those who respond well to that kind of challenge.' 'But I know certain people', she says, 'potentially fine scholars, for whom the timed approach is all wrong.'

'I gather that her term at Churchill College is unlikely to produce a manifesto for sweeping change, since Mrs Archer accepts that the O and A levels together form a reasonable but not by any means total prediction of later achievement. She might, she thinks, offer the basis of further long-term study.

'This opportunity comes at a particularly rewarding moment for King Alfred School, which is now celebrating its 75th anniversary.

'Mrs Archer thinks that democracy is the more secure so long as society supports exploratory situations like King Alfred 'where it's possible to question accepted values'. I hope nobody would want to question that.'

Churchill was founded in 1960 and introduced the scheme - at first for schoolmasters only - in 1962. Since that time there had been a series of thirty-four Schoolmaster Fellow Commoners at the College, and Nikki had the distinction of being the first Schoolmistress since the admission of women as students in 1972.

She was by no means a stranger to Cambridge when she first arrived, having for several years had regular contact with individual Colleges over KAS entrants, administration of GCE A level examinations, and occasionally the moderation of results. Doctor (later Professor) Jack Pole[73], an old Alfredian, was on the staff of Churchill; her friends Margot and David Holbrook [74] -then a Fellow of Downing College - lived on the outskirts of Cambridge, while Amy Shrubsole, whom she had known since the 1940s, was Principal of Homerton College.

The project that Nikki had chosen brought her a wide variety of contacts both inside and outside the College. She had access to various libraries and used them a great deal. But her particular habit of working between 5 and 9 a.m., when they were closed, made borrowing facilities at the University Library essential, and these, after some initial difficulty, were obtained as a special concession.

Early contact was made with the Cambridge Institute of Education, where she met several members of staff, was warmly invited to use the facilities, and talked with tutors at some length about the nature of her investigation. She emphasised that this was not concerned with substituting a new system for GCE A levels but with finding an additional alternative

---

[73] Honorary Fellow of KASS from 1978 and former Council member.

[74] q.v. Chapter 4 - Poet, author, educationist and critic, David Holbrook once spent a year as Writer in Residence at Dartington Hall School.

designed to provide divergent[75] thinkers with a greater chance of showing their full academic potentialities.

This initial discussion served to crystallise her ideas on the design and the structural limitations of her enquiry, and led not only to the development of a fruitful working relationship but also to the acquisition of a whole set of new friends outside Churchill. Partly in return for the help and advice she had received from her new colleagues, she agreed to conduct several seminars with their students during the remainder of her time at Cambridge.

Much of her time in the ensuing weeks was spent in the collation of statistical data, the study of assessment procedures, their validity and reliability, and analysis of the measure of correlation between A level grades and performance in degree examinations. These studies she supplemented by the construction of a questionnaire for distribution to a sample of students in Polytechnics and Colleges of Education.

The project was seldom entirely out of her thoughts, even at the informal social gatherings in College which marked the end of each working day. She would be asked about her special investigation and this would lead to the exchange of relevant experiences and, sometimes, the discovery of new and valuable insights.

Within the first week at Churchill Nikki started keeping a diary, in which she recorded impressions of the people she had met and descriptions of interesting encounters that had taken place.

Most of the new encounters she recorded took place either at dinner in Hall or before or afterwards in the Senior Combination Room. On several occasions she was invited after dinner with a few others to the Master's Lodge, and, at other times, joined students in the Junior Combination Room and discussed education in general and their own degree or post-graduate courses in particular. The following extracts from her diary give some indication of the discourse in which she now found herself daily immersed:

1st October. Only a few dons and Fellows dining this evening, as term has not officially started, Very interesting exchange between Jack Pole and Dr A about the moral imperative of protest against state oppression in the particular case of Sakharov, the dissident Russian scientist. Dr A cynical about both governments and press, inclined towards no action unless sure of evidence, but unwilling to attempt to gather it, on the grounds that we have enough to do to keep our freedom here, where we are at least in a better position to judge the facts. I said I felt balance of probabilities was that the accusations (of oppression) were true, and my conscience asked the question, if true, and if action would have helped and you did nothing, how would you feel? Limited myself firmly to two tentative remarks, and

---

[75] Hudson, L. Contrary Imaginations, Methuen, 1966, Considers two types of reasoning ability (`convergent' and `divergent') with implications for performance in intelligence tests and formal examinations.

then said goodnight at appropriate point, having I hope drawn a balance between no contribution and too much!

Dr A is tall, good-looking in the slightly unconvincing manner of so many English public school intellectuals. Has so many of the characteristics which irritate both foreigners and the left wing that I can imagine his being used as a prototype... yet he never for a second descends to caricature. It is just his gentle deprecatory manner and refusal to move from his own unadmitted but implied conviction that the wise and the well brought-up leave the rest of the world to muddle through alone and themselves pay strict attention to their own business, while remaining courteously indifferent to extremism of any kind. Suspect he is also very good at not letting anyone know what he feels. I have made him sound old. He isn't. Probably my own age.

This morning went round the centre of Cambridge and got to know the general lay-out of the shopping area. Also went mad in three bookshops and bought enough paperbacks and journals to last my time here; all germane either to my enquiry or the Sixth Form General Course for next term, but the feeling of guilty dissipation could not have been greater if I had bought six cases of Bollinger.

Professor Yvonne Brackbill[76], an Overseas Fellow, is a tall, slim and attractive American of middle years and gentle manner. She has a warm smile, pleasing voice, and incisive speech. Her subject is Psycho-physiology, and her line is research. She was discussing retardation of young animals after maternal deprivation. Later, asked her about dreaming in animals, especially what was known about pre-natal dreaming. She explained that, although it had been established that rapid eye movement in adult humans (over 25) was an accompaniment of dreams, there was no conclusive evidence to support the theory that the same thing applied with animals. Conversely, there was no proof that it didn't.

2nd October. When did the Middle Ages end? Dr Coleman, a young American medievalist, claims to have evidence supporting her contention that it ended in the 14th century but, as we agreed, it is an artificial concept anyway...all one can really do is trace the emerging growth of concepts which characterise the Renaissance amid the lingering attitudes of the 'moyen age', as the power of money rather than land and armies took over and allowed the significance of the individual in society to be recognised...as well as the new ideas of equity and justice.

7th October. I met the Master, Sir William Rede Hawthorne, although he did not come in to dine. Sat next to the Bursar and an Overseas Fellow, Dr Prager from Vienna, whose wife, as Mary Edwards, was once a teacher at KAS. He is an ex-LSE student, one of the '30s vintage of Marxist

---

[76] Professor of Psychology, University of Gainesville, Florida, USA. Friendship with Yvonne Brackbill outlasted Churchill and continues to the present day.

economists, and sat at the feet of Maurice Dobb et al. He is a very pleasant, friendly man and clearly sincere; and delighted to be able to tell his wife that he had met me. The Chaplain, Dr Richard Cain, who has come this term from Warwick, is an interesting man. Prager asked whether he was correct in thinking that Methodist and other non-conformist sects might be more rigid than the Church of England, and I suggested slyly that, the Church of England's heresy being earlier, they had had time to relax about it. Dr Cain said he would have to remember this for future use.

12th October. Guest night. John had a wretched journey across London and arrived here at 7.20 to change and get across to the Fellows' dining room for drinks at 7.30. We made it. I was ragged with nervous apprehension that he would be late and my first official occasion spoilt, so I was less than calm.

Dinner was delightful...conversation - wise, not food, which was as usual greater in intention than quality. I sat next to Professor Hewish (who discovered Pulsars) and had a lovely time. He is charming, and easy to get along with, young-looking for a professor. He tells me that Black Holes are now more or less universally accepted as fact, although not understood, and we discussed the way in which astronomy has moved into the realm of the fantastic which is fact...my words, not his. We discussed contact with students, mine and his, and the absurdity of hierarchies in research establishments, the nature of authority, the parallel qualities of Black Holes in space with non-logic as a positive form of thinking (vide my Korean professor)[77], and laughed at all kinds of things we both found amusing and which I cannot now remember. His wife, whom I have not yet met, is, John tells me, very agreeable and wants to see KAS. For dessert we sat at the other side of the table, and I was next to Dr McClintock, a criminologist, who is moving shortly to the new Chair at Edinburgh. He had recently attended a conference with representatives of East European countries on the problems of crime in late adolescence. Their problems, it appears, are very much the same as ours. The Maoists, of course, attribute all this to revisionism in the USSR.

16th October. After dinner I went along to the Senior Combination Room and spent some time talking to an American visiting Fellow who had some interesting, if rather ghastly, ideas on the subject of President Nixon and involvement in the Middle East war. Many people had dispersed after coffee, and I was left with the Master, Dr Prager, and another man whose name I failed to register. We established a friendly understanding about several subjects ranging from the real issues of the Common Market to

---

[77] The reference is to an incomprehensible lecture Nikki had once attended at the Institute of Education, London University, when a Korean Professor spoke about the adoption of non-logic as a type of intellectual reasoning at approximately the same time as the Greek philosophers were adopting formal logic.

eighteenth century inventions. Apropos of the latter, the Master had discovered references amid the papers of Horace Walpole to a primitive steam engine made in this country for an Italian in the early eighteenth century, long before the first recorded steam engine as such. This was apparently completely overlooked by the American scholars who sorted out and indexed all Walpole papers.

16th November. Took Sally Cockburn and Ilse Pole to lunch at the Three Horseshoes, Madingley, and Zoe Wanamaker (an Old Alfredian) arrived a few minutes later, to my great delight, as I thought she had perhaps not received my invitation. We had a lively lunch and enjoyed meeting again. I had seen Zoe in a delightful and vigorous production of Twelfth Night a few weeks before at the Arts Theatre, when she gave a fresh and attractive performance. After lunch she and I went on to David Holbrook's seminar where they were discussing Marvell's poem 'To A Coy Mistress'.

David, by the way, is angered by a new book recently published in which the idea of seducing nine-year old girls is recommended. I do agree that someone must speak up about this kind of destructive so-called freedom because it really does threaten young people quite genuinely.

7th December. Fellows' guest night. All very pleasant. Sat next to Professor Wole Soyinka and joined him in an argument with Dr Kenneth McQuillan (Vice-Master) and the Professor of Geography (whose name escapes me) about Yuri Geller. Soyinka took the whole phenomenon very much for granted and seemed amused that anyone should think it extraordinary. (Diary closes).

The Michaelmas term eventually drew to a close and Nikki had to take her farewells of all the friends she had made at Cambridge. The enormous goodwill she carried back to London with her was a measure of the success of the diplomatic mission her sabbatical had insensibly become. Subjectively, she had enjoyed every moment of her time at Churchill, and valued the privilege of having met some of those whose work was currently advancing the frontiers of knowledge.

A few months after the sabbatical, she received a letter from Captain Stephen Roskill, RN, editor of the Churchill Review, asking if she would write a short article on her views of the College and the value of the Fellowship scheme, 'since, of all our Schoolmaster or Schoolmistress Fellow Commoners, I know of non-one better equipped to write on their experience'. She was glad of the opportunity to express her genuine appreciation both of the imaginative foresight which had made the Fellowship possible and of the whole-hearted way in which the scheme was being implemented. She emphasised that she was writing from an entirely personal viewpoint, and made no claim to represent a general attitude.

'To most people who have never been there', she wrote, 'and perhaps to a few who have, the University and the life of its Colleges has a special and partly symbolic value based on a mixture of reality and fantasy. For me, Cambridge, more than any other centre of intellectual activity and academic excellence, stood for male privilege. I envisaged it as a stronghold of traditional masculine infallibility against which the increasing numerical strength of women members and the defection of three Colleges to the co-educational camp had made no noticeable impression. This is a widely held and obviously limited view, but I must admit to feeling when I arrived at the College on one of those cold, windy nights, not unknown in that part of the country, that I had strayed into a world designed by, and for, men, which is, of course, exactly what it was until two years ago, and traces of the basic assumptions implicit in that are easily discernible. (Rooms built round a courtyard are attractive, but have disadvantages for mixed residence unless you are a happy exhibitionist with a gregarious disposition). Opinions within the College differ about its design. I belong to the group which finds it architecturally interesting and attractive, but if anyone is looking for a set for a thriller they might do worse than try Churchill on a dark night, with the rain sneaking up around every corner, and the anonymity of the courtyard blocks, identifiable to a newcomer only by their numbers, rendered more sinister by the low-level lighting which casts a theatrical upward emphasis on the face of the occasional stranger as you pass. I had an attractive 'set', with enough cupboards and shelves for comfort, and a long window seat (made apparently of black marble salami) on which I could sit and see most of the campus. Naturally, the English phobia about vanity had ensured that there would be just one wall mirror, placed in the darkest corner of the bathroom at a height which gave me a reasonable view of my forehead. But my request for a full-length glass was taken as a matter of course, as most women students now have these in their rooms. (Presumably, in a world where the mind rules all, the men never feel the need to see themselves below the neck, as it were.)

'For the first time in my life I had a quiet (well, comparatively quiet) place in which to work, protected from the demands which are part of my normal working conditions; I doubt if many people get the opportunity to experience the intoxicating freedom of working without interruption, and this became one of the more addictive of my indulgences.

'During my stay I took the opportunity to pursue an enquiry of my own into certain aspects of A level examinations which brought me a wide variety of contacts both inside and outside the College. I had the entry to various libraries and made a great deal of use of them, but my particular habit of working between 5 a.m. and 9 a.m. made borrowing facilities at the University library essential and I was granted the necessary MA status (a concession which will now, I understand, be extended by Churchill to other SFCs). I wish I had enquired how the enlightened decision was arrived at not to require SFCs to justify their presence by completing some work during their time here; our normal assumption in western civilisation ranks the possibility of indolence as a major danger to be guarded against at all costs. As a teacher, I wonder about the validity of our arguments for the

204

ruthless organisation of educational time. Space, and a sense of perspective, are of inestimable value when you are driven by a personal interest, and I believe they are not compatible with the arbitrary division of the day into slices, for the better consumption of knowledge. It might be worth investigating the actual effectiveness of the conventional method as a preparation for sustained concentration on mental activity in later life.

'My function at Churchill was to have no function and in consequence (feeling rather like a living refutation of the principle of contradiction) I had no part to play in the actual work and life of the College and yet was completely immersed in it at several levels.

'Each term a number of Overseas Fellows forms part of the community and adds to that immense diversity of personalities, achievement, interest and scholarship from which the Senior Combination Room draws its impressive quality and vitality. Any lingering notions that the College might be a haven of prosaic pedantry and eclectic eccentricity died a swift and painless death in the first twenty four hours and I relaxed in the comfortable assurance that where everyone was an expert in some field, my own vast areas of ignorance were excusable

'I had every opportunity, through lectures, seminars and other functions, to meet and talk to postgraduate and undergraduate students, and, partly through them, I made contact with people from other Colleges. Apart from the stimulation of encountering various lively personalities, holding opposing attitudes to current issues which they expressed with vigour and lucidity, this provided me with insights into the nature of university life today which I could never otherwise have gained.

'I was interested to find how close was the parallel between areas of concern among university students and those who are still at the secondary stage of their education, and our discussions were valuable in helping to clarify my ideas about some of the problems we face in schools. There is a theory which maintains that all sociological questions can be reduced to statements about order and control within societies, and I think it is true to say that at the secondary level one of the urgent problems is the search for new patterns of authority and responsibility which would be relevant to the needs of today. Students are involved in seeking fresh concepts which relate to a swiftly changing society and in redefining roles and functions in the academic world where the traditional ones seem to them no longer adequate. It was fascinating to watch this process at work in a social group where there is a belief in the need for clear thinking and a genuine desire among the majority of Fellows and Commoners alike to extract from a wide range of conflicting theories some coherent policies for community life.

'The value of inviting other teachers to share in and observe this process for a time seems to me very considerable. I cannot agree with the view of some people I met who still see in it no more than a sociable way of informing the schools about the opportunities available and the standards of candidates for entry. Although this certainly came into it, the greatest gain for me was my day to day experience of the extraordinary vigour and growth, in intellectual and social terms, which the working life of the College generates. If any justification is needed for the continuation of collegiate universities this must surely be one of the major elements in the argument.

'To end on a personal note, my most lively memories are of the warm friendliness, humour and breadth of vision which is characteristic of the whole place and of the group of people I met and shared ideas with - a most uncommon fellowship of which I am happy to have been, for however short a time, a part.'

Churchill reciprocated by taking its first Schoolmistress Fellow Commoner to its heart. She had entered fully and enthusiastically into the life of the community and made in the process many friends, all of whom testified to the favourable impression she had made in such a relatively short time. In a period when political correctness was in its infancy, she was amused to learn that apart from being a 'good ambassador' she had been responsible for 'a revised view of schoolmistresses' and that at least one don had been 'cured of a phobia' (of schoolmistresses). Margot Holbrook recalls an occasion when, as Nikki's guests, she and David had dined at Churchill: The Vice-Master, 'a nice bearded Scotsman', turned to her and said in a confidential tone, 'Ach, she's very good value, isn't she?' Leading Margot to reflect that Churchill were evidently thinking they had made a good choice in taking Nikki on.

Nikki was not sure how much credence to attach to gossip suggesting a permanent Fellowship was hers for the asking. 'Although this is clearly nonsense', she said, 'it is most agreeable nonsense, and very pleasant to hear. I'm sure the report was genuine, but I also feel that someone had misunderstood the context.'

Also gratifying was the suggestion that she might spend a year as a tutor at the Cambridge Institute of Education. This had arisen as a result of a number of seminars she had done for them, partly in return for the advice she had received in connection with her research project. It was, she thought, an intriguing idea, albeit impracticable; but good to know that her collaboration would have been welcomed.

Her return to KAS required less in the way of adjustment than might have been expected. For, although the usual implication of a sabbatical is total separation from the normal working environment, it was clear that, in spite of having left Roy Greenfield to deputise, her responsibilities could not be entirely put to one side. Thus she was in regular contact with the school by telephone, and, at intervals, dealt with correspondence requiring her particular attention. This her secretary, Katie Munden, unwilling to risk the vagaries of the postal service, brought to her in Cambridge.

A.S.Neill had died in September shortly before Nikki had gone up to Cambridge. It was as if a light had gone out in the world of progressive education, but his death had not been much remarked upon at Churchill.

Nikki recalls talking about him to the Holbrooks and some of the tutors at the Cambridge Institute of Education. It was, for her, a time for reflection. The obituaries, she noted, had all paid tribute to his unique gifts and his major contribution to the gradual transformation of teachers' attitudes to children and to the best means of educating them. She thought his achievement rested far more on his charisma as a teacher, his love, trust and respect for children, than on the theoretical content of his published works, which had lent itself to such widespread misunderstanding and misapplication.

While Nikki herself knew only too well the unwitting harm that could be done to their children's education by ignorant or unco-operative parents, she nonetheless felt that Neill could have gone half way towards meeting parents' views and perceptions, instead of distancing himself and making no attempt to find a compromise.

His apparent scepticism about scholarship was also a weakness, in her view, but one born of the same basic philosophy which accounted for his greatness - a philosophy with its own epistemic assumptions about freedom, knowledge and the negative aspects of institutional domination.

She had a certain ambivalence towards his educational ideas because of the inconsistencies she found in his writings, but was also disarmed by his wit, sense of humour, and total integrity.

His pupils at Summerhill shared one characteristic with Freud's patients in Vienna: they were not a typical sample of the normal population. They had in most cases had a history of over-repression and, as a consequence, suffered a significant degree of neurotic anxiety, for which Neill's system provided an effective remedy. It was a system by no means appropriate to the needs of all children.

Another of Neill's admirable qualities was his unassuming nature. He acknowledged his mistakes and had no pretensions to being the guru his admirers wanted to make of him. It was partly for this reason that Nikki had reservations about the foundation in January 1974 of the A.S.Neill Trust 'in memory of the man whose writings and whose school, Summerhill, have become focal points for teachers throughout the world'.[78]

Although she attended the inaugural meeting in London, the heterogeneous nature of the groups and organisations represented (some of them politically assertive, and not conspicuously concerned with education) led her to the conclusion that membership would not be in the interests of KAS. Furthermore, she felt intuitively that it was the wrong kind of memorial to Neill, who should be commemorated by a continuation of the work he had begun, and the active development of his ideas, and not by establishing a shrine where his thought was carved in stone and his disciples endlessly turned over the old texts.

---

[78] Report of the inaugural meeting of the A.S.Neill Trust, 1974.

16   Alternative Realities

A matter of serious concern to both parents and staff at KAS since the 1960s had been the mounting evidence of drug abuse in certain sections of society and the potentially harmful influence of this on the health, education and moral development of young people.

The heart of the problem was the controversial issue of the so-called 'soft' drugs - in particular cannabis resin, over which even expert medical opinion was divided. In spite of prolonged research, there was still no conclusive proof that marijuana was physically harmful or addictive, albeit there was a strong presumption that dependence could develop in individual cases as a result of long and regular use.

Such research evidence as there was had persuaded the Government that the risks involved in using it for non-medical purposes were sufficient to warrant banning possession of the substance by law. In spite of or because of this, various libertarian groups cited their own experience as evidence that cannabis was no more harmful than smoking, and certainly less so than alcohol. The insidious appeal of these messages for many young people was reinforced when their 'pop' idols, the Rolling Stones, appeared in court charged with illegal possession; and when, on another occasion, the Beatles campaigned for its legalisation with a full-page advertisement in the Times, which began with the statement: 'The law against marijuana is immoral in principle and unworkable in practice'.

Whilst the charge of immorality was untenable, unworkability was manifestly a claim of more significance, and a matter on which, in the light of its educational principles, KAS was particularly well qualified to speak. For attempts to dissuade people by coercion, in the context in question, by reasoning from hypothetical premises, or by films or posters calculated to horrify, were examples of negative motivation, sometimes effective but often counter-productive.

A more positive approach was adopted in the formulation of KAS policy. The high staffing ratio, the close relationships between the staff and children and their parents, and the flexibility of the curriculum, provided a framework for the open and comprehensive discussion of the issues involved.

First among these was the fact of legal prohibition and the responsibility of the school for educating children to be aware of, understand and respect the law. Policy was thus unequivocal on this issue: possession of illegal substances could not and would not be tolerated on the school premises. Any decisions that might be taken outside were first and foremost the responsibility of the parents, but the complementary responsibility of the school was to ensure that, as far as possible, the children were apprised of the relevant knowledge they needed to make the right decisions for themselves. Chemistry, biology and social studies were the main sources of the data necessary for informed discussion, and in addition the school had recourse to leading experts, including Dr Derek Miller of the Tavistock Clinic (a KAS parent) and Drs Faith Spicer and Elizabeth Tylden, who came to speak not only to staff and pupils but also to groups of parents.

Nikki prepared the following paper for one of the periodic progressive school conferences at Dartington Hall, detailing the approach adopted at KAS towards this highly controversial issue: 'We recognise that most of our children from the age of twelve will be moving in circles where someone is experimenting with or even addicted to one or other of the drugs in current use and that many of them will be drawn into experimenting themselves.

'We think it most likely, on the basis of present medical and psychological findings, that only those children who are suffering from a severe sense of failure, or conviction of personal inadequacy, are likely to progress from experimentation to habituation.

'As the present attitude of society is highly ambivalent where drugs are concerned, it is extremely hard for schools to face the problem constructively, but it cannot be ignored.

'We feel it is essential to differentiate between experiment and the deliberate attempt to involve others, whether or not this is for financial gain. In the latter case it is usually a disturbed personality involved and if we have any proof, or sufficiently strong circumstantial evidence, we suspend them and refer them for psychiatric examination, having brought the parents in on the whole matter as early as possible. It has to be said that when some parents are themselves convinced that the smoking of cannabis should be legalised, it is extremely difficult to get them to realise the implications of the school's legal responsibilities. It would appear to be a peculiarity of progressive schools that there seems to be an unspoken assumption among a few such parents that we shall take a different view of an illegal activity from that taken by more conventional establishments. It is necessary, we find, to disabuse them of this at once.

'If the psychiatrist's report has suggested that there is really no reason to believe they are, as it were, 'pushing' drugs, and they are not felt to be fundamentally disturbed, we have then readmitted them, kept an eye on the situation, and maintained close contact with the parents regarding the children's subsequent behaviour and social activities.

'If the clinic reports that their behaviour is truly delinquent and that they show signs of real disturbance, and we do not feel able to readmit them, we inform the parents accordingly. This has been a rare occurrence up to now. We would, of course,. take all relevant factors into account when making our decision, one of the most important being the length of time the child has been with us, and the extent to which we feel the family can and will help.

'We are very concerned as to how we can best minimise the risk for the future. Clearly the problem is on the increase and whatever decisions are made at a national level about soft and hard drugs, the fact remains that the drug industry as well as the unofficial market, is too big and too powerful a commercial interest not to affect us all increasingly in the next few years. We see it as essential to tackle the social problem in the schools with every means at our disposal.

'It seems clear that neither prohibition nor reiteration of the dangers are likely to be effective in the long run, and, therefore we should be considering how best to enable children to withstand the fears, anxieties and frustrations they will encounter, without recourse to 'anxiety relief mechanisms' of this kind. We are considering, at present, various ways of tackling the situation, including some counselling, opportunity for group discussions, and extra information through the biology course.

'We also want to bring the parents of 12-14 year olds more fully into the picture through meetings not directly about drugs but about the whole field of adolescent stress.

'We held a meeting recently with heads of local schools to discuss what they do in such instances and have agreed to keep in touch over both general and particular issues. We have also exchanged the names of speakers on the subject who can be recommended (some speakers, however knowledgeable and well-meaning, approach the subject in a way which produces exactly the opposite effect from what is required) and medical and psychiatric experts with special knowledge and experience who will give advice and real help.'

In the late sixties Nikki had been a member of the Association for the Prevention of Addiction (APA) and was for a short time involved in the formation and development of its educational sub-committee. This collaboration between medical and educational professionals was initiated for the purpose of enlisting schools in a campaign for the prevention of addiction. Hitherto, the functions of the Association had been limited to medical advice and the dissemination of relevant information through public lectures and the distribution of pamphlets. The foundation of the sub-committee thus represented a major extension of its functions and directed the campaign where it was calculated to have the most influence - namely in the schools.

As a preliminary step, the education sub-committee conducted a survey to assess the current situation in schools regarding drugs education, and followed this up with a national conference of teachers held under the auspices of the APA in London. The conference was widely reported and an official conference report distributed. Shortly after this, due to pressure of work, Nikki had to discontinue her connection with APA, following her appointment as sole head at King Alfred. The campaign as a whole succeeded in raising public awareness, and many schools responded by making appropriate curricular adjustments.

But the good work continued, as was shown by a letter she received in 1975 from James Ferman[79], recently appointed Secretary of the British Board of Film Censors: 'Thanks so much for your letter of congratulations. I listened carefully to your contribution to the BBC 'phone-in' on censorship the other week and was most pleased to hear your sanity and, of course, your kind remarks.

'It is going to be an enormous job bringing clarity into the legal situation, as the self-appointed moral vigilantes are becoming active in a legal sense. So I shall need all your good wishes.

'I have just finished the fifth and last film in my drugs series and it contains a lot of you. Most people think it is the best film of the lot, so you must see it some time.'

In view of her commitment to the school's policy on drugs, it was ironical, to say the least, when in 1969 an application she had made for appointment to the Commission of the Peace was turned down (she heard later) on the objection of a member of the Interview Board who associated KAS with questionable ideas about authority and the law. A renewed application with references serving to correct this fallacy was more successful and she was appointed in March 1971 as a Justice of the Peace to the Barnet Bench in the Middlesex Area of Greater London.

At her final interview she had been asked what her attitude would be if a young person appeared in front of her charged with the illegal possession of drugs. Her reply was unequivocal: if there was evidence to show that the law had been broken, penalties were inevitably incurred. As to her political affiliation, the subject of a supplementary question, she could say with equal assurance that she had none.

During her years as a magistrate, besides dealing with general and motoring cases, which were the responsibility of all JPs, she was attached to the Domestic (including Matrimonial) and Juvenile Panels. Her appointment and subsequent career, during which she became a respected and valued member of the Bench, enhanced the popular image of KAS. While she was able to use her growing knowledge and experience of the law to the advantage of the school in terms of both administration and the curriculum.

The most serious implications for education posed by the non-medicinal use of drugs lay, in Nikki's view, not in childish experiment but in the possibility of habituation. The existence of deeply divided opinions on the nature and effects of cannabis in no way absolved teachers or parents from concern with the healthy physical and mental development of young people. It was difficult but not impossible to distinguish between signs indicating the use of drugs and those expressing anxiety or emotional

---

[79] Nikki had known James Ferman prior to his appointment to the BBFC and collaborated with him in connection with the APA campaign. The film in question had been of a 6th Form discussion at KAS.

tensions involving personal relationships with parents or peers. The resort to soft drugs might or might not have been the response to some unresolved conflict, but, whatever the case, it was a matter of concern to the school if there were occasional instances of individuals who had observably ceased to care about anything or anyone else, including themselves, apparently opting out from the life of the school.

In fact, Nikki had seen very little evidence of such behaviour at King Alfred during the sixties and early seventies, and, by the middle of the latter decade, she was more worried about the potential effects of alcohol than of drugs.

17 Spreading the Word

It had become fashionable in the sixties for professionals of various kinds to diversify their roles by occasional ventures into the media world, often with considerable benefit to all concerned. Television dons, for example, in their role as popularisers, were amongst the more visible and well-known of this new breed of media personalities.

While Nikki's professional responsibilities precluded her from aspiring to celebrity of this kind, she was nevertheless always ready to avail herself of any opportunity of publicising the school or of propagating the ideas of progressive education.

The new communications media provided access to a far wider audience than that available to her predecessors Russell and Wicksteed.

She was herself an experienced speaker, broadcaster and panellist, and had appeared in various radio, film and television feature programmes on the subject of education.

Her appearances at different times in the radio series 'You and Yours' and as the guest of Maggie Norden (Old Alfredian) on Capitol Radio preceded and were possibly instrumental in her being invited to join the panel of 'Petticoat Line' on a number of occasions in 1975.

'Petticoat Line' was a weekly radio programme in which listeners' letters were treated from a feminine (and only mildly feminist) point of view. It had been conceived in 1965 by the actress and singer Anona Winn, then star panellist of 'Twenty Questions', and ran for fourteen years until it was disbanded in 1979, in deference among other things to the growing pressure of militant feminism.

It was described as an amusing all-female version of Any Questions in which letters were discussed in a light-hearted vein, as the chairwoman Anona Winn explained, 'to get a little laughter, but sometimes something serious does creep in'.[80] The panel was composed of four members, three of whom varied each week, while the fourth, the resident member, was the 'earthy' Scottish actress Renée Houston (allegedly rationed to saying 'bloody' no more than three times per show). Nikki's vitality, humour, empathy and spontaneous wit made her a natural for the programme and she invariably evoked a sympathetic and encouraging response from the studio audience. She made a clear distinction between trivial and serious questions, adopting a light and playful approach to the former, but never failing to give a considered, intelligible and professional answer to the latter.

Among the regular panellists on the show were Sheila Van Damm, Barbara Cartland and the Observer columnist, Katharine Whitehorn.[81] Nikki knew the latter but, as it turned out, they never met on the same panel.

---

[80] Donovan, P The Radio Companion, BBC 1990
[81] Qqv. Chapter 11

Ahead of her Time

The co-panellists on her first appearance apart from Anona Winn and Renée Houston, were Nancy Wise of 'Pick of the Week' and 'You and Yours', and Margaret Powell, a newly celebrated author of books about her life in domestic service.

The first question was about insomnia. 'We have a newcomer with us', announced the chairwoman, 'Nikki Archer is headmistress of a co-educational progressive school. Nikki, do you ever have any sleepless nights?'

'As a headmistress, what would you expect?' Nikki replied, smiling and with a rueful emphasis that drew appreciative laughter from the audience. 'Yes, I do get quite a lot of sleepless nights. But one of the things I've learned is not to get worried about them because if you do, they only get worse. So, if you can make up your mind that what in fact you are doing is giving yourself that extra two or three hours you couldn't squeeze out of the day, you can really make use of them. I once prepared an exhibition of paintings in just a few months by getting up at 2 o'clock in the morning and painting till 4, and then going back to bed for a couple of hours' well earned sleep. And it does help, if you make up your mind that if you're not going to sleep you might as well use the time purposefully.

'And the other thing I do is write the sort of letters that I know perfectly well I shall never send because I should probably regret it for the rest of my life. But I can take enormous pleasure in sitting down and writing it and saying all the things I would like to say. I get it down on paper, and the next morning I come in and there it is looking at me and I read it through and think I feel much better, and I don't feel like saying any of those things now - so now I can tear it up.' (Laughter).

Anona Winn: 'Yes, that's the best thing to do with those letters, isn't it?'

Nikki: 'It's the only thing to do with them, yes. When you are young you send them, when you get older, you learn not to.' (Laughter).

Renée Houston suggested that because of the neighbours the insomniac listener could hardly get up and fry an egg, but she might try painting or writing poetry (something saucy to make her laugh) and concluded with the encouragement not to worry about insomnia, and 'do what you fancy, love. It isn't serious, so don't lose any sleep over it!' (Laughter).

Next came a question about corporal punishment. A male listener, this time, had written recalling a panel member who had spoken on the last programme in favour of abolishing caning in schools. Was this not just following a fashionable trend? And did not the panel agree with him it was unkind to encourage the young in the belief we didn't all need discipline?

Anona Winn: 'Well, we've got the right person. What could be better than having with us the headmistress of a co-educational progressive school? oooer!'

Nikki: 'I don't know why everybody associates headmistresses with caning. It's very sad.' (Laughter).

Anona Winn: 'I don't, I assure you. It's just that...are we being unkind if we don't assert that people...I mean children...need discipline?'

Nikki: 'Yes, I'm sure there is a sense in which we are being unkind if we aren't aware that we all need discipline in our lives. What I would disagree with absolutely is that caning would produce disciplined children in the real sense of disciplined, because I don't think for a moment that it would. Some people tend to assume that if you are going to be harsh you will produce one effect, and if you are going to be kind you will produce another, and it doesn't matter on which side of the fence they sit, they seem to go overboard with it, to go to extremes. Whereas what I think people need to be looking for in the upbringing of children is a sense of balance enabling them to recognise that there are times when they can't have their own way and times when they can. I can't think of anything more miserable than the sort of child who has never had no said to it. They're usually so miserable, it isn't true. I remember once meeting a little girl who had never had 'no' said to her and it fell to my lot to say no to her for the first time and really mean it. And she was so appalled that she lay down on the floor and screamed for five minutes, and I watched her with great interest. (Laughter). I just stood there and when she stopped screaming, because she'd lost her breath, I was still there, and she said, 'Do you still mean no?' and I said yes. She got up and we went off together and that was that. Now I do not think any sort of physical punishment would have had the desired effect in a situation like that...(Houston: 'No!')...and I think this is the difficulty...the mother who loses her temper and slaps the child is one thing, but I don't believe and never have believed in the use of corporal punishment in the school. My view is that education has been associated with harsh discipline for far too long. But that doesn't mean you should never say 'no' to children or that you should not make your 'noes' absolutely firm and make quite sure they understand what you mean by them.'

The selection of letters for discussion was not random but, like 'Any Questions', sometimes angled towards the interests of particular members of the panel.

A few minutes before each programme the panellists were told the subjects for discussion, but, apart from this, had to speak entirely extempore. The leitmotiv was clearly entertainment, although Anona Winn had originally envisaged a more serious format with the panel dispensing advice in response to listeners' problems. But, if discussion was a long way from high table at Churchill, it lacked nothing in wit, intellectual verve and practical philosophy.

18   Discipline

The frequency with which questions on discipline arose on 'Petticoat Line' and the more serious programmes in which Nikki had taken part was symptomatic of the current anxiety over a rising tide of crime and delinquency, and public concern over causes and remedies.

KAS, with its long tradition of child-centred education, had much in the way of valuable experience and knowledge to contribute to the public discussion of such matters. If, in the event, this proved to be an under-used resource, it was probably attributable *inter alia* to the proliferation of specialists in related professions and to the limited time available to KAS staff.

A democratic structure, shared values, and traditional loyalties were significant factors in maintaining the stability of the school during the volatile 1960s and '70s.

It was an essential condition of the relative freedom enjoyed by its pupils that rules should be kept to an absolute minimum. 'Too many rules are as bad as too few,' Nikki observed. 'In the latter case, children are confused because there are no guidelines to expected behaviour; in the former, more opportunities are created for deviant activity, with the risk of opening divisions between 'them' and 'us'. If the extended family image of the school means anything, then we should be able to talk of ourselves as 'we' and the rules as 'ours'.'

The voluntary acceptance of rules by children as their own, and not as objective and alien impositions, was fostered by rational persuasion, and explanation of the necessity for regulation in the interests of the community of which they were themselves members. Participation by older pupils in framing rules governing specific areas of school life reinforces compliance and social cohesion. It was by the same process that discipline, functioning unavoidably as external control in infancy and early childhood, could be transformed, with the growth of understanding, into self-discipline at a later stage of development. There was another component in this developmental process - that of learning the distinction between intrinsic and extrinsic values of moral conduct - the extent to which people do good for its own sake or alternatively for reasons of self-interest. Or, conversely, the extent to which wrong-doers regard 'being found out' as a far greater evil than the injury they may have done to others.

This process of socialisation has been described self-evidently from a normative perspective, and therefore cannot be taken as an absolute statement about the learning experiences of every child. Any number of social and psychological factors can account for the failure of socialisation in individual cases; for example, the child who resists even the most reasonable constraints, appears impervious to reason, and persistently interferes with the rights of other members of the school community.

Ahead of her Time

There were certain regulations over which pupils had no jurisdiction. These related to the curriculum, health, safety and other legal considerations and were the responsibility of the head, acting under the delegated authority of council. It is a truism that progressive schools are more vulnerable and exposed to lawsuits than many conventional schools, and KAS was no exception. The ethos of individual self-expression, minimisation of rules, and teaching methods emphasising discovery and experiment all represented added risk, requiring greater vigilance on the part of staff, and greater sensitivity to the need for accident prevention. There were situations in which formal disciplinary measures were essential; for example, in the science laboratories or physical education classes, in both of which behaviour was strictly regulated and special clothing mandatory. In an extraordinary case in 1958 a former pupil sued the school over a broken ankle sustained three years before, when two boys had rocked an electric radiator on which she was sitting, and tipped it over. The case for the prosecution included the contention that the pupils made all the rules. The judgment of the court went against her in the event, in spite of which, according to the report in the Observer, she shook Monty -Nikki's first co-head - by the hand and said she hoped they would remain friends, adding that her years at KAS had been the happiest of her life. In a period of affluence, change and innovation, new dangers materialised with disturbing frequency. Skateboards could not be used on school premises, and the practice of martial arts without supervision was forbidden. Tree-climbing was a traditional pastime at King Alfred, which, in spite of encroachment over the years, still retained some of its ancient woodland. Handholds were provided at a different height for each individual tree, on the principle that if children were able to get up to the first of these they could probably climb safely above them. And, as a rider to this precaution, lifting up small children to the lowest hold was not allowed. Despite the alarm and apprehension of some visitors who saw children of all ages in what appeared to be dangerous situations, the actual casualties were rare, and none of them serious. Nikki found that 'most children, left to their own instincts, trust themselves only as far as they feel they can do so with safety, and their judgment is remarkably sound'.

It was a sign of the times that walking barefoot - a virtual symbol of the progressive aesthetic - should become the subject of regulation, but such was the case, and it was not encouraged at Manor Wood except in the nursery playground. Concealed fragments of metal, glass and other debris - the residue of wartime occupation and years of school activity - constituted a perpetual hazard. As Nikki observed, 'Green and inviting though the school field undoubtedly was, the Garden of Eden it was not.

'The hippy movement and the phenomenon of 'flower power' were at their peak at the time, and freedom to go barefoot became a sensitive issue which we discussed fully in the pupils' and the Society's councils. Our case was unequivocal: while having no objection to anyone's exercising this freedom, we could offer no guarantee that children would not be injured by doing so. We could not therefore accept responsibility for the safety of the children without the collaboration of parents. We concluded that, if anyone wanted to walk barefoot on the school premises, they would require the written authority of a parent, and this was how the matter was resolved.'

It was the constant endeavour of the staff to foster socially acceptable behaviour by positive means whenever possible, and conversely, by the exercise of tolerance and discretion, to limit the incidence of negative sanctions to a minimum. Turning a blind eye to certain kinds of innocuous childish naughtiness had the effect of not only reducing negative suggestion but also averting social tensions and unnecessary conflicts.

The inevitable cases when 'no' had to be said were always accompanied by reasons and mainly reserved for emergency situations or where children's security was involved.

Nikki recalled with amusement an 8-year old boy chasing another child across the school field and shouting repeatedly at the top of his voice, 'Sex maniac: Sex maniac!' Quietly halting the pursuer in mid-career, she waited for him to recover his breath and then inquired calmly, 'What's a sex maniac?' The boy thought for a moment and replied somewhat bashfully, 'It's someone who likes girls'.

But not all minor transgressions could be managed with the same good humour and mutual respect. A 14-year old girl rushed up to her on one occasion and, in front of a group of other children, said angrily, 'I've got a bone to pick with you, Nikki!' But for the child's anger, Nikki's reaction would have been entirely different, probably something playful along the lines of, 'Well, let's take the bone to my room, shall we?' In the circumstances, she replied coolly, 'Very well, but not now and not here. Come to my room at 2 o'clock.' And, with this, she walked away. It was a rebuff she would rather have avoided, but the girl's behaviour had to be shown as unacceptable. If she was testing reality, it was important for her and the bystanders to learn that there were limits. As Nikki often pointed out to children, they had access to her at any time when she was available, and they were free to talk with her about anything they wished, on condition that it left both the child and herself with their self-respect intact.

In a climate of rapid social change, testing the limits to free self-expression was a common preoccupation of school children in Britain, but nowhere more pronounced than at King Alfred's, where it found implicit encouragement as an element in the developmental process. Any aspect of social behaviour could become the subject of some new challenge to which the staff had to respond, which they invariably did with tolerance and understanding. Dress was a case in point: the general feeling among staff and parents was that young people would always want to experiment with their appearance, and that this was a fairly harmless freedom which it would be a pity to interfere with. It was recognised that if it went to extremes the reputation of the school would suffer, and the heads retained the prerogative of requesting anyone they considered was exceeding the limits to modify their dress or appearance. All this was jam for the press, and many a reporter in search of copy used the school to provide articles which, whatever the intention behind them, were ammunition for the local critics of 'progressive' education.

Nikki recalled some of the instances which had precipitated her intervention: the girl who had to be prevailed upon not to wear an enormous cartwheel hat in the classroom, and a boy in the Upper School who walked down from Hampstead Heath wrapped in a blanket and wearing nothing but a pair of shorts underneath. Soon after the Rocky Horror Show opened in London a fourth form boy arrived at the school one day, when Nikki happened to be away, with his face painted white and wearing a torn tee-shirt fastened by thirty safety pins. As there was some ambivalence amongst the staff about this apparition, no action had been taken in the matter, with the result that he came in the following day wearing the same apparel. Nikki took one look and promptly made him wash the paint off his face and gave him a sports shirt to wear. The boy tried to mount a form protest but was stopped by Ivor Thomas, the head of Middle School. Some of the parents and staff took exception to her action, but she stood firm on a decision which had been taken in the best interests of the school and, ultimately, the boy himself. Subsequently, after a staff discussion on the incident, she sent a letter to all parents, enclosing revised guidelines on forms of dress acceptable at school, already regarded by many as being as liberal as they could be.

In October 1971, she addressed the Children's Council on certain disturbing events at the end of the previous term which had been of serious concern to the school: 'At the end of the summer term a few people brought alcohol to the school, which is not and has never been allowed, and they drank both here and in the park.

'They behaved stupidly under the influence of drink, and caused serious complaints from members of the public.

'They also made a nuisance of themselves in school and at sing-song. Staff were most concerned at this, and we all felt that intolerable behaviour of this kind, which is very bad for the reputation of the school and causes distress to members of the community, was absolutely out of keeping with King Alfred School tradition, and must never happen again.'

Concern for the needs and interests of individual children, an indispensable condition of the school's cultural ethos, came under its severest test in the case of bullying. The empathy so freely and spontaneously accorded to the victim was not, in extreme cases, so easily transferable to the bully. Yet, with encouragement and support derived from ethical values, it could be done.

'I don't believe in punishment, but treatment,' said John Russell, thus capturing something of the essence of these values. Like Spinoza's resolve not to judge but to understand; Augustine's distinction between loving the

222

sinner while abhorring the sin; and Homer Lane's unrealistic injunction to love both the sin and the sinner[82], they suggested a diagnostic and remedial rather than a retributive approach to bullies and bullying.

At the practical level, a problem which KAS shared with other schools was that of obtaining information about the incidence of bullying in the first place. It had been no easier for John Russell in the early 1900s, despite the fact that he had a much smaller school to manage. He clearly envisioned the school 'parliament' as a forum for the open discussion of anti-social behaviour and was frustrated by the reluctance of pupils to tell tales (as they perceived it) or 'sneak' on their friends. He rejected the concept of 'schoolboy honour', obviously regarding it as a spurious justification for silence, and failed to convince the children that it was their duty to tell on some occasions for the benefit of the school as a whole. 'One's friendship', he added, 'should be to the whole community and not only to one's intimate friends.' But this denied the reality of peer group dynamics: one boy expressed it all when he said, 'If you tell on someone, and it gets known, everyone will be against you.'

This aspect of the problem of identification was equally intractable in the 1970s. The school six, an elected group of senior pupils, were no more anxious to be cast in the role of informers (however rationalised) than John Russell's prefects before them. The school, on the other hand, did not ask this of them, but would have expected that, as members of a caring community, they would have intervened - just as staff would have done - in any cases of bullying they encountered, and subsequently reported the circumstances of their actions.

Since any bullying that occurred at KAS was typically verbal rather than physical, its detection was correspondingly more difficult, and more likely to come about through the reluctant evidence of victims than from any other source, and this only because their unhappiness could no longer be concealed from their teachers.

The high level of social cohesion in the school encouraged a positive expectation that anti-social behaviour would normally be the exception rather than the rule, and this was largely confirmed by experience.

The incidence of bullying was therefore perceived as a symptom of disorder in the system, in which both victim and perpetrator were involved, and in need of help and support.

Of course, the act of bullying, once established, had to be censured, but, once this had been done, the help that followed was calculated to support both parties, and designed to create conditions enabling the 'bully' to find his/her own way towards more altruistic behaviour.

Redemption, according to this philosophy, was not in the gift of the teacher or priest, but lay in the personal achievement of the autonomous individual. And by the same token, there was a reluctance to employ the

---

[82] Wills, D.W. Homer Lane. A biography (1964)

negative label 'bully' - with its implication of irredeemable stigma - and a resolute faith in the individual's capacity for change.

Teasing, also, was an elusive problem because, dependent on circumstances, it could be either a playful and acceptable form of social behaviour or a thinly disguised form of bullying.

Nikki considered the educational significance of this in a discussion paper for a parents' meeting on the subject: 'The extent to which teasing can develop into a form of torment is not always realised; and, where the motivation is aggressive rather than merely playful, and the teasing is carried to extremes, it can induce in the victim a state of isolation and despair.

'Because it is usually carried out in the presence of others, the victim is debarred from retaliating lest he be considered a 'poor sport'. The tradition that we must all be expected to endure teasing is to my mind a relic of tribal society and the ritual initiation ordeals that adolescents had to undergo to qualify for adult status.

'But, where it is no longer part of a formalised process of socialisation, it loses any constructive function it may have possessed, i.e., in the encouragement of self-control, and simply becomes a means whereby people can indulge the darker side of their own natures at the expense of others.

'Teasing an equal is a form of provocation which is excusable because there is always the possibility of immediate and vigorous retaliation in some form or another. And this kind of teasing is often indulged in by adolescents when the beginnings of sexual interest are driving them to try and capture the attention of a member of the opposite sex, without being fully aware either of the means they are adopting to achieve this or of the reasons for their desire to do so. The audience which participates in a campaign of teasing is usually half aware that something unpleasant is going on but the various reasons which prevent individuals from taking action to stop the teasing are only partly realised. The greatest of them, of course, is fear. As one small boy said to me when I had been talking to the School Council about the responsibility of bystanders in such a situation, 'But if we draw attention to ourselves by protesting, they'll turn round and tease us!' This is the eternal problem of the non-participant who is insensibly engaged in completing the process of bullying by the person who needs to bully. Shall he or shall he not risk incurring the same treatment by protesting on behalf of another person?

'It is the same problem on a smaller scale as that of peoples subjected to totalitarian government, and the answer to it can be found only in the possession of widely shared and strongly held ethical beliefs and the will to act on them. This was more easily said than done in Nazi Germany where, to protest against injustice required courage beyond the ordinary, life itself being at stake. But, in a democratic society, the risks involved are clearly not in the same order of magnitude, and therefore passivity in the face of injustice has, depending on the circumstances, less to condone it. Where there is no serious threat of physical retaliation, passive disinclination to be involved in helping others in distress takes on the appearance of moral cowardice.

'It is remarkable, if chilling, to reflect in the light of this, that the philosophy of the 'Beat' generation in the United States implicitly rationalises a deliberate withdrawal from all but the most superficial relationships. Man's mental isolation, it is claimed, must result in a day-to-day existence, and precludes all permanent forms of human relations. It is the antithesis of the social integration and solidarity epitomised in Donne's 'No man is an island'.[83] To the Beatniks each man is not even an island, but a mere floating straw in a chaotic whirlpool, so that it is hardly surprising if they feel cut off from all those normal forms of help and interdependence which most of us take for granted.

'To me it seems to be an anti-philosophy, likely to appeal more to immature young men than to any other category; as I think it unlikely that a woman would identify with its tenets once she had experienced childbirth, for this bestows, more than anything else can, a sense of the continuity of life and the interdependence of human society.

'If education is to be a balance as well as reflector of the community of which it is a part, it must pass on to young people the values which embody the rights and responsibilities of each individual person. If these values are to be more than merely theoretical, they have to be consciously worked for and cannot be left to chance, and this calls for active social participation. Dissociation, passivity and non-involvement have no place in a democratic society.'

What has already been said of progressive schools up to this point has indicated that they are not totally permissive institutions. To say that they are non-authoritarian is not the same as saying there is no authority, just as, to say that their pupils enjoy a large measure of freedom is not to claim they are subject to no restrictions or that their behaviour does not, at times, necessitate the imposition of sanctions. What has been stressed is that the sanctions themselves are not arbitrarily imposed but have evolved in the course of a democratic process, and are in theory legitimised by the whole community. In spite of this, attitudes to sanctions differ widely in the progressive movement, ranging from considering them as 'a clement necessity, to a total opposition to the idea as a violation of respect for the personality.'[84]

Those at the permissive end of this continuum find inspiration in Rousseau's dictum that 'Children should never receive punishment as such; it should always come as the natural consequence of their faults.'[85]

---

[83] Donne, J. Meditations, XVII
[84] Stewart, W.A.C. op cit. Chapter 8
[85] Rousseau, J.J. Emile. Everyman (Trans Dent.)

Ahead of her Time

One modern progressive school claims to discourage misbehaviour, not by punishment, but by creating a rational, egalitarian and happy environment in which children do not need to misbehave.

This is an admirable, if utopian, ideal and, while the attempt is clearly worthwhile, it is unrealistic to expect it will ever dispense with the need for sanctions, if this is genuinely the intention. Like Rousseau's discovery principle, it says nothing about the action to be taken when misbehaviour does, in fact, take place.

In part, this reticence stems from the semantic confusion surrounding the term 'punishment'. Probably because of its narrow colloquial connotation, 'punishment' has acquired a taboo status in progressive circles, rather as if its negative aspects were thought likely to contaminate the principle of positive expectation. Despite which, it continues to be used in the behavioural sciences, covering a wider spectrum of meanings, including the verbal and non-verbal expression of disapproval - even, in certain situations, saying 'no'.

One of the consequences of semantic imprecision and ambivalent attitudes towards discipline is that the sanctions, aims and objectives of a school may be vaguely expressed and therefore open to misunderstanding and misrepresentation. Another, potentially more dangerous, consequence is that, in the absence of clearly prescribed sanctions, pupils may be unintentionally lulled into the mistaken belief that breaches even of statute law enjoy special immunity in the protective environment of the school. For a pupil so placed, to discover the reality when it is too late must be to experience a bitter sense of disillusion and betrayal.

At KAS it was considered essential that pupils should have a clear understanding of existing sanctions and of the school's responsibilities under the law.

It was emphasised that the school's discretionary powers *in loco parentis* related only to its internal regulations and not to the law in general. There was nothing vague or equivocal in the school's position, and no inherent contradictions between its functions and the operation of the law. This understanding was essential if the school was to fulfil its responsibility to inculcate respect for the rule of law and the observance of the laws in practice.

For this reason the school encouraged parents to keep their children at KAS for the whole of their primary and secondary education, if possible. It provided the opportunity for a continuous and stable period of enculturation and development from which, other things being equal, most children could benefit enormously. Disciplinary problems not infrequently occurred in the case of children who had come to the school in their later years and experienced difficulty in adapting to a way of life so much at variance with anything they had known before.

There were instances of children, who, exulting in relative freedom after years of misery under a harsh regime, still thought KAS 'weak' in comparison to their former schools and enjoyed the novel experience of exploiting the supposed 'weakness' they thought they had found. Which is to say they had a lot of ground to make up if they were to fully understand what the school was all about.

Some had histories of maladjustment in other schools and of these a few had been recommended by educational psychologists in the hope of their benefiting from a more liberal regime. Past experience had shown that sometimes this could be spectacularly successful, but at other times it was manifestly not the case. There was clearly a limit to the length of time the school could contain those whose aggression and antagonism to rules threatened to cause disruption and who showed not the slightest intention of changing their uncooperative behaviour. The futility of efforts made to help these young people was compounded in some cases by the lack of co-operation and laissez-faire attitudes of some of the parents concerned. It was as if, in their seeming indifference to parental responsibility, they were, together with their children, acting out some parody of the progressive ethic, testing the limits of tolerance in a kind of anarchic charade, all unfortunately at the expense of the rest of the school. Reflecting on the rare cases of expulsion that had taken place during her time at KAS, Nikki observed that the staff had had to balance the school's needs against those of various individuals. There was a limit to the extent to which the majority could be sacrificed to one or two who were clearly in need of specialist treatment, and out of place in King Alfred School. 'These decisions were always taken, after consultation with staff, where we no longer had any alternative, if the school was to function as a serious educational establishment. No competent or responsible member of staff in any school could have done more than my colleagues in extending sympathy, tolerance, and helpful understanding towards children in difficult circumstances. We did not act in a spirit of moral censure; no grudges were borne or hard feelings expressed. We simply concluded that, after an exhaustive trial, the fact of incompatibility had finally to be accepted. The only positive answer was transfer to a more appropriate educational setting.'

Towards this end, Nikki always offered advice and practical help if required in connection with resettlement, being particularly concerned to ensure that no stigmatic record should be allowed to jeopardise an individual's chances in later life. Moreover, she was not alone in being impressed by the small but significant number of Old Alfredians who returned to visit the school from time to time, obviously having long outgrown their earlier developmental problems, talking frankly and without embarrassment about the 'odious children' they had been and the appalling time they had given the school. They had later recognised the value of what KAS had been trying to do, and could not understand why they had behaved as they had done.

19 Parents and Teachers: Limits to collaboration

The foregoing discussion of rules and sanctions has re-emphasised the importance of understanding and co-operation as the basic conditions of success in the conduct of a school like KAS. The effective promotion of these conditions requires the willing participation and collaboration of staff, parents and pupils, and this has been a constant goal of the school since the time of its inception.

The school's original aims included a clause designed to 'promote co-operation in the education of children between parents and teachers, amongst other ways, by giving parents who are members of the Society some representation in the management'[86]. Whilst this wording was doubtless unequivocal to the founders themselves, it was to lead to differences of interpretation in subsequent periods of the school's history and to definitional uncertainties relating to the respective areas of responsibility of the heads and the parent governors.

Historical accounts of the early years have stressed the dominant management role played by the founder parents and the reforming zeal which motivated them to succeed in keeping the school in existence against all the odds, where professional educators might well have failed. Given the indispensable professional advice they obtained from Professor Findlay in drafting the curriculum, theirs was the main driving force in the initial stages, and not that of the school's first headmaster, Charles Rice. The patronising attitudes and inexcusable behaviour shown by some of their number to the latter have been tentatively explained by preoccupation with the larger reformist movement in which they were engaged at the time, but it was possible also that the nature of their innovation was such as to suggest there were no precedents to guide them. However, they appeared 'to have no conception of the proper function of a headmaster' and 'it was for the next generation to solve the problem of smooth working between the headmaster and the governors'[87].

This came about in the period following the departure of Charles Rice and the subsequent appointment of John Russell, when a clearer definition of the areas of responsibility emerged, and a less hierarchical and more conventional relationship between Council and headmaster was negotiated.

With its parent-led antecedents, KAS stood alone amongst the progressive schools in recognising the positive benefits afforded by the participation of parents in the conduct of the school. By contrast, the boarding schools were criticised by a senior KAS member in 1900 as being

---

[86] Memorandum and Articles of Association, Clause 4(a), 1897.

[87] Montgomery, B., Hibburd, E.M., A Short History of the King Alfred School Society, KASS Archives, 1965.

instrumental in destroying 'the development of the natural and harmonious relationships between pupil and parent, and parent and school'[88].

It is clear that John Russell was expressing not only his own view of the limits of parental participation but also a general consensus of opinion when he wrote in 1908, 'Recognising that the parent - next to society - is in a position to exercise the most profound moral influence upon his own child, we encourage in all matters the fullest interchange of opinion and practical collaboration between school and home'[89].

By this time the majority of parents were content to limit their participation to either serving on Council, if elected, or to the various and at times vital, supportive roles that so notably sustained the school through the difficult years of its subsequent history. The functions of parent governors were concerned with policy, finance, overall supervision and general management, whilst the Head had *de facto* responsibility for the effective implementation of educational policy, being accountable to Council representing the parent body as a whole.

The imprecise nature of line management between head and parents was reflected in a press release in the Westminster Gazette of March 1923 under the headline 'Parents Run a School'. In this, KAS was described as an unusual school at which 'parental interference' was not merely welcomed but actively solicited. It had been suggested (it was not disclosed by whom) that there should be a meeting of parents with the governing body at which members of the school staff would not be present. The meeting was designed to provide an opportunity for the free interchange of ideas on the general conduct of the school. The response was negligible, and, in the event, no meeting was held; nor, according to further inquiries, did the parents want such a meeting. A number of reasons suggest themselves: It is possible that parents found the exclusion of teachers unacceptable, and were therefore making a silent protest; they may have wished to dissociate themselves from the tendentious notion of absolute parental control, as well as the equally objectionable suggestion of interference. They were anyway largely satisfied with existing arrangements for parent-staff meetings, and their own free access to classrooms at any time. If, as this incident suggests, the main impetus for this public representation of the school came from the parent governors, it would appear to have been against the current opinion of most parents, and certainly that of the headmaster, Joseph Wicksteed, who confided in correspondence with A.S. Neill his intention of 'running the school'. An intention which Neill approved, adding a caveat that Wicksteed's conduct of the school should agree with the laws of the Society. 'But again', observed

---

[88] The Highgate Express, 3rd March 1900.
[89] Russell, J., The Aims of KASS's Hampstead School, in Chapter 20, Executive Committee of Inquiry into Moral Instruction & Training in Schools, 1908.

19 Parents and Teachers: Limits to collaboration

Neill, 'in your shoes, I'd send the laws of the Society to the devil if they got in my way'.

The existence in the Russell-Wicksteed era of a supportive, co-operative, though not uncritical, parent body is well illustrated by the following extract from John Russell's valedictory address in July 1920:

'To those of you who have found and kept sufficient faith in us (seldom, I am glad to think, a quite unquestioning faith) I want to say two things: while thanking you for your co-operation, often so invaluable to the school, I could wish that it had been fuller, more constant, more universal, and, above all, that none of you had ever hesitated to come to me (as some of you generously have hesitated) for fear of adding to my anxieties. To know the worst in time is often the way to the best. Not to know all, or to know too late, is often loss irretrievable.'

To fully appreciate the implication of these words in the context of the period it is salutary to reflect that the school's numbers averaged about one hundred, and the conventional assumption of parents at large, and to a great extent of parents at KAS, was that the professional staff should be trusted to get on with the job, with the qualification in the case of King Alfred that parents reserved their constitutional right to hold the heads accountable if and when things went wrong.

It would, however, be simplistic to conclude that parent-teacher relations were at all times as harmonious as it might be supposed during this period. To do so would omit consideration of individual cases of non-co-operation on the part of parents, some instances of which have already been cited in previous chapters.

Parent-teacher collaboration in any real sense was virtually non-existent before the foundation of KAS, and has been an idea slow to mature in the present century in both the independent and state sectors of education. And, considering the fact that there are between parents and teachers potentially more causes for antagonism than rapprochement, the degree of successful co-operation at KAS can justifiably be regarded as a triumph for rationalism and pioneering enterprise.

The sources of tension and antagonism are well documented in psychological literature, but nowhere more trenchantly than in the writings of A.S. Neill. 'To the teacher the parent is an enemy', he wrote in 'The Dominie in Doubt'[90], an uncompromisingly blunt statement to which he added certain necessary qualifications in his later writings. Like other boarding school heads, he did not encourage parental involvement, but in his case this arose from his conviction that the parents of problem children were themselves inescapably part of the problem.[91]

The tragedy of such parents, in his view, was that they were always 'acting for the best', would not or could not acknowledge their own part in

---

[90] Neill, A.S., A Dominie in Doubt. Herbert Jenkins, 1920.
[91] Neill, A.S., The Problem Parent. Herbert Jenkins, 1932.

the causation of their children's emotional disturbance or social maladjustment, and were therefore unaware of the need to change the home circumstances which were at the root of the problem. 'An unloving matrimonial home', he noted, 'means an unhappy home - an atmosphere of psychic death to the child...This is why it is hopeless to try to cure a problem child when the home retains the atmosphere that made the child a problem.'[92]

Nikki was familiar with the subliminal tensions inherent in the parent-teacher relationship and had practical experience of some of the associated behaviourial manifestations. Of these, one of the most difficult to deal with arose when, after a long period of observation, it became necessary to recommend a child for psychiatric referral. Where some parents would unhesitantly consent to such a proposition, others would react with resentment and aggression, as if the suggestion itself was perceived as an insult to both child and parents. And how much greater was the appearance of outrage if, in accordance with developments in modern practice, it were suggested that parents and child could with advantage be seen together by the psychiatrist.

Tensions may also be generated where the parent is subconsciously jealous of the teacher and expresses this outwardly in the form of negative attitudes and unwarranted adverse criticism - all of which are liable to be assimilated by the child. The teacher, in consequence, becomes the innocent victim of hostile attitudes for which no rational explanation can be found.

Nikki recalled one case in which the circumstances suggested the operation of unconscious motives. It concerned a teacher of irreproachable character and exceptional professional ability who had to be protected against an unjustified campaign waged by someone intent on the teacher's dismissal. In the event, the campaign was unsuccessful, but left behind it a sense of shame for the incalculable distress to which an innocent person had been exposed as well as for the damage done, albeit temporarily, to parent-staff relations. It was against all that KAS stood for as a community bound together by shared values, first among which was concern for all its individual members, a concern which, in this instance, had been betrayed.

Clearly jealousy is a more complex emotional state than this single example would suggest, and, where fear, insecurity or prolonged frustration are part of the established pattern of family relationships, different forms of jealousy can develop, which may be unconsciously projected as a negative influence into the life of the school. Neill asserted that there was no need for rivalry between parents and teachers; if children felt unloved by their parents, it was to be expected that they would love elsewhere - it was thwarted love for parents that was showered on the teacher.[93]

---

[92] Neill, A.S., Summerhill. Gollancz. 1962
[93] ibid.

If, conversely, the child assimilated and acted upon the parent's hostility to the teacher, this could be interpreted as a negative way of trying to win at least the approval if not the love of the parent.

Another contentious issue over which an element of unspoken rivalry existed concerned responsibility for the implementation of educational policy. This had remained a relatively dormant issue since the early years of the century, appearing only intermittently when dissension arose over the rate and type of educational reforms. This reached its climax in the 1960s with the major controversy over the importance of science in the curriculum.

The issue surfaced again in the early 1970s, but this time in a different form affecting more directly the professional interests of the teaching staff. It was initiated by a few parents who questioned the long-standing convention which appeared to 'exclude' parents from discussion of certain educational matters - the curriculum, teaching methods, etc., - hitherto regarded as the prerogative of the professional teaching staff.

The reference in the Constitution of 1897 to 'giving parents who are members of the Society some representation in the management' they interpreted as a mandate for the joint management of all aspects of education by parent representatives and teachers.

In view of the consensus that had existed since the foundation of the school over the division of responsibility between parents and staff, this revisionist challenge evoked a cautious response from members of staff, who apprehended an extension of parental intervention in the practical implementation of educational policy, hitherto accepted as the proper function of the professional teaching staff - indeed the raison d'etre of their employment.

As Nikki pointed out, parents were already involved in the management of education through their elected members of Council, even more so if they were members themselves. If parents, some of whom were educationalists in their own right and had a valuable contribution to make, had questions to ask, recommendations to make or new ideas for discussion, alternative channels were open via the Parent-Staff Committee, and the heads and teaching staff, who were readily available, despite an ever-increasing workload.

There were many precedents for the participation of parents with different kinds of expertise contributing voluntarily to the educational process in the school and in the home, while parental collaboration and support had always been a source of inspiration and pride throughout the history of the school.

It was, however, necessary to be clear about the limits of collaboration, if it was not to become counter-productive. Diversion of a disproportionate amount of the teacher's time and energy to the interests of parents, at the expense of children, would clearly have been the least productive outcome of collaboration beyond a critical point.

'Parents and teachers have much to learn from one another', Nikki observed, 'but they have to be aware of what is needed. They can't help by trying to do each other's job. Despite the tradition of being *in loco parentis*, any teacher who knows his job doesn't try to usurp the parent's function, and neither should parents do the reverse.'

The problem of defining the limits of collaboration was aggravated by the inherently uncertain status of the teaching profession as a whole. Had it enjoyed the same kind of public esteem as the established professions, the question of limits would hardly have arisen. But, as Nikki recorded in an essay on the subject, teaching as a profession had certain unique characteristics. The child-rearing experience of parents, as well as their own experience as school children, had so familiarised them with the role of the teacher that teaching had little of the 'mystique' typifying 'real' professions. This justified parents in claiming to have knowledge of the early stages of learning behaviour and to have their own very definite ideas about the whole process of education. 'Everyone considers himself, as a matter of course, a complete adept in the science of education', wrote Arthur Hill in the 19th century, 'and it has been for some time held as an axiom, that the only good reason for sending children to school, is want of time on the part of their parents for their instruction at home. We doubt if a man could be found in the three kingdoms, sufficiently vain to make a similar avowal with respect to the repair of his old shoes.'[94]

Such ideas may be regarded as exaggeration but, in spite of the increasing professionalisation of teaching at all levels in the present century, they linger on to a surprising degree in the public consciousness. Nikki recalled many instances of parents who had said to her, when talking about a teacher, 'if only he would do this, or do that, he would have no problem; it's only because he does what he does that the class is difficult/my child is troublesome'. The variations were infinite, but the message was always the same...it's easy if you know how; anyone could do it, so why doesn't he? They would never dream of saying the same sort of thing of a doctor, lawyer or a research chemist, so why of a teacher?

Progress towards an all-graduate profession and the development of education as a multi-disciplinary field of degree-level study appeared to have made remarkably little impression on the misconceptions of those who clung to the idea of teaching as 'child's play'.

In a letter to Genevieve Sanua in the summer of '92 Nikki wrote:

'I am aware of the fact that the word 'professional' has now apparently become an unacceptable designation among some educationists. Doubtless Bernard Shaw would have been delighted (the dear old Irish iconoclast held that ' all professions are conspiracies against the laity'). I

---

[94] Hill, A., Public Education, quoted in Burke, V., Teachers in Turmoil, Penguin Special, 1971.

have always supported the idea that people who work in any job can have something valuable to offer in a school and we have always asked our parents, whose interests lie in a wide variety of fields to come and talk or take occasional classes,(or even weekly ones in lower school) and I don't think our sports section would have survived in the past had it not been for the generous and constant presence each week of one or two friends and past pupils who gave their time freely. The problem is that busy and interesting people rarely find time to come in on a regular basis, but when they do come they can be a tremendous asset

'Recently though I have observed a change in the attitude towards staff and heads generally. Comments I have read (and indeed heard expressed at meetings and conferences)seem to suggest that simply because they are professionals, they must be carefully supervised and put on enquiry (presumably by those who hold themselves to be non-professionals ?). Accountability is essential and desirable, and it already exists for teachers through the teachers' unions and the Dep. of Education, but I can't see anyone suggesting that other professions (doctors, lawyers, architects etc.) should be subject to a quite unregulated kind of scrutiny from outside.

'If parents in schools don't trust the teachers in charge of their children they have every right and indeed the absolute responsibility, to challenge the school, particularly if they are among those who have no choice. We are lucky because all our parents have chosen KAS and if we are not what they want they can take their children away (and we will help them to find a more suitable place, if there is a problem!) But when they appear to distrust the school and yet keep their children with us, this raises great problems for the children -and of course for the staff. Children need to be able to be loyal to their parents , but also to their school community and if the parents and teachers are in open opposition this can interfere seriously with their progress in school. There is also another aspect....if you are paying people to do a job you must either allow them to do it or, if they prove themselves incapable of doing it you must dispense with them and find others who are more competent. Sorry to load this on to you but I suppose it is the end of the academic year and a break will I am sure restore my confidence - particularly in those really wonderful and positive parents who are the real strength of the place'.

By contrast, at the other extreme were parents who, while in no way lacking in affection and concern for their children, seemed to expect the school to assume many aspects of what most parents would have regarded as their own responsibility. A wealthy parent once said to her: 'I hated myself when I was a child, but I hated my teachers even more, and I've come to your school because I don't want my son to go through the same experience. I don't care how much it costs, I'll pay it. He's got to be happy'. It quickly became apparent to Nikki that 'what it costs' was only to be understood in terms of money. 'The things that any child needs more than luxury - time with his parents, love and approval, a regular pattern of life, continuity of care and basic respect for him as a person - were not going to be provided because they would have involved a curtailment of the father's freedom. The parents separated shortly afterwards, but fortunately the mother, a warm, sane and responsible woman, was able to hold the family together, while the father continued a lucrative career as a fulfiller of expensive dreams.

'Another couple, chain-smoking throughout one interview in my room, complained bitterly of our inability to stop their daughter from bringing packets of sweets to the school and eating them when she was on a drug-assisted diet for obesity. I pointed out that dependence on a comfort habit was not uncommon, and usually went with feelings of acute anxiety. But it was clear that they never connected their own state of mind with hers. As far as they were concerned, we should be able to stop her somehow. I felt about this as I felt about other instances of a similar kind, that parents who expected us to exact from their children a degree of obedience or to exert a measure of control which they were unable or unwilling to undertake themselves were virtually asking the impossible, at least in a school like King Alfred's. Whilst sympathetic counselling might temporarily evoke some degree of outward conformity from a child, and this only when under supervision, it would do nothing to remove the underlying causes of compulsive behaviour.'

Whatever elements of conflict or dissent may have been suggested by the foregoing discussion, Nikki felt absolute confidence in the validity of her assessment of parent-staff relations in the mid-1970s: 'Fortunately for everyone, the majority of parents are honestly concerned for their children and anxious to give them the best possible chance of developing well. They support the school and the staff, and give their young people a coherent and positive sense of the value of education. They give up their time to be on the governing body and the parent-staff committee, organise meetings and other activities and help with projects, visits and camps whenever they can find the time. These people are the guarantee of a happy and successful school'.

Accepting the impossibility of complete consensus, she nevertheless emphasised that a large measure of consensus was essential to the achievement of the goals of the school. This she saw as threatened by aggressive confrontation and destructive forms of conflict but as enhanced by positive forms (e.g., the conflict of ideas, as a source of progress and change), always provided these were regulated by the conventions of civilised discourse.

The indirect influence of KAS in the development of parent-teacher collaboration in the maintained schools is traceable through the foundation in 1930 of the Home and School Council, under the wing of the New Education Fellowship. 'Parents and Teachers', the official journal of this organisation, had a nursery-infant bias and was designed to promote parent-teacher co-operation. This was followed in 1956 by the institution of the Confederation of Parent-Teacher Associations, welcomed by Lord Hailsham, the Minister of Education, with the caveat: 'Parents cannot run schools. What I hope the Federation is going to do is to encourage the fullest co-operation between home and school, leaving the precise organisation to those on the spot.'

The growing recognition of the educational importance of parents received a further boost with the publication in 1967 of the Plowden Report - 'Children and their Primary Schools'.[95] Research commissioned for the inquiry was quoted in the report showing that, of all the variables associated with attainment in schools, parental attitude was by a considerable margin the most significant. While Plowden made no recommendation to suggest that Parent-Teacher Associations should be mandatory in schools, it clearly pointed the way to a more active parental involvement in the educational process, and the formation of a new Home and School Council was an early outcome of this. Three years before the publication of Plowden, the KAS Parent-Staff Committee included the following comment in its annual report to the Annual General Meeting:

'At a time when there is much discussion in educational circles regarding the desirability of parents and staff working together, it is not considered immodest to assert that KAS is in the forefront of schools practising this policy. The association of parents and staff at this school is, with all its imperfections, probably a model of what educationalists would like to see achieved in most other schools.'[96]

The movement gathered pace in the years which followed, and liaison between home and school became the subject of further educational research, practical experimentation in primary schools, and a voluminous literature calculated to promote innovations.

Nikki herself was active in establishing contacts with some of those involved in the movement. In 1975 she engaged in a wide-ranging correspondence with Mia Kellmer-Pringle[97] on the importance, in a period of rapid social change, of children's having a stable home background; and, in 1977, appeared in a Thames TV discussion with Eric Midwinter[98] when he introduced a new scheme called Home Link.

At this stage, the development of parent-teacher collaboration in state schools contained a large element of voluntaryism and was relatively apolitical in character. At a time when parents often complained of the instability of an educational system periodically liable to reorganisation with each parliamentary election, this at least appeared to be free from partisan considerations. But it was not destined to remain like this.

---

[95] Central Advisory Council for Education (England & Wales). Children and their Primary Schools. The Plowden Report. HMSO, 1967.
[96] KASS Annual Report, 1964.
[97] Kellmer-Pringle, M., Director of the National Children's Bureau.
[98] Midwinter, E., Head of Public Affairs Unit, National Consumers' Council.

The seeds of political intervention were germinated indirectly in 1977 by the report of the Taylor Committee of Enquiry into the government of maintained primary and secondary schools in England and Wales.[99] This recommended that the composition of governing bodies should be determined by democratic election, and provided for equal representation from the four categories: Local Education Authorities; staff including the head ex officio; parents, and the community served by the school. These recommendations were subsequently incorporated into parliamentary legislation and thereby gave statutory force to parental representation on governing bodies.[100]

The relationship between the four representative groups was clearly envisaged as one of partnership and co-operation, and the provision for equal numbers was designed to ensure that no one group should be able to dominate others. In the knowledge that certain teachers' associations were against the report, Taylor emphasised that it was to be regarded as a discussion document. And, anticipating some of the grounds for objection, pointed out that many of the recommendations were not new but merely involved the reactivation of extant, though widely inoperative, statutory powers invested in governing bodies.

The curriculum, for example, was a legitimate area of concern to governors, and the assumption that it was the preserve of teachers had absolutely no foundation in history or in law. The committee accepted, however, the importance of teachers' expertise in implementing curriculum policies, and acknowledged that governors could bring to the task 'no more than can reasonably be expected of informed, interested, and responsible lay people.'[101] Governors, noted Taylor, should see classes at work not as 'inspectors', but to provide themselves with greater insight into their work. Joan Sallis, a parent member of the Taylor Committee, elaborated on this later in a salutary book on school government, stressing the value of the 'ordinariness' of parent governors, 'casting a precious and healthy light on expert affairs'. The role of the parent, she suggested, was not to shadow teachers as 'pretend' inspectors, trainee managers or imitation accountants, but to have the information and confidence needed to be effective in their 'ordinariness'.[102]

The Taylor Report showed a sensitive understanding of the problems involved in making partnership work in practice. Give and take were going to be necessary on all sides. If teachers tended to be defensive, many were so for good reasons, having had poor experiences of the old system. On

---

[99] Report of a Committee of Enquiry appointed by the Secretary of State for Education & Science: `A New Partnership for our Schools.' (The Taylor Report) HMSO, 1977.
[100] Education Acts, 1980, 1985.
[101] Taylor Report, op cit.
[102] Sallis, J., Schools, Parents and Governors. Routledge, 1988.

the other hand, heads needed to be tolerant of the inexperience and nervousness of the new parent governors 'who, waiting for a turn, often make an innocent question come out all wrong and sound aggressive. Our only enemies in the school are clumsiness and misunderstanding.'[103]

While the moral was clear for all those prepared to heed it, the expectation of partnership envisaged proved to be based, in practice, more on hope than experience, for factional domination was far from being eliminated.

Preliminary research into the operation of the new governing bodies showed a tendency for parent governors to be uncertain of their position and to be overawed by both Local Education Authority and school professionals.[104]

Conversely, Joan Sallis commented on the growing confidence of parent governors and increased awareness of their roles. 'It is common to find that giving people some involvement stimulates the demand for more', she noted, and went on to quote examples of parents 'who were outraged by any limitations placed on their participation or by any effort to suppress debate'.[105]

These examples of self-assertion were among the first indications of a new and more political element in the relations between parents and teachers, an element which was incompatible with the 'partnership' principle envisaged by Taylor.

The parents' movement generated during this period several pressure groups of varying degrees of militancy in whose membership women represented a majority and whose rhetoric included a number of new concepts like 'empowerment' and 'parent power'. Finally, all these developments were reinforced by the publication of a number of books relating to the new role of parents in education and of a series of self-help manuals designed to equip parents with the necessary knowledge and skills to obtain the maximum benefit from their children's schools.

Although the actual role of parent governors was not prescribed by the terms of reference of the Taylor enquiry, Nikki was convinced that the evidence presented to the Committee should include a statement of the unique experience of KAS in this connection. It was clearly going to be necessary to volunteer the information, since the enquiry was exclusively concerned with the maintained system and not with independent schools, and, if it was to find its way to the Committee in time, it would need influential support.

At the suggestion of Alan Wood, the chairman, she wrote first to a mutual friend in the Cabinet - John Silkin, MP[106] - and then to Lady

---

[103] Taylor Report, op cit.
[104] Kogan, M., et al. School Governing Bodies. Heinemann, 1984.
[105] Sallis, J., op cit.
[106] Minister of Agriculture and Fisheries.

Falkender,[107] whom she had also met. As a result of these initiatives the proposal was referred to Shirley Williams, the Secretary of State for Education, who invited the school to submit a paper on the subject, including suggestions on how KAS experience could be most usefully applied in a wider context.

Nikki accordingly drafted the requisite paper, modified it following discussion with the chairman, and forwarded the final version to the Department of Education and Science for onward transmission to the Taylor Committee.

Detached from background details of the history and organisation of the school, the relevant paragraphs concerning the historic role of parents at KAS read as follows:

'There is no doubt that the close involvement of parents in the life of the school determined to a large extent both the direction and quality of its development. Many of the crises which the school passed through in its early days were directly attributable to over-enthusiastic participation by amateur educationalists in a way which diminished both the status and authority of staff and at times rendered their position untenable.

'Gradually, growing experience and the fortunate influence of a series of outstanding individuals among both parents and staff led to a more genuine understanding of the division of responsibility and the proper functions of parents and teachers.

'As a result of my experience over the last eighteen years, I have reached certain very definite conclusions about the advantages and disadvantages of parental involvement in the running of a school, and these are as follows:

'I consider that success or failure will depend almost entirely on the voluntary nature of the professional/amateur partnership. If either side has no choice but to accept the conditions, then the chance of a good understanding developing is minimal. Legislation should not be used except as a last resort. The aim is co-operation and this is only likely to be achieved within a comparatively free and flexible atmosphere, in which individual differences and needs can be recognised and catered for.

'Because of economic realities it is highly unlikely that any really significant choice of school can be given to the majority of parents in the maintained sector. For this reason, power given to parents over the staff of a particular school to which those parents must send their children is probably going to be exercised with less subtlety and discretion than it should be, if the staff are not to be put under intolerable stress.

'While an ordinary, responsible parent may be, and usually is, well able to judge what would be best for his child, the same parent may be no better able to make judgments on behalf of other people's children than any other

---

[107] Private Secretary to the Prime Minister, Harold Wilson.

untrained person. To give him the power over the professional person, who will ultimately be held answerable, is a risky procedure.

'Parent opinion should be heard on an equal footing with that of the teachers, in the context of the area planning authority, where they can be involved as individual members of the community rather than as parents of a particular child in a particular school.

'Parent participation at each school should be encouraged by any means acceptable to the head and staff, and should be allowed to take shape and grow in the way, or ways, which are most helpful to children, staff and parents. The children's needs will not be met in any satisfactory way if there is fear, suspicion and resentment engendered by a compulsory yoke under which teachers and parents have no choice but to work. One result of such a system can be seen in American education, where teachers are often passive and submissive.

'Parental involvement in the community outside the school through their own work, interests and skills is a rich source of experience for a school. Children's horizons can be widened and their transition from child to working adult made easier, and more worthwhile, if the wisdom and knowledge of adults in their area are made available to them.

'Teachers must be prepared to communicate with parents as part of their professional responsibility. This, in turn, means that their own training must involve courses which help them to understand their function in terms both of the classroom and of the wider community outside the school.

'My opinions are based on long experience, albeit in a small school. I do not for one moment pretend that what I can offer is 'evidence' in the sense in which the word is used by researchers and statisticians, but I would be happy to appear before any committee considering matters of this kind and to answer questions on this or any related topics.'

The outcome of her initiative was disappointing. The Taylor Committee had reached a definitive stage in their work and announced that they were consequently unable to take any further evidence from the public. It was understood they had received copies of her deposition from the Department of Education and Science, but whether these had been considered by the Committee was not known. In a final letter from the Department she was assured that the Secretary of State would bear her offer of assistance in mind when the views and recommendations of the Taylor Committee were known.

When, in the event, nothing further was heard either from the Department or the Committee, it was concluded that Nikki's evidence, for all its relevance, had been considered of marginal importance to the Enquiry, particularly in the light of the recommended quadripartite composition of governing bodies which the Report ultimately disclosed. The effect of this, as far as the maintained schools were concerned, was that 'parent power' was from the first exposed to the checks and balances represented by other sectional interests on the governing body.

This reduced the sense of urgency with which the KAS evidence had been invested hitherto, but, if Taylor had proved to be a blind alley, there was still a case to be made in the growing public discussion of new parental powers and responsibilities.[108]

Towards this end Nikki redirected her efforts through the medium of the press in the novel form of a multiple choice quiz addressed to school parents and posing the basic question 'How do you score as a parent?' It appeared in the Look! section of the Sunday Times on January 22nd, 1978. Nikki had provided an introductory article which is reproduced here but was not, in fact, used in the feature, owing to lack of disposable space.[109]

'When the recommendations of the Taylor Report are implemented', the article began, 'parents whose only previous experience of education finished in their teens will find themselves with the opportunity of becoming involved in the government of their own children's schools. The nature of their contribution to this vital and complex task of management will depend on a great many factors, but a major consideration must be their personal opinions of schools and teachers. And these may be based on feelings not always fully realised.

'If your own school days were happy and successful, you are likely to assume that the approach which worked well for you is the right one for your own child and most other children as well. If your experience was unsatisfactory and has left you with feelings of resentment or sadness, your attitude may well be that teachers and schools are not to be trusted and must be checked up on at every turn to make sure they do what they should and give your child a better chance than you had - and very understandable too.

'The only difficulty is that 'see what teacher is doing and tell him not to' makes it hard to create the kind of atmosphere in which children and teachers can work in freedom from unnecessary anxieties, and put all their energies into the friendly co-operative team work which makes good education possible.

'Your attitude to children and to what growing up is all about is another important factor in the situation. Do you see children as people or as possessions, as little adults or overgrown babies? Do you think it is your job to bring up your children with professional help from the school in areas you can't deal with or do you think that the schools should be responsible for the whole business of education, control and instruction? These are

---

[108] The Education Act 1980, the first stage of enacting legislation, was only a diluted response to the Taylor recommendations, almost all of which were, however, implemented in the Education Act (No.2) 1986, together with extra places offered to parents at the expense of LEA governors.

[109] Details of the Quiz, scoring, and assessment of results are shown at Appendix C.

important issues and most of us hold views which fall in between the extremes.

'This article is a plea for what is considered in some circles to be an educational heresy: that is the view that, no matter how intelligent a young person may be, he is not at the age of 13 an adult and should not be encouraged to think of himself as such, let alone be exposed to the same kind of demands which society quite properly makes on adults.

'Quite recently a parent related, with some amusement, how her daughter had asked her, in connection with an invitation she had received and which she did not in the least want to accept, 'Couldn't you say you won't let me go?' 'Well, of course, I couldn't, could I?' she said, 'After all, her father and I have always left her to make her own decisions about things and she has to take her own responsibilities.' As the girl in question was not yet 14, I suggested that she might still need to lean a little on adult authority as a way out of a situation she found difficult. If you can say 'My parents won't let me', you don't lose face with your group, and hopefully, by 16 you will have learnt both the technique of saying no and the strength of character to follow your own wishes. The idea that the earlier you can make a child perform like an adult the earlier he will become one, has been shown to be far from reliable in all kinds of contexts...on the contrary, a child who is not allowed to be a child at the appropriate age often acts out the behaviour of a child in later life, to his own disadvantage.

'I am not seeking to defend a mindless, insensitive authority over anyone, least of all children; there is far too much of that in the world already, and not only over the young. But it would help if we adults could somehow call up from some depths within ourselves the courage to be adults in relation to our children, and give them some experience of facing both refusal and failure to get one's own way without being permanently thrown off course by it.

'There are few more pathetic sights than the child to whom no-one has ever said an effective and final 'no'. Frightened by his own power, which he can see no end to, he cajoles, blusters and tears his way through the delicate web of his relationships with others, trying to find someone or some situation stronger than himself to reassure him. After all, if you are more powerful than your parents, your friends, and all the adults you know, who is left to protect you if ever you need it? Which most of us feel we do at some time.

'All this is fairly well established by psychologists and observably instinctive in the behaviour of most parents. Both human and other animals realise the need to give protection if necessary by thwarting the tendency of offspring to follow their noses into danger by showing clearly and unequivocally the limits of acceptable conduct.

'Unfortunately, in a society which grows progressively more threatening and destructive, the most thoughtful and well-intentioned adults can become so uncertain of their role and their own feelings that they have to find intellectual justification for preventing children from taking really dangerous risks, and even then they suffer from guilt about being repressive.

'Even people with strong views and social consciences go on record as being at a loss when it comes to saying 'you must' or 'you must not' to their own children. Take, for example, Margaret Drabble, the well-known writer and broadcaster, and someone who it is very hard to imagine being ambivalent about anything.[110] Writing in the Observer recently, she was emphasising the need to teach children actively rather than allowing them to flounder in a sea of self-discovery and then blaming them for not knowing how to do things; a point of view with which I am very much in agreement.

'Yet, faced with a young boy smoking in a lift, she was quite unable to do what she feels the schools ought to do, and express her disapproval on the perfectly sensible grounds of danger to heath. It was left, she tells us, to a lift attendant to adopt the adult role of caring authority and say to the child, 'Son, what are you doing to yourself?'

'How many of us, today, faced with the same circumstances would have had the courage to comment openly? Most people would I think mentally shrug their shoulders and assume that it was up to the child to make the choice. In her article, she expresses what is in my experience a very common view.

She wants the schools to be more repressive than she can herself bear to be and feels both shocked and let down if they cannot adopt the role of authority which she so clearly dislikes in her own role as a parent. One often hears people say how much they hate to be repressive and how they want to give their children the things they never had themselves; both understandable and natural feelings, but not good enough reason surely for giving in feebly to demands we know should be refused for the child's sake as much as for ours.

'Most people are quite clear about what they feel is part of the school's job, namely to insist on certain standards of behaviour from the children in their care. But most teachers know only too well the double standards in society by which what is expected of them is, in some cases, barely attempted by the adults who are closest to the children and could most easily prepare the way for the work the schools must try to do later. A great many good, experienced and devoted teachers have reached the stage where they feel they must leave the profession because they can no longer face the task of dealing with disruptive pupils whom they were not trained to handle. One might ask, who is so trained? Even social workers, who are in theory prepared to deal with the problem-makers among the young, only take on such confrontation in a one-to-one situation and not in a thirty-to-one class.

---

[110] Drabble, M., `Elders and Betters'. The Observer, 9th October, 1977.

'What is really alarming is that the children who are not troublesome, the children who want to learn and would enjoy the kind of education we should like to provide for everyone, are gradually losing out more and more because the social controls are slipping further and further out of our hands.

'Once co-operation fails then we are left with no alternative but confrontation. But only if adults are prepared to exercise the normal adult role, and allow children to learn about growing up gradually rather than thrusting an unnatural and precocious image onto them before they are ready for it, can we learn what living together in a caring society really means.

'Children's views of society and its values are developed as a result of their composite experience in which both home and school play a major role. Friends of their own age group rapidly become a strong influence in early adolescence, but even this can be modified at home if the relationship with parents is one of love and trust. Children are very aware of the attitude their parents have towards their education. They know, without being told, if their parents' expectations of them are high, and when the parents are indifferent to their progress this is soon reflected in their own attitude. Luckily, the majority of parents care deeply about their children, about their education and their future, but they are not always able to relate this clearly to the need to be firm, supportive and yet flexible where the child's developing sense of independent judgment is concerned. The most well-meaning and concerned among us can be surprisingly imperceptive when something happens which makes us anxious, and this is often reflected in the way in which we react to things which happen at school.

'Rigidly authoritarian parents are comparatively rare nowadays, and so are really indifferent ones, but between these two apparent extremes comes a whole range of approaches from firm and supportive to downright subversive, and we all get trapped by our own attitudes at times.

'For the parent who is interested in comparing other people's experiences with his or her own, the quiz[111] which follows offers a series of five situations and six different ways of dealing with each one. In case anyone considers them far-fetched, I would ask you to accept that each one is drawn straight out of personal experience of school life.'

Nikki was indefatigable in availing herself of every opportunity to foster at KAS not only the sense but also the reality of community, recognising the principle that community, like friendship, happens not by accident but has of necessity to be worked for. Her desire to encourage and reinforce positive forms of parental collaboration was one aspect of her wider concern to preserve a communitarian ethos which had endured as a tradition of the school since its foundation in 1898. Actual experience of the shared values inherent in the concept of community - co-operation, caring

---

[111] Vide Appendix C.

and concern for all its members - was in her view an essential condition for the creation of a genuine learning environment for children. King Alfred's role as a day school and its long tradition of parental collaboration clearly favoured the development of an authentic community structure. The visible signs of this were to be seen in the informal relationships between staff and pupils, the individualised teaching methods, and the exceptional contribution made by parents to the life of the school.

Social events connected with vital fund-raising activities as well as those centred on conventional anniversaries and festivals provided not only the opportunity for communal interaction but kept alive a sense of the continuity and strength of the school's importance for second and even third generation families.

A less public aspect of the persistence of community ties was the contact maintained by those past pupils, teachers, and even parents who wrote to send news, ask for references, express appreciation (and at times criticism) of the school as they had known it. Many of the staff kept in touch with those they had taught in the past, and former pupils - some now with families of their own - formed a sizeable minority at all times.

A significant number of school leavers took a year abroad with organisations like Voluntary Service Overseas before continuing with their higher education, and their letters from all over the world made particularly interesting material for class discussions with their teachers by pupils still at the school.

Inevitably there were those families who found themselves in financial straits and faced with the prospect of having to take their children away as they could no longer meet the ever-increasing fees which continuous inflation made necessary if the school was to survive. During the years before the second world war the school had welcomed many children whose parents had been driven from their homes in Europe and sought refuge in England, and they had greatly strengthened and revitalised the sense of international understanding which the school sought to foster. Because the school had kept its fees as low as possible at the beginning and had spent everything as it came in on providing the equipment and buildings needed by the increase in numbers, money was always in short supply. Unlike the great independent public schools, KAS had no funds invested by former generations to provide scholarships for future students. Nevertheless, whenever it could, the school did its best to help by remitting fees, or a part of them, particularly when the children concerned had been there from the age of four or five.

Sometimes parents themselves who had the means to do so helped individuals over difficult times and in a few urgent cases this help was arranged by Nikki or through the Council.

As a catalytic agent, her active facilitation of mutually helpful and supportive networks served to enlarge the aggregate of productive relationships and to enhance the sense of communal identity. She saw it as the diffusion of creative energy, cumulative in its effect.

Earlier discussion has already established that the fullest consensus in any social organisation is seldom if ever complete. This by no means weakened her persistent efforts to contain and, where possible, to partially resolve the negative and potentially disruptive dissensions which occurred from time to time. This was largely achieved by using every opportunity to stress the vital importance of consensus over the aims, objectives and methodology of the school, and over the kinds of parental support most likely to help the teaching staff perform their tasks effectively. Support of this kind was a logical expectation, being implicit in the initial decision of parents to send their children to the school. In spite of which, Nikki was intermittently prompted by events to re-emphasise in her annual reports the principle of co-operation, while aware that her words were directed in particular to only a very small minority of the assembled parents.

20 KAS and the National Curriculum

The end of the 1970s at KAS was a period of relative calm in which it was possible to assess and consolidate recent achievements and to consider plans for the school's development during the next ten to fifteen years.

On Nikki's recommendation, and after careful consideration, Council decided as a preliminary step to commission a comprehensive independent survey of the school, in order to provide an assessment of its current practices and the quality of its work as a basis for decisions about future development strategies. 'It is hoped', she announced in her Head's Annual Report for the academic year 1978-1979, 'that this assessment will enable us to evaluate our present performance in relation to our professed educational aims, and also help us to establish priorities in the matter of building and the provision of new facilities.'

The team which carried out the inspection consisted of five people, four of whom had been members of Her Majesty's Inspectorate and who had between them experience which spanned the whole field of primary and secondary education. They spent three days in the school at the beginning of May 1979 and considered every aspect of school life, as Nikki observed, 'from dialectic to drains'.

The generally favourable and positive nature of their preliminary report was a source of satisfaction to Council and staff, especially their comments on the children; 'Their individuality is very apparent when one observes them at work in the classroom or meets them outside. They are friendly, fairly uninhibited, and articulate. They easily establish relationships with adults and readily support one another. As they grow up, the majority appear to apply themselves conscientiously to their school work, and one was particularly impressed by the maturity and poise of many of the Sixth Formers. All these characteristics speak well for the way in which the school is being true to its aims.'

Of all the comments made by the inspectors, this was perhaps the most gratifying since it went to the heart of the school's traditional ethos, testifying to the successful achievement of the founders' aims, from which some doubters feared KAS had deviated under the pressure of social change.

'It was a good year for the school', Nikki reported, 'in that we were able to follow through and develop ideas and plans which had begun in the previous year. We were also able to consider the recommendations made by our team of expert advisers and to implement some of them immediately. Others were the subject of further consideration in relation to future plans, both short and long term.'

The survey also occasioned a review of the school's progress towards the achievement of objectives first outlined in the 1960s, among which were the phased increase in the school's size from 230 to a maximum of 430 pupils, extensive curriculum development and innovation, and a building programme designed to provide the necessary accommodation and facilities to meet this expansion.

By 1975 the target figure for pupil numbers had been substantially accomplished but implementation of the building scheme was seriously delayed as a result of rising inflation, the increasing cost of materials and services, outstanding bank loans and a temporary decline in fund-raising. These factors, together with two large salary awards, necessitated the introduction of new and stringent economies, bringing in their train an inescapable increase in school fees.

Fresh target dates had to be projected and a scale of building priorities determined. The main casualty had been the planned P.E. building, long overdue as far back as 1971 because the only accommodation available for Physical Education was the central hall, already insufficient to meet the many other demands made upon it, including the serving of school meals.

By the late 1970s, thanks to the foresight and prudent management of Bernard Igra, the Honorary Treasurer, together with the Finance Committee, the financial position was sufficiently restored for Council to authorise the construction of the long-awaited P.E building, now redesignated as a Sports Hall.

Funding the project remained a problem, the resolution of which was ultimately expedited by a generous donation of £60,000 from the Swiss charitable foundation Hermes Sweeteners through its president, Mr Peter Graff, a KAS parent.

Largely owing to the drive and energy of another school parent, Cecil Lush, the school's architect, the new facility was completed a year ahead of schedule and within its budget in December, 1981. With the official opening the following January, it became operational, with plans to make it available to disabled people at times when it was not being used by the school.

It became apparent during this period that the fall in the birth rate, with its consequences for primary and eventually for secondary education, was affecting local schools, both state and independent, and that KAS was not immune. The number of children in Lower School had shown a small but significant decrease and entries at the lowest age group declined slightly, but waiting lists existed at all age levels and there had been no difficulty in filling vacancies when they arose. The total picture was one about which the school could be reasonably optimistic. However, as Nikki pointed out, there was no room for complacency and KAS had to take a realistic view of its market situation in an increasingly competitive economy, and this meant ensuring the provision of educational services which parents were willing to pay for at a level of fees they could afford.

Another implication of the competitive element concerned the public image of the school. Whilst this had never been a matter of indifference to King Alfred, it acquired a new significance in the changing economic climate. The reputation of the school was of vital importance to its survival. It was no time for mock modesty about the school's advantages and achievements but called for a revival of some of the active propaganda characterising the early years of its existence. In the final analysis, it could no longer afford a laissez-faire attitude to the kinds of delusional misinformation to which Nikki had referred in her Annual Report of 1975:

'A number of parents still approach the school firmly convinced that we find all rules and restraints unnecessary and undesirable and, although we spend a good deal of time explaining this is not so, it remains a lively folk legend.

'Another myth is that we prepare for examinations with reluctance and pass them without distinction. In fact our excellent record with the universities continues, not only in the number of places we obtain but in the steady increase in the number of higher degrees our former pupils achieve. The reputation we have established for sending up well-informed students with a mature outlook is one of the pleasing side-effects of our approach to education, and the good impression this creates benefits all our applicants. We have been reluctant to single out and publicise these achievements in the traditional way, as they represent only one aspect, although an important one, of the total life of the school, and because we value equally all the different kinds of achievement that can occur in a comprehensive framework like our own.'

The election of a Labour Government in 1974 reawakened fears for the survival of the independent schools. KAS in particular was concerned that legislation might be introduced to rescind charitable status, in which event the school's financial viability would have been seriously threatened. At Nikki's instigation, Council initiated inquiries with a view to joining the Governing Bodies' Association. It was an unprecedented step for KAS but a worthwhile precaution in the light of the current political uncertainties.

The school had particular reason to value its independence at this time, when public education had become a central arena for the political and ideological conflicts which had superseded the large measure of consensus marking the post-war recovery period.

In 1975, in a speech at Ruskin College, Oxford, James Callaghan, then Labour Prime Minister, voiced growing public disquiet about flaws in the educational system, particularly so-called 'progressive' curriculum innovations which had appropriated time from learning basic skills, and led to a general decline in standards of number and literacy. He went on to attack 'fashionable' teaching methods, called for a national 'core curriculum' of English, Maths and Science, and expressed the hope that his speech would promote a national debate on education, throwing light on the 'secret garden' of what was taught in schools.

Nikki drew attention to these developments at the annual general meeting of KASS IN 1976:

Ahead of her Time

'The current debate about a common core curriculum, and the very understandable fears about ineffectual or irresponsible teaching methods, has given a new and unfortunate twist to the use of the word 'progressive'. I have never made any secret of my deep distrust of labels and have avoided, as far as I could, using a word whose precise meaning is so impossible to define. It is now being used widely to indicate anything from a method of which we ourselves, as responsible teachers, might approve, to extremes of casual inefficiency or deliberate failure to educate. There are those in education today who would, in the name of populism, deny to children the very rights they have themselves enjoyed. I feel we should reject both the well-intentioned vagueness of the 'de-schoolers'[112] and the dogmatism of political prophets who would like to make everyone subservient to their particular versions of education. Each generation may have to write its own history, but it is clearly lunacy to throw it away. Some people still make the assumption that because we rely on co-operation, rather than coercion, we must be either naive or irresponsible.'

The Prime Minister's speech received a large measure of support from the general public, and, in due course, the national debate took place, organised around a series of regional conferences. It met, however, with strong disapproval in the education establishment, and the National Union of Teachers expressed their indignation about political interference so vehemently that more than a decade passed before a Conservative government felt able to introduce legislation on the national curriculum.

The debate, which started with limited objectives concerned with raising educational standards, widened out during the moratorium to include a range of conflicting ideologies - all seeking to influence the content of the curriculum. The polar extremes of this continuum constellated around ideas broadly associated with traditional and 'progressive' political and educational values.

For the traditionalists the main priorities were raising standards and promoting academic excellence, laying down and enforcing both a core curriculum and standards of attainment, improving the training of teachers, and a return to traditional methods of teaching.

'Progressives' advocated a more radical reform, adapted to the conditions of the modern world, Eurocentric and internationalist in outlook, responsive to the educational needs of a multi-cultural society and the implications of cultural relativism.

KAS could afford to remain detached and to look on with equanimity as the successive stages of the dialectical process unfolded, free to make its

---

[112] Advocated the abolition of compulsory education, the dissolution of school systems as such, and the alternative provision of individual choice from a network of community-based learning resources. Vide Illich, I. Deschooling Society.

own curricular decisions in the best interests of the school, and not according to dictates of ideology.

Nikki commented on the position of KAS in relation to the curriculum debate in her Annual Report of December 1980:

'As long as the major parties continue to treat education as a political shuttlecock, we can only guess at what the future holds for the independent sector. Leaving aside legislative discrimination, we must remember that our survival depends on parental choice. No matter how laudable our philosophical ideals, we shall have no chance to attain them if parents do not wish to buy the service we offer.

'We must ensure our survival by being responsive to parental expectations, and we have to prepare ourselves for changing social needs by looking carefully and analytically at three main areas: academic standards, curricular relevance and management efficiency. All three must be viewed within the context of the school's educational approach, and that, in turn, has to be carefully examined and reinforced.

'High academic standards we already have, and they are just as important for the less, as for the more, intellectually able child - a point which many people in education have lamentably failed to appreciate in the past two decades.

'Any curricular change needs to be approached with great care. The current debate about the common core and responsibility for aims are, despite the wide publicity they have received, not particularly relevant to us. We are, and always have been, concerned primarily with the individual child's potential, because unless that is recognised, respected and developed, education is debased and becomes little more than an aspect of social engineering.

'The new technological approaches to learning methods appear to offer interesting possibilities, but we must maintain the balance between the broadly-based tradition of proven methods of teaching and the new techniques. Innovation needs to be preceded by careful evaluation.'

In fact, the KAS curriculum accorded to a marked degree with the principles of curricular design that had issued from the original conferences in 1977, before more radical perspectives had begun to influence the ongoing debate. As the nature and extent of these transpired - exemplified by revolutionary ideas concerning the English literary canon, the status of standard English and the value of grammar - the attitude of the Conservative government, at first inclined towards liberal reform, hardened in favour of a return to traditional orthodoxy.

The long-awaited legislation on the National Curriculum appeared eventually in the Education Reform Act of 1988.[113] While it laid down the

---

[113] Vagueness and lack of guidance in the National Curriculum were blamed as recently as 1995 for the failure of schools to lay the foundations of basic mathematics. Report of the London Mathematical Society, 1995.

compulsory subjects to be taught in primary and secondary schools in the maintained system, it did not specify the content of programmes of study in the component subjects, delegating this responsibility to Working Groups set up for the purpose. Largely appointed from and dominated by the academic establishment, including a significant number of influential 'progressives', these groups became a source of increasing embarrassment to the government. Only by redistribution of the membership over a period of time did it eventually reverse some of the less desirable consequences following the 'hi-jacking' of the National Curriculum, and succeed in restoring to it a synthesis of less controversial elements. Notwithstanding, some of what were considered more acceptable principles of the suggested 'progressive' reforms were retained and were implemented in schools when the Act became operational.

Free to determine its own curriculum according to the needs and interests of its pupils and the progressive tradition it represented, KAS was under no obligation to be concerned with, let alone influenced by, the development of the National Curriculum. It could not, however, remain indifferent to contemporary events in the academic world, and the implications of the conflicts and compromises involved in the curriculum debate had to be addressed.

As expected, individual teachers and parents found that they could identify with some curricular principles but not others in both the traditional and the 'progressive' camps. This was complicated by the semantic problems to which Nikki had drawn attention: were the 'progressive' reforms advocated by the academic establishment progressive in KAS terms?

On the one hand there were aspects of the traditional approach which were manifestly alien to everything the school represented, but there were also others based on sound educational principles with which progressive teachers had little cause to take issue.

The same was true, on the other hand, of the so-called 'progressive' reforms in the National Curriculum: some were unobjectionable in KAS terms, while others, in spite of their novelty and sense of 'avant-garde', were regarded with scepticism.

Whilst there were inevitable differences of opinion, it was clearly important that these should be discussed thoroughly, seeking areas of consensus and isolating broad principles on which curriculum decisions could be made and consistency of content and teaching methods ensured.

A large measure of agreement existed, for example, on the eclectic use of a range of teaching methods best suited to the needs of individual pupils, as distinct from the indiscriminate application of uniform stereotyped methods.

There was also provisional agreement on the need for mastery of basic numerical skills as prerequisite to mathematics; grammar as essential to English language; facts and dates as the necessary concomitants of history. These were principles confirmed by long tradition and, notwithstanding the recent challenge to their authority, widely acknowledged in contemporary pedagogy as having enduring validity. As Nikki, with a twinkle in her eye, once remarked to John Izbicki, 'nowadays, it's progressive to be reactionary'. The proviso was that the teaching methods employed should reflect progressive educational principles and not formal traditional approaches. Grammar, as one instance, was not transmitted formally as a body of knowledge but learned experientially in the process of using language.

Insistence on the priority given to basic skills and emphasis on the chronology and context of history in no way precluded exploration of the more abstract reaches of New Maths, or engagement in guided historical research and discovery assignments. They were not mutually exclusive and time was made for both as complementary elements in a balanced curriculum.

There was no doubt that consensus on the principles of curriculum design had become more difficult to achieve since the ideological conflicts surrounding the National Curriculum. Some of the younger teachers had been introduced to the more radical 'progressive' ideas at their training colleges and came to KAS with doubts, if not convictions, about the legitimacy of traditions concerning grammar and the centrality of standard English. A few contended that, having specialised in subjects other than English, they had studied no grammar at college, were therefore unqualified to teach it, and expected this to be the responsibility of the KAS English Department. The implications of such a clash of expectations could not be ignored and Nikki and other experienced members of staff were obliged to make explicit the principle that 'all teachers responsible for specialist subjects had an additional responsibility for their pupils' use of English in the academic discipline concerned. This meant that some form of in-service remedial training was essential if the teachers concerned were to fulfil such an obligation.

Even some of the children, exposed in the metropolis to the influence of populist ideas, diffused in the school a counter-culture in which the use of 'bad' English like blue jeans stood for a gesture of solidarity with the working class. It caused no serious concern, since they were constantly exposed to the dominant influence of standard English both at home and in school.

The widening spectrum of conflicting values at KAS - a relatively new phenomenon - aggravated not only the problem of consensus but also the process of curricular decision-making, placing a premium on thorough discussion and careful evaluation.

By virtue of its independence the school had always been able to regard the development of the curriculum as an organic growth and not as an imposed theoretical construct. It had been principally determined by the needs and requirements of all the children in the educational process. But, in spite of its independent status, it had also been subject to other constraints, and these too had increased over the years. The school's educational aims, pressures of social change, and restrictions imposed by the law were clearly foremost among these, but there was also the pragmatic consideration of those conditions on which the survival of the school depended. 'It had to be accepted', Nikki recalled some years later, 'that there were always two opposed educational ideologies represented in the school, so that head and senior staff had the responsibility of achieving a balance between them - a compromise enabling us to attain the goals which were the guarantee of our continued existence.

'Our curriculum was innovative but not undiscriminating, and the choices which had to be made were invariably based on the best interests of the school. The definition of these interests had to take account of existing conditions in the educational system and not of some hypothetical system envisaged by the more radical 'progressives'. This was why, in spite of the arguments of cultural relativism, we gave priority to standard English and grammatical correctness. Whether or not they were relative or intrinsically correct was for all practical purposes irrelevant. The status quo required mastery of these skills as a condition of democratic participation, equal opportunity, and progressive educational achievement. Suppose, for sake of argument, we had considered incorporating some of the more radical ideas being advanced at this time into our curriculum. These were ideas whose positive consequences were untested by research, development, or evaluation. Their negative consequences, being anti-traditional, were only measurable years later when the decline in educational standards in the state system to which they had contributed became glaringly apparent. In the circumstances it was not a risk we could have undertaken.

'Nuffield Science, one of our major innovations, had by contrast met all the KAS criteria, being the product of the kind of action research which characterised the new procedures in curriculum development.'

The issues raised by cultural relativism which met with the most critical response at KAS were those concerned with practical implications for the content and methodology of the curriculum. There were, however, other more general questions of wider social and educational significance which were perceived at KAS as in no way new or radical, but as merely a restatement of values consistently maintained and propagated since the time of its original foundation.

These values were inherent in the school's commitment to democratic ideals, its theosophical heritage, international outlook, and the multi-ethnic composition of its population. All had a bearing on the major problems of the contemporary world and seemed to be inspired by some teleological vision of a more equitable world order. Asked to define the essence of the theosophical tradition, an Alfredian might envision an ideal world order in which universal human rights prevailed and there were in consequence no longer any wars. If this was the ultimate goal, then the affinity and sympathetic involvement of the theosophist with the intermediate questions of cultural relativism - identity, minority rights, equal opportunity, prejudice and negative discrimination - could be taken for granted.

The circumstances which had driven the state schools to introduce a 'multicultural curriculum' in the late 1960s had no equivalent at King Alfred's, with the result that the introduction of a similar curriculum was considered inappropriate and unnecessary. Although the intake of the school was technically non-selective and comprehensive, the numbers of children both from and within ethnic minority groups were too small to warrant such an innovation, and this was compounded by the fact that, even had it been practicable, it would not have been welcomed by most of the parents concerned. The multicultural curriculum had evolved in the maintained schools in response to the social and demographic changes resulting from post-war immigration from New Commonwealth countries. New educational problems were posed by the rising numbers of minority children in the major conurbations. These problems were not at first appreciated and only gradually became apparent. Growing evidence of the extent of racism and racial discrimination in contemporary Britain and of the inter-ethnic tensions, amounting in some cases to violent conflict, called for comprehensive reform of the education of both indigenous and minority children.

The outcome in some schools was a less ethnocentric curriculum designed to include aspects of the cultural backgrounds of the larger ethnic minorities. In the case of indigenous children , the aim was to develop knowledge and understanding of other cultures and to inculcate the respect due to them as equal though different in status. A secondary aim was by means of these positive strategies to inhibit as far as possible the formation of racial or ethnic prejudice. In the case of minority children the intention was to reinforce cultural identity and self-confidence, thereby increasing the level of motivation and raising the standards of academic achievement.

At KAS the existing curriculum provided ample opportunity for learning about other cultures; racial and ethnic prejudice and discrimination were virtually non-existent, and children had apparently no doubts as to their cultural identity or, if they had, were at least in an environment likely to successfully resolve them.

Another social problem which had been thought to warrant intervention in the curriculum of state schools was that of sexual discrimination. And, here again, the tradition and present circumstances of King Alfred's argued against the adoption of measures which would have been inappropriate and superfluous. It could not be claimed that instances of gender prejudice and discrimination were unknown in the school, but they were more likely to have been the result of maladaptation to social change or subconscious motivation than of conscious and hostile intention.

Ahead of her Time

The same free and egalitarian principles which influenced inter-ethnic relations were seen to operate also in the relationships between the sexes. They were reflected in the content of the curriculum by representation of the achievements and legitimate aspirations of women, and the sensitive observance of equal opportunity in classroom teaching and organisation. Staff discouraged gender stereotyping, and curriculum options were free of gender restrictions - boys could opt for needlework and girls woodwork, if they so wished.

When during the 1970s the findings of research into classroom interaction were published, indicating a tendency for teachers to discriminate by asking more questions of boys than of girls, Nikki was prompted to remark, with understandable irony, 'If that had happened here, the girls would have very quickly put a stop to it'. She had not forgotten the apparent difficulty of certain parents and even one or two teachers in accepting the equal status of the co-heads during her first ten years at the school. It was an inconsistency she had grounds for believing had been substantially eliminated by the time of her retirement.'

21   History Repeated

Council had every reason to feel well satisfied with the achievement of the school during the previous decade. Targets for expansion outlined in the 1960s had been successfully accomplished; the notional political threat to survival had receded, the recurrent apprehensions about financial viability had been contained and, by dint of astute management, superseded by a period of budgetary stability.

Realistic adaptation to the new market situation had involved a reappraisal of the significance of good public relations, as a result of which the school benefited from a rationalisation of those aspects of school life which were considered capable of undermining them. In spite of competition, maximal pupil numbers were maintained and waiting lists at most levels testified to a continued demand for places. Educational standards across the whole curriculum, whether in academic creative or technical subjects had risen steadily. 'A' level results were comparable with those of leading public schools and, with each succeeding year, the number of university places obtained was rising significantly, as was the general standard of degrees and post-graduate qualifications achieved.

The Inspectors' enthusiastic and highly favourable report, particularly their commendation of the ways in which the school was proving faithful to its professed aims, served both to boost morale and to confirm the genuine progress that had been made.

The school had come through a period of accelerating social change in which traditional values were challenged, authority was questioned, and alternative ideas and lifestyles proliferated. The educational challenge was enormous and without precedent. To be able to respond to it effectively called for cool heads, independent thinking, objective judgment and professional expertise. All these qualities were represented in full measure at KAS and had been tested to the utmost in the dialectical process involved. But the prime source of motivation, without which these qualities would have lacked focus and direction, was an implicit belief in the ethos of the school and the propriety of its aims and objectives. These provided the objective criteria against which the new ideas could be evaluated and the basis on which rational decisions could be made.

The shared experiences and endeavours involved in adaptation to a rapidly changing society had strengthened the ties of community at KAS and revived a sense of collective identity and common purpose.

If all descriptions of dynamic processes are best understood as snapshots taken from a constantly changing scene, the school was at this point in its history at the culmination of a fruitful period of development. It was by any standards a highly successful school, one, moreover, where the measure of success was incontrovertibly more exacting by virtue of its progressive heritage and comprehensive intake.

259

Ahead of her Time

The achievement of its major goals owed much to the dedicated and highly qualified teaching staff, the large element of consensus over educational values, and the indispensable support and collaboration of parents. It also benefited from elimination of the factional disputes which had undermined social cohesion some years before. The absence of conflict now unloosed reserves of teachers' creative energy for their rightful purpose - the education of KAS children.

Open Day, high point of the school year, and always a 'showcase' for the quintessential King Alfred School, was, according to some observers, a far more spectacular occasion in 1980 than any they had known in the past.

The Manor Wood landscape had, of course, recently undergone a considerable change with the implementation of the building programme, but the usual features of Open Day remained essentially the same as in previous years. These included exhibitions of school work, a performance in the open air theatre, auctions, stalls and side shows. Teas were served in the school hall, which in 1980 was transformed into a Palm Court complete with pupils' orchestra. There was the customary quota of celebrities, and visitors included the Mayors of Camden and Barnet accompanied by their wives.

The organisation and presentation of the event was, as always, impeccable, a tribute to the Parent-Staff Committee and to the collective efforts of volunteer parents, staff and children. So what was the special quality of this particular occasion? Description compels recourse to qualitative terms like 'atmosphere', 'euphoria' or to even more esoteric concepts like 'subtle energies'. There was the temptation to suggest it had evolved from a collective awareness that the school had something to celebrate - namely the consummation of a genuinely remarkable period of growth and development.

Predictably, it was a state of equilibrium not destined to last. The scene changed and new conflicts of interest emerged, threatening to unbalance the fragile status quo. This was invariably a cause for some apprehension because, while some forms of conflict could be resolved by discussion and compromise, others, less tractable, could become the object of a kind of power struggle. Whereas the former were positive and to be welcomed, the latter were potentially disruptive, jeopardising the social integration and harmony on which depended the functional efficiency of the school. The problem was: how the conflicts would develop, and whether they could be regulated within the democratic process. This was always a sensitive issue for Nikki, who had for years persistently striven to build and maintain social consensus: 'Things had been going right for KAS and it had been a long process to get it that way'.

'On its past track record', wrote R Brooks, 'Council by 1979 was long overdue for a period of heightened political tension'.[114]

And, whilst not inevitable, this proved to be a prediction largely borne out by subsequent events. Fortunately for the school, the tensions and the conflicts to which these eventually led were to a great extent contained within the confidential proceedings of Council and thus not communicated to the rest of the community. This was just as well, because the vast majority of parents, whilst seriously concerned with the education of their children, did not want to be involved in school politics in the sense of power relations and the exercise of power. The 'political passion' of which Brooks speaks found its expression in Council and not, in normal circumstances, in the school as a whole. Most parents had the same reasons as Nikki herself to deplore confrontational power struggles and had the same vested interests in preserving the stability of the social environment on which the functional efficiency of the school depended. When such conflicts could not be contained and parents became necessarily involved, their disapprobation was not slow to follow. Aggressive tactics at an Annual General Meeting were criticised for having generated bad feeling, some of which had spilled over into the Parent/Staff Committee, whose Chairman, Bob Parvin, deplored the fact that political in-fighting had become commonplace. Concerned parents were worried by the apparent contradiction between bitter and uncompromising attitudes expressed in Council and the rational principles on which the school was founded. 'A general meeting', it was asserted, 'should not be expected to fight the battles of individual Council officers and members.'

Council appeared in the view of some observers to have acquired a more 'political' character in the early 1980s, and there were those who saw in this the influence of contemporary changes affecting the role of parents in education and in the government of schools in the state system. In this connection, the Taylor Report, the new role of parents on governing bodies, and the concept of 'parent power' have been discussed in Chapter 19, as has the influence of the guide books for parents which were published during the period under review.

The aim of much of this literature was to provide parents with information and advice about the education system, schools and teachers, which would enable them to take a more active part in the education of their children. It was addressed primarily, if not exclusively, to the parents of children in maintained schools and covered a wide range of topics, including school government, choice of schools, and parents' rights in education. Some of the studies had in common a critical approach of the kind already firmly established in the social sciences at this time.

---

[114] Brooks, J.R. King Alfred School and the Progressive Movement. 1898 - 1998. University of Wales Press. 1998

This sceptical approach had the effect of exposing heads and teachers to a new kind of scrutiny, designed to evaluate the significance of their behaviour in relation to the changing role of parents in education.' You need to know', the reader is informed in one publication, 'how school, LEA and DES work, if you want to put a spanner in the works. This section (How Things Get Changed) discusses the machines and gives tips on the best way to wield the spanner'.[115]

The results of diagnostic procedures showed numerous instances of behaviour which could have led to frustration of the legitimate aims of the school parents. Role behaviour which would have previously attracted little or no comment was now invested with an entirely new significance.

Heads were a major focus of most inquiries and the source of many of the examples cited. The essence of what was to transpire was, incidentally, well captured in an observation by R.Bourne in 'Choosing a School' that 'All heads are conscious of the need for good public relations - not unfortunately the same as really open relationships with parents.[116] Some, it was shown, could be 'evasive', liable to 'procrastination'; others could be 'reactionary', apprehending the possibility of 'parents running schools', and in certain instances capable of exerting 'manipulative pressures' to achieve their ends. One example of this sort of pressure was where 'Heads have been known to suggest that lack of co-operation in participating in out-of-school activities may affect the reference given to the university'.[117]

In a second (revised edition of 'Choosing a School' it was noted that 'Some heads only pay lip-service to Parent-Teacher Associations, equal opportunities and partnership with parents.[118]

By inference, getting to know the head was a priority in assessing the degree of co-operation the parent could expect to receive.

It was important not to be overborne, 'have the wool pulled over one's eyes', or deflected from the pursuit of one's legitimate aims as a school parent. All writers apparently discouraged what Bourne called 'ill-considered exercises 'in parent power' and, in their own way, advised parents to show patience, respect, courtesy and reasonableness in their relationships with heads and teachers. Conversely, as Bourne pointed out, 'parents don't want to sit idly by, if convinced that French teaching is bad.'

Advice was given on the kinds of action parents could take to counter instances of staff intransigence in response to their requests. Bourne's advice appeared to be limited to direct action within the school. Other writers went further by suggesting, if direct action failed, a range if indirect alternative strategies enlisting support from external sources. It was implicit

---

[115] Stone J, Taylor F. The Parents' Schoolbook Penguin. 1976.

[116] Bourne R. Choosing a School. Advisory Centre for Education. 1975.

[117] Stone J, Taylor F., op cit.

[118] Taylor F. Choosing a School. 2nd (revised) edition Advisory Centre for Education. 1981

that actions of this kind would need to be considered only if prior representations to the head had clearly been of no avail.

Information was given on ways of complaining, organising appeals, pressure groups, campaigns, and on recourse to higher authorities from governing body, through Local Education Authority and Members of Parliament, to Secretary of State and Ombudsman.[119]

Accepting that the proposals contained in some of this literature were realistic in the context of state schools, it seemed nevertheless to the author that there was an element of risk in the suggestion of quasi-political remedies for the parental problems in question. Arguably, this risk lay in the possibility that parents could develop negative expectations in relation to heads and teachers in general, irrespective of whether or not any evidence existed to justify them. If this were the case, it was reasonable to suppose that such expectations could in turn foster the growth of suspicion, tension and distrust in parent-staff relations. And this would almost inevitably tend to affect the way in which children and students regarded the school.

The claim that parents were free to make up their own minds as to what use they made of the information would of course depend on whether or not they had a genuine choice of schools.

If, as some writers seemed to indicate, confrontational strategies might be the only realistic means of achieving parental objectives in the maintained schools, it had to be said that such strategies had no relevance to schools like King Alfred's.

Conceding, with reservations, that strategies of the kind under consideration may have been applicable in the maintained sector of education, Nikki felt that they were alien to KAS, where the powers of parents were built into the Constitution, but exercised, by common consent and tradition, only in those areas deemed to be appropriate. Most parents would have agreed with her that what amounted to political pressures and the adversarial conflict they engendered were incompatible with the ethos of the school. She took the opportunity of pointing the moral when giving the head's annual report in 1981 :

'The state system is only now experimenting with a process which has been familiar at this school from its inception: the involvement of parents in the government of schools. Because of the nature and complexity of the state system, this involvement is still little more than an attempt by a comparatively small number of people to compel a powerful bureaucracy to pay at least some attention to their views in areas which affect their children's education. Working from a position of comparative impotence, it is hardly surprising that, in trying to make a minority voice heard, that voice becomes occasionally a little strident and sometimes reflects suspicion of, rather than confidence in, teachers and heads. We at King Alfred School are in a totally different position. We give our parents full

---

[119] Taylor F., ibid.

opportunity to interest themselves in the life of the school and we rely on their good sense and understanding to recognise the limits which are necessary if staff are to fulfil their proper professional role under the direction of the head.'

Nikki was within a few years of retirement and had been glad of an earlier period of relative calm in the proceedings of Council, enabling her to review the state of the school in anticipation of handing over responsibility in due course to her successor.

She was not at first unduly disturbed by the rising political tensions in Council; her knowledge of the history of the school had led her to the conclusion that periodic and potentially damaging conflicts were endemic and that all she could do was try to prevent these as far as possible from harming the school.

But she was soon apprised of the fact that a new and unprecedented situation was developing and that, so far from the events of this period being the latest manifestation of a familiar pattern, they threatened to precipitate a crisis more serious than anything the school had experienced before.

The focus of political activity, which in the 1960s had concerned the relations between Council, parents, teachers and the pupils' Council, had shifted to Council itself and the relations between Council and Head, in which the key question was the redistribution of their respective functions, a highly charged issue. Nikki found herself at the centre of the kind of power struggle she dreaded, because of the damage it could inflict on the school, but one in which she knew she had no option but to engage, on account of her responsibility to the children, the staff and the 'silent majority' of parents.

R. Brooks identifies political and economic changes which were probably significant in setting the scene for these critical developments. Financial crisis and economic recession had necessitated the introduction of stringent government policies emphasising criteria of efficiency, accountability and value for money, 'heralding the ideology of the Thatcherite eighties'.[120]

These issues, together with what were perceived by some, on questionable grounds, as threats to open government, came to dominate KAS Council politics.

In the early 1980s a number of Council members formed a caucus which was instrumental in politicising Council to an unprecedented degree. Whilst they shared with more conservative members a belief in the need for changes in response to the recession, they differed on the means of putting these into effect. In particular, they rejected the assumption that the new governing bodies in maintained schools were as remote from KAS experience as had been supposed. On the contrary, they argued, King

---

[120] Brooks, R., op cit.

Alfred, with inadequate communications and information-processing, was lagging behind LEA schools, which had developed a model of school government from which KAS could learn and which it currently needed to secure its own future. This model, it was contended, gave parent governors an enlarged role in the management of schools, extending even to those areas thought to be the special responsibility of the head and teaching staff.

This contention represented a challenge to the consensus over the appropriate limits to parental collaboration which had obtained for some eighty years, a consensus which had become a part of the ethos of the school, and one which Nikki had stressed both in her deposition to the Taylor Committee and in the Annual Report of 1981.

Actuated by what they saw as the relevance of the Taylor model of school government to the needs of KAS, the dissidents drafted a set of proposed reforms with the aim of developing what they saw as a more democratic framework of open government and increased accountability. They sought greater participation by parents in the management of all aspects of school life, and the fullest use of the expertise represented on the parent body as a whole and especially on Council.

The dissident caucus claimed that there was an inner circle in Council which, they believed, denied much of the information other members required if they were to make an effective contribution to decision-making.

The reaction of the moderates was to repudiate strenuously the charge of undemocratic procedures, and to insist that the role of parent governors in LEA schools was irrelevant to KAS because their circumstances were fundamentally different: all KAS parents, for example, had been free to choose the school for their children and were equally free to find an alternative if they were not satisfied.

One parent is said to have queried - (on the Cockney principle 'if it ain't broke, don't mend it') - whether a root and branch restructuring of the school's organisation was either necessary or desirable. It was a sentiment echoed by the moderate governors, who pointed to the existing and clearly defined responsibility structure, open lines of communication, and easy access to information - the Head's ever-open door as the last resort - and asserted that the opposition were exaggerating both the amount of work Council and Committees had to do and the scale of innovation needed.

Council was thus largely divided by conflicting ideologies. Both wings could justly claim to be conforming with the democratic tradition of the school, but, whilst sharing certain goals and values, had different perspectives on others. Broadly these could be differentiated by whether they placed greater emphasis on the spirit or the letter of the democratic process.

The moderates could be said to emphasise the spirit in their contention that most of the parents were interested in having a well-organised school, responsive to their educational needs, but not being involved in detailed everyday control. Satisfaction of these criteria was in their view ensured at KAS by understanding and teamwork between Head and Council, a collaboration best achieved by consensus and not amenable to the formal procedure of resolutions and votes. Responsiveness to the wishes of parents was further secured through the agency of the Parent/Staff Committee, while there remained the ultimate control exercised by parents in their role as electors of the Council membership.

With the exception of the Finance Committee, which merited permanence, they favoured a flexible system of sub-committees, including those of an ad hoc nature, consistent with the consensus principle of reinforcing success and pursuing policies that worked; with the corollary that committees which had outlived their usefulness should be phased out.

The consensus model had evolved with the school, and what some perceived as its comparatively relaxed approach was in fact a highly effective form of government. It was concordant with the progressive ethos of the school, dedicated to the creation of a harmonious, anxiety-free, stable and supportive educational environment. To accord with this ethos, Council required not confrontation but a collegiate style of decision-making based on rational discussion, negotiation, willingness to compromise and seek consensus. It was an approach based on the supposition that the Council and the school formed one organic whole and were not to be regarded as two separate entities. The prevailing climate in Council indirectly affected the school as a whole, which was why prolonged conflicts were potentially so damaging.

The ideology of the dissidents grew out of a reaction against some of the value assumptions implicit in the status quo. Their values and the goals deriving from them were in consequence opposed in a number of ways to those represented by the moderates.

The proposals to change the structure of school government at KAS and to extend parental intervention into areas hitherto considered the responsibility of head and teaching staff were clearly the most prominent as well as the most controversial of these goals. Not being a total ideology, it was of the kind not obliged to be logically consistent, nor necessarily in accordance with facts. For example, the actual powers of parent governors in state schools (compared to parental powers at KAS) were negligible in the face of the countervailing powers of LEA, community, and staff representation on governing bodies.

The moderates were concerned because they thought the dissidents might be seeking a change in the bureaucratic balance of the school government. Such an eventuality, they conjectured, could presage a shift in Council - Staff relations, emphasising hierarchy rather than partnership

The text of at least one of the various papers on proposed structural changes was couched in what for King Alfred School was an unfamiliar, impersonal and legalistic style and included references to rules of procedure, duties and authority relations. Much of the content was unexceptionable but the tone of its presentation had an alien quality which aroused some apprehension. The incongruity was remarkable because authority had always been inherent at KAS but, in order not to impair the special quality of teacher-pupil relationships, relatively inconspicuous in general discourse and official correspondence, though familiar as a topic in sixth form philosophy seminars.

Another marked change in the conduct of Council business was a new and unwelcome increase in the level of acrimony, while, in individual cases, the asking of questions took the form of a relentless cross-examination which one Council member described as 'inquisitorial'. Some of the questions addressed to Nikki struck her as adversarial in tone yet unsubstantiated by any specific grounds, suggesting a negative motivation which looked to find something wrong instead of positively seeking and encouraging what was conspicuously going well. It all suggested the existence of a collective attitude of suspicion and distrust which was deeply disturbing to both the head and staff representatives on Council. 'If you look hard enough', Nikki observed, 'you can always find something to criticise. The trouble is this can so easily become a habit of thought and negative expectation.'

It was suspicion and distrust that had induced dissidents to claim that Council was being manipulated by a 'cabal', by which term presumably they implied involvement in secret intrigues, in particular the withholding of information and resistance to democratic reform. Because of her implied association with the supposed 'cabal', Nikki was presented as exercising disproportionate power in the decision-making process. All this bore no relation to the facts. The truth of the matter was that the appointment of working parties composed of parents and staff, selected for their expertise and answerable to Council, had a long tradition at KAS and had been shown to work successfully. Their continued existence was legitimised by the general consensus of most of the parents in the school. As to the power of the head, Nikki was inclined to be apolitical, concerned to preserve only such powers as were essential to the fulfilment of her professional responsibilities. If procedural reforms were demanded, there was nothing to prevent these from going through the normal democratic process of discussion and resolution, first in Council and then, if necessary (e.g., at the level of constitutional reform), in plenary session of the Society.

This was the position in early 1981, with Council divided on ideological grounds and by apparently irreconcilable policies on the future development of the school. The dissident faction which had by this time established itself in a powerful position on Council was still in a minority, and the precise dimensions of their programme of reform had yet to be declared. In fact, much of their time was preoccupied with resisting a major constitutional reform initiated in 1980 by a working party originally set up to study the inspectors' report on the 1979 survey. The working party proposal had been conceived in response to the report and to the current political and economic situation, and sought to 'reconcile democracy with efficiency' by reducing the size of Council from 21 to 11 elected members.

In his formal presentation of the proposal, Bernard Igra, the Honorary Treasurer, argued that 21 members, with the addition of the Head and staff representatives, made Council an unwieldy body, ill-suited to taking executive decisions. In practice, the executive duties had been delegated to sub-committees authorised to act on behalf of Council, but this practice had in recent years become functionally less effective. For this reason, it was proposed that the practice of working through sub-committees should be terminated and that the executive function should be vested in the suggested smaller Council. The more detailed arguments adduced against the existing size of Council were that it was inefficient, inordinately time-wasting, repetitious, and involved an additional workload for staff representatives. Against the claim by the opposition that a smaller Council would reduce the scope for democratic participation by parents it was countered that, in practice, the large Council often exemplified the ways in which 'democracy could be its own worst enemy'.

The debate continued throughout the period 1980-1982, during which time it came to be the central focus of the ideological conflict dividing Council. In the early stages it appeared that the arguments in favour of change would prevail, but alterations in the membership following annual elections resulted in a shift in the balance of power. By the end of 1981 deadlock had been reached, with an equal number in Council voting for and against the reform proposals. Nikki, who together with other staff representatives, did not have voting rights, supported the case for the resolution, expressing her opinion that 'teamwork between Council and Head could be much improved through the creation of a smaller Council. Not only did large numbers prolong discussion past the point of efficiency, but they sometimes necessitated the laborious repetition of discussions for the benefit of those who had missed previous meetings. All this reduced the amount of business that could be conducted, and left one with the impression that nothing could ever be regarded as conclusive. Some time later, a kind of statute of limitations was introduced to correct this anomaly.'

In April 1982 an Extraordinary General Meeting (EGM) of the Society was called in order to resolve the long-protracted controversy, and the two sides presented their arguments before the whole parent body.

Self-evidently, the proposals advanced by those who had been for many years involved in the Society, and were known to have the full support of the teaching staff, carried considerable weight.

However, the well-organised campaign which had been conducted beforehand by the opposing group had concentrated on the idea that the proposal to create a smaller Council was designed to reduce democratic representation, and that this was a deliberate aim of the proposers. The charge was, of course, repudiated by the proposers, who stressed the importance of improvement in administrative efficiency and of making

Council 'an effective decision-making body without delegation to committees or sub-committees'.[121]

Anecdotal accounts were agreed that attitudes shifted during the course of the meeting, swayed first by one side and then the other, so that the outcome was uncertain up to the time when the issue was put to the ballot.

The resolution was defeated by a small majority, thus reaffirming the continued existence of a Council of 21, non-voting teacher representatives, and the system of sub-committees. Those who had voted against the resolution may have been reassured that broad representation and wide expertise had been preserved, but one moderate member of Council criticised the continuing presence of 'an oversize body of interfering parent-governors wanting to turn the school into some form of co-operative'.

In the statement of their objections to the proposed reduction in the size of Council, the opposition had outlined their own alternative proposals concerning the organisation of Council business and the relationship between Council and Head. These included the introduction of an Education Committee through which the Head would become responsible to Council for decisions hitherto regarded as within her own discretionary powers.

Although the EGM vote did not extend approval to these counterproposals, the latter clearly took on a new significance as a statement of intent on the part of the dissidents, seeking to extend their power base in Council.

Encouraged by the result of the ballot, they applied their campaigning skills to securing all six Council vacancies at the 1982 Annual General Meeting (AGM), a contingency which the moderates had neither expected nor attempted to emulate. All the dissident candidates were elected, giving them in consequence a majority on Council.

In an account of the events of 1982/3, the President, Sir William (Alan) Wood, describes how the new majority at once began to act 'like a political party with a mandate for revolutionary change'. But no manifesto had been presented to the electorate (the KAS Society) 'and the votes which had elected the new members of Council, though numerous, were very far from a majority of the Society's membership'.[122]

In spite of this, the new Council began to implement the programme foreshadowed at the EGM in April, but now including a new and totally unexpected plan involving the early retirement of the Head, as soon as terms could be arranged, 'to make way for the appointment of a Head who would be more amenable to the new regime'.[123]

---

[121] Council Minute. 18th March, 1980.

[122] Wood, Sir William. A Time of Trouble, 1982 to 1983. KASS Archives, November 1988.

[123] Ibid.

Ahead of her Time

The moderates on Council were shocked not only by the nature of this disclosure but also by what appeared to be unseemly haste in parting with a Head who had served the school so long and with such distinction.

The majority, though acting within their constitutional powers, apparently did not consider a decision of such significance warranted informing the membership of the Society or indeed the parent body, reserving their announcement until arrangements for Nikki's retirement had become virtually a *fait accompli*. Equally peremptory had been the communication of Council's intentions to Nikki herself. When asked in early 1982 about plans for her eventual retirement, she replied that she wished to retire in 1984 or 1985 and undertook to give Council at least a year's notice when the time came. As no comment had been made, she assumed that her proposals were acceptable and henceforth regarded the matter as settled.

The subject, however, came up again, and then only informally, in a personal letter from the chairman of Council in November 1982 in which he wrote of her 'looming retirement, regrettable though it is', and the need to consider well in advance the appointment of her successor. The process of retirement, he had learned from experience, 'was painful in some way before the event, but almost pure bliss afterwards. It's my wish, early days comparatively though it is, to help minimise the pain for you and increase the bliss! For that to happen, you must gradually and gracefully let go.'

It was getting towards the end of a very busy term and, as the letter was presumably concerned with forward planning for 1984/5, and therefore not urgent, she resolved to do nothing more than acknowledge its receipt. She heard no more until the second week in January, 1983, when she received the following communication from the Chairman:

'At its meeting last night the Council resolved that the time was ripe for a change of Head to be arranged. It instructed the President, the Treasurer and the Chairman to discuss and agree with you the date and terms for ending your engagement and to report the results of this discussion for Council's approval at a further Council meeting to be held on 8th February.

'The three of us agreed that to save time Alan Wood would get in touch with you at once in order to arrange a meeting with you at his house. No doubt he will have done this by the time this reaches you.'

Shock and disbelief were her immediate responses but, after she had thought about it, her chief concerns were for the school's well-being and her own future.

It was now quite clear that the kind of politics which so threatened the stability of the school was an inescapable reality. Having consistently worked for harmony and consensus during the whole of her career at KAS, she was now involved in and at the centre of that reality. It seemed to her that she must have been the target of a deliberate organised campaign and, since no explanation had been given for Council's action, she had no alternative but to speculate on the causes of a decision she found incomprehensible.

There had been differences of opinion, and occasions when she had expressed her reasons for objecting to some of the plans put forward by the new majority, but these hardly constituted grounds for demanding her retirement. There had also been the matter of her age, when it was claimed that, having reached the age of 61, she was already overdue for retirement. Questioned during a Council meeting as to why she had not informed anyone of her 60th birthday, she replied that, as there had never been any age limit for retirement at KAS, it had not occurred to her to do so. The age of retirement did not feature in staff contracts, it was customarily decided on an individual basis, and there were examples of both men and women teachers throughout the school's history who had retired at ages well above 60. When reminded of all this the Chairman exclaimed, 'Lucky for us, then, isn't it?' For Nikki the implication was that henceforth the age of retirement would be what Council decided it should be, and it served their convenience now. Although, in accordance with traditional practice at KAS, her age provided no reason in itself for urging her retirement, she had nevertheless been exposed to an unfounded accusation that she had concealed her age, with the implication that she should have retired at sixty. This despite the fact that, as she told members of Council, all the details of her age, qualifications etc. were held in the Secretary's office and available to any member who might have wished to check them.

The injustice of this humiliating experience remained for her one of the bitterest memories of this troubled period in the school's history.

Having come to the conclusion that she was seriously under attack, she decided that it would be prudent to inform her professional organisation - the Secondary Heads' Association (SHA) - and to ask for their advice and comments.

'The Association members to whom I applied were puzzled by the bizarre story I had to impart to them. Such a dismissal might, I knew, occasionally be used as a last resort where a gross breach of professional conduct was involved, but was unheard of in normal circumstances.

I pointed out that by all applicable standards the school was running well, the exam results were excellent, our staff hard-working, united, and extremely competent professionally and the atmosphere at the school, as usual, busy, friendly and orderly.

'The SHA representatives expressed astonishment at the incongruity with which the whole affair had been managed: the exceptionally brief initial period of notice (one term, after 24 years' service, later renegotiated to two terms); the fact that there was apparently no crisis in the school to explain such precipitate action and no history hitherto of anything but good relations existing between heads, staff, parents and governors during my tenure of office. I could not blame them for finding it incomprehensible, because it was exactly my own reaction. I was fairly certain that they were waiting to establish the facts when they visited the school.

'After two meetings with committees of Council my representatives came to the conclusion that my account was entirely correct and advised me accordingly. From the guarded comments that were made to me I realised that their considered view of KAS Council as then constituted, and of its procedures, was not a flattering one.

'By this time I had resolved that there were only two options open to me. I could either leave with whatever my advisers decided was a satisfactory settlement, or I could fight my case openly at the cost of involving the whole school, the staff, and the parent body in a protracted and potentially disastrous public conflict.

'I believe that, had I chosen the second option, I would have been able to complete my last two years as originally intended, but the cost of a public quarrel would have been too great.

'It was altogether too like a reprise of the situation in 1959, when the school had been split down the middle by a power struggle between two factions, affecting staff, parents and children; and here I found myself twenty-four years later with the school once again facing the same kind of crisis. Moreover, I was not oblivious to another historical precedent - the resignation of Charles Rice in 1901.[124]

'To stay and fight (which I had been strongly urged to do) and risk dividing the school again could not fail to have attracted adverse publicity, causing damage to the reputation of KAS which the staff and I had worked long and hard to stabilise, and threatening our continued existence as an independent school.

'Conversely, I could lend my support to ensuring a peaceful changeover, with the hope that influential friends on Council would be able in due course to reverse some of the changes that had been made, and frame new and less vulnerable conditions for my successor.

'I chose the latter course and have never regretted doing so. The young people's interests had to come first if the school was to remain true to its traditions. If it had not been for the unwavering moral support I received from our President, Alan Wood, a long-time KAS parent and personal friend, I do not know what would have happened.

'Of my last two terms at King Alfred I can only say that they were hard to endure. I suffered a constant stream of prohibitions, including on one occasion being told that any expenditure over £10 was to be vetted by a committee and passed by the Chairman of Council personally. Considering that in the previous summer I had been responsible for obtaining a gift of £60,000 for the school funds, I found this ironic.'

It was this kind of pervasive intervention by the new regime which seemed to confirm Nikki's initial reservations about their plan to redistribute

---

[124] Vide Chapter 9

the functions between Council and Head. Their claim that this would not involve interference with the roles of the Head or the teaching staff did not seem to be substantiated by subsequent actions, and certainly at odds with Council discussions initiated later to consider alternatives to headship, e.g., a college of teachers on the Steiner model or the control of education by a parents' co-operative. Whether such alternatives would have appealed to the parent body or not, the fact of their being discussed at all suggested the trend of some of the thinking in Council at this time.

R.Brooks suggests that the dissident group could with advantage have studied the history of KAS and thereby avoided repeating the dangerous mistakes of the past.[125] A rival hypothesis suggests itself: that they were fully aware of that history, positively identifying with it, hankering after the parent-dominated movement of the school's beginning, and at the same time rejecting the consensual ethos institutionalised in the Russell era. Speculative as this may be, it could explain why some observers described the new regime as 'adopting the rhetoric of democracy and partnership but acting autocratically in practice'.

In the period between the communication of Council's decision to Nikki and the public announcement of her retirement, rumours circulated, feeding on themselves and growing in the absence of any definite knowledge or accurate facts. Nor was the prevailing uncertainty entirely removed when the official statement eventually appeared because rumour now focused on the circumstances surrounding Council's decision and whether, if legitimate under the constitution, it was to be regarded as final or open to negotiation, even reversal. Most of these questions were resolved in the second week of March, 1983 with the following official announcement of Nikki's retirement with effect from the end of August:

'It is with very great regret that Council has to announce that our Head, Nikki Archer, will shortly be retiring. Discussions have taken place and it has been agreed that she will retire with effect from August 31st, 1983, in order to allow the Council to appoint a new head in time for the start of the academic year 1983/4,

'We hope the children, staff, parents, Old Alfredians and other members of the King Alfred School Society will join with Council on a day near the end of the summer term to celebrate the very great contribution Nikki Archer has made to King Alfred School.'

Alan Wood gives a graphic account of the danger facing the school at this time, stressing the dependence of good schools on the reputation of the Head and a co-operative relationship between the Head and the governing body. The wider implications for policy at KAS were that interference with the Head's professional judgment would inevitably cause conflict between Council and Head, weakening the latter's authority with the staff, and making it very doubtful whether the school could attract a new

---

[125] Brooks, R., op cit.

Head of the required quality and experience. 'The Staff, too, as they saw the tightening grip of the Education Committee, were not slow to understand the threat to their own professionalism.'[126]

The news of Nikki's retirement produced the same kind of response among the parent body as that earlier experienced by the moderate members of Council. Shock, dismay and concern were expressed over the precipitate and incongruous nature of Council's actions. A number of new parents who, having chosen KAS principally because of Nikki's reputation and the expectation of her remaining as Head at least for a few years longer, now felt they had been badly let down.

There were those representing the silent majority who expressed their feelings more actively by writing directly to Council through its chairman or more widely to the membership of the Society as a whole. Notable among these were Jack Pole, John Izbicki, Bob Parvin, Peter Graff, Mike and Mana Brearley, the collective impact of whose efforts was greatly reinforced by a personal deputation of three parents - Kay Gallwey, Mana Brearley and Marie-Elena Vafiadis - who, in the hope of receiving some answers to the questions many parents were by then asking, confronted the chairman in his own home.

At first some parents clearly thought another EGM should be called to review the situation, but it was too late for this, as Nikki had by now accepted, for the sake of the school, that she had no real alternative but to resign.

Letters of protest ranged from those which deplored the insensitive and incongruous manner in which the Head had been treated to those accusing Council of having exceeded, if not its constitutional authority, at least its implicit mandate. Indeed, one writer felt that few at the last AGM in November, 1982 could have suspected that the issues included a sudden change of Head or the redistribution of functions between Head and Council. John Izbicki wrote to members of the KAS Society, 'Nikki Archer who, for a quarter of a century, directed KAS with great skill, expertise, benevolence and kindness, did not 'retire' or 'resign', despite notices to the contrary. She was forced to go, driven out by a Council, some of whose members were openly antagonistic towards her and her administration of the teaching staff and methods.' His suggested remedy was for the Society to demand the resignation of the Chairman and elect as new a Council as possible under current rules, with a mandate to restore the *status quo ante*.[127] Bob Parvin, a moderate governor, denounced the personal animosity directed against Nikki at Council meetings by certain members. 'Shameful in any context,' he wrote. 'but in the governing body of a school,

---

[126] Wood, Sir William. op cit.

[127] Izbicki, J., Letter circulated to all members of the KAS Society, 18th November, 1983.

the main reputation of which lies in its caring attitude to its pupils, it is grotesque'.

Other grounds for concern were that no reasons had been given for Council's extraordinary decision, and that insufficient time had been allowed for the appointment of a successor, towards which Nikki's collaboration and advice should have, but had not been, invited.

Professor Jack Pole, honorary fellow and former Council member of KAS. writing to the Chairman before Nikki's agreement to retire, said that it was easy to see how she might well be willing to step down. 'She has behind her a magnificent achievement and must rank as one of the outstandingly successful school heads in London in the last twenty-five years or so.

'Far from being thanked, she has become the victim of a carefully organised campaign of personal opposition among members of the Council, whose conduct does not inspire confidence in either their experience or judgment and who seem likely to precipitate the most serious crisis in the schools history.

'In the circumstances I have urged upon Nikki my own view that her duty is to remain at her post. The best service she can do for the school which she has served so long and loyally is to resist her own natural wish to withdraw from the struggle, and instead to try to keep the school together - and to keep the staff together - until this storm blows itself out.'

Representations by staff were subject to implicit constraints and for this reason Nikki had not expected her colleagues to mount any kind of petition on her behalf. She was therefore touched to learn that, in fact, the following appeal had been addressed to Council shortly after the announcement of her retirement:

'Dear Members of Council,

We feel that our silence over the last few weeks may have conveyed to you our tacit approval of the policy relating to Nikki's retirement.

'Whatever criticisms may be levelled at her, it cannot be disputed that she has very often gone to great lengths to support members of staff in times of personal stress, and has shown tremendous humanity and understanding. We have also been able to rely on her for professional support.

'We are distressed that we have been unable to return this support at a time when she herself is under personal stress. We have not voiced our concern over recent events before because we wished to avoid drawing parents' attention to disharmony within the school, which would reflect so badly on KAS. However, the letters circulated by certain parents has made our silence unnecessary.

'We would like you to know that we do care about Nikki and are deeply concerned about how she must feel at the moment. We appeal to you to allow her to retire with dignity.'

Ahead of her Time

In his reply, the Chairman claimed to have found the teachers' letter 'mysterious' and asked in what way Council could have prevented or be preventing Nikki's retiring with dignity. Arrangements were being made 'for occasions to wish her farewell with plaudits'; 'prolonged and civilised negotiations' had preceded the drawing up of terms for her retirement, and 'great pains had been taken to avoid painful confrontations.' He therefore failed to see what more could have been done, or done better. However, if there were any more of the letters of the kind that had been circulating, Council might have to make 'a full statement of the events leading up to Nikki's retirement'. The teachers' letter, he concluded, must inevitably bring that possibility nearer. 'There is no reason for Council to remain silent under attack.'

Nikki's response when she was told about this later was to say, 'I should have thought the silence of Council was precisely what people, including myself, had been complaining about. Had I been told what I was supposed to have been doing wrong, I would at least have known what it was all about but despite great pressure from both myself and the Secondary Heads Association the committee involved maintains they have no criticisms of any kind and are only concerned (for the first time in the school's history!) with the fact that the Head is now 61'.

Margaret Maxwell, who had left the school the year before, also intervened on Nikki's behalf, sending her the following letter, addressed to the King Alfred School Council. But, in the event, Nikki, who was anxious to spare Margaret any uncomfortable repercussions, persuaded her not to go through with it, and the letter was never delivered. The text was, however, reproduced in the souvenir programme of the May Fair held at the school on the 14th May, 1983.

'Having known personally every head of King Alfred School except the first (Mr Rice), and knowing the various crises through which the school has passed since its inception, I believe I am in a unique position to comment on the achievements of Nikki Archer.

'She is the head who has overseen the school to its present size (or, in view of the recession, its potential size), its basic stability and its reputation in academic circles. She has made it a highly professional place in which staff of high calibre are and have been glad to teach.

'She is a woman of vision with a continually updated sense of long-term needs in a volatile social climate, in both general and specifically educational spheres. Her capacity for efficient and humane organisation has made it possible for the staff to work at their best.

'She has a breadth of understanding and an acute knowledge of the children of every age, as well as sympathy for old Alfredians, parents and staff. This is a knowledge that no one else connected with the school is called upon to possess - or could, perhaps, sustain. She is particularly skilled as a teacher of teachers, seeing the special gifts of individuals and showing them how to achieve their potentials (often without their being aware of it); and in practical terms giving them the means to do so.

'She is also a woman of deep compassion, spending long hours, in and out of school hours, helping children and staff in need; and outstandingly tolerant about the current social neurosis which envisages anyone in authority as self-seeking and interested only in power. I have never, in twenty-four years, known her own, even legitimate, interests come before those of the school. In her period of co-headship she always acted co-operatively and unselfishly.

'From my experience both at King Alfred School and in other schools, I know that she has given fuller and more acute time to school affairs, and is more available to parents, staff and children, than any other head with whom I have worked. Because they take it for granted as part of the school's ethos, many are, I believe, unaware of their privilege in being able to raise and discuss any topics they wish and to take part in decision-making without, of course, having to carry the long-term, full responsibility. Whatever sentimental tradition suggests (which always sees 'the old days' as more liberal than now), I know, from my knowledge of the school, that this has been almost entirely due to Nikki's initiative. I know that I would not have stayed so long and so happily at King Alfred School if she had not been there.

'She has, in a school that has never made conditions easy for its head, remained longer than any other, probably at the most difficult period in education. In view of the large number of independent schools that have gone under in recent years, I believe that without Nikki the school might now be no longer in existence.

'For her many years of wisdom, practical sense and productive devotion, she deserves Council's considerable gratitude and respect.'

The Chairman and certain individual members of the Council majority replied to the letters of protest with a comprehensive denial of all the charges levelled against them. There was no attempt to compromise nor any concession that anything they had done might conceivably be grounds for adverse criticism. It was asserted that, while not denying 'the paramount importance' of the Head's position, the real strength of the school lay in the constitution, the ethos, and the Council.

Two parents were admonished for presuming to judge Council on the basis of only two years' experience, and must be supposed to have been misinformed through listening to 'all the wrong people'; they were, misguided enough to have been supporting 'the personality cult' rather than the school.

The Chairman denied suggestions that he was not impartial or that he was one of the leaders of the caucus. There had been no question of forcing Nikki's immediate retirement; following the satisfactory negotiation of severance terms, her decision to resign had been entirely voluntary. During the time he had been on Council he could recall no instance of interference in the Head's sphere of authority or with the powers which it was proper for her to exercise.

As to the allegations that she had been subjected to cross-examination at Council meetings, he had never seen her treated with anything other than courtesy, or asked any but perfectly reasonable questions.

In conclusion, the Chairman hinted that, if there were much more niggling about

'shabby treatment of the Head, and suchlike nonsense', Council might feel obliged to tell the Society 'the full details' of what had happened and been hitherto undisclosed. And, once again, Nikki was prompted to comment that these 'dark hints' were precisely what she and everyone else wanted to know about. It was clear that an impasse had developed in the relations between Council and the growing number of those who were concerned about recent changes in the conduct of the school. Council claimed that the concern was unwarranted and based on misinformation, but it was difficult to reconcile such assurances with the evidence of progressive marginalisation of the Head, increase in the number of committees, meetings and inquiries, and the consequent burden of extra work falling on an already hard-working teaching staff. Nikki was told that some members of the teaching staff had been puzzled to receive specific instructions about their teaching duties from members of Council, a development concerning which she had herself been neither consulted nor informed.

The moderates on Council were faced with a dilemma: they knew their belief in the traditional organisation of government at KAS was shared by the majority of parents, but they were now in a minority and therefore precluded from calling for another EGM to appeal to the Society, because of the conflict that would ensue and the damage that might be done to the school's reputation. The only course left seemed to be one of containment, continuing the struggle in Council in the hope of changing the balance of power at the next AGM.

22   The Turning of the Tide

In the months that followed, the conflict over policy continued both in Council and in the now increased number of committees. On many of the contentious issues there was little or no progress and any hope of compromise, let alone agreement, seemed as remote as ever.

However, in the discussion of new draft principles for the school, the moderates had some success when they persuaded Council to abandon the description of KAS as a 'parents' co-operative'. This term, it was argued, had connotations that would be unwelcome to a large number of current and prospective parents. The Memorandum of Association established quite clearly that it had never been the intention of the founders to set up schools dominated by parents, but it had been to promote co-operation between parents and teachers 'by giving parents some representation in the management'.

The decisive struggle, however, began, as Alan Wood points out in his archival paper, 'in quite a muted fashion in the selection committee for the appointment of the new Head'.[128] He had at first been in a minority of one in recommending a contract on the model issued jointly by the Governing Bodies Association (GBA) and the Headmasters' Conference (HMC). This agreed in large measure with the form of contract drafted by the majority on Council 'but was at variance with their specific limitations on the Head's powers of appointment, promotion, and dismissal of staff, as well as the provision for an appeal to Council before a pupil could be expelled'. He had argued that, if the school was to attract candidates of the required quality, it would seem advisable to follow the GBA/HMC model, which was, incidentally, in accordance with traditional practice at KAS.

When, during this period, Gabbitas Thring were appointed as consultants to the school, their representative supported Alan Wood's recommendation, with the result that 'after much discussion, the majority reluctantly agreed to leave the form of contract open for negotiation with the successful candidate'.[129]

The appointment of Nikki's successor was followed by further debate, turning on the crucial issue of the Head's academic freedom, before the contract was eventually signed largely in the form recommended by the GBA/HMC.

Mobilisation of the silent majority had been gathering momentum, and, by the time of the AGM in the autumn term, an election strategy had been determined, private meetings held, candidates chosen and briefed. At the meeting, which was marked by an unprecedently large turnout, there were fourteen candidates for seven vacancies, each of the two sides in Council

---

[128] Wood, Sir William, op cit.
[129] Wood, Sir William, ibid.

having put forward a full complement of contenders. The outcome of the election was an overwhelming victory by a margin of two to one for the moderate candidates. 'The losing side', noted Alan Wood, 'were stunned by this decisive verdict on their year of office.'[130]

As a result of the shift in the balance of power on Council following the election, a process of reversing certain recent policies was initiated. Amendment of the new Head's contract had already restored the responsibility for overall management, teaching and curriculum within general policy and financial limits approved by Council. There followed the abolition of the Education Policy Committee (described by a moderate as like a 'Star Chamber') and its replacement by the more flexible alternative of a 'think tank' or educational forum; while the Publicity Committee was suspended, its subsequent operation being conducted on an informal basis without the need for regular committee meetings.

The number and length of Council and residual committee meetings, which had become burdensome and tiring under the previous regime, were reduced. 'Under a new chairman the Council returned to orderly discussion and decision by consensus. Normality had been restored without a public row - but also without any public debate, which would have made the issues plain for all time.'[131]

It was principally to inquire into these issues - and the reasons for the recent deterioration in relations between Nikki and Council - that a working party was set up at the request of her very able successor, Francis Moran. In the event, this initiative proved inconclusive and, in the absence of an agreed report, the project was abandoned by Council in order to avoid any further acrimony or recrimination. In the final sentence of his paper, Alan Wood explains its function as one of supplementing 'what has otherwise to be read between the lines of the official record'.[132] And it was the same recognition of the historical importance of a supplementary record which prompted Nikki and her biographer to pick up the inquiry where the working party had left off and to place on record their own perceptions of the events of this time.

Not for the first time in the school's history, a small group of parents had acted in ways which appeared in certain respects to be incompatible with the cultural ethos of the school. Historical precedents suggested that this could have had adverse consequences for the stability of the school and, indirectly, the education of the children. Once again the potentially damaging crisis had been averted by the forbearance of those who were prepared to put the interests of the children and the staff before their own.

Some of the events of the period 1981 - 1983 had, for diplomatic reasons concerned with the welfare of the school, been necessarily

---

[130] Wood, Sir William. ibid.
[131] ibid.
[132] ibid.

glossed over. Now, fifteen years later, they could be seen in perspective as the temporary aberration they really were.

At the time, however, these events had threatened to precipitate a crisis more serious than anything the school had experienced before. The abandonment of the working party's inquiry had left the real circumstances of Nikki's retirement unresolved, and thus open to speculation and doubt. Except for the announcement of her retirement, the actual complicated history of her resignation was never formally recorded and the problem of avoiding the recurrence of periodic crises of this kind remained largely unexamined.

We began our analysis with the political conditions of the early 1980s, which were in various ways exerting pressures for change in the organisation of the school. Adverse demographic trends and economic recession were once again raising questions of financial viability and competition for pupils, and these in turn placed a premium on greater efficiency and accountability, two characteristics, of the dominant Thatcherite philosophy. This meant that both factions represented on Council shared the common goal of reorganisation, but had different ideas about the methods of bringing this about. The bitter controversy over the proposition to reduce the size of Council had been a case in point: many were persuaded that a smaller Council would have been more efficient, but the motion was defeated in the end on the ground that it would have reduced the number of parents having access to democratic representation. The fact that Nikki supported the resolution has been seen as pivotal in explaining the deterioration in her relations with the dissident faction on Council. But, whilst this might have seemed to be a sufficient cause for them to regard her as antagonistic, it was far from being an adequate one. She had supported the motion on the basis of personal conviction, but, when the vote went the other way, she abided by the result with equanimity, accepting it as part of the normal democratic process.

Another factor which had been overstated was the supposedly inevitable clash of personalities in a relationship where the strong individualism of some Council members confronted a Head 'whose firmness of resolve would not allow her to stand aloof from the political arena when the future of the school was at stake'.[133] Unlike Mrs Thatcher, Nikki was an educationalist and only reluctantly a political animal, having no interest in personal power beyond that which was necessary to fulfil her responsibilities. Her tough-mindedness expressed itself in situations where she thought the interests of the school and its members were at risk and it was balanced by a tender-mindedness to which many Alfredians would bear witness. Her leadership style was democratic and anyone less like 'the iron lady' would be difficult to imagine.

---

[133] Brooks, R., op cit.

Misperceptions of this kind seemed to her to arise from the confrontational politics which now dominated so much of Council business. If in discussion she had reason to disagree with members of Council she sensed that this was in some cases interpreted as evidence of political antagonism. Whereas, to her, it was no more than the exchange of ideas in the process of decision-making, where her professional experience had an important contribution to make.

While opposed in principle to some of the new policies, she co-operated with them fully, never questioning that this was her duty as an employee of the Society, acting under its duly elected Council. In this respect her role was like that of the civil servant who provides the same impartial service to whichever party is in government.

But this was clearly not the perception of the Council majority, apparently suspicious of her motives and believing her to be implacably hostile to their objectives, if not actually working to frustrate them.

These considerations led us to the conclusion that the explanation of the rift was less to do with an inevitable clash of personalities than with a misperception of the actual degree of opposition Nikki represented. Had her opponents been less dedicated to an ideology of 'parent power' and less inclined to perceive her as an obstructive and manipulative head, they would have found that she was none of these things, but one who was always open to discussion and absolutely sincere in her quest for reconciliation and consensus.

The problem was that their identification with notions of parent power appeared to find expression in values, attitudes and policies which were incompatible with certain traditions of the school. The politics of confrontation, for example, threatened a return to factionalism and, by implication, the rejection of the consensus principle in decision-making. These were two developments which Nikki had always apprehended and attempted by positive suggestion to contain, concerned as she was to foster social cohesion and stability in the school. Nothing, in her view, demonstrated more clearly the alien nature of factional politics in education than the way in which divisions could weaken the bonds of community and convert relationships based on trust and co-operation into those characterised by suspicion, discord and conflict.

Objectively, she acknowledged there was a sense in which politics was indissociable from the government of schools, but still regarded its conflictual form as a contradiction of the ultimate meaning of education.

It was an opinion with which the majority of parents were in agreement, seeing adversarial politics as a distraction from the proper functions of the school and a potential threat to the education of their children.

Members of staff had memories of an unfortunate example of parent power which had taken place some years before . A small group of parents had drawn up and circulated a petition listing complaints against some of the teaching staff on grounds which were shown in the event to be entirely unjustified.. In a joint letter of protest addressed to the then Chairman of Council, the teachers expressed their concern for the preservation of good relations between parents and staff which they feared had been undermined by the actions of the parents concerned. 'Behind-the-scenes activity', they wrote, 'is entirely contrary to the spirit and tradition of KAS and represents a real threat to the stability and unity of the school.'

The final and, in effect, the most significant departure from tradition was the challenge to the long-standing consensus over the limits of parental collaboration and the related issue of the division of responsibilities between Council and Head. Significant because it portended an unprecedented extension of control by Council beyond its traditional concern with policy and into the process of teaching itself. This foreshadowed restrictions in the role of the Head and, less directly, in the roles of the teaching staff, which could have seriously undermined the ability of both to fulfil their professional responsibilities adequately.

Generations of past parents had been content to leave the teaching staff to do the job for which they were employed without interference, and Heads from John Russell onwards had been able to depend on this. Only in the late 1970s and early '80s had Nikki found it necessary in the face of criticism from a small minority to re-establish this principle. She had twice made reference to it in her annual reports and stressed its importance in her deposition to the Taylor Committee.

The new policy was implemented only gradually, so that it was not easy to determine the ultimate form and proposed extent of Council intervention in the educational process. But, despite consistent denials that there was any intention to interfere, or that the Head's powers would be in any way restricted, their actions suggested otherwise. Obviously they were not presuming to assume the role of the teacher, but clearly intended to be involved in the process in many ways short of this in both classroom and committee. All of which diverted an increasing amount of teachers' time and energy from their proper function in relation to the education of the children.

The trends appeared ominous and it is probable that, had Council encroachment gone as far as Nikki anticipated, she would have found herself compelled on principle to resist, in the interests of both children and staff. In the event, she had left before such a decision had to be made, and, with the next AGM, the balance of power on Council changed, leading to the reversal of those policies which had been the cause of so much concern. It was concluded in post-mortem discussions that lack of trust had had a great deal to do with the breakdown in relations between the Head and her opponents. If this implied that both parties were in some measure responsible, it did less than justice to Nikki, for, to her, trust was at the heart of her efforts to build and maintain community and consensus, just as it was a central moral value, indispensable to any worthwhile form of education. Distrust appeared, in her opinion, to have arisen in council comparatively recently with the development of adversarial relations and factionalism. She felt that untrustworthiness was being attributed to her by some individual members of Council and was, of course, deeply concerned by this. It was not to be the only adverse personality trait ascribed to her by those who had become opponents during her last years at the school.

She was accused variously of overreacting, being defensive, hostile to reasonable questioning - even paranoid. The reality, as she experienced it, was a period in which she felt constantly harassed and exposed to an apparently orchestrated programme of interrogation. There was, in fact, no reason to pathologise her defensive reactions against verifiable threats. There are verifiable threats, just as there are conspiracies which are not myths. In the circumstances, Nikki's reaction was no different from that of any other Head: it was to become more defensive than was in character and more circumspect than usual.

If at times she became impatient, it was exceptional and uncharacteristic, the result of specific situations where she had been exposed to an intolerable degree of stress.

Attempts to explain what went wrong have up to this point been restricted to the structural elements of the situation (the social context, the polarisation and conflict of ideologies) and to some of the group and personal characteristics of the protagonists. Marginally overlapping this, one final perspective - the group dynamics of the Council majority - remains to be considered, providing a narrower focus on the motivational factors which could have been involved.

Among their defining characteristics were efficient organisation and broad agreement on policy and objectives, notwithstanding a strong individualism that precluded total unanimity or absolute commitment in all cases. Their shared goals were idealistic and sought to introduce a greater measure of structure and regulation in the government of the school, calculated, in their view, to lead to more efficient, democratic, and accountable procedures. Unexceptionable in principle, these appeared less acceptable in practice when Council arbitrarily introduced the first of their more radical changes.

It was a policy which, with its implicit rejection of the consensual approach to school government, appeared paradoxically to be introducing a less rather than a more democratic regime. There was something about it which traditionalists found 'unAlfredian'.

The dominant ideas motivating the new majority on Council, inferred from their deeds and words, seemed with varied emphasis to have been inspired by the evolving ideology of 'parent power'. With its stress on political activism, understandable in the context of state schools, it had been repudiated by Council as irrelevant to the needs and interests of KAS, when it had come up for discussion a few years before.

At a time of expansion in the numbers of women in positions of authority, and when equality of opportunity was a matter of general concern, the question in Nikki's mind was : 'Would all this have happened if

I had been a man?' There was , after all, compelling evidence in society at large to show some persistence of latent - and not exclusively male - prejudice against women in authority.

She could not arrive at a final answer to this question, but reflected with amusement on the irony that 'if a man were to be accused of defensiveness, it would tend to be accepted as his right; whereas, in the case of a woman, it is more likely to be attributed to hysteria.'

Where potential causes of personal animosity were concerned, it was significantly a woman friend who drew attention to the complex emotion of jealousy. 'I could see what some women felt', she said, 'Nikki had everything - wit, charm, intelligence, beauty. Although she got on well with both men and women, there would always be those who, whilst not overtly grudging her what she had, resented it at some sub-conscious level.'

At this point, the returns of a motivational analysis that was becoming more speculative than evidential were of diminishing value to our inquiry. Little was to be gained from further exploration of the sources of individual motivation, other than the discovery of more complex and largely hypothetical explanations of the underlying causes of the debacle. At the outset of our inquiry, Nikki had intended, in principle, to avoid recrimination - to understand and not to judge. This proved to be more easily said than done, for, if there were any lessons to be drawn from the events of this period, it would have been difficult not to express some criticism of the actions for which the Council majority were collectively responsible. As she saw it, the basic flaw in those policies which had so patently departed from the ethos and tradition of King Alfred School stemmed from a lack of historical insight and sociological imagination.

By reference to historical precedents, they could have avoided repeating the mistakes of the past which had precipitated conflicts threatening to the survival of the school. It was a basic error of thinking which led them to create a false analogy between the state system's need to give parents some representation and King Alfred's well-established tradition of co-operation between parents and professional staff - including the Head. The result of this was the introduction of an acerbic, confrontational dialogue in which anyone who disagreed was by definition an enemy, and this extended even to the staff who were teaching their children.

The consequences were evident in the emergence of factional disputes which put in jeopardy the harmonious relationships, community, and consensus, on which the functional efficiency of the school depended. Significant also was their failure to appreciate that the curriculum, properly understood, comprises all that a school is and does - all, in other words, that is to be learned from all that happens. Not to have understood this was to have failed to comprehend the essential meaning of education, progressive or otherwise.

Ahead of her Time

The ultimate error of judgment, it was concluded, was the assumption that the main parent body did not need to be consulted about the radical changes being introduced, in particular the arbitrary decision concerning the premature retirement of their Head. It may have been in accordance with the letter of the Constitution but it could hardly be described as consistent with the spirit.

In his preface Jack Pole notes that it would be regrettable if the history of this important period in the school's life were made to turn on the way Nikki's headship came to an end. And it was clearly more appropriate that the focus of her last year at KAS should be turned more positively on the events celebrating the end of a distinguished career as its longest-serving head. These represented a reaffirmation of the school's belief in itself, its traditional values, and its sense of destiny.

Jack Pole refers to her success in maintaining 'the twin KAS values of personal compassion and intellectual excellence' as well as proving that 'reasonable expectations are compatible with - indeed are best served by - an atmosphere of confidence and happiness'.

Tributes of this kind were later to be followed by a flood of letters from parents, staff, pupils past and present, all expressing affection, appreciation of her achievement and regret for her departure. She was particularly moved by gifts she had received from pupils representing all departments of the whole school: a large earthenware pot made for her and signed by everyone in the Upper School; a glazed dish signed by the Sixth Form; and a farewell book compiled by the Middle School containing individual portraits, pressed flowers and original writing. 'These and the enchanting cards painted by children in Lower School', wrote Nikki in a letter of thanks, 'have been very greatly admired by everyone who has seen them, and are a welcome reminder of the lively and happy community with which I have had such a good relationship for so many years.'

On Saturday, March 19th the school presented 'Razamataz', a spectacular revue described in the publicity as 'a grand fund-raising event for stage and hall improvements'. This was organised by Parent-Staff Committee members with the help of Ian Davidson, a parent and Council member, script editor of the Two Ronnies and other TV productions, who compiled the sketches.

Many members of the school, pupils and staff, took part, as well as a number of parents, including the actor Alan Bates. Nikki was in her element, some measure of which could be gauged from the report which appeared some weeks later in the KAS Bulletin:[134]

'King Alfred School's gain when Nikki Archer became its head was certainly the musical comedy stage's loss, as she proved on March 19th. 'See members of staff in a totally different light' read the advertisement for 'Razamataz', and the capacity audience of parents and pupils saw just that

---

[134] K.A.S.Bulletin Summer 1983

when Nikki, complete with school hat, mini-skirt and black tights, gave a dazzlingly professional performance as a schoolgirl in one of the sketches. 'She was really fantastic, really brilliant', gasped a first former in wonder. The cause of this astonishment was an archetypal revue character who suddenly appeared from somewhere in the auditorium exclaiming:

'I say!...this is King Alfred School, isn't it? Oh super! (Looks around) I'm Debbie Ffoliot-Psmythe (two small f's and a silent 'p'). Oh, Golly Gosh! What a lot of people! Actually I've come for an interview. You see I'm at Debenham Ladies' College and I want to take 'O' levels here because I hear you're simply fab at getting people through. The only thing is, I have to meet your Head, and I've heard she's the most frightful old dragon! Oh Darlings, headmistresses are a great mistake...in fact I believe they're absolutely OUT these days. I think you ought to press for a computer instead...they're so much easier to programme! Anyway, my problem you see is like this:

Deb's Lament
I'm bored with my school, it's so terribly kitsch
and they won't let me train as a technical witch.
So I'm going to apply for a Polytechniche,
but I need an 'O' level in Spells.

I'm trendy and groovy with up-to-date gear,
Industrial spying's my chosen career.
But I haven't much chance of succeeding, I fear, without
an 'O' level in Spells.
Grandpa's in the City, he chairs lots of Boards.
Mummy runs after pop stars, collects them in hordes.
Dad's a Labour M.P., so he'll end in the Lords,
but they can't fix an 'O' level in Spells.
Wherever there's trouble, I'm sure to be found,
I have no fear of flying and jetting around.
My hang glider's black and it's wired for sound,
but I must have 'O' level in Spells.
If all systems go is the name of the game,
I've an Equity card and I'm looking for fame,
and I'd get there as fast as an Honours List Dame,
if I had an 'O' level in Spells.
So pity me, darlings, in spite of the flip.
I'm sad but I keep a brave smile on my lips.
If I lose out I'll hand in my silicon chips and to hell with 'O'
level, it can go to the devil, they can keep their 'O' level in
Spells.

On which note, and with the parting words 'Bye darlings, have lots of fun!' she made her exit, to tumultuous applause, through the main door.

With a change of costume and entirely different persona, she appeared again later in a *pas de deux* with Bob Parvin in which they danced and sang to Jerome Kern's tuneful score of 'Pick Yourself Up', the pertinence of whose lyrics by Dorothy Fields was not lost on those who knew something of the inside story of Nikki's retirement:

'Nothing's impossible I have found, for when my chin is on the ground, I pick myself up, dust myself off, start all over again.'

(and)

'Will you remember the famous men who had to fall to rise again? So take a deep breath (singers breathe audibly), PICK YOURSELF UP, DUST YOURSELF OFF (stage business), START ALL OVER AGAIN.

Another highly successful event - the May Fair - took place on the 14th May. A masterpiece of organisation, it was the result of a year's hard work by a seven-strong committee under the inspired chairmanship of Diane Meyersohn. It involved an exceptionally large number of KAS parents, staff and pupils in running a wide range of stalls, sideshows, and catering facilities with marquee accommodation for no less than two restaurants of unquestionably professional quality. Copies of a splendid souvenir programme were on sale and included several references to Nikki's retirement. She had herself written the preface, entitled 'Will the real King Alfred please stand up...!' in which she gave a synoptic view of the school, its history, aims and objectives; disposed of the myth that it was or ever had been a 'do as you like' school, emphasised the qualities which had, on the contrary, made it a highly respected educational establishment, and expressed satisfaction that she was leaving it in a strong and successful state for her successor to take over in due course.

Margaret Maxwell's elegant and moving tribute - 'Twenty-Five Years'[135] - also appeared in the programme, while the adjoining page was set apart exclusively for the following testimonial:

'Parents, staff, and pupils past and present take this opportunity to thank Nikki for 24 years of dedicated work and inspiration, and wish her happiness and fulfilment for the future.'

Kearsley Airways, sandwiched between advertisements for heating oil and haute couture, tendered in giant capitals their 'Best wishes to Mrs Nikki Archer for a happy retirement', whilst the wine importers Mascaro UK wished her the same, and KAS a successful May Fair.

The climax of the celebrations was marked by a farewell party held at the school on 29th June. Some five hundred people attended, comprising parents and pupils, as well as members of staff, Old Alfredians and friends. Thanks to the prodigious voluntary efforts of the Parent-Staff Committee -

---

[135] Maxwell, M., op cit.

for whom this was indeed an *annus mirabilis* - and other well-wishers, an excellent supper, organised by Sharon Goodman (an Old Alfredian), was provided for this multitude. 'Acres of lasagne' were served on trestle tables in a school hall stretched to capacity, with excess numbers estimated at around a hundred being catered for outside on what proved to be one of the coolest evenings of the summer.

Before the ceremonies took place, James Drew-Edwards of the music staff entertained the congregation with a medley of light music on the piano, setting the tone of the occasion and contributing to the sense of mounting excitement and anticipation.

Nikki sat facing the main entrance to the hall, flanked on one side by Sir William (Alan) Wood, President of the KASS Council, and on the other by some of her Sixth Formers. The hall itself was so crowded that for many there was standing room only, whilst a number of the younger children clustered at various levels on the wall bars. There was an interlude when Nikki, Sir William and others went up on to the stage, not, as it turned out, for the presentation ceremony, as some of the audience at first expected, but to provide an opportunity for press and other photographs to be taken. When the time for the ceremony arrived, they were once again back at their tables, but not before a group of people had surged in at the last moment through the rear entrance, having failed to penetrate the crowd at the front.

In a speech proposing a toast to the guest of honour, the President referred to Margaret Maxwell's tribute in the Bulletin as a definitive account of Nikki's achievements during her twenty-four years, first as co-head and later as sole head of King Alfred School. He mentioned the outstanding and well-deserved reputation of KAS which owed so much to her tireless activity both within and outside the school, through contact with schools and universities, speaking engagements and participation in conferences. Candidates applying for the vacant post of head had come from a wide range of distinguished schools in the public as well as the private sectors and included a number of existing school heads, further testimony to the growing prestige of KAS in the world of education.

The contributions towards her parting gifts, he said, had gone 'beyond the dreams of avarice' and were a clear indication of the high esteem in which she was widely held. He spoke of the lasting worth of Nikki's achievement and the enduring character of her contribution to the school which had for so long been the centre of her professional career.

His speech was greeted with a storm of thunderous applause, which continued unabated for several minutes. Nikki, visibly moved by this, responded by thanking Sir William, expressing her appreciation for all the support she had received and her gratitude for the generosity that had been shown to her. She went on to delight the audience with a lightly humorous reminiscence of her early days. 'Did I want to be a teacher? No! Did I want to be a head? No!' She had come to KAS because of what she had heard about it, and thought it provided the kind of education in which she profoundly believed and with which she wanted to be associated. One's teaching, she said, was at the same time a process of learning, of growth and development. It was, above all, about relationships between people, and it could not be repeated too often that in education it was the children who were of central importance. This was followed by prolonged applause (not a few people were observed to be in tears) and, shortly afterwards, by a spontaneous standing ovation.

A Sixth Former took the floor to make a brief speech on behalf of the pupils, expressing appreciation for all she had done for the school, and saying how much she would be missed after her retirement. It was a memorable and, for Nikki, a reassuring as well as heart-warming experience, not least because it had the ring of authenticity to it, being direct, spontaneous and genuine. The real King Alfred was standing up...and this, in the light of recent comparatively unreal events in the school, was all she needed to know. The enduring traditional values of KAS were vibrantly alive and would prevail.

Her only regret with respect to the party, as she was to say later, was that Lady Zoe Wood, owing to ill-health at the time, had not been able to attend.

Three weeks later, on a warm summer's evening in July, a final celebration took place, when Peter Graff gave a private dinner party in Nikki's honour at Kenwood House, to which she was able to invite members of her family and close personal friends, including Old Alfredians.

The coda to these celebratory events came in November when, engaged in preparation for her Indian tour,[136] she received notification that Council had at its last meeting elected her an Honorary Fellow of the King Alfred School Society.

Family retrospective

Our extended family had grown significantly during the 1970s both in size and closeness of association, creating an integrated pattern of supportive relationships.

In 1972 my mother, who had always valued her independence, was finally persuaded owing to declining health to join our household in Finchley. After two successive strokes, however, she needed the constant care and attention we could not provide and we arranged for her to move into sheltered accommodation in Whetstone, two miles away. The following summer her condition deteriorated further and she was admitted to Barnet Hospital, where she remained until her death in March, 1974, at the age of eighty-three.

Meg, Nikki's mother, died in the same hospital three years later, shortly before her eighty-sixth birthday, mourned not only by her family and friends,

---

[136] Vide Epilogue.

but also by the local branch of the Society of Friends, of which she had been a valued member for the last ten years of her life.

Then, sadly, in 1980 Paul, who had left Hampstead the year before to live in Somerset, also died, leaving us all with a deep sense of personal loss. In her annual report of the same year Nikki included the following tribute to a truly remarkable man:

'Artist, poet, scholar, for many years a member of KASS and a friend and supporter of the school, C.W. Paul-Jones died recently after retiring to a new home in Somerset. It was he who produced the illustrations in the KAS prospectus and, just before his death, was engaged in compiling and illustrating a collection of anecdotes about his Edwardian childhood. These included a description of the time when, as the son of a doctor in Knightsbridge, he travelled daily by horse bus to the prep school he attended before going on to St Paul's.

'At seventeen he decided that he wanted to paint and, to the consternation of his family, attended the Art School in Vienna instead of the Medical School to which he had been sent.

'In later years he often said that he had received a good and competent training at school but would have been better educated, in the true sense of the word, if he had been fortunate enough to go to KAS, where independence of thought and creativity were fostered and recognised.'

Also in commemoration, we went to a ceremony in the same year denoting both the sixtieth anniversary as well as the dissolution of the Kibbo Kift movement with which Paul had been so long associated.[137] This event was held at the Museum of London, which was to provide henceforth a permanent home for the archives, insignia, and artefacts of the now moribund organisation.

The children of our two families grew up, adapting successfully in their own ways to a rapidly-changing and uncertain world. Most of them married, some formed partnerships, and nearly all had families of their own - our present count of grandchildren being ten.

Miranda trained and qualified as a nurse, working in hospitals until 1971, when she married Nick Scholefield, a graduate in textile chemistry. They made their first home in Nottingham but later moved to Somerset where Nick took a job as a research chemist with a prominent firm in the south-west.

Miranda made the choice of staying at home in the traditional role of wife and mother during the dependent years of their three sons, until 1990, when she embarked on a five-year training as a psychotherapist.

Richard, naturally gifted and of an independent disposition, adapted singularly well to the uncertain conditions of employment in the '70s. On the completion of his studies in further education, he broadened his experience by taking a series of different jobs, eventually settling into a diversified

---

[137] Vide Chapter 6.

career in which his intelligence, creativity and managerial skills could find their authentic expression and fulfilment.

23   Epilogue

Ahmedabad
13th December, 1983

'Everything in India is an adventure - especially crossing the road. At 6.30 this morning a rickshaw took me, plus escort, a serious and silent security man who works as a night guard, to my yoga class at a local ashram. The rickshaw most in use here is a bone-shaking mechanical wolf in pram's clothing - in other words a converted Lambretta with a hood and seats for three passengers. The drivers weave in and out of the seething mass of cycles, cars, pedestrians, lorries, camels, bullock carts, wandering cows and holy men and hoot their way along to the accompaniment of black looks and protests from most other road users. The driver, in this case a cheerful young man with a flying helmet and a pretty shawl (who indicates a right turn by sticking his right foot out, as his right hand is usually on the horn and his left hand on the handlebars) took us to the ashram, with only one wrong turning; after which he executed a delicate balletic spin and I nearly knocked my solemn escort out of the seat beside me, being unprepared for the manoeuvre.

My guru is called Swami Manuvarya and he teaches yoga free to anyone who wishes to come. There are usually twenty to thirty energetic men every morning and about eight or nine women and girls who do their exercises in an upstairs room. The Swami decided that as I was there for only a limited time he would supervise my work personally instead of leaving it to his assistant teachers. So you may imagine me, prone on a rug in his office, tying myself into a series of knots while he and a stream of people come and go, in and out of the room by one or other of the two doors. As it is a very small room I upset their progress but in typical Indian fashion, no-one is in the least put out by this arrangement - and I merely close my eyes firmly while working at my poses (asanas) and leave them to walk over or around any stray bits of me which happen to lie in their path. In between some of the more strenuous exercises I lie still and relax, and sometimes Swamiji comes in and talks about Hindu philosophy with me - or, if the mood takes him, advises me about anything from laxatives to longevity - not as far apart as one might suppose, I gather - and questions me with great courtesy and simple curiosity about my life, my career, and my family. He is a delightful old gentleman.'

Ahead of her Time

Nikki had come to India, after her retirement, at the invitation of Gautam Sarabhai, to whom she had been introduced by his daughter, Mana Brearley.[138]

An eminent industrialist and philanthropist, Gautam was a gifted man of wide interests among which was included the B.M. Institute of Mental Health in Ahmedabad, of which he and his late wife were the original founders. The Institute provided services for adults and children whose disabilities ranged from mental retardation and emotional disturbance to acute psychiatric illness.

A component part of the organisation, although in a separate location, was Balghar Primary School, providing a frame of reference - an 'ethos of normality' - to which other services could relate, achieving a measure of integration benefiting all interests. It was to Balghar that Gautam Sarabhai had specifically invited Nikki in the role of educational consultant and it was here that she spent the greater part of her time in India.

As a dynamic research centre, at that time the only one of its kind in India, the B.M. Institute was accustomed to regular visitations by professional experts and specialists from other countries working in the same or related fields of investigation. One of her predecessors, also with KAS connections, was Dr John Bowlby,[139] whose wife, Ursula, kindly provided her, before she left England, with much information and advice that was to prove useful when she got to Ahmedabad. Her visit was therefore welcomed as part of an established pattern of cultural exchange and mutual enrichment.

Concerned to set the tone of her collaboration with the staff of Balghar School, she wrote in advance to Sumant Majmudar, chairman of the B.M. Council:

'I hope, in sharing our knowledge and experience, we may all learn together.'

To which she received a gratifying reply expressing 'a sense of close affinity between some of your thoughts and the direction of our efforts at Balghar'. She was to learn later that it had developed as a progressive experimental school along the lines prescribed by its founder, Mrs Kamali Sarabhai, herself a qualified psychoanalyst.

A provisional programme was agreed, allowing time for Nikki to observe the work of the school before taking part in a series of group meetings and discussions with the teaching staff. These were designed to cover as comprehensive a range of topics as possible under the headings of education (curriculum, examinations, methodology and resources), behaviour (discipline and the role of parents), and administration.

---

[138] Mana Brearley. Vide Chapter 21.

[139] Dr Bowlby's daughter-in-law, Xenia Bowlby, a Council member, and her children, were all educated at King Alfred School.

Time was also reserved for her to visit three local secondary schools: Udgam, which was co-educational, Loyola (for boys only) and Mount Carmel (girls). It was at the latter that quite by chance she saw pupils abseiling under the supervision of their PE teachers from the roof of one of the school buildings.

Implementation of the final programme proved in the event to be more demanding than previously anticipated, and it became clear that more time was needed if prescribed goals were to be accomplished. As a result, Nikki decided to curtail her original sightseeing itinerary and agreed to an extension of her stay in Ahmedabad.

In addition to group discussions with teachers and the observation of classes in progress, she gave lectures (one of these to parents) and seminars, assisted in the evaluation of new textbooks from England, and drafted suggested schemes for project work.

The conclusion of this exacting yet highly productive schedule was marked by an all-day workshop designed to develop skills in the production of educational aids and resources. To this end she suggested that teachers with the relevant expertise be invited from other schools and institutions to contribute their knowledge and experience, and this was arranged. The workshop was an unqualified success, and valuable publicity accrued to the B.M. Institute when the Indian Express, with one of the biggest circulations in India, splashed a large picture of Nikki ('guiding a primary teacher in the production of a teaching aid') across its front page, including inside an account of the interview she had given their staff reporter.

Much of her leisure time in the evenings and at weekends was spent as a guest of the Sarabhai family, of whose hospitality she could not speak too highly. In one of her letters home she wrote, 'The family are kindness itself, and deserve a whole book to themselves; suffice it to say, they are all remarkable in any terms.'

She was taken to see the Sarabhais' cotton mill and the small but exquisite Calico Textile Museum nearby; attended two weddings, a festival of classical Indian dance, and a spectacular fashion show (with models from Bombay) initiated by Gautam and the first of its kind to be held in Ahmedabad. Then there was an exposition of *son et lumière* at Gandhi's ashram in Sabarmati, the symbolic annual kite-flying festival in Ahmedabad, and a day visit to an experimental organic farm. All of these events she enjoyed enormously, but none more than the hours she spent with members of the family in the peaceful surroundings of their beautiful estate outside the city.

She was given letters of introduction to writers, artists, educationalists and other professionals; had escorts for her personal safety when required, and assistance with every detail of her travel arrangements.

When she fell ill at Christmas they were concerned to ensure that all the medical care and attention she needed was made available. She was also fortunate enough to have the daughter of her doctor in London, (Dr.Chandra Sharma)also a doctor, living near Bhalgar. In consequence she soon recovered and was able to make the 5-day tour of Rajasthan which had been planned for the Christmas recess. This involved travel by air-conditioned bus (in which she was very cold), dormitory accommodation, and included visits to Udiapur and Mount Abu.

Before the tour, owing to the reluctance of the male staff to take on the role, she played the part of Santa Claus at the children's Christmas party, complete with a red robe, hood and cotton wool whiskers, distributing gifts and performing a spirited impromptu dance. Contrary to her subsequent feeling that this had all been a mistake, her performance was in fact enthusiastically received, and served to enhance the popularity she had already acquired with the parents, staff and children of Balghar School, some indication of which was shown by the large number of handmade greetings cards she later received.

The remainder of her stay in Ahmedabad passed quickly, and, all too soon, it was time to take leave of the Sarabhais and all her new friends at the B.M. Institute. It had been planned that she would finish her tour in Delhi, using this as a base for local sightseeing, including Agra and the Taj Mahal, as well as a brief excursion to Nepal, before her return flight to the U.K.

By the last week in January she was in New Delhi as the guest of Mr and Mrs Sheth Vasant, to whom she had received an introduction from Michael Peraticos of Pegasus Shipping. Her arrival was just in time for the anniversary of Republic Day and the celebrations which always marked this occasion. The main and most spectacular event of these was the gala parade in which Mrs Gandhi, the Prime Minister, took part, together with representatives of the armed forces, civic bodies and schoolchildren.

The pageantry was both exhilarating and vividly colourful - from the tipsy flying elephant (a helicopter camouflaged with legs and a pink trunk), which preceded the fly-past, to the cavalry and infantry regiments in their dazzling uniforms and the massed bands of the three armed services - and in an attempt to photograph everything she soon ran through all her reserves of film.

The excursion to Agra was a great success: the Taj Mahal 'an amazing poem in marble'. On the trip to Nepal she was glad to have the company of Pallavi, Gautam's niece, with whom she stayed in Kathmandu at the Yak & Yeti Hotel ('A Classic Combination of Comforts, Convenience and Convention') and made the mountain flight to see Everest. This was followed by two nights in Pokhara, north of Kathmandu, from where they had a fine view of Annapurna and the profile of adjacent mountains which Nikki likened to 'a magnificent council of high peaks which look as though they were in silent conclave about the business of the stars and planets'. An outing to a village in the hills several miles from Pokhara led to their discovery of a tiny school, where Nikki took pictures of the children with their head teacher, the last photographs of her tour.

The following day they took the night flight from Kathmandu to Delhi, where she parted from Pallavi, who returned to Ahmedabad, and picked up her onward connection to London.

Ahmedabad
4th January, 1984

'India is indeed a remarkable and fascinating experience for me. I am surprised by nothing, although, as I expected, there is much to sadden me. The most memorable thing is the quiet depth one finds in the most 'ordinary' people and the sense of fun which is never very far below the surface of most social encounters. There is a lovely little lady of about four feet two who comes to give one of the guests here a massage each day and now gives me one too when I am free. She is a tremendous character and full of wit and a kind of wisdom. We cannot talk in a common tongue and have to rely on sign language, with occasional hilarious results, as when she poured tea onto a saucer of massage oil for me under the impression that this was a curious foreign custom. Heaven knows whether she expected me to drink it or rub myself with it - but she broke into peals of laughter when she saw from my face that it was wrong and rocked to and fro and laughed until she was wiping tears from her eyes. Later, I gather, she told the whole story to a friend with graphic descriptions of my face and expression. She has a hard life, I think, but is full of courage and humour and with no self-pity at all.

There are encampments of farmers and their families from North India who come here every year to the dried river bed and grow water melon crops between November and the start of the monsoon season in June. At present they are living in makeshift tents but in a month's time I am told they will build huts and, as a result, present a quite different appearance. The women wear bright saris and carry their brass water pots with grace and skill. They have a beautiful carriage of the body and seem energetic, healthy and calm.

Perhaps I lack sensitivity but much of the 'shack' living I have seen strikes me as less appalling than the soulless and unsympathetic blocks of flats in bare spaces where the inhabitants cannot spread out and create their own territory.

I am not unaware of the physical discomfort nor of the fact that I am seeing it all from a very comfortable position. I also know that for me, with my western background and expectations, such a life would represent misery and deprivation. Yet they seem in some sense insulated from such a view. They behave with dignity, are clearly capable of enjoying life, and their children seem happy and solemnly engaged in tasks in a way that some of our more privileged children in the west do not. How does one measure human happiness? Any Marxist would consider my view outrageous I am sure but - starvation and cruelty excepted - is a man to be pitied if he does not pity himself? Is he poor if he does not see himself as poor? I wish I knew.

It is so fatally easy to be patronising without knowing it, and the reformers can sometimes be as guilty of this as the upper class they criticise. I can only say that I feel grateful without guilt for being able to come here and see things from a fairly comfortable position - I know that I am past the age when dirt and danger hold any fascination for me!

> B.M. Institute of Mental Health
> Ahmedabad
> 7th January, 1984

I had a most interesting talk with Gautum Sarabhai on Sunday morning when he came over to Shyama's for breakfast and told us all about his father's relationship with Gandhi. One of his father's two sisters had been given in marriage to a man she had no wish to marry. When strategies of evasion proved unavailing, she left India in the early 1900s for England, where she spent the next eight years of her life. During this period she met Sylvia Pankhurst and joined the suffragette movement, adopting the western style of women's lib prevailing at this time.

She returned to India after her betrothed had married someone else, and looked for a way of life, a goal and an outlet for her energies which did not include marriage. She asked her brother what he thought she could do and he suggested that she should go with him to meet Gandhi, who, in turn, urged her to start a trade union of the textile workers. This she did, giving rise to a paradoxical situation in which she, as president of the union, and her brother, as owner of the textile mills as well as chairman of the mill owners' association, used to attend meetings as opposing powers and afterwards climb into the same car and drive home together.

When the famous first strike took place, backed by Gandhi and the union president, Gautam's father was angry with Gandhi, but still liked and respected him. Gandhi urged the workers to hold out for higher pay and better conditions, in spite of which, one of them reproached him at a public meeting, saying, 'When our meeting is over, you go back to your ashram and drink your milk; the president of our union goes back to a luxurious meal, but our children's bellies are empty and we cannot feed them, and they are crying with hunger!' Gandhi replied, 'You are right, and therefore I will fast until the strike is over.' Gautam's father accused him of blackmail, and Gandhi acknowledged that he could understand how it might appear so, but he could see no other choice for himself 'but that of sharing the workers' hunger as long as they remained on strike.'

I have heard so many fascinating anecdotes which throw new light on the whole Gandhi scene, and I realise more clearly than ever before the amazing contradictions and contrasts, ambiguities and illogicalities which make any kind of final judgment quite impossible even to attempt. Gandhi's utopian view of the caste system seems a little less absurd when you see caste in an Indian rather than a European context. I must admit to being amused on visiting C.N.Vidyala School yesterday (a school run on Gandhian principles) to discover that girls were not allowed to learn carpentry!'

Ahmedabad
19th January, 1984

It will amuse you to learn that I have an inflated and largely undeserved reputation as a story-teller here, on the basis of one extremely protracted and complicated version of 'Rudi and the Snow Queen' which I enlarged upon from memories of past reading.

The small group of five children who are learning through the medium of English, as opposed to Gujarati, which the rest of the school uses, feel a little isolated and I had adopted them slightly because I felt they needed a little extra attention. On one occasion a teacher was absent and I offered to tell them a story in order to help out. As my memory was uncertain, I started inventing all kinds of extra characters and situations to pad out the time required and found they were so absorbed and lost in the story that we went way past the time for their lunch break without noticing. Then, of course, we were only half way through the story and I had no further opportunity to finish it until today. They, in the meantime, were convinced I had forgotten and that they would never hear the end of the tale, so I was particularly keen not to let them down.

I took with me a magic banana (one which had been cut into six slices without opening or breaking the skin, a favourite of mine for mystifying the very young) and told them that, before they heard the end of the story, it was very important to believe just a little bit in magic, and if you could not guess how something was done that was a kind of magic for you. We had a lovely time and, although my voice is now slightly hoarse after two long sessions, I feel happy with the day's work.

Ahead of her Time

B.M. Institute
Ahmedabad
22nd January, 1984

I am sitting typing against the infernal racket made by a few hundred birds which every evening sit in the trees outside my room and have a last get-together before settling down for the night. They also do the same in the morning, squabbling, whistling and chirping, and being generally as raucous and noisy as a set of Glasgow fishwives. There are jays and green parrots. Crows and jackdaws, sparrows, finches and pigeons, and a soft grey-brown kind of thrush, woodpeckers and starlings, and probably a great many other types I have not identified, and they are deafening! Probably thousands would be nearer the mark than hundreds when you count the number of trees which are all black with them, jostling and protesting, contending for the best perches.

The wedding today was a very superior affair. The bride's father is a high-caste Brahmin apparently and she is marrying into a lower caste family, as her husband belongs to a caste who are mainly, it seems, agriculturalists and merchants, and this is, even today, considered unusual for a girl of such a family. The embargo on caste seems to have made absolutely no difference to the majority of people who still live largely by its rules despite the efforts made to eliminate its more pernicious consequences. She made her own choice (again quite unusual) and he is training to be a psychiatrist - a very nice as well as a very handsome young man. They had an enormous marquee and about three hundred guests, and the bridegroom arrived looking very impressive in a cloth-of-gold turban and lovely curly-toed shoes and a beautiful silk tunic. The bride was in a rose pink and gold sari with lots of gold ornaments, and looked very lovely. The marriage ceremony, during which we all sat, chattered and talked, or wandered around doing anything and everything except watch what was going on under the marriage canopy, was very long, and involved the bride and groom walking seven times around the sacred fire.

There was a very curious incident during the celebrations, which involved a visit by a group of Castrati dressed (very gaudily) as women, who turned up at the gates and were sent away with, my informant said, a gift of money to prevent their embarrassing the guests. This ancient 'sect' has a long and extraordinary history and claims the right to visit confinements and and even in some circumstances remove and 'adopt' children whose physical sexual orientation is uncertain.

Recently we were taken to meet a famous Indian artist - Piraji Sagra - who has exhibited all over the world. He was born into an illiterate village family and started painting when he was ten. He is now fifty-three, a friendly, powerfully-built and happy man of character and simplicity - I took to him very much, in spite of the language barrier. His work - or some of it - made me want to go away and do the same! It was all very powerful in content and form, no matter what the subject, and his latest series of portrait heads were strange, touching, evocative and not at all what one would call beautiful, but they attract one's attention irresistibly. He thinks Rembrandt was the greatest painter of all time, and says quite simply, 'For me Rembrandt is God'.

Appendix A: Bran Mash for Breakfast

(Broadcast by Nikki Paul-Jones, Woman's Hour, 1960)

When I was thirteen my father read a book. It was not his first, in fact he was addicted to the habit, but it was important in a way that most of his books were not, for it literally changed our lives. We were a Yorkshire family who liked good food and even in the south of England where the butchers called joints by the wrong names, my mother kept what she felt was a 'fair table'. Unfortunately, my father enjoyed ill-health and in the course of it had recently spent some time at an expensive establishment which reduced its patients to quiescence by restricting their food intake to two pints of orange juice daily. The cure thus effected did not last, as the necessity to return to normal living put him once more on bad terms with his colon and he greeted this new book on diet (it had the unprepossessing title of 'The Cauldron of Disease') with enthusiasm. Soon he went to London to meet the author and arranged for my mother to join him at the doctor's establishment so that she might learn the new way of life: I perforce accompanied them.

My recollections of the first evening are confused by the fact that all meals eaten there were equally dreadful, but I do recall being gently reproved when, finding the soup lacking in all the qualities I had come to associate with edible liquids, I asked for some salt. 'Do not worry', said the doctor comfortably, 'we must educate the palate gently.' I don't know what he meant by gently, but I never enjoyed another meal for nearly four years.

This remarkable man believed that certain foods produced putrefactive (and therefore harmful) bacilli in the intestines and that, by careful adherence to the rules laid down, one could effect a cure in about three years. The snag was that one relapse into bad habits put you back at the beginning again.

He had drawn up a list of forbidden foods, a kind of cook's *Index Expurgatorius*, which started with fish, meat, eggs and cheese and went on to prohibit white bread (stale brown was allowed) salt, pepper, white sugar, spices, sauces, cakes, pastry, jam, chocolates and sweets, and ended with a grave warning against any food which was either very hot or very cold.

Morning ritual...no-one who has ever experienced it could call it breakfast, consisted of a gritty poultice made of two cupfuls of bran (the sort that horses eat), one of raw oats and one of boiling water, eaten, after two minutes soaking, with black treacle, or sour milk for light relief. It seems unbelievable to children today that I should have accepted meekly such a horrifying curtailment of all the things one likes to eat, but I was a sober-minded only child with a desire to live up to my father's definition of intelligent judgment, and I managed to persuade myself that I agreed with

303

Ahead of her Time

it, endured the tasteless soups and ubiquitous soya beans and rock-hard bread...and voluntarily gave up sweets.

Gradually I became a social outcast among my contemporaries, for I was always sent visiting with a list of things I could not eat (this usually comprised the whole of the meal provided) and a list of those I was allowed (which, understandably, non-one would admit to having in the house). Of course, none of my friends ever came to tea with me a second time, as guests were also subject to the same laws.

The end really came for me, however, when my mother, who had flung herself into the business with fervour for my father's sake, served, on the first Christmas Day A.D.(after diet), a turkey of nutmeat rissole, soya stuffing with no salt, and vegetarian gravy. After this, as my longing for the wrong things grew, my adherence to honesty weakened, and the guilt-ridden ice cream devoured secretly, the pork pie bought with my sixpence pocket money ceased to be occasional symbols of a depraved nature and became ordinary occurrences. I have vivid memories of the day when my father found a toffee paper in the W.C. and I, hardened in sin, told him with convincing penitence that it was my first false step.

About three years after we started, my mother caught undulant fever and nearly died. She was ordered chicken juice and the nurse disposed of my father's protests with a glorious burst of professional, and Irish, indignation; and my mother never returned to the diet.

By the time she was about again, my grandmother, a diminutive woman with a face like a baby eagle and a will to match, was running our household. She decided that my father needed meat and meat he was going to have, so she mixed his nutmeat rissole with raw minced liver and added beef gravy to his soup, which I am sure did him no good but eased her mind, and left him innocently surprised by her skill at flavouring soya beans.

My mother was by this time convalescing in Italy and when she heard by chance that our dietetic expert had rented a villa in the hills above the bay, she decided to visit him, hoping I think to get advice about returning to ways of grace. Always impulsive, she went without warning, and finding him absent, left a letter. On the way back, however, she met him coming up the path from the bay, carrying in his arms a large cheese and a basket of new-laid eggs. That was the end. His bland explanations found no response with my mother, for whom truth was all, and, as she wrote in her letter home that night, 'It was such a big cheese!'.

My father's faith in humanity was badly shaken by this, and it was months before he regained enough to investigate a new American religion which promised spiritual and physical regeneration for a mere ten dollars.

Appendix B: Case Study of a Gifted Child

(under the pseudonym 'Karl') by Nikki Archer

Preamble:
When children of exceptionally high intellectual ability come from a family where there are siblings of comparable ability, there is a strong probability that they will find it easy to form relationships outside. The support of others who understand them, and the existence of a loving group to which they can turn for sympathy and sensible explanations when things go wrong, make a great deal of difference.

The child who is really unhappy is often the only child, or the only very gifted child in an ordinary family and quickly becomes isolated.

If the parents are themselves intellectually gifted, and place high value on intellectual achievement, they may expose him (or her) to an almost unendurable strain by relating to him only at the highest level of his mental ability, paying little if any regard to the relative immaturity of the child in terms of physical, mental, social and emotional development.

With parents like this, the teacher is often at a loss to know how best to help. Experience has suggested to the child that to obtain parental love and approval it is necessary to behave like an adult at all times. Feeling is undervalued and thinking overvalued. The result is that the child who needs to be a baby first dare not live out his childish needs and impulses, sensing all too clearly that they do not fit with the 'gifted' intellectual image his parents expect.

Case Study:
'Karl' Age: 16 IQ:160
Karl, an only child, used the school to express feelings and indulge in patterns of behaviour which were not acceptable at home. These had to be expressed somewhere, if he was to gain any kind of emotional stability.

His mother was deeply impressed, as mothers tend to be, by his obvious and exceptional intelligence. She insisted on 'stimulating' him lest he became 'bored' and arranged a constant programme of mental activity for him, from museum visits to extra lessons in a variety of subjects. We protested in vain. Karl responded by behaving like a three-year old in class and was intolerable, or barely tolerable, for a long time.

His father, less concerned with his son's intellectual ability, nevertheless wanted him to be an adult long before his time, and was only prepared to spend time with Karl on things which he personally found interesting, like going to the theatre, listening to lectures, and discussing books, which Karl, at the age of seven, could read and discuss, though they were beyond his emotional experience and comprehension.

He was a sad child, who denied his feelings and insisted on subjecting everything to a process of analysis. It was as though he enjoyed nothing directly but only through the intervention of his conscious intellectual appreciation.

At the same time, he displayed certain obsessional habits of movement which appeared to give him momentary relief. He could hardly be said to enjoy them. He would play endlessly with mud, as do many children; but in his case the play which so absorbed him at the age of four persisted up to the age of fifteen. He would do page after page of work of a repetitive kind, which seemed to reassure him in times of stress.

He was always alone both in class and out of it, and it was many years before he learned to respond normally to comments or overtures from others of his own age, even those of an ability comparable to his own. He could hardly be said to form relationships even with those teachers he trusted and whose intellectual stature he could respect, or whose expertise was obvious enough for him to feel safe in accepting them. He 'used' them when they were necessary to him.

His 'technique' was interesting to watch, and staff became skilled in dealing with it as soon as they realised what was needed. He would approach someone for 'help' with a problem to do with his work. He never followed instructions and always worked on his own schemes, but, as he clearly knew what he could and could not do, we accepted this and gave guidance only when it was essential...sometimes it was accepted. When the 'help' was volunteered he then proceeded to tie the unfortunate person up in logical knots of his own devising. If he was allowed to do this, and enabled to demolish his 'victim' in argument, all was well. At first, we were stubbornly unwilling to accept what was often a contrived stratagem. Then we realised what was needed, and accepted his terms of play. Almost immediately after 'winning' he would return to the person involved and offer the comment that perhaps they had a point after all. This was for him the equivalent of a friendly overture, and we gradually learnt to make use of these episodes in the interests of general peace.

Endnote: 'Karl' later went on to complete 6th form studies, gained three GCE 'A' levels, entered university and graduated with distinction. A certain eccentricity of manner persisted, but he had gained immensely in social maturity and emotional stability in his final year at KAS.

Appendix C: Parent + Child + School = ?

A Quiz for Parents, featured in Look: The Sunday Times, January 22nd, 1978

What part of your child's upbringing would you leave the school to deal with? What would you deal with yourself? And when, and how, should you intervene in problems between your child and its school? This quiz, which concerns itself largely with the predicaments of young people in their early teens, was conceived by Nikki Archer, head of the King Alfred School in north-west London. In it she invites you to examine your attitudes.

1. Your child complains that he is expected/forbidden to wear an article of clothing which he particularly dislikes/wants to be seen in. Do you:

   a) Tell him there is probably a fairly good reason why this is so and talk over what it could be while remaining firm over the need to co-operate with the rules.
   b) Say of course he may/need not wear the article in question and prepare to do battle with the school on behalf of what you feel are his (and your?) rights.
   c) Tell him you want to hear no nonsense and if that is the rule it must be obeyed without question or discussion.
   d) Make a plea to the powers-that-be to treat your child as a special case because 'after all, it doesn't really matter terribly to anyone, does it, and most rules are made to be broken, aren't they?'
   e) Take no particular line and hope the whole question will resolve itself without involving you.
   f) Show him how to make things as awkward as possible for the school and get a protest going while remaining quietly in the background yourself. 'I've always taught the children to question everything and not accept any rules unless it makes sense to them.'

2. Your 12-year old daughter comes home and announces her intention of going to a friend's for an 'all-night party' and informs you with great conviction that 'everyone is going' and she will be an outcast for ever if she is not allowed to, and 'it is on a Saturday night and will not interfere with school on Monday'. Do you:

   a) Say no without qualification and refuse to discuss it further.
   b) Say yes, however grudgingly, 'because if everyone in her class is going, you can't really say no, can you? And she does keep on so.'
   c) Say no firmly to the all-night bit (and remain unruffled by pleas and tantrums alike); contact the parents who are giving the party to

check the facts and say what time you will (i) collect her or (ii) expect her to leave for home.

d) Leave her to make the decision and take no further steps in the matter beyond providing her with money for the occasion.

e) Start by saying no and then say yes but only until midnight, but give in when she calls at some time during the evening to say they are all staying and the au pair is there, and can't she please stay.

f) Encourage her to go, expect she'll get drunk and put it down to experience.

3. Your child complains several times in a row that a particular teacher is too strict/not strict enough/unfair to him. Do you:

a) Believe everything he says implicitly, 'because he never lies to you', and assume the teacher must be wrong.

b) Assume that what the teacher does must be right because that was how it was when you were at school, and refuse to listen.

c) Go round to other parents you know, collecting information about this particular teacher so that, if possible, you can go to the Head with a number of complaints and 'get something done about it'.

d) Wait, listen and see whether the next complaints involve the same thing about another teacher, or whether it is always the same one, in which case there may well be something which needs looking into, and you make an appointment to see someone at his school.

e) Stop listening and just say, 'Yes, dear' until he stops telling you.

f) Alternate, according to your mood, between believing him and thinking he is exaggerating, and never give him any definite response.

4. Your child complains about being forced to spend time doing a subject which she can see no immediate purpose in, and at which you also were unsuccessful at the same age. Do you:

a) Sympathise with her wish to drop it and tell her of your own experience; and that she probably can't do it because you couldn't, and then write to the school suggesting that she should be allowed to discontinue the subject.

b) Sympathise and share your own experience, pointing out that it still remains a failure in your mind and you wish someone could have helped you to get something out of it, and perhaps if you work together on the problem, you may find that you are both a bit cleverer than you thought, even if she still can't see an immediate reward herself (yours is helping her).

c) Tell her it's part of the school curriculum and she'd better get on with it and not worry about what it's for.

d) Agree that unless you know exactly why you are doing something you should not be asked to do it, and try to arrange a parents' meeting to get the subject taken off the curriculum, or made voluntary, on the grounds that the consumer view is all-important.
e) Tell her that it's her problem and suggest that she and her friends who feel the same run a passive resistance campaign against working in that lesson until staff are forced to take notice of their demands.
f) Tell her that you'll do something when you next visit the school and then feel unable to tackle it when you get there.

5. Your child comes home and tells you that friends of his have been stealing/smoking pot/drinking alcohol in school. You can see that he is intrigued, half admiring and half afraid. Although his tone is virtuous, you suspect he may know more, or be more involved in the incident than he confesses. Do you:

a) Invite his friends round for a drink, 'because they will do it anyway and at least they will be safe with you' and try to act as unofficial counsellor on the understanding that everything they tell you is entirely confidential.
b) Assume he is making it up, and ignore it.
c) Without pointing a censorious finger directly at your child or his friends, discuss with him the issue in a broad sense: ask whether he thinks it's right or wrong, safe or dangerous - and add your views to the debate, in the hope that he'll make a note of them when he makes up his own mind.
d) Threaten him that if you find out he is mixed up in the matter there will be immediate retribution and you will inform the police.
e) Say, 'I don't know what the schools are coming to these days', and tell everyone except the school what you know, while suggesting that it might be even more widespread than it seems.
f) Tell him that you must inform the school and leave them to investigate the matter, without saying where your information came from unless you have real proof. Assure him that if he is not involved he will be all right, and if, in fact, he is involved he had better tell you so, because if he is with people who break the law and he knows it, or suspects it, he will also be held responsible.

You + Quiz : Results

Score:		a	b	c	d	e	f
	Q1.	a-8	b-4	c-10	d-6	e-1	f-2
	Q2.	a-10	b-4	c-8	d-1	e-6	f-2
	Q3.	a-4	b-10	c-2	d-8	e-1	f-6
	Q4.	a-4	b-8	c-10	d-2	e-1	f-6
	Q5.	a-4	b-1	c-6	d-10	e-2	f-8

Ahead of her Time

If your score is between:

50 and 41:
You're a firm believer in discipline: you probably see it as a great character-builder. But you could be paying the very high price of alienating your child completely. If you constantly reinforce every school rule, no matter how difficult or upsetting he finds them, he will see you as siding with 'them' and - at best - feel desperately alone.

40-31:
You seem to strike a good balance between your own clear values and beliefs and a recognition of the fact that your child has his own ideas. If you continue to respect those ideas - while keeping a guiding hand - your child will see both home and school as places in which to develop happily.

30-21:
You are caught between a tendency to indulge your child rather more than you know you should do and a timidity of the school system which seems to you to be over-harsh. Perhaps you separate yourself off too much from the school: if you made an effort to be more involved, to know the teachers as people and familiarise yourself with the rules and the reasons for them, you'd find a compromise of attitudes easier to work out.

20-11:
You obviously feel very aggressive towards your child's school and are prepared to take issue with them on many points. While it can be a good thing to show that you want to be involved and consulted, excessive interference and bickering could kick back on your child - 'the one with the difficult mum'. You should work out if there is something in you which generally resents authority, or if, in fact, you believe the school to be particularly bad. If that's the case, a change might even be in order.

10 or under:
If you drift from passionate indignation on your child's behalf to total disinterest in his school life, you ought to realise that there will really be no winners at all. He'll either resent you, or the school, or both - and, whichever way, he won't be happy. Some deep thought on your part is much overdue.

Reproduced by kind permission of the Sunday Times